A World Without Hunger

Josué de Castro and the History of Geography

Liverpool Latin American Studies

Series Editor: Matthew Brown, University of Bristol
Emeritus Series Editor: Professor John Fisher

Liverpool Latin American Studies, New Series 25

A World Without Hunger
Josué de Castro and
the History of Geography

Archie Davies

LIVERPOOL UNIVERSITY PRESS

First published 2022 by
Liverpool University Press
4 Cambridge Street
Liverpool
L69 7ZU

British Library Cataloguing-in-Publication data
A British Library CIP record is available

ISBN 978-1-80207-720-9

Typeset by Carnegie Book Production, Lancaster
Printed and bound by CPI Group (UK) Ltd, Croydon CR0 4YY

Contents

A alma da fome é política
[The soul of hunger is politics]

Herbert de Souza, aka Betinho

Acknowledgements

This book began life as a PhD dissertation supervised by Alex Loftus at King's College London. Alex's influence as a thinker and as an extraordinarily kind and generous teacher can be found on every page. No doctoral student could hope for more than he has given me. At the beginning and end of this project I was lucky to work with two wonderful geographers in Jenny Pickerill and Tariq Jazeel. At Sheffield, Jenny was the platonic ideal of an academic mentor in the last phase of this book's gestation, and Tariq carefully supervised a very different Master's dissertation at UCL, before Josué de Castro entered my life. I am grateful to both for their wisdom and advice. Elleke Boehmer first taught me nearly fifteen years ago and has continued to be an inspiration.

The most important periods of archival research for this book were undertaken in Recife in 2017 and 2019. The Fundação Joaquim Nabuco was an excellent place to do archival research, and on both visits I was cared for, and inspired by, the members of the research group on Social Movements and Urban Space at the Universidade Federal de Pernambuco (UFPE). Cláudio Jorge Moura de Castilho introduced me to the vibrant field of contemporary Northeastern geography while gently guiding me around its history. Katielle Susane do Nascimento Silva has been a warm friend and colleague; I will always be grateful to Eduardo Ascensão in Lisbon for putting us in touch. Júnior, Carolina, Vinícius, and many others all made me feel hugely welcome in Recife and Olinda. Thanks in particular to Rafa and his wonderful students in Cabo, and to Andrea for putting me up in Rio. José Arlindo Soares hosted me in his flat in Recife, and Ana Maria de Castro kindly responded in writing to questions about her father's life and work.

I would also like to thank archivists, researchers, and librarians around Europe and Latin America, including: Elizabeth Accioly at the Instituto de Nutrição Josué de Castro in Rio de Janeiro; the libraries at the Universidade Federal do Estado do Rio de Janeiro and the Universidade Federal de Pernambuco; Sandro Vasconcelos at the Museu da Cidade do Recife; María Rita Garda and colleagues at the Escuela de Nutrición in Buenos Aires; Fabio Ciccarello at the FAO in Rome; the archive of the Câmara dos Deputados in

Brasília, the Pernambuco state archives and the Arquivo Nacional in Rio de Janeiro; the Ibero-Amerikanisches Institut in Berlin; Julio Cazzassa at Senate House Library in London; L'Institut mémoires de l'édition contemporaine in Caen; and La Contemporaine in Nanterre.

I received useful responses to elements of this work at the International Conference of Historical Geographers in Warsaw, the London Group of Historical Geographers, the American Association of Geographers in New Orleans and San Francisco, and elsewhere. Breno Viotto Pedrosa, André Reyes Novaes, Mariana Lamego, Guilherme Ribeiro, João Sarmento, and, in particular, Federico Ferretti have been generous and stimulating interlocutors on Josué and the history of Brazilian geography. At King's I was also grateful for the time and insight that Jeff Garmany lent this project. Ruth Craggs was an inspiring reader at an early stage and has continued to be a hugely supportive colleague. Thanks also to Anthony Pereira, David Featherstone, Jess Dubow, and Eric Olund for ideas and responses at different points along the way. Undergraduate and Master's students at King's, LSE, UCL, Sheffield, the Universidade Federal Rural do Rio de Janeiro, and UFPE have all asked me probing and profound questions about Josué de Castro, some of which I hope are answered in this book. Thanks also to Alain Bué, Chloe Johnson at LUP, and Rosie Wood for the index. The research for this book has been funded by the UK Economic and Social Research Council, the Leverhulme Trust, and the Department of Geography at the University of Sheffield.

I thank Prue, Howard, George, Amélie, and Caro for their love and support, and indeed for their moments of bafflement, which have always sharpened my thinking. Tom Cowan and James Angel have been vital intellectual friends in corners around London, and Hashim Reza, Marie-Do Reza, Philip Knox, Venetia Thorneycroft, Lotte Johnson, and Ed Thornton have, sometimes unconsciously, helped bring this book into being. I am grateful to Ed in particular for his peaceful, ruminative companionship and for always having another way of thinking about things – whether that be lunch or humanism.

Alexandra Reza's restless intelligence has constantly pushed me to think more carefully and critically, and the ideas in this book owe a huge amount to her. From Recife to Rome, Lisbon, Buenos Aires, Berlin, and Paris, she was always there in a bar at the end of the day. Thanks to her, the years of writing this book were full of love and joy.

Introduction

Hunger and the Militant Humanist

In the midst of the Covid-19 pandemic, from a very high base, food insecurity and hunger in Brazil exploded. In March 2021 9 per cent of the population – 19 million people – went hungry every day. Nearly another 100 million suffered from food insecurity of some kind.[1] This hunger has a geography. In the Northeast over 73 per cent of households suffer food insecurity.[2] Hunger is distributed in lock-step with racialized, gendered, and spatial inequalities. The facts and faces of hunger compel attention and action in the immediate present, but this book places the analysis of the geography of hunger in a long historical context and a broad intellectual framework. Because, just as hunger has a geography, so geography has a lot to learn from hunger.

What follows in the first four chapters of this book is the biography of an idea, the geography of hunger, through the life of one man, Josué de Castro. It traces that idea through and beyond his writing and practice to see how it changed shape in the different places and times in which it intervened. Chapters 5 to 7 move in a different direction. They follow Castro's biography to raise new questions about twentieth-century geography through the lenses of the region, the intellectual, and finally the emergence of an anticolonial international environmentalism in Paris in the aftermath of May 1968. In telling a story of the geography of hunger this book is in one sense a history of geography and, in another, a biography of Josué de Castro, a Brazilian geographer, diplomat, writer, and international political activist. But it carves an unconventional path through both those domains. It travels from the clean desks of early twentieth-century nutritional laboratories to the muddy shores

1 Rede PENSSAN, 'VIGISAN: National Survey of Food Insecurity in the Context of the Covid-19 Pandemic in Brazil' (Instituto Vox Populi, March 2021), accessed 14 June 2022, olheparaafome.com.br.
2 Eryka Galindo et al., 'Efeitos da pandemia na alimentação e na situação da segurança alimentar no Brasil', Food for Justice Working Paper Series, 2021, doi:10.17169/REFUBIUM-29554.

of Recife, via the modernist halls of post-war global institutions. Within this journey is the continuous trouble brought by the idea of the geography of hunger: the claims that hunger is not natural, that it has a history, that it is contingent, that it is spatial, and that it is done by some unto others. Yet the greatest trouble that the notion of the geography of hunger brings with it is its utopian charge: the proposition of a world without hunger.

I propose that reconstructing Castro's geography of hunger – placing it in the context of his practice, and in its intertexts – can yield interventions of lasting importance for the history of geography and a geographical understanding of hunger. Castro trained as a doctor but became a nutritional scientist and then a geographer, politician, and international diplomat. Above all, he sought to demonstrate that hunger was a social rather than a natural condition. His innovative, anticolonial work can be seen as a precursor to critical geography and to political ecology. Exiled in 1964 by the Brazilian military dictatorship, Castro died in Paris, as a professor at the University of Vincennes, in 1973.

Castro made a methodological movement from nutritional and metabolic science to geographical method, from the internal workings of the body to the production of space and nature. Empirical natural scientific experiments, social scientific surveys, and clinical medical practice lay behind Castro's geographical method and his '*biosociologia*' [bio-sociology]. As a natural and social scientist, he performed research in laboratories, in urban field sites, and in doctors' surgeries. His interdisciplinarity is therefore a central concern for me here, not least because of the long history of the interconnection between Euro-North American natural science and enlightenment humanism.[3] Beginning from the positivist traditions of French regional geography,[4] Castro developed the notion of a negative geography. Though he never fully articulated the theoretical contours of this negative geography, he helped capsize his adoptive vessel of regional geography by moving from a description of geographical forms as they appear on the surface of the earth to a spatial analysis of negation and lack.

The dynamics of this lacking are central to Castro's concerns and are underpinned by his being, in the words of his friend the communist organiser and rural sociologist Clodomir Santos de Morais, 'a loyal and permanent militant of humanism'.[5] His ideas of hunger and humanism were intrinsically connected. He defined hunger in terms that were both political and biophysical, both normative and relative. His understanding of hunger was

3 Sylvia Wynter, 'Unsettling the Coloniality of Being/Power/Truth/Freedom: Towards the Human, after Man, Its Overrepresentation—An Argument', *CR: The New Centennial Review* 3, no. 3 (2003): 268–70.

4 Denis Cosgrove, 'Towards a Radical Cultural Geography: Problems of Theory', *Antipode* 15, no. 1 (1983): 2–3.

5 Santos de Morais Clodomir, 'Josué de Castro: brasileiro e cidadão do mundo', News, *A Nova Democracia* (blog), February 2005, accessed 15 June 2022, https://anovad-emocracia.com.br/no-23/690-josue-de-castro-brasileiro-e-cidadao-do-mundo.

based in a situated deployment of nutritional science, but this normative baseline informed a broader analysis of relative hunger and undernutrition. In attending to the absolute foundations of human survival, he did not reduce poverty to absolutes but emphasized the material bases of human flourishing. He produced a geography of hunger, not a geography of food, never losing sight of suffering and survival even while he was interested in the cultural, historical, and social dimensions of food provision. He enacted a twin intellectual and political movement that was at once positivist – insisting that basic nutritional needs are absolute, and must be central to political demands – and radical – insisting that the proper fulfilment of these needs would require historical, structural, and systemic social transformations. His work does not exhaust the possibilities of this movement, nor does it manifest as a fully formulated set of theoretical propositions, but, as this book shows, it can nevertheless advance contemporary geographical ideas about hunger.

In 1952 Castro wrote, 'I believe in the biological and social power of necessity, which at the most critical moments in history always leads man towards survival.'[6] Hunger is a fundamental human drive. As Kathi Weeks puts it, in a way that chimes with Castro's writing and practice across his career, hunger is a 'thoroughly historically variable' that 'urges humans forward to extend themselves and become more'.[7] The biology of the human is reciprocally bound into social processes. Castro's own understanding of hunger as a drive is influenced by his reading of Freud and Spinoza:

> it is strange to find that [hunger's] narrow aspects of sensation, what Spinoza called the impulse and instinct that has served as the motive force of human evolution, have been ignored; but it is even more curious to observe the oppressive silence that has surrounded its broader influence as a universal calamity.[8]

These two ways of seeing hunger are both important. Hunger as a worldwide calamity is the sweeping subject of his work, but hunger as 'impulse and instinct' underpins it in important ways and helps explain Castro's idea of social change.

This concept of 'biological and social' necessity should be correlated with his argument elsewhere that 'it is through hunger that the *latifundio* [plantation] proceeds'.[9] Hunger is mobilized, in this formulation, as a tool

6 Josué de Castro, *Geography of Hunger*, 1st ed. (London: Victor Gollancz, 1952), 28.

7 Kathi Weeks, *The Problem with Work: Feminism, Marxism, Antiwork Politics, and Postwork Imaginaries* (Durham, NC: Duke University Press, 2011), 249. We find aesthetic expressions of hunger as an extending force in Castro's *homem-caranguejo*, the family of Graciliano Ramos' *Vidas Secas*, and in the other novels and films Castro draws upon, such as Knut Hamsun's *Sult*.

8 Castro, *Geography of Hunger*, 14.

9 Josué de Castro, *Geografia da Fome: O Dilema Brasileiro: Pão Ou Aço* (Rio de Janeiro: Edições Antares, 1946), 31.

of oppression. Castro provided a clear political analysis of why he thought hunger as a social calamity had been overlooked: 'it was to the advantage of economic imperialism and international commerce, both controlled by profit-seeking minorities, that the production, distribution and consumption of food products be regarded as purely business matters rather than as phenomena of highest importance to society as a whole'.[10] In terms of impulse and instinct, on the other hand, Castro figures the drive to conquer hunger as a positive force of necessity. He writes that 'hunger itself will be the guiding force, the mainspring of a social revolution that can gradually draw the world back from the abyss which threatens to swallow our civilization much more greedily than the oceans threaten to swallow our soils. This faith makes me an optimist.'[11] This is a curious kind of optimism, founded in a particular kind of humanism. While it might seem an under-theorized idea of social change, the depth of his analysis of hunger as a biological and sociological force – its nutritional and geographical ontology – should be read into this idea of 'guiding force'. However, the transposition of necessity into politics is not straightforward: it is a question of political struggle, even as the drive to survival has a structuring power.

Castro's ideas changed and developed. Yet they were in many senses limited and underdeveloped: his conception of race initially lacked a sociology;[12] his silence on gender is deafening; his analysis of capitalism and class is at times rudimentary; and his account of the feudal remnants of Northeast Brazilian plantation society is contestable. But I find a great deal in both his theory and praxis that remains compelling for thinking through how uneven embodiments are made through, and in relation to, the uneven production of nature and space. By following both his theory and his praxis we can work towards an ecological, relational, humanist geography of hunger that offers novel formulations for contemporary geography.

Castro's insistence that hunger should be the starting point for geographical enquiry is salutary today. In global and local contexts of persistent hunger (according to the World Food Programme, 860 million people are suffering from hunger at the time of writing,[13] and around 2 billion people suffer micronutrient deficiencies of various kinds[14]), malnourishment, starvation,

---

10 Castro, *Geography of Hunger*, 7.

11 Castro, *Geography of Hunger*, 28.

12 Though it is worth noting that by 1958 he had a more sophisticated conception of race, writing that 'race is an anthropological abstraction without real existence'. Josué de Castro, *The Compass of China* (Venice: Société Européene de Culture, 1958). See also Josué de Castro, *Ensaios de biologia social* (São Paulo: Editôra Brasiliense, 1957), 131–52.

13 'HungerMap LIVE', accessed 25 August 2021, https://hungermap.wfp.org/?_ga=2.110786054.243136831.1629886323-1405136313.1629886323.

14 Ty Beal and Daniel Ervin, 'The Geography of Malnutrition', *The Professional Geographer* 70, no. 1 (January 2018): 47–59, doi:10.1080/00330124.2017.1310623.

and lack should remain central and urgent concerns for radical geography. While there is inspiring work done across many disciplines, including geography, to analyse and address hunger – a significant part of it cited in the pages that follow – geographical thought and practice rarely puts hunger at the centre of understandings of human relations with nature. Indeed, it can be strangely overlooked in geographical education.[15] Rereading Castro today, we should continue to be struck by his belief that the profound, widespread, and still permanent condition of hunger, shared by a very significant minority of people around the world, must be the starting point of geographical inquiry because it is the starting point of the human relationship with nature. We do not need to accept every element of Castro's formulations, or leave his theoretical interventions as we find them, to see the political force of this contention. If this book is part of an effort to put Castro's work into closer articulation with anglophone geography, it is above all his straightforward, urgent, unceasing political commitment to creating a world without hunger that remains the most inspiring, and most challenging, of his legacies.

Josué de Castro and the Geography of Hunger

The geography of hunger was not Josué de Castro's idea alone. The spatial, social, and political contingency of hunger is a broader notion than that. Regardless of whether he claimed that it was his invention, the political insistence that hunger is not inevitable precedes and exceeds Castro. Yet there remains much to be gained by exploring the idea through the life and work of this charismatic Brazilian, not only because it provides another string to the bow of anti-imperialist histories of knowledge production but because of the new angle of thought which it supplies to familiar topics. This book has two tendencies throughout: one epistemological, aimed at the construction of geographical knowledge as a collective and political project; the other ontological, directed towards the content of that geographical knowledge and practice. The book insists on the importance of writing histories of geographical knowledge that are multilingual, in translation, and from the south. More importantly, it insists that geographical ideas need to be followed across languages, over disciplinary boundaries, and beyond the confines of disciplinarity.

Castro's academic reputation has waxed in the last two decades in Brazil as not only a scholar of hunger but an inspiration for social movements and a leading interpreter of Brazilian social reality in the twentieth century.[16] As Jacqueline Rose reasoned, 'you read a historic writer not for what they

15 Barney Warf, 'Textbooks in Human Geography: An American Perspective', *Area* 50, no. 1 (2018): 55–58, doi:10.1111/area.12401.

16 See, for instance, Rosana Magalhães, *Fome: uma (re)leitura de Josué de Castro* (Rio de Janeiro: Editora Fiocruz, 1997); Manuel Correia de Andrade, ed., *Josué de Castro e o Brasil* (São Paulo: Editora Fundação Perseu Abramo, 2003); Mercês de Fátima

failed to see, not for the ideological blindspots of their writing [...] but for the as-yet-unlived, still shaping history which their vision—which must mean the limitations of that vision—partially, tentatively, foresees and provokes'.[17] It is in this spirit that this book goes back to an anticolonial geographer from the south. However, this is not a story about internationalizing a subjugated voice; as the book will show, Castro was a profoundly international subject and had access to substantial institutional power and social and cultural capital. He was mobile, networked, and prominent. Nevertheless, there is an unequal and complex set of relations of power and knowledge involved in writing an intellectual history of Castro's geography. The relationship between the knowledge about and through Josué de Castro that I am engaged in producing, and the knowledge that Josué de Castro himself produced, is fraught. It is worth articulating this book's stakes in what Adrienne Rich calls the politics of location.[18] My own position is relatively clear: I write from within the British university system, as a white man with access to signifi- cant intellectual capital, and my work is enabled by various kinds of cultural, social, and economic advantage. I write about Castro not only out of curiosity but out of a conviction that he has important things to say to contemporary academic and political practice in geography. While there are very real problems in importing anticolonial voices into the circuits of a university and publishing sector that remains compromised and colonial, in writing about Josué de Castro this narrative needs to be specific and balanced. For a start, there should be no pretence that he was a subaltern figure. He was a middle-class man, and, though he occupied an ambivalent place in the complex structures of Brazilian racism and white supremacy, nothing, to my knowledge, in the archival record suggests that he suffered from racial discrimination or disadvantage. From a relatively early age he had access to institutions of privilege and status in Brazil and from middle age accrued a global, international prestige. In terms of public status, he reached the pinnacle of academic and diplomatic life. A *relational* politics of location is necessary here; where Castro wrote and acted 'from' was itself multiple and contingent. He was from Brazil, from the Northeast, from Recife, from Madalena by the Capibaribe,[19] but he also wrote from Geneva, Paris, Naples, and Rome. His own relationship with his public prominence was ambivalent: he seems to have enjoyed his public profile, and he leveraged any celebrity

dos Santos Silva, 'Josué de Castro: Um Autor Do Legado Esquecido?' (Universidade Estadual de Campinas, 2016).

17   Edward Said, *Freud and the Non-European*, ed. Christopher Bollas (London and New York: Verso, 2003), 67.

18   Adrienne Rich, 'Notes towards a Politics of Location', in *Feminist Postcolonial Theory: A Reader*, ed. Reina Lewis and Sara Mills (New York: Routledge, 2003), 29–42.

19   Tânia Elias Magno da Silva, 'Josué por ele mesmo: o diário', in *Josué de Castro: Memória do saber*, ed. Tânia Elias Magno da Silva, 1st ed. (Rio de Janeiro: Fundação Miguel de Cervantes, 2012), 55.

he had endlessly in his work against hunger. But he also seems to have been plagued by poor mental and physical health, and – as chapter six explores – the sufferings of exile. To see him as a 'southern' scholar is a complex determination whether we use the south to refer to either a geographical or a metaphorical space.[20] Rather, I place him in the anticolonial tradition of militant intellectuals. In terms of a politics of location, therefore, as much connects me and Josué de Castro as distinguishes us: he wrote, like me, largely from a position of institutional privilege, and his anticolonial, radical politics, though they emerged from his praxis as a doctor, were essentially based on solidarity, commitment, and action, not on position, subjectivity, or identity. To the extent that he was involved in political movements, it was as an intellectual and a politician. As I explore later in the book, in Gramscian terms he was more a traditional than an organic intellectual. Therefore, while the project of writing Castro into contemporary anglophone geography needs to be cautious and self-reflexive, the political contours are to be found in the limitations of colonial institutional and linguistic historiographies of geography, not in Castro's own subjectivity of marginalization. In a sense this is to emphasize the limitations of this book, and Castro's work, in terms of projects that seek to 'decolonise' geography. As Tuck and Yang emphasize, decolonization is not a metaphor,[21] and it remains unachieved. Securing Castro's place in the ensemble of anticolonial geography is to add another instrument to the orchestra, not to declare victory.

I go back to Castro, therefore, not exactly to find new answers to old questions, but to expand disciplinary horizons, contest accepted histories of thought and offer views along paths not taken. As Neil Smith put it in 1988, 'the "history of geographic thought" [...] should by any and all standards be one of the most intellectually stimulating branches of the discipline'.[22] I hold to this enthusiasm while, like Smith,[23] treating the boundaries of the sub-discipline as extremely flexible. I progress more broadly from the premise that we can still learn from reading – closely, contextually, tangentially – an 'old' geographer for his insights, and use Castro's theory and praxis to explore the material and imperial histories of geographical ideas, particularly those around food and hunger. I aim to be both grounded and expansive in this reading, neither anachronistic nor hagiographic. I use Castro's lifepath and work to explore theoretical, as well as historical, problematics in geographical

20 Chandra Talpade Mohanty, '"Under Western Eyes" Revisited: Feminist Solidarity through Anticapitalist Struggles', *Signs* 28, no. 2 (2003): 505–06, doi:10.1086/342914.

21 Eve Tuck and K. Wayne Yang, 'Decolonization Is Not a Metaphor', *Decolonization: Indigeneity, Education & Society* 1, no. 1 (2012).

22 Neil Smith, 'For a History of Geography: Response to Comments', *Annals of the Association of American Geographers* 78, no. 1 (March 1988): 159, doi:10.1111/j.1467-8306.1988.tb00200.x.

23 In, for example, Neil Smith, *American Empire: Roosevelt's Geographer and the Prelude to Globalization*, vol. 9 (Berkeley: University of California Press, 2004).

thought and, in particular, political ecology. Though he does not use its contemporary anglophone lexicon, I follow Latin American geographers in placing Castro's work as a precursor to political ecology, and go beyond both biography and the history of geography to attempt to rethink some of political ecology's core concerns from the perspective of a Pernambucan geographer and the spaces in which his work emerged. In this book, therefore, I will consider a global history of nutrition, but from Latin America, and I will read the workings of the United Nations and the emergence of political ecology from the standpoint of a Third Worldist intellectual.

Castro's geographical theory and praxis put political and economic power at the core of an analysis of the uneven distribution of resources. For Castro, the human always exists in relationship to their particular geographical context, above all through the mechanism of food as an active relationship with the environment.[24] In this relationship people suffer not because an abstract 'nature' cannot provide but because social relations structure unequal access to resources. It is in this sense that his geography of hunger is perhaps most immediately recognizable to contemporary anglophone geographers as a *political ecology* of hunger.[25] Prior to, and somewhat distinct from, the tradition that Raymond Bryant and Sinéad Bailey articulate,[26] we can read his work as part of a Third Worldist tradition of political ecology that speaks, in Enrique Dussel's terms, from an 'epistemological location, that of the victims, the south of the planet, the oppressed, the excluded, new popular movements, ancestral people colonized by Modernity, by globalized capitalism'.[27] Castro's work takes its place in the Third Worldist thought that Enrique Leff has described as 'a discursive amalgam between academic and political actors, between theoretical thought, participatory research and the imaginaries of the peoples, in alliance with resistance movements and their emancipatory strategies [...] historically, theoretically and politically committed to a sustainable future and other possible worlds.'[28]

'Third Worldist' captures the historical and geographical specificity of Castro's work and, although he did not use the term from the beginning of his writing, by the end of his career it was a crucial framework.[29] However,

---

24 See also Castro, *Ensaios de biologia social*, 39–41.

25 For example, the access to resource frameworks found in Nancy Lee Peluso, *Violent Environments* (Ithaca: Cornell University Press, 2001).

26 Raymond L. Bryant and Sinéad Bailey, *Third World Political Ecology* (London and New York: Routledge, 1997).

27 Enrique Dussel, *Politics of Liberation: A Critical World History*, trans. Thia Cooper (London: SCM Press, 2011), 549–50.

28 Enrique Leff, 'Power–Knowledge Relations in the Field of Political Ecology', *Ambiente & Sociedade* 20, no. 3 (September 2017): 237, doi:10.1590/1809-4422asocex0004v2032017.

29 F. Alburquerque, 'Tercer Mundo y Tercermundismo En Brasil: Hacia Su Constitución Como Sensibilidad Hegemónica En El Campo Cultural Brasileño-1958–1990', *Estudos Ibero-Americanos* 37, no. 2 (2011); see also, for example, Josué de Castro, 'De

more than just Third Worldist, I read Castro as an anti-imperialist and anticolonial geographer. He practised a counter-hegemonic politics at many scales, struggling against hunger in the Northeast, in Brazil, and internationally. It is in this sense that his was, as Manuel Correia de Andrade put it, a *geografia combatente* – a combatant geography or, better, a militant geography.[30] Andrade's formulation suggests Castro's place in an alternative history of geography: a militant geography set against Felix Driver's history of 'geography militant', the handmaiden of imperialism and state expansion.[31] Castro's is a geography in alliance with popular movements against colonial oppression, not in alliance with the colonialist impulse and imperial states that foster it. It is in this sense that Castro's geography is militant: the militancy of the movements of decolonization as a whole, from their intellectuals and their partisans.

Nik Heynen has argued that political ecology and, by extension, critical geography needs to develop an abolitionist, anticolonial bent by 'drawing on work outside for the sake of growth'.[32] Slightly differently, by positioning Castro's work within an open field of political ecology, I suggest we can find the kind of anticolonialism the field needs in its own history. Turning to sources outside the history of geography – whether Said,[33] the subaltern school,[34] or the Black Panthers[35] – is the bread and butter of those seeking more radical and emancipatory geographical ideas. My suggestion here is that we can find those ideas and practices within the history of geography itself, particularly if we are open to its intertwined multilingual histories. This presupposes pushing disciplinary and linguistic confines. Producing more emancipatory geographical knowledges, and more emancipatory conditions of possibility for geographical knowledge production, is not as simple as valorizing the work of anticolonial geographers or geographers from the South. Nevertheless, thinking deeply with the work of anticolonial geographers from the past can form part of a wider set of theoretical and practical interventions seeking to fracture Anglo-European hegemony and

Bandung a Nova Dehli: A Grande Crise Do Terceiro Mundo', *Revue Générale Belge, Brussels*, no. 4 (1968).

30 Manuel Correia de Andrade, 'Josué de Castro e Uma Geografia Combatente', *Diario de Pernambuco* (March 1981): 460, CEHIBRA.JdC.

31 Felix Driver, *Geography Militant: Cultures of Exploration in the Age of Empire* (Oxford: Blackwell, 1999).

32 Nik Heynen, 'Urban Political Ecology II: The Abolitionist Century', *Progress in Human Geography* 40, no. 6 (December 2016): 840, doi:10.1177/0309132515617394.

33 Joel Wainwright, 'The Geographies of Political Ecology: After Edward Said', *Environment and Planning A* 37, no. 6 (June 2005): 1033–43, doi:10.1068/a37166.

34 Tariq Jazeel and Stephen Legg, eds, *Subaltern Geographies* (Athens: University of Georgia Press, 2019).

35 Nik Heynen, 'Bending the Bars of Empire from Every Ghetto for Survival: The Black Panther Party's Radical Antihunger Politics of Social Reproduction and Scale', *Annals of the Association of American Geographers* 99, no. 2 (2009): 406–22.

open the discipline towards a political and intellectual future orientated towards liberation. The Sista Resista collective have emphasized the dangers of empty appropriation of the terms of decolonization,[36] and the exchange of geographical knowledge is deeply unequal and attended by 'epistemic expropriation'.[37] Certainly, there are very significant theoretical, political, and epistemological challenges raised by attempts to 'decolonize' the discipline.[38] In spite of these problematics of audience, institutionality, the geopolitics of knowledge, and expropriation, I proceed on the basis that multiplying intellectual histories can open more pathways for radical critique, offer new concepts, and enact an egalitarian politics of knowledge production.

I share Juliet Fall's conviction that 'it matters how and where we do things as geographers. It matters where ideas come from and then where people think about, discuss, and publish them. It matters where ideas are read, how they are spread, how they get picked up, and where they are ignored.'[39] Through her concept of 'disciplinary Orientalism' she argues that geography 'both draws heavily from foreign critical thinkers, often removed from the spaces of debate they are/were writing in, and simultaneously ignores foreign geographical traditions and contributions'.[40] The case of Castro falls into both halves of this simultaneity. On the one hand, where he is referred to in anglophone geography it is without being embedded in a political context, and, on the other hand, the Brazilian, and more specifically Northeastern, tradition of which he is a part is rigorously ignored in mainstream anglophone geography.

In the rest of this introduction, I outline the ways in which Castro's life and work has been archived, canonized, and scrutinized up to now, and the sources available for his biography. This leads me to a consideration of doing biography in the history of geography, and an analysis of its scope and limits as a methodological and historiographical approach. I connect these crucial guide-posts of my work to the problematics of generating an anticolonial mode of thought in political ecology and critical geography.

36 Sista Resista, 'Is Decolonizing the New Black?', sisters of resistance, July 2018, accessed 15 June 2022, https://sistersofresistance.wordpress.com/2018/07/12/is-decolonizing-the-new-black/.

37 Sam Halvorsen, 'Cartographies of Epistemic Expropriation: Critical Reflections on Learning from the South', *Geoforum* 95 (2018): 11–20.

38 James Esson et al., 'The 2017 RGS-IBG Chair's Theme: Decolonising Geographical Knowledges, or Reproducing Coloniality?', *Area* 49, no. 3 (2017): 384–88; Tariq Jazeel, 'Mainstreaming Geography's Decolonial Imperative', *Transactions of the Institute of British Geographers* 42, no. 3 (2017): 334–37.

39 Juliet J. Fall, 'Reading Claude Raffestin: Pathways for a Critical Biography', *Environment and Planning D: Society and Space* 30, no. 1 (2012): 174.

40 Fall, 'Reading Claude Raffestin', 173; see also P. Hubbard, Rob Kitchin, and G. Valentine, 'Editors' Reply to Book Review Forum: Review Essays on: Key Thinkers on Space and Place', *Environment and Planning A* 37, no. 1 (2005): 161–87.

Archives, Biography and the History of Geography

Castro's life and work is available as an object of study thanks to two, at times contradictory, practices: publishing and archiving. He was published and archived both during his lifetime and after his death. Both kinds of practice have been conducted in uneven, at times confusing, ways. Alongside his published work he left a rich personal archive, as well as traces in various repositories in Paris, Rio de Janeiro, Brasilia, Rome, and elsewhere. Josué de Castro's own archive, now at the *Fundação Joaquim Nabuco* in Recife ('Fundaj') was previously housed at the *Centro Josué de Castro*, which was founded in Recife in 1979 and is now winding down, retaining only a proportion of memorabilia of Castro's life.[41] These institutions set out to repair Castro's legacy, much of which was silenced during the Brazilian military dictatorship, which limited study of his work.

The archive comprises around 30,000 documents relating to Castro's life, from newspaper clippings to correspondence and manuscript drafts.[42] They were collated largely by Castro's wife, Glauce, but with assistance not only from Castro himself before his death but also friends in the years after. Castro's library, of around 9,000 volumes, is still in the process of being organized for research.[43] The archive houses some remarkable documents – a telegram sent to Castro by the Cuban government the morning after the Bay of Pigs invasion – and some funny ones – a sardonic note about coverage of the Northeast to the editor of *Time* magazine – but it inevitably contains much of what Brent Hayes Edwards calls 'the inexorable production of the ordinary'.[44] While the archive has an index, it is often inaccurate and incomplete, so the process of research produces unexpected synergies and many scraps of texts that are difficult to date, place, and, in many cases, identify.

Castro was an inveterate launcher of projects and maker of plans. Some of these projects are identifiable in fragments in the archive, but others appear lost. Ill health explains some of the abandoned projects, while, in other cases, things remain obscure. While the Castro archive in the Fundaj is extremely extensive, it is also partial. For instance, Castro kept a diary in the 1950s that would be a valuable resource for further historical research, and the Brazilian police archives of the *Delegacia de Ordem Política e Social* (DOPS) remain

---

41 Helder Remigio Amorim, '"Arquivar a própria vida": o acervo pessoal Josué de Castro como instrumento para a pesquisa histórica', *Interfaces Científicas – Humanas e Sociais* 6, no. 1 (July 2017): 135–44, doi:10.17564/2316-3801.2017v6n1p135-144.

42 Helder Remigio de Amorim, '"Um pequeno pedaço do incomensurável": a trajetória política e intelectual de Josué de Castro', PhD thesis (Universidade Federal der Pernambuco, 2016), https://repositorio.ufpe.br/handle/123456789/23349.

43 Amorim, '"Arquivar a Própria Vida"', 139–40.

44 Brent Hayes Edwards, 'The Taste of the Archive', *Callaloo* 35, no. 4 (2012): 946, doi:10.1353/cal.2013.0002.

difficult to reach. One researcher – Tânia Elias Magno da Silva – has had access to the family archive, for a limited period of time, under supervision.[45] It is held by Josué de Castro's daughter, Ana Maria de Castro. An intimate biography of Castro would need to draw on these personal materials in depth. This book, however, is somewhat less concerned with Castro's inner life than with his contextual manifestation in the world. Evidently, this not a stable or useful binary in itself – the personal is always political, and the political personal – but it is a relevant starting point for considering my own angle on the archive, which has skewed towards the public and the published.

One way of giving a sense of the nature of the archive and how I use it in this book is to zoom in on a single file. File 545 of the personal collection held in the Fundaj is a typical example of the archive in its richness, its randomness, and its indeterminacies. The file is given the title 'Miscelânia não é correspondência', an enigmatic formulation that could be translated as 'Miscellania is not correspondence'. The missing dash gives an endearingly aphoristic quality to the title.

I want to name the contents of this single file's miscellany. The first document is a series of fragile typed pages, which are not gathered under a title page but appear to be a Portuguese-language version of notes from the November 1951 meeting of the Executive Council of the Food and Agriculture Organization (FAO). They are on paper from the Brazilian Ministry of Work, Labour and Commerce, presumably because Castro held one of his many advisory roles there at various points. (Castro kept and reused headed paper from a variety of institutions, and these headers can be red herrings in identifying the sources and dates of documents; just because the headed paper says University of Brazil does not mean that the document in your hand is from his period at that institution, it could be from a decade later). This document is typical in its multilingual and enigmatic quality: Castro worked in French at the FAO and Portuguese wasn't one of the official languages, so was this a translation made for Brazilian colleagues? It is unclear. Underneath this are official, English-language FAO papers from the same conference and formal instructions from the Brazilian Foreign Secretary on the position for Brazil to take up at the FAO conference. Below these papers, we jump forward two years to two identical copies of a press release by the US Senator James E. Murray on the question of an International Food Reserve. Underneath that is an undated, hand-signed petition, 'a Manifesto to the Pernambucan people' calling for a formal celebration to be held in honour of Castro's 50th birthday (so, it is from 1958) at the Teatro Santa Isabel, the main theatre of Recife. It is signed by a group of students. Next is a syllabus for a specialist medical course on 'alimentação e nutrição' [diet and nutrition] for the University of Brazil, taught by Castro, covering clinical metabolic science, physiology, and dietetics. It is

45 See Silva, 'Josué por ele mesmo: o diário'. However, it is worth noting that Silva's access was also constrained, so hopefully a fuller consideration will one day be possible (personal communication, March 2017).

likely to be from the mid-1940s. After a series of formal state papers dealing with the relations between Brazil and the FAO is a strange document: it is a 'report' by an un-named author written in the early 1960s. It seems to be by one of Castro's political consigliere, and it contains a polemical assessment of the state of Northeastern politics and a detailed plan for how 'we' will advance, politically, through the means of ASCOFAM, Castro's proto-NGO active in the Northeast of Brazil from the 1950s. It places Castro in the heart of internal struggles in the Partido Trabalhisto Brasileira [Brazilian Workers Party] and as a political ally on first-name terms with the President of Brazil at the time, João Goulart, aka 'Jango'. After that is a press release, seemingly from the World Association of Parliamentarians, dated 16 October 1963, which describes a speech by Castro that 'caused smoke to curl out of the windows of the annex to the Old League of Nations' Palais Wilson', in which Castro 'yanked the audience into contemporary reality' and 'thundered' over the need for 'an Einsteinian perspective in the Nuclear Age'. Beneath that is a programme, in English, for a stay in Moscow, then fragments of a paper related to the post-war peace movement and the Pugwash conference. Tucked in among this is a brief note, unsigned and undated, in English: 'Idea for a book': 'There is no book (that I know of) which gives a graphic presentation country by country of the actual daily life of the peoples of the world in terms of the three necessities of life: food, shelter, and clothing.' Next is a speech in French by Castro on Khrushchev's proposals for general disarmament, in which he advertises 'Le Plan Vert International' [The International Green Plan] of the Association Mondiale de Lutte contre la Faim [the World Association Against Hunger]. It precedes what seems to be an annotated proposal in French for a film called 'Terre Humaine', unsigned and undated, though apparently written by Castro shortly after 1960. The film tells the story of the twentieth century and the global geography of hunger through a series of vignettes, moving from 'Guerre et Bidonvilles' [War and Shantytowns] to 'UNICEF-OMS' [UNICEF-WHO]. It seems that the film was probably planned within the auspices of Castro's work with the World Campaign Against Hunger in the early 1960s, but it's hard to be sure. The next document is sheet music: 'A BRAVE NEW WORLD: Hymne of the world citiezens, Dedicated to Jos[u]é de Castro, Président of the world citiezens' [sic]. The lyrics run: 'When peace is in your heart, then Peace will reign the World, Let's all reach hands, unite the nations, And forge a brave new world.' It is followed by a version of the lyrics in Esperanto. Next is a lengthy proposal for four conferences on the geography of Latin America: in Spanish, unsigned, undated, on blank paper. It seems possible that this document is connected to one of Castro's late publications, 'Adonde va la América Latina?' [Where is Latin America Going?].[46] That document, probably from around 1966, precedes a 'Proposed Programme for Second World Congress of Doctors

---

46 Josué de Castro, *Adónde va la América Latina? Dinámica del desarrollo, cambios y resistencias sociales* (Lima: Editorial Latino Americana, 1966).

for the Study of Present-Day Living Conditions', dated April 1956. Castro was associated with that congress – a kind of international pressure group for progressive doctors that worked to draw public attention to the relation between health and nutrition – for a few years, including acting as its President. Finally, there is a twelve-page homage, in English, to Lord John Boyd Orr. I will come back, throughout this book, to certain elements of this motley assortment, but as a whole it testifies to the nature of Castro's life and work, and to the nature of doing archival work on Castro's life and work. It is full of tantalizing possibilities and unexpected connections. Many of the threads, when pulled, come apart in your hands; others lead to deep wells. My approach to this book has been to rely on this archive's idiosyncrasies and to enjoy its frayed edges.

My interest in Castro began, of course, not in the archive but in the world. Most specifically, I came to him in his use by the *mangue beat* movement of the early 1990s, based in Recife. The first question I asked about Castro was not about his geographical theory but about why this youthful, innovative, urban musical movement of the early 1990s named a long-dead nutritionist and geographer as a figurehead. It was out of an interest in the organic qualities of Castro's intellectual journey and the regionally specific qualities of his radicalism that I began my enquiry. Looking for discussion of his work in anglophone geography, I found a few references to Castro – by scholars such as Ben Wisner, Nancy Scheper-Hughes, Keith Buchanan, and Michael Watts – but, though they all stated his significance and his radicalism, they did not develop any more detailed analysis or put his geographical writing to work. This specifically passing kind of interest in Castro piqued my curiosity: if he is cited as a significant predecessor for the analysis of the political economy of hunger, why has his broad range of work remained relatively unexplored? I approach the archive, then, from the outside in, not from the inside out. I have not sought to correct the record of other versions of Castro's life, but to dwell on the ways that his full and manifold biography can stand for a new political history of geography in itself. The biographical drive of this book is precisely metonymic: I read Castro's geographical life and work as an alternative history of geography itself in the twentieth century.

Research in historical geography in English has recently emerged on Josué de Castro,[47] above all a series of important articles by Federico Ferretti, but he has long been an important figure in Brazilian geography and political

47   Archie Davies and Federico Ferretti, 'Josué de Castro', in *Geographers: Biobibliographical Studies*, Vol. 40, ed. Elizabeth Baigent and André Reyes Novaes (London: Bloomsbury, 2022); Federico Ferretti, 'Geographies of Internationalism: Radical Development and Critical Geopolitics from the Northeast of Brazil', *Political Geography* 63 (March 2018): 10–19, doi:10.1016/j.polgeo.2017.11.004; Federico Ferretti and Breno Viotto Pedrosa, 'Inventing Critical Development: A Brazilian Geographer and His Northern Networks', *Transactions of the Institute of British Geographers* 43, no. 4 (May 2018): doi:10.1111/tran.12241; Eric D. Carter, 'Population Control, Public Health, and Development in Mid Twentieth Century Latin America', *Journal of Historical Geography* 62 (April 2018): doi:10.1016/j.jhg.2018.03.012.

thinking, particularly in Recife and the Northeast. Renato Carvalheira do Nascimento sees Castro's reception in four phases.[48] The first pertains to the democratic opening of Brazil in the 1970s and 1980s, when Castro was written about as a significant figure in establishing connections between medicine, public health, and the social sciences. Secondly, an institutional upsurge of interest in Castro and the mapping of hunger then came in the early 1990s. Thirdly was his use by the Lula government as an intellectual and political figurehead of the *Zero Fome* [Zero Hunger] project both at home and abroad.[49] Finally, there was a resurgence in historical interest in the late 2000s.[50] The Brazilian process of democratization and opening up, and the leftward turn under Lula, were fruitful contexts for this rediscovery and reassessment of Castro's work.

Much of the Brazilian work on Castro can be seen as variegated attempts at canonization. This process began during Castro's own lifetime with the publication of a collection of essays on his work to coincide with his 50th birthday,[51] and continues in more recent collections.[52] An important figure here

48 Renato Carvalheira do Nascimento, 'O Resgate Da Obra de Josué de Castro, Onde Estamos?', *Revista Cronos* 10, no. 1 (2012).

49 Eduardo Matarazzo Suplicy, 'Programa Fome Zero Do Presidente Lula e as Perspectivas Da Renda Básica de Cidadania No Brasil', *Saúde e Sociedade* 12 (2003): 61–71; Markus Fraundorfer, *Brazil's Global Fight against Hunger and Poverty* (London: Palgrave Macmillan, 2015), 86–131; Luiz Inácio Lula da Silva, 'Twenty-Ninth McDougall Memorial Lecture', Thirty-Ninth Session of the Food and Agriculture Organization of the UN (Rome: FAO, 2015); Luiz Cláudio dos Santos, 'Da Geografia da Fome ao Fome Zero' (Doutourado, Universidade Estadual Paulista (UNESP), 2009).

50 Helder Remigio de Amorim, 'Em tempos de guerra: Josué de Castro e as políticas públicas de alimentação no Estado Novo', *Revista CLIO* 1, no. 35.1 (August 2017): 51–75; Helder Remigio de Amorim, 'Entre o Intelectual e o Político: a Participicação de Josué de Castro no Partido Trabalhista Brasileiro Durante o Segundo Governo Vargas', in *Democracia Liberdades Utopias* (2018), 14; Helder Remigio de Amorim, '"Sete Palmos de Terra e Um Caixão": Escrita e Práticas Políticas Na Trajetória de Josué de Castro', in *XXVII Simpósio Nacional de Historia* (Conhecimento histórico e diálogo social, Natal-RN, 2013), 1–13; Maria Letícia Galluzzi Bizzo, 'Ação política e pensamento social em Josué de Castro', *Boletim do Museu Paraense Emílio Goeldi. Ciências Humanas* 4, no. 3 (2009): 401–20.

51 Miguel Herédia and Souza Barros, eds., *O Drama Universal da Fome* (Rio de Janeiro: Livraria Francisco Alves, 1958).

52 Andrade, *Josué de Castro e o Brasil*; Tânia Elias Magno da Silva, *Josué de Castro: Memória do saber* (Rio de Janeiro: Fundação Miguel de Cervantes, 2012); Bernardo Mançano Fernandes and Carlos Walter Porto Gonçalves, *Josué de Castro: Vida e Obra*, 2nd ed. (São Paulo: Editora Expressão Popular, 2007); Anna Maria de Castro, ed., *Josué de Castro: Semeador de Ideias* (Veranópolis: Iterra, 2003); Marcelo Mário de Melo and Teresa Cristina Wanderley Neves, eds, *Josué de Castro*, Perfis Parlamentares 52 (Brasília: Câmara dos Deputados: Coordenação de Publicações, 2007).

is Manuel Correia de Andrade,[53] a geographer working in Recife, who took up the strands of Castro's work as part of his own long-term project to understand the agrarian economy of the Northeast and, through a politically engaged geographical practice, to advocate for radical land reform in Brazil.[54] Silvio Tendler's documentary *A Cidadão do Mundo* [The Citizen of the World][55] collates many remarkable interviews – from Dom Hélder Câmara to former President of Portugal Mario Soares – discussing Castro's impact and oeuvre. In the film, Darcy Ribeiro describes him as 'the most luminous Brazilian intelligence of the twentieth century'.[56] Castro's legacy within Brazilian geographical thought has always been a contested and political question, but his place in the Brazilian geographical canon is now secure.[57] Such canonization is in part a response to an earlier sense of loss after Castro's exile, the political repression of his work, and the banning of his books in Brazil. As Arnold Niskier put it, remembering Castro's work has become a 'question of honour'.[58]

In English, in the last few years, Ferretti's work has placed Castro squarely in an expanding field of the history of geography from the south. He has not only shown Castro's contributions to an early version of critical development studies but articulated Castro's work within the context of mid-twentieth-century decolonization and geopoetics. This attention to Castro as a geographer, and to the Northeast as an important region in the history of critical geography not only in Brazil but also globally, has been late in arriving to anglophone geography. My own focus, in an extended dialogue with both Ferretti's work, and that of contemporary Brazilian scholars working on similar questions, including Helder Remigio de Amorim, Breno Viotto Pedrosa, Mariana Lamego, and others, picks up and develops these themes through the particular lenses of translation, political ecology, and a theoretical concern with the place of humanism in geographical approaches to hunger. It owes a huge amount to the rich flourishing of contemporary scholarship on Castro in Brazil, particularly in Pernambuco, and aims to pick up points of dialogue with contemporary Brazilian scholars throughout, while bringing a distinctive

53 Manuel Correia de Andrade, 'Lembrada morte do pensador', *Diario de Pernambuco*, June 1983, Domingo edition, sec. P.
54 Federico Ferretti, 'Decolonizing the Northeast: Brazilian Subalterns, Non-European Heritages, and Radical Geography in Pernambuco', *Annals of the Association of American Geographers* 109.5 (2019): 1632–50.
55 Sylvio Tendler, *Josué de Castro – Cidadão do Mundo*, 1994, accessed 15 June 2022, https://www.youtube.com/watch?v=fQrwW1sjHyI.
56 Irineu Guimarães, 'Josué de Castro: Um Cientista Que Soube Amar Seu País Mesmo Conhecendo a Verdade', *Jornal do Commercio*, February 1997, Domingo edition.
57 André Roberto Martin and Mônica Sampaio Machado, eds, *Dicionário Dos Geógrafos Brasileiros* (Rio de Janeiro: FAPERJ, 2014); Rui Ribeiro de Campos, 'A Presença Na Geografia de Josué de Castro', *Revista Geográfica de América Central* 2 (2011): 1–23.
58 Arnold Niskier, 'Ano Internacional de Josué de Castro', *Jornal do Commercio*, June 1993, Quinta-feira edition.

emphasis on Castro's life, legacy, and theory-making. This is not only the first English language book-length study of Castro but the first to systematically address his work, as this book's chapters do, through the lenses of the body, translation, the region, exile, and political ecology. The book attends to the theoretical dimensions of the geography of hunger in a novel way, in particular in developing the question of humanism and its geographies, which emerge as a central thread in my analysis of Castro's work. Though also motivated by the history of geography, my approach therefore travels outside historiographical concerns and connects the history of disciplinary geography to ideas circulating in critical geography and political ecology today.

There is an important distinction to be drawn between Castro's Northeastern, Brazilian, and international legacies. These scales inter-relate in complex ways: regional disciplinary histories are implicated in international ones. Keighren, Abrahamsson, and della Dora ask whether a canon of human geography exists, what role it might play, and what its importance is to understanding the history of geography.[59] If the canon of human geography exists, it is multiple, and it has a geography, a history, and a historical geography. One way of approaching these historical geographies of knowledge is through biography.

Castro's life and ideas took unexpected turns and emerged in unexpected places. I investigate his biography to explore how his geographical concepts, positions, and engagements, particularly around hunger, had extremely variable outcomes at different scales and in different institutions and conversations. My approach brings together scholarship on biography within the history of geography[60] with work on anticolonial geography. Biography can contribute to recalibrating the history of radical geography away from anglophone and anglo-North American histories and towards a more imbricated, anticolonial trajectory of mutual influence and exchange between North and South and between theory and praxis. With the recent publications of collections such as *Spatial Histories of Radical Geography: North America and Beyond* (2019) and *Decolonising and Internationalising Geography* (2020), the multiplication of histories of critical geography is in full swing,[61]

59 Innes M. Keighren, Christian Abrahamsson, and Veronica della Dora, 'On Canonical Geographies', *Dialogues in Human Geography* 2, no. 3 (2012): 296–312.

60 Cheryl McGeachan, 'Historical Geography II: Traces Remain', *Progress in Human Geography* 42, no. 1 (February 2018): 134–47, doi:10.1177/0309132516651762.

61 Trevor J. Barnes and Eric Sheppard, eds, *Spatial Histories of Radical Geography: North America and Beyond* (Hoboken, NJ: Wiley-Blackwell, 2019); Federico Ferretti and Breno Viotto Pedrosa, 'Alternative Geographical Traditions from the Global South', *Geography Directions* (blog), June 2018, accessed 15 June 2022, https://blog.geography-directions.com/2018/06/12/alternative-geographical-traditions-from-the-global-south/; Bruno Schelhaas et al., eds, *Decolonising and Internationalising Geography: Essays in the History of Contested Science*, Historical Geography and Geosciences (Cham: Springer International Publishing, 2020), doi:10.1007/978-3-030-49516-9.

and biographical approaches are central to this.[62] This book aims to make contributions to this field of debate in two methodological veins. First, I use the question of translation as a crucial theoretical orientating point for my approach. This brings to bear a rich field of work in and beyond geography on the history, practice, and theoretical significance of translation in the history of knowledge. I approach translation as a mode of thinking about the history of geographical ideas at lexical, political, theoretical, practical, and historical scales. Secondly, drawing on feminist historiographies of geography, such as that of Avril Maddrell, and the histories of Black feminist thought, such as Saidiya Hartman's recent *Wayward Lives*, I build on the idea that research on the history of ideas must go beyond texts to consider the theoretical significance of lifepaths, fragments, and praxis. This is an approach to biography and the history of geography that shares much with other vital work that intertwines biographical research with theoretical investigation: Susanna Hecht's work on Euclides da Cunha and Neil Smith's on Isaiah Bowman are two shining examples.[63] The biographical drive of this book, therefore, argues that Castro's work on public health, activism, regional and national legislation, international peace activism, and world food policy are all part of his contribution to geographical knowledge. I use the development and traction of his idea of the geography of hunger as a lens through which to refract the history of geography itself. This does not mean telling a disciplinary history as such, but rather stitching together a story about how one geographers' ideas moved and changed, not only in themselves but in the world and in practice.

Geographical ideas emerge unevenly across linguistic space. Keighren, Abrahamsson, and della Dora write that 'engagement with multilingual canonical texts can lead to the rediscovery of forgotten networks, alternative historiographies, and thus new ways of recounting geography's past [...] it can also lead [...] to new ways of engaging with the present and, more significantly, imagining and shaping possible futures'.[64] Castro can find a place alongside Reclus, Kropotkin, Penck, Geddes, and Ghisleri in the early twentieth-century internationalist networks that the authors of 'on canonical geographies'

---

62 Federico Ferretti, 'History and Philosophy of Geography II: Rediscovering Individuals, Fostering Interdisciplinarity and Renegotiating the "Margins"', *Progress in Human Geography* 45, no. 4 (November 2020), doi:10.1177/0309132520973750; Daniel Clayton, 'Historical Geography I: Doom, Danger, Disregard – Towards Political Historical Geographies', *Progress in Human Geography* 45, no. 6 (2021), doi:10.1177/03091325211011664.

63 Susanna B. Hecht, *The Scramble for the Amazon and the 'Lost Paradise' of Euclides Da Cunha* (Chicago: University of Chicago Press, 2013); Smith, *American Empire*; see also Gavin Bowd and Daniel Clayton, *Impure and Worldly Geography: Pierre Gourou and Tropicality* (London: Routledge, 2019).

64 Keighren, Abrahamsson, and della Dora, 'On Canonical Geographies', 306.

highlight: his trajectory from Pernambucan concerns to an avowedly globalist position by the 1960s is worth charting in part to understand the folds and flows of internationalist exchange. His trajectory reveals, too, a particular moment at which visionary utopian projects to solve global hunger were underpinned by particular historical and geographical imaginations. Castro's work connects this history with the disciplinary development of geography. The 'situated messiness'[65] of Castro's biography offers a path through an alternative disciplinary history.

There is a rich and well-trodden path of work in 'lifepaths' and biography in the history of geography,[66] which works on the basis that 'the arts of geography and biography are historically connected'.[67] Longstanding projects such as the *Geographers: Biobibliographical Studies* and *Geography and Geographers: Anglo-American human geography since 1945* attest to this. Biography can also help internationalize the discipline and its history, challenge its anglophone bias, and draw attention to the sites and places of the production of geographical knowledge.[68] Anne Buttimer's pioneering *The Practice of Geography* (1983) and her work for the International Geographical Union was pushing, nearly forty years ago, for a broader understanding of the discipline through geographers' biographies.[69]

Biographical approaches can also challenge the masculinist history of the discipline, drawing attention to how geography has written its own history, challenging who counts as a geographer and how geographical knowledge is

65 David Livingstone, *The Geographical Tradition: Episodes in the History of a Contested Enterprise* (Oxford: Blackwell, 1993); see also David N. Livingstone, 'In Defence of Situated Messiness: Geographical Knowledge and the History of Science', *GeoJournal* 26, no. 2 (1992): 228–29.

66 Innes M. Keighren, *Bringing Geography to Book: Ellen Semple and the Reception of Geographical Knowledge*, vol. 4 (London: IB Tauris, 2010); Innes M. Keighren et al., 'Teaching the History of Geography: Current Challenges and Future Directions', *Progress in Human Geography* 41, no. 2 (2017): 245–62; Charles W.J. Withers, 'History and Philosophy of Geography 2004–2005: Biographies, Practices, Sites', *Progress in Human Geography* 31, no. 1 (2007): 67–76; Trevor J. Barnes, 'Lives Lived and Lives Told: Biographies of Geography's Quantitative Revolution', *Environment and Planning D: Society and Space* 19, no. 4 (2001): 409–29; Trevor J. Barnes, 'History and Philosophy of Geography: Life and Death 2005–2007', *Progress in Human Geography* 32, no. 5 (2008): 650–58.

67 Stephen Daniels and Catherine Nash, 'Lifepaths: Geography and Biography', *Journal of Historical Geography* 30, no. 3 (2004): 449.

68 Juliet J. Fall and Claudio Minca, 'Not a Geography of What Doesn't Exist, but a Counter-Geography of What Does: Rereading Giuseppe Dematteis' Le Metafore Della Terra', *Progress in Human Geography* 37, no. 4 (August 2013): 544, doi:10.1177/0309132512463622; see also Fall, 'Reading Claude Raffestin'.

69 See, for instance, her series of video interviews with geographers from non-anglophone traditions, discussing national geographical disciplines.

constructed.[70] These approaches complicate a historiography of the discipline that sees the 'spatialization of tradition as a transparent territory'.[71] However, I do not set out to make a detailed critique of such disciplinary history not only because I find this to be a fertile and enlightening field of contemporary scholarship but also (and more importantly) because I want to tell Castro's story from beyond a preconceived set of anglophone and francophone ideas about what the history of twentieth-century geography is. I always start from Castro, putting his trajectory at the centre of geography, rather than in relation to a centre that is elsewhere and already established. Through this I am trying to tell an alternative history of geography, not trying to change an existing history of geography. In the rest of the book, the reader will therefore find fewer statements about disciplinary histories of geography than they might expect in a book that is also a history of geography. The feminist critique of the history of geography remains troubling for an alternative history that seeks to take Josué de Castro seriously: this book is littered with men. Articulating the relationship between, for example, Milton Santos and Josué de Castro risks reproducing the 'dutiful son' model of academic masculinity. Yet there are good feminist reasons – discussed below, including anticolonialism, polylingualism, translation – why it is important to place Josué de Castro's work in dialogue with anglophone histories of geography. One means of responding to feminist historiographies of geography is to fracture the disciplinary history of geography beyond its recognized spaces and texts and into the messier realm of the history of geographical ideas. This is a more diffuse and complicated category. This does not resolve the problem: masculinist histories of knowledge are not so easily resolved. What it does suggest, however, is the importance of a broader field of praxis to the production of geographical knowledge.

Josué de Castro's own relationship with the disciplinary history of geography was very explicit: he sought to intervene in the development of geographical ideas in association and dialogue with great geographical thinkers of the past, from all kinds of school of thought and areas of the world. He also partook in what José Borzacchiello da Silva calls French geography's 'hegemony' in Brazil, established not only through the dissemination of the Vidalian tradition but also through the personal intervention of Pierre Monbeig, a major figure in mainstream Brazilian geography, who was key to the establishment of the modern discipline in

---

70 See, for example, Mona Domosh, 'Toward a Feminist Historiography of Geography', *Transactions of the Institute of British Geographers* 16, no. 1 (1991), 95–104; Avril M.C. Maddrell, 'Scientific Discourse and the Geographical Work of Marion Newbigin', *Scottish Geographical Magazine* 113, no. 1 (1997): 33–41; Janice Monk, 'Women, Gender, and the Histories of American Geography', *Annals of the Association of American Geographers* 94, no. 1 (2004): 1–22.

71 Gillian Rose, 'Tradition and Paternity: Same Difference?', *Transactions of the Institute of British Geographers* 20, no. 4 (1995): 415.

Brazilian universities and particularly in São Paulo.[72] Though not a fully signed-up participant of the 'Vidalian' school of Brazilian geography,[73] in Milton Santos' words 'within Geography [Castro's] position was that of an authentic possibilist'.[74] He was committed to moving geographical analysis out of disciplinary confines and into wider political, intellectual, and public discourse. For him, geography was always *both* disciplinary and expansive. It is this openness – and his attention to an ecological way of thinking[75] – that Manuel Correia de Andrade argued was Castro's crucial inheritance for Brazilian geographical thought.[76] Castro himself emphasized that he learned from the people of the marshes, novelists, the landscape, and ecology. As well as picking up on a Vidalian trope of the centrality of fieldwork[77] and the claim to authenticity through realism,[78] we can also place this practice in the long-term relationship between intellectual and political practice in Latin America, particularly over questions of land. For instance, he was part of an earlier stream of scholars of underdevelopment and dependency that laid some of the ground for contemporary scholarship within the paradigm of modernity/coloniality/decoloniality. Given the wealth of research in this field, it is a propitious moment for geography to reassess Castro. Indeed, the intellectual history pursued here could inform what are often foreshortened accounts of modernity/coloniality/decoloniality itself.

Castro's biography is an instigation to take seriously a variety of geographical practices and geographical knowledge making, and to add new textures and sources to the history of geography. My approach follows what Barnes notes is biography's task to walk along the 'knife-edge between social context (structure) and personal creativity (agency)'.[79] Mine is not a project dedicated to following the details of Castro's life. More often than not I prioritize Castro's political statements and practice, and his explicit scholarly engagements, using his life as a way of reading his wider social context more than the other way around. Yet this is only part of the story. I have been selective in my archival analysis, focusing in particular on his

72 José Borzacchiello da Silva, *French-Brazilian Geography: The Influence of French Geography in Brazil* (Cham: Springer, 2016), 25–29.
73 Andrade, 'Josué de Castro e Uma Geografia Combatente', B-7.
74 Milton Santos, 'Josué de Castro e a Geografia da Fome', in *Geografia da Fome*, by Josué de Castro (Lisbon, Portugal: Instituto Superior de Psicologia Aplicada, 2001), 21.
75 See 'Preface' by André Mayer in *Josué de Castro, Géographie de la faim: le dilemme bresilien: pain ou acier*, trans. Jean Dupont, 2nd ed. (Paris: Éditions du Seuil, 1964).
76 Andrade, 'Josué de Castro e Uma Geografia Combatente', B-7.
77 Gavin Bowd and Daniel Clayton, 'Fieldwork and Tropicality in French Indochina: Reflections on Pierre Gourou's Les Paysans Du Delta Tonkinois, 1936: Fieldwork and Tropicality in French Indochina', *Singapore Journal of Tropical Geography* 24, no. 2 (June 2003): 147–68, doi:10.1111/1467-9493.00149.
78 Orain Olivier, *De Plain-Pied Dans Le Monde* (Paris: L'Harmattan, 2009).
79 Barnes, 'Lives Lived and Lives Told', 415.

international commitments, networks, and travels, and on his regional, Northeastern concerns. This has meant, for instance, less attention to important dimensions of his life – for instance, his role in Brazilian national party politics. These emphases will emerge clearly throughout the book, but I note them here as a methodological premise; this is not an exhaustive biography, but biography as a means to trace, populate, and analyse the history of ideas. This is a variant on what Hodder has called 'a different kind of biographical work, one that is less concerned with knowing a life per se than how those experiences can cast light on the wider social and cultural worlds that a life inhabits'.[80] I principally read Castro's biography for what it has to tell us about the twentieth-century geography of hunger, and its history, even though, at times, that story needs to be told through the intimate, quotidian details of a lived life. Unlike Barnes' access to a deliberative set of oral interviews with geographers, my project relies on a body of archival material. Hodder notes that biography can be a means for controlling for archival abundance, and this is certainly true in many cases. The archive of Castro's life, however, is copious and highly mediated, so a unified life is elusive, even if a historian were to set out to reconstruct one. I zoom in and out of the archive, finding moments of density in the record that I put to use (in chapter 2, for instance), skirting around other episodes that produced a wealth of archival material and elsewhere putting a lot of emphasis on scraps and fragments (as in chapter 7). I put together this motivated intellectual biography through setting Castro's archive in conversation with his published output and the many traces of his political practice.

Jazeel argues in favour of 'present[ing] texts from different geographical origins to the Euro-American readership in ways that effectively realign the axis of global comparativism'.[81] These texts can have many forms, and this process of realignment should be relational. It involves reconfiguring the spatial imaginaries of where geographical thinking takes place, and the texts and contexts through which it does. Feminist geographers have laid out the need to do away with the fraternal/paternal schools of institutional knowledge production and to recognize the multiple heritages of how geographical knowledge is to be understood as situated, multiple, and gendered.[82] This book enacts these insistences by making visible the spatialities and contradictions of tradition and the hierarchies of knowledge production. It finds geographical theory in mobile and fragmented places. Nevertheless, I bring forward a male geographer whose notion of the political subject is masculinist. It therefore propagates a patrilineal history of

80 Jake Hodder, 'On Absence and Abundance: Biography as Method in Archival Research', *Area* 49, no. 4 (December 2017): 453, doi:10.1111/area.12329.

81 Tariq Jazeel, 'Between Area and Discipline: Progress, Knowledge Production and the Geographies of Geography', *Progress in Human Geography* 40, no. 5 (October 2015), 661.

82 Rose, 'Tradition and Paternity'.

geographical thought, and this is a shortcoming of the book. Innes Keighren argues that 'our shared goal as historians of geography should not be definitiveness but nuance; our task is not to agree a particular narrative, but to disrupt established accounts and to find new ways of telling our stories'.[83] Thinking with Castro and his legacy seeks to contribute to that project.

Chapter Overview

This book has seven chapters, which proceed in loosely chronological, biographical order, but which are each held together by thematic concerns that emerge out of a contextual and intertextual reading of Castro's life and work. The chronological drive tracks the changing nature of the geography of hunger through its multiple texts and contexts and against the landscape of Castro's life. This is a fruitful backdrop for an alternative history of twentieth-century geography, following Castro from his place in a French-influenced Brazilian tradition through to putting geography into less familiar sites at the UN and the FAO, and in the radical regionalism of the Brazilian Northeast and the proto-revolutionary Parisian 1960s.

In the first chapter I emphasize that the history of critical geographical thought is tangled up with histories of humanism. I show how Josué de Castro's geographical methodology and geographical politics were inseparable from his commitment to a reformulated humanism aligned with the project of liberating the peoples of the Third World. This focus on humanism is, I hope, a significant contribution to contemporary geographical work that positions itself within, against, or beyond various kinds of post-, trans-, or anti-humanism. I will return to this in the conclusion. The intersections between histories of radical humanism and histories of radical geography are productive areas of enquiry. So too are the histories of nutritional science, and its intersection with histories of agriculture, which I explore through Castro's work. I show how Castro himself moved, at the level of both theory and praxis, from a nutritional to a geographical methodology, and how this shift continues to be a powerful challenge to geographies of the body, food, and hunger. My analysis suggests that geographies of nutrition, agriculture, and food could be more closely integrated. I do not, here, address Castro's urban geography, which emerged in a patchwork of texts across his life. As I have argued elsewhere, his contributions to urban thinking and to geographical approaches to landscape can be deeply insightful for geographical work on the Northeast of Brazil and on the relations between landscape and infrastructure.[84]

In chapter 2 I use Castro's work and biography to make a different kind

83 Keighren, *Bringing Geography to Book*, 4:7–8.
84 Davies, 'The Racial Division of Nature'; Davies, 'Landscape Semaphore', 2021; Archie Davies, 'On the Coloniality of Infrastructure', *Environment and Planning D: Society and Space* 39.4 (2021): 740–57.

of intervention, into the history of geography. By exploring the publication, translation, and reception of Castro's work I argue that analysis of the history of geography could attend in more detail to the mobility of ideas, and more precisely to the historical and philological questions of translation. This intervention takes further work in the history of geography that is premised on analysis of the movement of knowledge. In reflecting on the twenty-fifth anniversary of his *The Geographical Tradition*, David Livingstone intimated that the process of translation of his own work 'made [him] far more aware of the need for careful attention to the practices of translation in the circulation of knowledge'.[85] This is an important realization on the part of probably the most influential anglophone historian of geographical thought. While there has been some interest in questions of translation in geography, my analysis shows that this lens changes our conception of how geographical ideas have developed, how processes of canonization and readership function, and how the historiography of the discipline must take account of the mobility of ideas and the material and intellectual frictions through which they travel. The forms by which this mobility and friction affect ideas are themselves sources of theoretical insight. So too, I argue, are the interstices between languages. Geographical theory-making can proceed through the complex, grounded, and highly theorized practice of translation. The movement of the idea of the *geografia da fome* out of Portuguese and into other languages is attended by theoretical potential. For instance, drawing on the language Castro used, what does a *geografia da alimentação* – an alimentary geography – offer to contemporary anglophone work on food and hunger? It presupposes, I suggest, an attention to the specific somatic needs of diet as well as the practised, necessarily social functions of feeding. It is by thinking through translation that we can raise such questions for geographical enquiry.

In chapters 3 and 4 I approach the geography of hunger as an open and intertextual set of ideas, which manifest through Josué de Castro's practice and in the work of his interlocutors in the spheres of art and politics. Addressing first the aesthetic dimensions of the geography of hunger, I take forward the questions raised in the first chapter on humanism and the spatial qualities of the body. In chapter 4 I focus on Castro's grounded and prosaic attempts to make hunger into a meaningful kind of universalism through the mechanics of post-war international institutions.

In the second half of the book I analyse the intellectual history of the Northeast of Brazil through the lens of Josué de Castro's life. This takes me both to, and far beyond, the Northeast itself. I argue that the history of critical thought from the Northeast offers new formulations for political ecology at the scale of the region, through not only the region's material history but how that history was interpreted by the Northeast's thinkers in

---

85 Livingstone in Ruth Craggs et al., 'Intervention: Reappraising David Livingstone's *The Geographical Tradition: A Quarter of a Century On', *Transactions of the Institute of British Geographers* 44 (2019): 438–43.

the mid-twentieth century. I suggest that the scale of the region is one that cannot be overlooked, and must be historicized, in political ecology. I open up some of the ways in which the intellectual history of the Northeast can contribute to Gramscian geographies. Much further work – in particular through analysis of the writing and praxis of Francisco de Oliveira, as well as of the dependency school – could expand and deepen this contribution. I argue that thinking about Castro as a public intellectual makes a contribution to assessment of the public role of geography and its status as a discipline. The problematic of why Castro – as a high-profile left-wing intellectual at a particular moment in twentieth-century history – has not been made part of the international history of critical geography leads me to question how geography has conceived of itself. Castro's biography, I argue, gives new angles on the scales and forms by which intellectual work is, or becomes, political praxis in specific historical geographies. This analysis contributes, I suggest, an expanded framework and an alternative historical context for the tasks and antinomies of being a public geographical intellectual.

Castro's archive yields a potent set of documents – many fragmentary – with which to reconstruct an important episode in the history of critical geography through analysis of the geography department at Vincennes. By putting these fragments at the front of my research I am able to show, in chapter 7, not only how an important passage in the history of political ecology developed but also the intersections between place, pedagogy, collaboration, and institutions in the history of geography.[86] This puts a Southern scholar at the centre of the development of geographical thought in a Northern institution. Through an analysis of the first UN conference on the environment, in Stockholm 1972, at which Castro was an important player, the chapter shows that anticolonial and Third Worldist critiques of Malthusianism were a vibrant feature of the emergence of international environmentalism. Finally, in the conclusion, I return to anticolonial metabolic humanism by reading Castro's negative geography of hunger as a contribution to a new, radical geography of survival.

86 See Sharp, 'Practising Subalternity'.

CHAPTER 1

1930–1946: The Geography of Hunger and Metabolic Humanism

It was not at the Sorbonne, or at any other seat of learning,
that I came to know the anatomy of hunger, but
rather in the marshy land of the poor parts of Recife.

Josué de Castro, 1970

Introduction

In this opening chapter I uncover the roots of Castro's idea of the geography
of hunger in order to reconstruct an argument for its continued relevance
today. I interpret Castro's trajectory of thought as he moved from the study
of the hungry body in Recife to an anticolonial geography of hunger, and
return to the nutritional foundations of his work. One of the finest definitions
of the European Renaissance tradition of humanism is that of making 'man'
'the measure of all things'.[1] Particular ideas of the body emerge alongside
particular versions of humanism, and I argue that Castro's work in nutrition
and medicine underpin his own unique version of a humanist geography.
Nutrition is a way of measuring not just the human but the human's depend-
ence on the natural world through the necessary condition of hunger and
through food as the interface between the human and the world. This is
why, for Castro, geography, as the privileged study of the human relationship
with nature, was from the ground up a geography of hunger. By reading the
development of his work, I draw out of it a metabolic humanism in tune with
political ecology's present concerns.

Castro described his endeavour as 'a tragically strange geography which,
instead of describing the earth feeding man, presents man serving simply
to feed the earth'.[2] This kind of dramatic formulation was both a marker of

---

1 Denis Cosgrove, 'Historical Considerations on Humanism, Historical Materialism
and Geography', in *Remaking Human Geography*, ed. Audrey Kobayashi and Suzanne
Mackenzie (London and New York: Routledge, 1989), 194–95.
2 Castro, *Geography of Hunger*, 32.

Castro's rhetorical, literary style and grounded in his regional worldview. The telluric and tragic quality of his geography is captured in the title of his late work on the Northeast, *Sete Palmos de Terra e uma Caixão* (1965). The book is usually translated as *Death in the Northeast*, but both a more literal and poetic rendering would be 'seven handfuls of earth and a coffin' or, as the title of the first chapter of the English version has it, 'six feet under and a coffin'. Castro's fascination with hunger brings with it a geographical interest in death. Yet through his strange, negative, metabolic geography, Castro's geography of hunger is resolutely intertwined with his militant humanism.[3] Read in this way, Castro's geography of hunger comes into view as a disruptive theory that, in Adam David Morton's words, written in relation to Antonio Gramsci, 'has to be grasped in the place and time out of which it emerges as a part of that time and then subsequently related to the places where it might be put to use'.[4] Castro's demand for a world without hunger was a demand for a whole new social, ecological, and economic system, because he understood hunger not merely as a consequence of socio-economic forms but as a necessary precondition of their propagation. Overcoming hunger would require a new space in which humanism could flourish, against the dehumanizing forces of exploitation. We should take Castro's radical humanism seriously not least (to follow Richard Pithouse on Frantz Fanon) because Castro himself did.[5]

Food is a 'tenacious force', he wrote, as early as 1936.[6] Twenty years later, as the global politics and geography of hunger had changed drastically – with his involvement, as chapter 4 explores – so too Castro's conceptualization of the geography of hunger had developed. He had come to the argument that 'it is perhaps through the nutritional link that the environment – soil and climate – even though indirectly, exerts its most decisive influence on the physical vigour, productive capacity and resistance to disease of human groups'.[7] This means that the socioeconomic structure of society is crystallized and reproduced in the body. Hunger is 'biological slavery'; 'the formative pressures of economic and cultural forces make themselves felt [...] through the biological mechanism: it is through the nutritional deficit that monoculture imposes itself'.[8] All of this moves the body more

---

3 Clodomir, 'Josué de Castro: Brasileiro e Cidadão Do Mundo'.

4 Adam David Morton, 'Traveling with Gramsci: The Spatiality of Passive Revolution', in *Gramsci: Space, Nature, Politics*, ed. Alex Loftus et al., 1st ed. (Chichester: John Wiley & Sons, 2013), 60.

5 Richard Pithouse, '"That the Tool Never Possess the Man": Taking Fanon's Humanism Seriously', *Politikon* 30, no. 1 (2003): 109.

6 Josué de Castro, *Alimentação e Raça*, 1st ed. (Rio de Janeiro: Civilização Brasileira, 1936).

7 Josué de Castro, *Geopolítica da Fome: Ensaio sôbre os Problemas de Alimentação e de População do Mundo*, 4th, revista e aumentada ed., vol. 1 (São Paulo: Editôra Brasiliense, 1957), 5.

8 Josué de Castro, *Geografia da Fome: A Fome No Brasil* (Rio de Janeiro: Emprêsa Gráfica 'O Cruzeiro' S.A., 1946), 31.

resolutely to the centre of thinking about space and nature than elsewhere in mid-twentieth-century geography and anticipates recent configurations of the corporeal in political ecology.

This chapter sets the methodological tenor of the rest of the book as I return to Castro's intellectual trajectory to formulate and reform the idea of the geography of hunger. I do not intend to tell a disinterested history of Castro's life. Rather, my approach is a motivated attempt to draw out of his ideas, praxis, conflicts, mistakes, and misapprehensions a set of useful provocations for thinking about the history of geography and the geography of hunger today.

1930s: From *Antropofagia* to Nutrition

In the autumn of 1930 political life in Brazil burst into crisis with a military coup led by Getúlio Vargas. Vargas, from the state of Rio Grande do Sul, had been the liberal opposition candidate, running against Júlio Prestes, a conservative who would have continued the Old Republic and its longstanding politics of *café com leite* [coffee with milk], in which the coffee elites of São Paulo state allied with the dairy interests of Minas Gerais. In 1930, Vargas put an end to this Old Republic and began a long period at the pinnacle of Brazilian state power. Under Vargas the state began to centralize, and some of the old élites were challenged. Corporatist politics gained an – albeit often untrustworthy – voice in the centre of state politics,[9] and various movements for national development clicked into gear. Yet Vargas moved with the winds of politics as much as he commanded them, swaying from liberal to populist to autocrat and back again during his initial fifteen years as President, and then again from 1951 until his suicide in 1954.

The first decades of Castro's own political career were intimately tied to Vargas'. In Pernambuco the revolution of 1930 had seen significant political tumult, not least because the politician João Pessoa, who was Vargas' candidate for the vice-Presidency in the 1930 elections, was assassinated in *A Glória* sweet shop in Rua Nova, in the centre of Recife. Pessoa's murder was one of the triggers of Vargas' coup. The first five years of the new republic was marked by instability, and in 1935 there was a short-lived communist uprising, one of whose centres was Recife. Following this, amid Vargas' increasingly authoritarian rule and the installation of the *Estado Novo* [New State], Recife was the centre of a quasi-fascist government, until the installation of the Second Brazilian Republic in 1946. Throughout this period Recife was also a regional centre not only of left-wing politics but of Brazilian cultural and intellectual life.

9 John D. French, 'The Origin of Corporatist State Intervention in Brazilian Industrial Relations, 1930–1934: A Critique of the Literature', *Luso-Brazilian Review* 28, no. 2 (1991): 13–26.

Figure 1. Josué de Castro at the Palatine Hill in Rome, 1939.
Source: Acervo Fundação Joaquim Nabuco – Ministério da Educação – Brasil

It was in this political milieu that Josué de Castro came of age as an intellectual. During the late 1920s and early 1930s Castro moved between Recife and Rio de Janeiro, studying, writing and working in both, as well as travelling to Mexico, the United States, Europe, and Argentina (Figure 1). He was a passionate follower of cinema and an aspiring poet, writer,[10] and social commentator.[11] In early adulthood, hunger was not his primary concern.[12] He knew Oswald de Andrade and Mário de Andrade, the leading modernists who changed the face of Brazilian culture. Castro published an underwhelming romantic poem in the famous *Revista de Antropofagia*[13] [The Magazine of Anthropophagy], the outlet for the anthropophagic movement, which saw the destiny of Brazilian modernism to be in cannibalizing European culture and confronting the epistemological challenge of being

10 See, for example, Josué de Castro, 'A Poesia de Manoel de Abreu', *A Nação*, June 1936, 110, CEHIBRA.JdC; Josué de Castro, 'Introducção Ao Estudo de Philosophie', *A Nação*, February 1936, 110, CEHIBRA.JdC.

11 See, for instance, Josué de Castro, 'Assistencia Social', *A Manhã*, August 1936, 110, CEHIBRA.JdC.

12 Normando Jorge de Albuquerque Melo, 'Josué de Castro Antes da Fome', *Revista Aurora* 4, no. 1 (2010): 140–42.

13 Josué de Castro, 'Namôro', *Revista de Antropofagia*, November 1928.

(European) in the Americas.[14] Before 1930, Castro had expected a government post in education,[15] but the revolution altered his fortunes and instead he established a medical practice in his hometown. In a series of twists of fate he became a specialist in nutrition.[16] Nutritional knowledge was undeveloped in Recife: Castro later said that there was only one relevant book on nutrition in the medical faculty library, an obscure German handbook on internal medicine by Falle Umber.[17] Castro was employed as a factory doctor in 1930, and it was at this time that his interest in hunger solidified. Although they presented themselves with various kinds of illness, Castro realized that his worker–patients were chronically malnourished. With this insight a swathe of work began that was to culminate with the 1946 *Geografia da Fome*.

In 1932 he conducted the first nutritional survey ever undertaken in Brazil,[18] commissioned by the Department of Public Health of the State of Pernambuco and published as *As Condições da vida das classes operárias no Recife* [The Conditions of Life of the Working Classes in Recife] in 1935.[19] This was a Brazilian manifestation of a rising concern with nutrition around the world,[20] with which Castro would increasingly involve himself in the decades to come, but which in the early 1930s was still nascent, and with which Castro did not, at that point, demonstrate a concern. Rather, this early work came from his position embedded in a progressive political moment in Brazil, and in Recife. The book's Engelsian title is not accidental, and tells us a lot about Castro's critical attitude to prevailing social structures, but it does not indicate he was a Marxist. His early work was to prove a constant touchstone for his studies on hunger: 'it was not at the Sorbonne, or at any other seat of learning, that I came to know the anatomy of hunger, but rather in the marshy land of the poor parts of Recife'.[21] His early scientific knowledge of nutrition came from primary urban sociological fieldwork. Most of the workers and unemployed whom the survey covered lived in informal settlements ('*mocambos*') in the interstices of the mangrove-lined,

---

14 Melo, 'Josué de Castro Antes da Fome', 141.

15 Fernandes and Gonçalves, *Josué de Castro*, 28–29.

16 Melo and Neves, *Josué de Castro*, 52.

17 Melo and Neves, *Josué de Castro*, 52.

18 Jorge Luiz Alves Natal, 'A Questão Alimentar-Nutricional Na Politica Economica (1930–1976): Um Vai-Vem Na Periferia Da Agenda Publica', Master's thesis (Universidade de Campinas, 1982), 23–25.

19 On the interesting publication history of the short book see the introduction to Josué de Castro, *As condições de vida da classe operária no Recife: estudo econômico da sua alimentação*, ed. Rita de Cássia Barbosa de Araújo Araújo (Recife: Editora Massangana, 2015), 7–9.

20 Michael Worboys, 'The Discovery of Colonial Malnutrition between the Wars', in *Imperial Medicine and Indigenous Societies*, ed. David Arnold (Manchester: Manchester University Press, 1988), 208–25.

21 Josué de Castro, *Of Men and Crabs*, trans. Susan Henterlendy, 1st ed. (New York: Vanguard Press, 1970), ix.

deltaic, muddy, infrastructural landscape of Recife.[22] Castro saw that hunger had immediate effects and was a proximate cause and exacerbating effect in the spread of infectious diseases.[23] He described this urban socio-ecological landscape of Recife as 'the cycle of the crab': people lived in metabolic relation to their urban environment, catching crabs for subsistence, while the crabs lived off human detritus. This diet left people malnourished and hybrid – imbued with their environment through their metabolic relation to it: 'humans fashioned of crab meat [...] foster brothers to the crab'.[24] Castro never lost sight of the cycle of the crab. This particular regional metabolic relationship remained the cornerstone of his thought. In the crab cycle human relations with nature are direct and metabolic, familial and corporeal.

Condições initiated an interdisciplinary analysis of the biological and social life of Recife's working class, an approach Castro termed *biosociologia*. This was a rich interdisciplinarity embedded in Castro's own unique skillset and background: he was practising as a social scientist, a natural scientist, a writer, and a medical doctor in this period. It was as a factory doctor that he began his investigations into hunger. Indeed, we have an intriguing image of Castro at this time in his thinly fictionalized autobiographical story 'Assistência Social', written in the mid-1930s. It follows a young liberal doctor working in Recife in a factory confronting a hypocritical factory boss who refuses to pay for the most basic services for their staff.[25] When Castro wrote *Condições* he calculated the cost of living – a healthy and adequate diet, but also clean water, rent, and electricity (the metabolic necessities of life) – and juxtaposed it with actual wages and available diet. He found food fundamentally lacking not only in quantity but also in vitamins, minerals, and nutrients: 'there is only one way of feeding yourself worse than this: not to eat at all'.[26] In *Condições* Castro began to develop a metabolic critique of everyday life. However, the book does not address the social reproduction of life or the division of labour of food provision. Nor did that book offer what Castro would later produce: a geographical understanding of hunger. Castro started to promote his ideas on public nutrition across Brazil – specifically in Rio, São Paulo and Recife.[27] As his status grew, Castro sought to embed nutritional study in academic institutions and to bring nutritional science into

22 I explore Castro's particular conception of landscape in Archie Davies, 'Landscape Semaphore: Seeing Mud and Mangroves in the Brazilian Northeast', *Transactions of the Institute of British Geographers* 46, no. 3 (September 2021): 626–41, doi:10.1111/tran.12449.

23 Magalhães, *Fome: uma (re)leitura de Josué de Castro*, 29–35.

24 Castro, *Of Men and Crabs*, xii.

25 Josué de Castro, *Documentário do Nordeste*, 2nd ed. (São Paulo: Editôra Brasiliense, 1959), 41–44.

26 Castro, *As condições de vida da classe operária no Recife*, 22.

27 Anonymous, 'A Nota Literária', *Jornal do Recife*, July 1934, Quarta-feira edition.

public policy.[28] He was involved in establishing the Faculty of Philosophy and Social Sciences, teaching not only Human Geography but also courses in Social Biology.[29] *Condições* also marked Castro's entry point into public policy, in particular in relation to the minimum wage. He became involved in various public health initiatives in Recife, including against alcohol as well as about diet.[30]

Involved in nutritional labs, libraries, union meetings, and protest marches, Castro was the embodiment of connections between political movements and medical scientific controversies over nutritional science. Tracing his work as a nutritional scientist and the development of Latin American sciences of nutrition is important not least because traditional anglophone histories of the discipline see it as an insistently Northern, and indeed imperial science.[31] Much nutritional science saw the colonial world as an open laboratory for nutritional experiments.[32] With important exceptions discussed below, even avowedly postcolonial histories of nutrition argue that 'nutritional medicine came of age under imperial rule',[33] and overlook histories of science in the global south. It was in the middle of the 1930s, and thanks to his work on the connections between labour, public health, and nutrition, that Castro started to become an important figure on the Brazilian left. In the context of President Vargas' corporatist policies, he made the important connection between the labour and peasant movements campaigning for agrarian reform, nutritional intervention, and a minimum wage, both in public discourse and through legislative efforts.[34] Castro challenged what was known about hunger, by whom, from what sources, and in what forms. He wrote: 'when we speak of the national politics of food [...] it is a grave embarrassment to that policy that so little is known of the origins of our humblest classes'.[35] In his interests in Afro-Brazilian food

28 Magalhães, *Fome: uma (re)leitura de Josué de Castro*, 26–30; see also Manuel Correia de Andrade, 'Josué de Castro: O Homem, o Cientista e Seu Tempo', *Estudos Avançados* 11, no. 29 (April 1997): 169–94, doi:10.1590/S0103-40141997000100009; Mônica Sampaio Machado, 'A Implantação Da Geografia Universitária No Rio de Janeiro', *GEOgraphia* 2, no. 3 (2009): 123–40.

29 Josué de Castro, 'Educação', *Jornal do Recife*, April 1934, Domingo edition.

30 Josué de Castro, 'A Semana Anti-Alcoolica Doi Iniciada, Hontem, Em Todo o Brasil', *Jornal do Recife*, October 1934, Terça-feira edition.

31 For a general history of nutritional science see Carpenter's four part series for the *Journal of Nutrition*, beginning from 1785: Kenneth J. Carpenter, 'A Short History of Nutritional Science: Part 1 (1785–1885)', *The Journal of Nutrition* 133, no. 3 (March 2003): 638–45, doi:10.1093/jn/133.3.638.

32 Worboys, 'The Discovery of Colonial Malnutrition between the Wars'.

33 John Nott, '"How Little Progress"?: A Political Economy of Postcolonial Nutrition', *Population and Development Review* 44, no. 4 (2018): 2.

34 See, for example, 'Projeto de lei elaborado pelo deputado federal Josué de Castro' in Magno, *Memória Do Saber*, 'Combate Ao Latifúndio e Reforma Agraria Para Acabar Com a Fome No Brasil', *Diario Trabalhista*, December 1946, Combate.

35 Castro, *Documentário do Nordeste*, 124.

knowledges and the food cultures of the Northeast, Castro was an early activist scholar along the lines of Vandana Shiva and Carlos Walter Porto-Gonçalves, who continue to insist that the politics of food and agriculture is also necessarily a politics of knowledge.[36]

Nutritional science itself was deeply political in the emerging New Republic. Castro was at the centre of a public debate with Gilberto Freyre, the hugely influential Brazilian intellectual, and, to a lesser extent, Nelson Chaves, an important figure in public health in Pernambuco.[37] Gilberto Freyre and Castro were both from Recife, but the former's infamously rose-tinted view of racial relations in his epic *Casa Grande e Senzala* paints a very different picture of the Northeast, and Brazil, to that in Castro's work. These differences were methodological and geographical. Castro built his analysis on detailed surveys and demographic and medical methodologies. Freyre's style was more arm's length, touring principally rural areas by car.[38] Freyre argued that in colonial Brazilian society most people were well fed – including enslaved people. Castro had a much more critical view of the relationship between race and nutrition; his analysis makes clear that the harmonious society Freyre appeals to does not and did not exist. At stake was not only social history but the constitution of the body politic – who they were and what they ate. Freyre publicly criticized Castro's doctoral thesis on nutrition in the 1930s, attacking him for attempting to go beyond his remit as a nutritionist and a doctor into the realms of social science. Castro responded that Freyre did not have the necessary scientific understanding to critique his analysis.[39]

The exchange generated more heat than light, but two important conclusions emerge from it. The first is that, as Silva notes, there is 'no doubt' that 'it was Josué de Castro who since 1932 initiated this debate [about hunger] in a serious fashion in Brazil. With his socio-geographic method and approach dealing not only with physiological, but with cultural and economic questions.'[40] The second is that it demonstrates the centrality of food and hunger to the national question in the 1930s.[41] Freyre responded aggressively to Castro precisely because

36 For example, Carlos Walter Porto Gonçalves, 'Geografia Da Riqueza, Fome e Meio Ambiente: Pequena Contribuição Crítica Ao Atual Modelo Agrário/Agrícola de Uso Dos Recursos Naturais', *Revista Internacional Interdisciplinar INTERthesis* 1, no. 1 (2004): 1–55.

37 Francisco de Assis Guedes de Vasconcelos, 'The Nutritionist in Brazil: A Historical Analysis', *Revista de Nutrição* 15, no. 2 (August 2002): 127–38, doi:10.1590/S1415-52732002000200001.

38 Maria Lúcia Garcia Pallares-Burke, *Gilberto Freyre: Um Vitoriano Dos Trópicos* (São Paulo: Editora UNESP, 2005).

39 Melo, 'Josué de Castro Antes da Fome'; Amorim, 'Em Tempos', 67–68.

40 Mercês Santos Silva, 'Gilberto Freyre e Josué de Castro: dois Brasis?', XXVII Congreso de la Asociación Latinoamericana de Sociología. VIII Jornadas de Sociología de la Universidad de Buenos Aires (Buenos Aires, 2009), 9.

41 Todd A. Diacon, *Stringing Together a Nation: Cândido Mariano Da Silva Rondon and the Construction of a Modern Brazil, 1906–1930* (Durham, NC: Duke University

Brazilian national identity was at stake. Meanwhile, in *Alimentação e Raça* (1935) Castro lacerated the racism of those arguing that laziness, eating habits, and physical inferiority were responsible for the poverty of Afro-Brazilians. In both the Brazilian and British cases, food and nutrition were inextricably questions not only of science and knowledge but of economics and culture. In part, these debates about food were freighted precisely because they coalesced around the Northeast. This region has often been characterized by Brazilians as the most Brazilian – and originary – place in Brazil. This has always had a bitterly ironic dimension, in the sense that the region is both the epicentre and the periphery of Brazilianness. Freyre was one of the key figures in this regional history. Albuquerque Junior wrote that for 'Freyre, the birth of the region came before that of the nation'.[42] I will return to the region in Chapters 5 and 6. What is key here to recognize is that from early in his career Castro was committed both politically and intellectually to the question of the region, and willing to go toe to toe with Gilberto Freyre over how the Northeast was to be understood.

In 1934 Castro further developed his theoretical lens with his first major work, *O Problema da Alimentação no Brasil*. The book was prefaced by the Argentine nutritionist Pedro Escudero. Escudero, the major figure of nutritional science in Latin America at the time, was an important mentor for Castro.[43] In 1928 he had established the *Instituto Nacional de la Nutrición* in Buenos Aires with a radical mission statement connecting metabolic life to political life:

> The basis of the conservation of life [...] is nutrition: life, vigour, reproduction, spirit, society and morality depend on nutrition. Therefore, this Institute understands by 'Nutrition' not only the study of the life of man as a physical and moral entity but the study of the society which constitutes man. The National Institute of Nutrition is not only a hospital (though we treat the sick), nor is it only a biological laboratory (though we study life), nor is it a centre of social studies (though we investigate society), nor an agency of social action (though we help the needy), nor a school (though we teach), nor a pulpit (though we preach). It is all these together.[44]

Press, 2004); Mercês de Fátima dos Santos Silva and Everardo Duarte Nunes, 'Josué de Castro e o Pensamento Social Brasileiro', *Ciencia & Saude Coletiva* 22 (2017): 3677–88.

42 Durval Muniz de Albuquerque Jr, 'Weaving Tradition: The Invention of the Brazilian Northeast', *Latin American Perspectives* 31, no. 2 (March 2004): 51, doi:10.1177/0094582X03261187.

43 José María Bengoa, 'Nutrición En América Latina. Algunos Eslabones de Su Historia', in *Historias de La Nutrición En América Latina*, 1st ed. (Caracas: Sociedad Latinoamericana de Nutrición, 2002), 14–34; Maria Letícia Galluzzi Bizzo, 'Latin America and International Nutrition', in *Beyond Geopolitics: New Histories of Latin America at the League of Nations*, ed. Alan McPherson and Yannick Wherli (Albuquerque: University of New Mexico Press, 2015), 223–39.

44 Pedro Escudero, 'Instituto Nacional de La Nutrición', *Revista de La Associación Argentina de Nutrición, Buenos Aires* XVII, nos 65–66–67–68 (1959): Cover.

Escudero's statement reiterates the potential political significance of nutrition in this conjuncture. His voluminous collected works are primarily scientific studies of nutritional illnesses and the biochemistry of metabolism. The *Instituto* published the journal *Revista de Dietologia*, which interlaced discourses on social welfare with scientific investigations of metabolism.[45] Escudero sought to intervene in public policy and published widely on both the science and politics of nutrition.[46] At the Institute women did most of the work and – as Janet King shows of North American female nutritional scientists – largely remain unaccredited.[47] Practical nutritional science was often relegated to the domestic sphere and care of household nutrition was seen as women's work. As feminist scholarship has shown, the labour of care and social reproduction is vastly undertaken by women,[48] and the gendered dismissal of nutrition as domestic knowledge may help explain why academic histories of nutrition have not been widely incorporated into geographical thinking about the body. Just as Social Reproduction Theory has demystified the production of labour power as a commodity, so critical research can demystify the gendered dynamics of both nutrition and nutritional science. Certainly, the subject and target of nutritional research in early twentieth-century Latin America was predominantly the labouring (or potentially labouring) male body. The female body was largely figured as a producer of nutrition through breastmilk, not its subject.

My interest here is in articulating the social and political valency of nutritional science in this particular conjuncture. The politics of increasing nutritional knowledge were simple: these scientists were showing that society as it was constructed was unable to adequately feed many – perhaps most – of its people. They were coming up with new empirical, quantitative, and verifiable methods and discourses that appeared to demonstrate the failure of an economic system in the most basic and visceral terms. Castro's own survey work was done in 1932. Similar analytical approaches, which produced similar political ructions, were concurrently being undertaken elsewhere, not least in Britain, with the 'nutritional controversy' and the Hunger Marches of the 1930s.[49] Exposing that actual wages and welfare could not provide adequate

45 Laura B. López and Susana Poy, 'Historia de La Nutrición En La Argentina: Nacimiento, Esplendor y Ocaso Del Instituto Nacional de La Nutrición', *Diaeta* 30, no. 140 (2012): 39–46.

46 Pedro Escudero, *Métodos de Cálculo Para Determinar El Valor Calorico Total*, 1st ed. (Buenos Aires: Instituto Nacional de la Nutrición, 1938); Pedro Escudero, *Los Requerimientos Alimentarios Del Hombre Sano y Normal y Las Encuestas de Alimentacion*, 1st ed. (Buenos Aires: Instituto Nacional de la Nutrición, 1943).

47 Janet C. King, 'Contributions of Women to Human Nutrition', *The Journal of Nutrition* 133, no. 11 (2003): 3693–97.

48 Katie Meehan and Kendra Stauss, *Precarious Worlds: Contested Geographies of Social Reproduction* (Athens: University of Georgia Press, 2015).

49 Madeleine Mayhew, 'The 1930s Nutrition Controversy', *Journal of Contemporary History* 23, no. 3 (1988): 445–64; David F. Smith, 'Commentary: The Context and

nutrition to the working classes threatened the stability of state and capital structures and fomented radical politics.[50]

As an investigative natural scientist, Castro's early work studied how the tropical climate influenced basal metabolism. The white, masculine working body at the base of Northern metabolic science was replaced in Castro's work with the hungry migrant from the *sertão*. In this movement we can see, too, indications of his humanistic approach, for which the measurable body of nutritional science is a crucial subject. But, following Castro, a different nutritional body emerges for humanism.[51] Leonardo da Vinci's Vitruvian man is replaced by another eight-limbed figure, the *homem-caranguejo*. The charts and tables of his nutritional surveys are a different kind of measure of all things. This is a different approach to overturning humanism from Aimé Césaire's attempt to reconstruct a new humanism made to 'the measure of the world'.[52] Indeed, it can be put in that company. Castro did not utterly break out of the inheritance of European humanism in the biological sciences and the 'biocentric narrative [which] unevenly imbues the science of the body and the science of knowledge with race'.[53] Castro's theory and praxis of the geography of hunger can nevertheless offer a nutritional, geographical, ecological understanding of the body, which can contribute to the struggle to 'redefine Marx's class struggle in the terms of a "politics of being"'.[54] Castro's *homem-caranguejo* can be lined up against Leonardo's Vitruvian Man in the struggle 'waged over what is to be the descriptive statement of the human'.[55]

The practice of medicine was a threshold for Castro's political commitments. Though Castro's context was very different to the Algerian doctors

Outcome of Nutrition Campaigning in 1934', *International Journal of Epidemiology* 32, no. 4 (2003): 500–02; Charles Webster, 'Health, Welfare and Unemployment during the Depression', *Past & Present*, no. 109 (1985): 204–30; Wal Hannington and T. Mann, *Unemployed Struggles 1919–1936. My Life and Struggles Amongst the Unemployed. [Introd. by T. Mann]. With 42 Illustrations* (London: Lawrence and Wishart, 1936).

50 Hannington and Mann, *Unemployed Struggles*; For similar, roughly contemporaneous metabolism controversies in Germany see Corinna Treitel, 'Max Rubner and the Biopolitics of Rational Nutrition', *Central European History* 41, no. 1 (2008): 1–25; Jakob Lederer and Ulrich Kral, 'Theodor Weyl: A Pioneer of Urban Metabolism Studies', *Journal of Industrial Ecology* 19, no. 5 (2015): 695–702.

51 Wynter, 'Unsettling the Coloniality'.

52 Pithouse, '"That the Tool"', 110–11.

53 Katherine McKittrick, 'Axis, Bold as Love: On Sylvia Wynter, Jimi Hendrix, and the Promise of Science', in *Sylvia Wynter: On Being Human as Praxis* (Durham, NC: Duke University Press, 2015), 146.

54 Katherine McKittrick, *Sylvia Wynter: On Being Human as Praxis* (Durham, NC: Duke University Press, 2015), 319.

55 McKittrick, *Sylvia Wynter*, 319.

studied by Frantz Fanon under conditions of colonial war,[56] Castro's Third Worldist *scientific* work nevertheless attempted to re-form the natural science of the body in the circumstances of the Northeast of Brazil. Fanon, of course, was also a clinician.[57] The Brazilian literary critic Roberto Schwarz described the uptake and adaptation of European enlightenment ideas in Brazil as *'ideias fora do lugar'* – 'out of place ideas'.[58] For Schwarz, the fundamental premises of European liberalism came upon a profound unreality in Brazil, what he called 'an ideological comedy',[59] a formulation that recalls Castro's own argument, made in 1930, that the Brazilian intellectual elite lacked 'serious people'.[60] For Schwarz, whereas in the European context production relied on relations of exchange, in Brazil it relied on enslaved labour and the vast landscapes of the *latifundia*. For Schwarz these structures had their true object beyond Brazil, so rendering national social life and cultural production hollow and even farcical. Arbitrary relations of 'favour' came to underpin a social economy built on fundamentally meaningless grounds: 'in matters of rationality, roles were shuffled: economic science became fantasy and morality, obscurantism equalled realism and responsibility, technical considerations were not practical, and altruism sought to bring about the exploitation of labour'.[61] Schwarz's analysis recalls that of Sérgio Buarque de Holanda, who sees Brazilians as 'exiles in [their] own land':[62] 'in the process of reproducing its social order, Brazil unceasingly affirms and reaffirms European ideas, always improperly'.[63] Schwarz argued that slavery unsettled the bases of liberal humanism, but in an improper way. Abolition came about because wage labour became more profitable than enslaved labour. In this way 'the confrontation between humanity and inhumanity, in which no doubt there was a question of justice, ended up in a more earthbound way as a conflict between two modes of investment'.[64] Schwarz argues that these conditions determined Brazil's intellectual life well into the period of dependency in the twentieth century.

56 Frantz Fanon, 'Medicine and Colonialism', in *A Dying Colonialism* (New York: Grove/Atlantic, Inc., 1965), 121–45.

57 Richard C. Keller, 'Clinician and Revolutionary: Frantz Fanon, Biography, and the History of Colonial Medicine', *Bulletin of the History of Medicine* 81, no. 4 (2007): 823–41.

58 This is my translation. On other translations of 'ideias fora do lugar' see Introduction to Marilena Chauí, *Between Conformity and Resistance: Essays on Politics, Culture, and the State*, trans. Maite Conde (New York: Palgrave Macmillan, 2011).

59 Roberto Schwarz, *Misplaced Ideas: Essays on Brazilian Culture*, trans. John Gledson, 1st ed. (London: Verso, 1992), 20.

60 Melo, 'Josué de Castro Antes da Fome', 146.

61 Schwarz, *Misplaced Ideas*, 36.

62 Sérgio Buarque de Holanda, *Roots of Brazil*, trans. Daniel E. Colón (Notre Dame, IN: University of Notre Dame Press, 1936), 1.

63 Schwarz, *Misplaced Ideas*, 47.

64 Schwarz, *Misplaced Ideas*, 36.

'Ideas out of place' can serve to contextualize Castro's confrontation with European natural science and its inherited conception of 'man', filtered through the tropes of Brazilian racial anthropology. Castro's own ideas were 'out of place' or 'improper' precisely because they emerged in this Brazilian intellectual context. In *Condições da Vida das Classes Operárias no Recife* he contested the biologism of racial anthropology in Brazil,[65] writing on the first page of his 1932 book that the lack of productivity of the racialized working classes of Brazil *'não é mal de raça, é mal de fome'* – 'is not a flaw of race, but of hunger'.[66] Underpinning this argument is Castro's humanism, insisting on the inclusion into society of those who were racially maligned as naturally inferior. It was also a class-based humanism: aligning himself with an intellectual and political role model, he quoted the quasi-biopolitical words of doctor and founder of the Argentine socialist party Juan B. Justo: 'nowadays you cannot murder the proletariat, but you can legally make it die of hunger'.[67] His nutritional approach rearticulated how European and North American natural science methods could be brought into Brazilian social contexts and laboratories, against racial anthropology. In the rest of this chapter I will show not only how these insights led to further developments in Castro's own ideas but also how this nutritional starting point became a geographical commitment.

From Nutrition to Land

Castro's debate with Freyre came at a delicate time in his public intellectual life and helped him earn a reputation as an independent-minded figure.[68] After his move to Rio in the mid-1930s he became part of the Faculty of Philosophy at the University of Brazil and developed relationships with key intellectual figures, including the anthropologist Roquette Pinto and the writer Mário de Andrade, with whom he maintained a long correspondence.[69] His work on nutrition and the minimum wage threatened the corporatist pact between the élite and the emerging working classes in Brazil. Thanks to rising labour organization, but also directly in response to Castro's *Condições* and other studies that followed it, in 1940 the Brazilian Minimum Wage was introduced.[70] However, its level was inadequate, and it was largely not

---

65 See Eronides da Silva Lima, Mal de Fome and Não de Raça, *Gênese, Constituição e Ação Política Da Educação Alimentar: Brasil–1934–1946* (Rio de Janeiro: Editora da Fiocruz, 2000).

66 Castro, *As condições de vida da classe operária no Recife*, 11.

67 Castro, *As condições de vida da classe operária no Recife*, 12.

68 Interview with Francisco Bandeira de Melo, Recife, 1997 in Magno, *Memória Do Saber*, 653–69.

69 Castro, *Semeador de Ideias*, 21; Ana Maria de Castro in Fernandes and Gonçalves, *Josué de Castro*, 28–29.

70 Preface by Rita de Cássia Barbosa de Araújo in Castro, *As condições de vida da classe operária no Recife*.

implemented, particularly in the Northeast. That law marked only a staging post in the struggle against hunger in Brazil, to which Castro dedicated his life, which continues today, still informed by Castro's legacy.

However, the connection between income and nutrition in Castro's work did not yet constitute a structural critique of hunger, and Castro's analysis developed through the 1940s. *Alimentação e Raça* (1936) began with metabolism: 'all the phenomena which take place in our organism consume a portion of energy, and this energy does not come from some mysterious place inside the living being. It enters the human machine with the food that we eat.'[71] He began to incorporate a geographical attentiveness into his study of vitamins. Emerging knowledge of vitamins shifted nutrition in the early twentieth century from energetics to a more broadly bio-political field in which the environment and the body were in dynamic, non-determinist interconnection by which food provides 'metabolic functions distinct from the supply of sustenance' and the body is understood as relational and contingent on and implicated in its environment.[72] For Castro hunger was not monolithic but always precisely instantiated. How it manifested – as a lack of vitamins, protein, or minerals – was an indicator of the particular historical geography in which the body was embedded. In 1937 he published *Alimentação Brasileira à luz da Geografia Humana* [The Human Geography of the Brazilian Diet] and his field of enquiry had grown: 'penetrating the dark and complex thicket of the living phenomena of nutrition, [... consists of a] serious and complicated study, with its roots buried deep in the fields of sociology and philosophy, with influences that spread far into the most varied corners of life'.[73] He therefore turned to geography in order to study hunger 'no more in its partial aspects, but as a whole [...] based on the methods and principles of human geography, capable of allowing a total view of the subject'.[74] As Lima put it, he sought to give 'universal status to the close ties between the biological body and the social body'[75] – the ecological humanism introduced above. For Castro, geography was always an *abrangente* project – open, broad, and totalizing; he set himself, often polemically, against fractured or partial forms of knowledge. As Clayton has demonstrated, the question of

71 Castro, *Alimentação e Raça*, 17.
72 Robyn Smith, 'The Emergence of Vitamins as Bio-Political Objects during World War I', *Studies in History and Philosophy of Science Part C: Studies in History and Philosophy of Biological and Biomedical Sciences* 40, no. 3 (2009): 182.
73 Josué de Castro, *A Alimentação Brasileira à Luz Da Geografia Humana*, 1st ed. (Pôrto Alegre: Livraria do Globo, 1937), 17.
74 Castro, *A Alimentação Brasileira*, 13.
75 Eronides da Silva Lima, 'Quantity, Quality, Harmony and Adaption: The Guiding Principles of a Society without Hunger in Josué de Castro', *História, Ciências, Saúde-Manguinhos* 16, no. 1 (2009): 171–94; Ferretti, 'Geographies of Internationalism'; Mateus Litwin Prestes, 'O Pensamento de Josué de Castro e a Geografia Brasileira', *Revista Geográfica de América Central* 2 (2011).

the fragmentation or totality of geographical knowledge has recently become a concern for historical geography and historians of geographical thought, as the Anthropocene reinsists on the total qualities of the planetary.[76]

Increasingly committed to this holistic quality of geographical thought, by the early 1940s Castro was at the cusp of his geographical theory of hunger. *Geografia da Fome* constructed a cartography of the spatial distribution of ecologies, landscapes, and agriculture with the spatial distribution of hunger in Brazil. Nutrition and agriculture – both understood spatially and historically – were put into the same analytical frame. For Castro, geography was the most encyclopedic and universalist of sciences. In *Geografia da Fome* he wrote:

> I have tried to find a method of study that would give the broadest view of the problem, a perspective in which the implications, influences and connections of its multiple natural and cultural factors could be made intelligible. The only method that might offer such a panorama without uprooting the question from the field of social reality was [...] the interpretive method of modern geographic science.[77]

Part of the holism he found in the geographical method crystallized around an application of 'extensão' – 'extension' – derived from Ratzel, but shed of environmental determinism.[78] Bertoldo Kruse Grande de Arruda has argued that Castro's geography had five analytical–critical intentions. First, geography facilitated a selective description of the world embedded in scientific discourse. Secondly, Castro wanted to reinterpret classical geography and insert it more directly into the problems of society. Thirdly, he wanted to rid geography of its technocratic tone. Fourthly, geography enabled him to produce valid generalizations at the scale of the regional, while opening up geographical investigations to political analysis. Finally, he believed that geography was a path to unravelling uneven spatial development.[79] This multi-faceted approach to rebuilding geography – going beyond Vidalian depoliticization – underpinned the 1946 *Geografia da Fome*, a book that remains 'lively, polemical and seductive' to this day.[80] Reading Castro's work up to and including *Geografia da Fome* helps to articulate new spatialities and scales of the body's geography. As André Mayer's preface to *Geografia*

---

76 Clayton, 'Historical Geography I'.

77 Castro, *Geografia da Fome: O Dilema Brasileiro: Pão Ou Aço* (1946), 34.

78 Linda Peake, 'Anthropogeography', in *The International Encyclopedia of Geography: People, the Earth, Environment, and* Technology, ed. Noel Castree et al. (Chichester and Hoboken, NJ: John Wiley & Sons, 2017), 1–4.

79 Bertoldo Kruse Grande de Arruda, '"The Geography of Hunger": From Regional Logic to Universality', *Cadernos de Saúde Pública* 13, no. 3 (September 1997): 547, doi:10.1590/S0102-311X1997000300031.

80 Francisco de Assis Guedes de Vasconcelos, 'Josué de Castro and The Geography of Hunger in Brazil', *Cadernos de Saúde Pública* 24, no. 11 (2008): 2717.

da Fome made clear, the book represented a geographical progression from a history of nutritional knowledge.[81]

In the *Geografia* Castro deploys his biosociological analysis of hunger as a 'complex of manifestations [which are] simultaneously biological, economic and social'.[82] Deploying the 'fertile concept' of 'ecology',[83] he argued that hunger is not natural, but the product of social and economic conjunctures. Hunger was created and maintained as an act of violence by the powerful, and manifested in bodily metabolism as starvation, as well as in chronic and hidden forms that impede specific groups not only from flourishing but from surviving. Biology emerges through socio-spatial processes and the history of colonialism. Food is a 'tenacious force':[84] 'it is perhaps through the nutritional link that the environment – soil and climate – even though indirectly, exerts its most decisive influence on the physical vigour, productive capacity and resistance to disease of human groups'.[85] The socio-economic structure of society is crystallized and reproduced in the body. As hunger is 'biological slavery', 'we will not defend, therefore, any primacy in terms of Brazilian social evolution: either the primacy of the biological over the cultural, nor of the cultural over the biological'.[86]

By the time of *Geografia da Fome*'s publication in 1946, Castro's work on hunger was more than ever associated with a praxis of public nutrition. Through attending to the recursive relationship between Castro's praxis and his theory we can get a sense of the multiple scales at which nutritional politics play out. Castro published *Geografia da Fome* in the same year that he founded the *Instituto de Nutrição* (IN). The IN mirrored the *Instituto* he had visited in Buenos Aires a few years before: a charismatic male scientist led it; women activists, educators, and scientists did the work, often anonymously.[87] The impact of the Argentine institute on the Brazilian was formative; even the calorific tables used in research and teaching in Rio were those developed by Escudero and his colleagues in Buenos Aires.[88] The IN took up a public, pedagogic, even 'civilizing' role.[89] Castro was part of a wider

81 Josué de Castro, *Geografia da Fome (O Dilema Brasileiro: Pão ou Aço)*, 8th ed., vol. 1 (São Paulo: Editôra Brasiliense, 1963), 1–2.
82 Castro, *Geografia da Fome* (1963), 19–20.
83 Castro, *Geografia da Fome* (1963), 21.
84 Castro, *Alimentação e Raça*, 140.
85 Josué de Castro and World Federation of Scientific Workers, *Hunger and Food* (London: WFSW, 1958), 5.
86 Castro, *Geografia da Fome: O Dilema Brasileiro: Pão Ou Aço* (1946), 40.
87 The successor of the IN, now part of the Federal University of Rio de Janeiro, bears his name and its archive was consulted for this paper.
88 The archive of the IN includes blank versions from the early 1940s.
89 Maria Letícia Galluzzi Bizzo and Nísia Trindade Lima, 'O Projeto Civilizatório Nacional Do Instituto de Nutrição Da Universidade Do Brasil (1946–1960)', *Perspectivas: Revista de Ciências Sociais* 37 (2010).

Brazilian discourse. For example, Dante Costa was a colleague of Castro's at this time. He wrote on nutrition and society (e.g. *Alimentação e Progresso*, 1951) as well as on socialism in Brazil (*O Socialismo*, 1954). His *Tratado de Nutrição* (1947) told the history of nutrition from Antoine Lavoisier to Justus von Liebig; yet, unlike Castro, Costa emphasized the effects of nutrition on society rather than the systemic forces creating malnutrition. Costa, however, articulated the spatiality of the newly formed discipline in terms of what he called the 'triple aspect' of nutrition: 'the clinical, in hospitals; the experimental, in research laboratories; the social, in the organization of public services of food'.[90] Costa leaves out the domestic sphere, where most nutritional activity, knowledge, and politics occur. Yet Castro spanned the other three fields as director of the public institutions that became the *Serviço Técnico da Alimentação Nacional* (The Technical Service for National Food Supply) (STAN) and the *Serviço de Alimentação da Previdencia Social* (Social Security Food Service) (SAPS).

In 1944 Castro launched the journal *Arquivos Brasileiros de Nutrição*, which he edited, initially through SAPS and after 1946 through the IN. It published nutritional science, metabolic biochemistry, and political analysis. In the first editorial Castro lauded the creation of an internationally recognized Brazilian school of nutritional science capable of confronting the new urban–industrial society emerging in Brazil. Like Escudero, Castro sought to intervene across public life, placing nutrition at the centre of analysis of Brazilian politics and society. As Helder Remigio Amorim has shown, his work during the Second World War had seen him in a sometimes-tense relationship with the state. He worked on behalf of the state to improve the food industry's techniques in support of producing a better-fed army. He visited the United States and worked inside state institutions. However, as Amorim notes, after the war there was a significant shift in both his analytical perspective and his relationship with the state.[91] This can be traced in his editorial role at the *Arquivos*, which became increasingly critical.

He called, in the second edition, for a National Vitamin Campaign, citing surveys (not least his own) showing vast nutritional deficiencies among the population (1944, vol. 1.2). He demanded Ministers of Agriculture address the imbalance between food supply and exploitative agriculture for export (1946, vol. 2.2), critiqued national educational plans by pushing for the inclusion of nutritional education in their remit (1947, vols 3.4 and 3.2), sought to regularize school lunches (May 1948, vol. 5.3), and discussed national agricultural production (e.g. 1949, vol. 6.5). Despite attention in public policy and scientific research, and increasing state activity in direct feeding and education, the crisis of hunger in Brazil remained vastly beyond the reach of these interventions.[92] School lunches and workers' canteens

90 Dante Costa, *Tratado de Nutrição* (Rio de Janeiro: Guanabara, 1947).
91 Amorim, 'Em Tempos', 60.
92 Costa, *Tratado de Nutrição*, 23.

were particular sites of debate. As in Vernon's account of the school meal in modern Britain, measurements of hunger and dietary standards for children were bound up with not just the creation of the welfare state but visions of the good society.[93] Foucauldian histories of the authoritarian modernism of the *Estado Novo* regime have seen nutritional science as a form of disciplinary state action.[94] Certainly, Castro's practical activities unfolded at the nexus of science and politics,[95] but he was not always aligned with an authoritarian state that was in any case fractured and contested.

Analysing Castro's work in this period finds him often in the laboratory, conducting empirical natural scientific experiments. It is important to place this kind of work within flows of colonial, neocolonial, and imperial power and resources. I will return to these questions below, in particular in relation to the FAO, when Castro is involved in an attempt to insert Third Worldism into international institutions themselves. Critically, for Castro from the 1930s onwards, nutrition and nutritional science was a site of radical critique and praxis. But, above all, in his work in Brazil, the nub of this radicalism was land, understood in broad political and historical terms.[96] The significance of this cannot be overstated. Castro made life-long enemies of the reactionary Brazilian plantation elites.[97] He saw in the *latifundia* the nutrients of Brazilian soil being exported abroad as coffee and sugar to be stirred into European cups or as cotton to be worn on European backs. The vast land-holdings of the *latifundia* system – inherited from colonialism and tied to international capital[98] – imposed hunger on the Brazilian poor through its control of national economic policy and enforcement of landlessness. The *latifundia* violently suppressed both subsistence agriculture and economic reform to maintain its low-productivity, high-land-use system, based on the exploitative rural labour relations. Protein and vitamin deficiency, goitre, tuberculosis, infant mortality, and kwashiorkor were therefore not only outcomes but

93 Lynne Phillips and Suzan Ilcan, '"A World Free From Hunger": Global Imagination and Governance in the Age of Scientific Management', *Sociologia Ruralis* 43, no. 4 (2003): 436.

94 José Arimatea Barros Bezerra, 'Educação Alimentar e a Constituição de Trabalhadores Fortes, Robustos e Produtivos: Análise Da Produção Científica Em Nutrição No Brasil, 1934–1941', *História, Ciências, Saúde-Manguinhos* 19, no. 1 (2012).

95 Francisco de Assis Guedes de Vasconcelos and Malaquias Batista Filho, 'História Do Campo Da Alimentação e Nutrição Em Saúde Coletiva No Brasil', *Ciência & Saúde Coletiva* 16 (2011): 81–90.

96 For a related discussion of the anticolonial concepts of land in Amílcar Cabral's work see Amin Parsa, 'Review: Amílcar Cabral, Resistance and Decolonization', *Leiden Journal of International Law* 30, no. 4 (December 2017): 1032–34, doi:10.1017/S0922156517000334.

97 Francisco Julião, *Cambão – The Yoke: The Hidden Face of Brazil*, The Pelican Latin American Library (Harmondsworth: Penguin Books, 1972), 50–51.

98 Josué de Castro, *Death in the Northeast: Poverty and Revolution in the Northeast of Brazil*, 1st ed. (New York: Random House, 1966), 86–116.

necessary factors in this system. Plantations were more than merely economic apparatuses. They were totalizing institutions of enormous political, social, ecological, and spatial power in the region of the Northeast of Brazil. George Beckford – one of what has been called the plantation school of economic historians of the University of the West Indies in the 1960s and 1970s[99] – theorized plantations as 'instruments of colonization':

> where wealth was to be provided by the supply of agricultural produce, much more was usually required of the colonizing country. In addition to military and administrative organization, an institutional framework for the bringing together of land, labour, capital, management and technology had to be provided.[100]

In Castro's writing and praxis the role of the plantation – a reasonable translation of *latifundio* – is profoundly important to the geography of hunger. Indeed, it is the subject through which his interdisciplinary approach emerges most clearly, and through which he elucidates how he integrates the natural and the social in geographical explanation:

> Seeking to appreciate biological factors is not to denigrate the importance of cultural factors, internal to the character of the agrarian–feudal planta-tions that have so deformed the development of Brazilian society. These are undeniable. What we will try to show is that the shaping power of economic and cultural forces make themselves felt on man, and on human groups, in the final analysis through a biological mechanism: it is through nutritional deficiencies that monoculture imposes itself, through hunger that the plantation regenerates, and so on.[101]

This important passage places physiological hunger within a broader field of social analysis. Biological hunger is created by socio-economic forces, but that biological hunger plays into the socio-economic system through the specific textures of those forces' effects on bodies. This is not a determinist approach, but an idiosyncratic kind of materialist, geographical, and scalar form of socio-biological analysis. The plantation is at the heart of this. In both *Geografia* and *Geopolítica da Fome* Castro examines the *latifundia* as a form of spatial control, both in Brazil[102] and other areas of hunger. He analyses the American South, bringing together the ecologist Howard Odum and the Swedish sociologist Gunnar Myrdal to articulate 'that vicious circle of misery – monoculture, tenancy, soil exhaustion, and erosion'.[103] Castro is at pains

99 David Scott, 'The Re-Enchantment of Humanism: An Interview with Sylvia Winter', *Small Axe* 8, no. 120 (2000): 119–21.

100 George L. Beckford, *Persistent Poverty: Underdevelopment in Plantation Economies of the Third World* (New York: Oxford University Press, 1972), 30–31.

101 Castro, *Geografia da Fome: O Dilema Brasileiro: Pão Ou Aço* (1946), 27–28.

102 Castro, *Geography of Hunger*, 88–89.

103 Castro, *Geography of Hunger*, 116.

to emphasize the connections between hunger and soil erosion: 'caught in this net of negative factors – inadequate production, worn out soils, and low salaries – the human beings of the region necessarily suffer from [...] a diet both insufficient and incomplete'.[104] In Brazil, meanwhile, 'hunger has been chiefly created by the inhuman exploitation of colonial riches by the *latifundia* and one-crop culture which lays waste to the colony, so that the exploiting country can take too cheaply the raw materials its prosperous industrial economy requires'.[105] Castro's analysis can be placed alongside the history of plantation scholarship traced and deployed by Katherine McKittrick, Clyde Woods, and Sylvia Wynter.[106] Such work on the historical geographies of colonial extraction and its spatial forms offer another genealogy for scholarship that can attest to and challenge the geography of hunger.

In the Northeast, the plantations overwhelmingly grew sugar. Up to the end of the twentieth century sugar was the dominant social force in Northeast Brazil, defining its political economy and human geography.[107] Castro saw Latin American sugar as the foundation of European capitalism.[108] Sugar has been at the heart of many of the most important social struggles in Northeastern political history,[109] and interpretations of the role of sugar in national economic life have long been central to Brazilian social thought. From Sérgio Buarque de Holanda to Caio Prado Júnior and Manuel Correia de Andrade, the nature of the Brazilian plantation system – as feudal, pre-capitalist, mercantile, or capitalist – has been at the crux of some of the most important analyses of the Brazilian condition and the structure of the national economy. In the Northeast sugar furnished the elite with wealth, and the society that its plantation form produced was the subject of Gilberto Freyre's seminal sociological mystifications of Brazilian social history. Castro's own analysis argued that there were feudal remnants within the plantation society of the Northeast, and he placed an even greater emphasis on the role of colonialism and imperialism than on capital. As Gadiel Perruci argued in 1978, the sugar society of the Northeast fixed in place structures of domination inherited from the colonial period.[110] *Mutatis*

104 Castro, *Geography of Hunger*, 117.

105 Castro, *Geography of Hunger*, 116.

106 Beckford, *Persistent Poverty*; Scott, 'The Re-Enchantment of Humanism'; Katherine McKittrick, 'On Plantations, Prisons, and a Black Sense of Place', *Social & Cultural Geography* 12, no. 8 (2011): 947–63, doi:10.1080/14649365.2011.624280.

107 See Manuel Correia de Andrade, *The Land and People of Northeast Brazil* (Albuquerque: University of New Mexico Press, 1980).

108 Josué de Castro, 'A La Recherche de l'Amérique Latine', *Esprit (1940–)*, no. 340 (7/8) (1965): 72.

109 Thomas D. Rogers, *The Deepest Wounds: A Labor and Environmental History of Sugar in Northeast Brazil* (Chapel Hill: University of North Carolina Press, 2010).

110 Gadiel Perruci, *A República Das Usinas: Um Estudo de História Social e Econômica Do Nordeste, 1889–1930*, vol. 2 (Rio de Janeiro: Paz e Terra, 1978).

mutandis, the systems of agro-capital in place today across Brazil continue to be a barrier to social transformation.[111] Even today, urban Northeast Brazil is racked by a double nutritional crisis associated with sugar: malnutrition both associated with poverty and in the form of diabetes. The populations affected often overlap.[112] Brazil has the fourth highest absolute number of diabetes cases in the world, and the burden of disease from diabetes and hyperglycaemia is projected to rise by 144 per cent by 2040.[113] Brazil has a double metabolic crisis – of undernutrition on the one hand and of diabetes, obesity, and hyperglycaemia on the other. The distribution of land remains critical to the failure of the current agricultural regime in Brazil to deliver food security, particularly in rural contexts, and in terms of the rights of people to remain on their land.[114] This is to emphasize the continuing importance of the connection between nutrition and agriculture. The intellectual intersection between these two fields – in terms of both geographical enquiry and agricultural practice – is more necessary than ever as the contemporary food system is penetrated by technological capital, industrial foodstuffs, and mass production at growing scales.

Drawing on Castro, Nancy Scheper-Hughes describes how the connections between hunger, drought, and race in the Northeast can be mapped by both the production and consumption of sugar: it is 'a particularly predatory crop that has dominated both the natural and the social landscape'.[115] It is around sugar that Castro's ecological and biological concerns move towards one another, seeing the land and its population as suffering the same metabolic disease.[116] One of the crucial features of the sugar economy can be found exactly at the point of meeting between nutrition – diet – and land. In the most basic terms: sugar workers could not grow their own vegetables, not only because they were working low wages on long hours but because they were explicitly banned from doing so. As the North American documentary made about the Northeast in 1964 put it, 'sugar is almost everywhere. Vegetables for

111 We can cite, for instance, the vital importance of the well-organized *ruralista* block in the Brazilian congress, who were key to the impeachment of Dilma Rousseff. This goes beyond sugar, but its historical continuities are clear.

112 Muriel Bauermann Gubert et al., 'Understanding the Double Burden of Malnutrition in Food Insecure Households in Brazil: Dual-Burden Malnutrition and Food Insecurity', *Maternal & Child Nutrition* 13, no. 3 (July 2017): e12347, doi:10.1111/mcn.12347.

113 Bruce Bartholow Duncan et al., 'The Burden of Diabetes and Hyperglycemia in Brazil: A Global Burden of Disease Study 2017', *Population Health Metrics* 18, no. S1 (September 2020): 9, doi:10.1186/s12963-020-00209-0.

114 Gonçalves, 'Geografia Da Riqueza, Fome e Meio Ambiente'.

115 Nancy Scheper-hughes, *Death Without Weeping: The Violence of Everyday Life in Brazil*, new ed. (Berkeley: University of California Press, 1993), 122.

116 For further discussion see Archie Davies, 'Unwrapping the Oxo Cube: Josué de Castro and the Intellectual History of Metabolism', *Annals of the Association of American Geographers* 109, no. 3 (2019): 837–56.

the peasants would crowd out the landowner's cash crop.'[117] This, Castro and his successors have argued, was one of the reasons for hunger and malnutrition in the sugar zones.[118] The later dependency theorist Ruy Mauro Marini argued that imports of cheap sugar to Britain can be directly articulated with the super-exploitation of bodies in Latin America and the Caribbean. Marini argues that the calorific boon to Northern industrial capitalism was enabled by the further encroachment on the bodily integrity of the plantation labourer.[119] In one sense, Castro provides the geographical analysis underpinning precisely Marini's argument.[120] It is those labourers, too, who form the foundation of Castro's analysis of the geography of hunger.

His analysis also prefigures the works of more recent historians of hunger, such as Mike Davis' *Late Victorian Holocausts*.[121] Davis makes one passing reference to Castro, citing him citing someone else, but it seems that he has not read his work. Rather, Davis makes Michael Watts' *Silent Violence* his key precursor. This takes us to Castro, as Watts, writing in 1983, gave Castro a big billing: 'the brilliant Brazilian geographer spent much of his academic life wrestling with [the changing forms of the human appropriation of nature] [...] freeing the discussion of Third World peasant food supply from its Malthusian shackles and situating it within the context of the political economy of underdevelopment'.[122] While Watts does not develop this reference further, Castro can be seen as a precursor to scholars in political ecology, and those working on the production of scarcity, vulnerability, and hunger amidst abundance, such as Philip McMichael[123] and David Nally.[124] Attesting in another way to the lasting value of Castro's theory of hunger

---

117   Helen Rogers, 'The Troubled Land', DVD (New York: ABC News, 1964).

118   Robert Linhart, *O açúcar e a fome: pesquisa nas regiões açucareiras do nordeste brasileiro* (Rio de Janeiro: Editora Paz e Terra, 1981), 42–52.

119   Andy Higginbottom, 'Underdevelopment as Super-Exploitation: Marini's Political Economic Thought Revisited', in *Crisis and Critique, 7th Annual Conference* (Historical Materialism, SOAS: unpublished, 2010), accessed 15 June 2022 , http://eprints.kingston. ac.uk/23279/8/Higginbottom-A-23279.pdf; Jaime Osorio, 'Dialectics, Superexploitation, and Dependency: Notes on The Dialectics of Dependency', *Social Justice* 42, no. 1 (2015): 93–106; Adrián Sotelo Valencia, 'Latin America: Dependency and Super-Exploitation', *Critical Sociology* 40, no. 4 (July 2014): 539–49, doi:10.1177/0896920513479616.

120   Ruy Mauro Marini, *Subdesarrollo y Revolución* (México: Siglo XXI Editores, 1974), 21–25.

121   Mike Davis, *Late Victorian Holocausts: El Niño Famines and the Making of the Third World* (London and New York: Verso, 2002).

122   Michael J. Watts, *Silent Violence: Food, Famine, and Peasantry in Northern Nigeria* (Athens: University of Georgia Press, 2013), xx.

123   Philip McMichael, 'Feeding the World: Agriculture, Development and Ecology', *Socialist Register* 43 (2007): 170–94.

124   David Nally, '"That Coming Storm": The Irish Poor Law, Colonial Biopolitics, and the Great Famine', *Annals of the Association of American Geographers* 98, no. 3 (2008): 714–41.

are vast swathes of rural resistance spear-headed by the Landless Worker's Movement, the *Movimento dos Trabalhadores Rurais Sem Terra* (MST). These have shown the centrality of land to rural social justice in Brazil. As explored further in chapter 5, below, Castro was involved in the precursor of the MST, the Northeastern Peasant Leagues of the 1940s and 1950s.[125] The Peasant Leagues, which established the MST's most powerful tactic, land occupation, sought radical agrarian reform and were perceived by the Brazilian right and the United States in the early 1960s as an existential threat. The MST's leaders still cite Castro as an inspiration.[126] The Leagues, however, faded in significance even before the coup of 1964, challenged by both the church and the rise of rural unions.[127] Castro himself was increasingly distanced from them by the early 1960s.

Nevertheless, his political and scientific work connecting nutrition and agrarian reform was far reaching. The disciplinary shift from nutrition to geography placed the dietary metabolic relation to nature in direct articulation with spatial, socio-economic, and political processes in particular historical geographies.[128] This constituted a metabolic critique of society that can complement and extend the history of political ecology's understanding of socio-natural metabolism.[129] It was from and through an attention to the precise metabolic condition of hunger and malnutrition that he articulated his socio-political critique of hunger as produced by uneven relations between nature and society.

Towards a Metabolic, Anticolonialism Humanism

One of Castro's most important successors and another key Northeastern geographer,[130] Manuel Correia de Andrade, emphasized Castro's heterodox geography: 'he didn't participate in the Association of Brazilian Geographers [...]

125 For a critical history of rural movements from 1961 see Anthony Pereira, *The End of the Peasantry: The Rural Labor Movement in Northeast Brazil, 1961–1988* (Pittsburgh, PA: University of Pittsburgh Press, 1997).

126 João Pedro Stédile, *A questão agrária no Brasil: História e natureza das Ligas Camponesas, 1954–1964* (São Paulo: Editora Expressão Popular, 2005).

127 Anthony Pereira, 'O Declínio das Ligas Camponesas e a Ascensão dos Sindicatos: As organizações de trabalhadores rurais em Pernambuco na Segunda República, 1955–1963', *Revista CLIO* 2, no. 26.2 (2008), accessed 15 June 2022, https://periodicos.ufpe.br/revistas/revistaclio/article/view/24184.

128 Jose Jakson Amancio Alves, 'A Contribuição de Josué de Castro No Estudo e Combate à Fome e Sua Repercussão Científica e Política Na Geografia', *Revista de Geografia* 25, no. 2 (2008): 98–112.

129 For a discussion of how this work on metabolism connects to contemporary political ecologies of the body, sugar, and social reproduction see Davies, 'Unwrapping the Oxo Cube'.

130 On the connections between Andrade and Castro see Ferretti, 'Decolonizing the Northeast'.

his line of thought was different, emerging from studying the Brazilian problematic itself, through non-geographical pathways, but which led to Geography, above all in terms of epistemology and methodology'.[131] Castro's geography was, in Andrade's felicitous formulation – providing an inversion and alternative history to Driver's 'geography militant' – 'geography combatant'.[132] Its militancy emerged politically in the connection between land and nutrition, and intellectually in the movement from the physiological study of metabolism to the geographical analysis of underdevelopment.

Castro's thought and praxis, therefore, went through a methodological transition from a political and scientific focus on nutrition to a fully geographical cast of thought. The geographical intervention of his most famous work, *A Geografia da Fome*, was built on his training in nutrition. He placed food and hunger at the heart of a politically engaged reworking of the relationship between people and nature, and hunger was at the centre of his surpassing of a French, possibilist vision of regional geography. His work can be seen as a precursor of the transition to the 'new geography' that Milton Santos laid out in the 1970s.[133] His disciplinary shift from nutrition to geography put the dietary metabolic into direct articulation with nature, as well as with spatial, socioeconomic, and political processes.[134] As a scientist, Castro investigated how the tropical climate influenced basal metabolism, a question that was concurrently being investigated by Wallace Aykroyd and others in India.[135] However, he moved beyond the somatic scale. Sociospatial processes, and the history of colonialism, he argued, produce hunger. It was from and through an attention to the precise metabolic conditions of starvation, malnutrition, and endemic hunger that he articulated his critique of the uneven relations between nature and society. This is a productively different trajectory for metabolic analysis for Marxist-orientated political ecology.[136] Castro saw the metabolic malnutrition of the Brazilian masses – both urban and rural – as the material manifestation of underdevelopment.

Analysing Castro's work opens a new set of intersections between the history of geography, political ecology, and underdevelopment. Clearly, Castro is not the only scholar to have connected nutrition and geography, but thinking with Castro can shed light on the problem of how the human body is unequally produced in uneven environments. As this book explores, there are multiple different scales embedded in this notion of unevenness, from the

131 Andrade, 'Josué de Castro e Uma Geografia Combatente'.
132 Andrade, 'Josué de Castro e Uma Geografia Combatente'.
133 Milton Santos, *Por Uma Geografia Nova: Da Crítica Da Geografia a Uma Geografia Crítica*, 6th ed. (São Paulo: Editora da Universidade de São Paulo, 2004).
134 Magalhães, *Fome: uma (re)leitura de Josué de Castro*; Alves, 'A Contribuição de Josué de Castro'.
135 Wallace Aykroyd, *Les Progrès Des Travaux Sur La Nutrition Dans l'Inde* (Paris: Office International d'Hygiène Publique, 1938).
136 Davies, 'Unwrapping the Oxo Cube'.

nutritional/somatic to the global/international. Most explicitly, I will explore this question of scale in chapter 3 on the international, and chapter 5 on the region, but it is implicit everywhere the geography of hunger lands. Recently, sub-disciplines such as Urban Political Ecology and the Political Ecology of the Body have explored how socio-environmental processes materialize in bodies. This recalls one of Castro's key and lasting insights: hunger is a question not only of calorific flows but of vitamins, minerals, protein, culture, identity, and sociality. The type of food eaten, who produced it, how, and where, all leave traces in the body. Deploying a concept of metabolism that emerges from histories of nutritional thought can add to approaches that embed the body in the production of uneven geographical environments.

Rereading the geography of hunger today brings to mind the co-extensiveness of eco-social and physiological metabolism. It puts the coproduction of social and environmental injustice, bodies, nature, and society in the foreground of geographical analysis. Uneven nature is immanent to bodily, social, and political life and the body's sensory qualities can be at the root of an ecological politics of praxis and everyday life.[137] Nik Heynen, for instance, has connected hunger, the metabolic body, and political radicalism in his work on the Black Panthers' breakfast club.[138] Adding Castro's legacy to such productive approaches to the geography of hunger opens new historical paradigms for anglophone scholars of radical ecological thinking and praxis. For Castro, nutrition is always already political, and the body is a process in which other processes congeal and reform. As metabolism determines the spatial, temporal, and ecological dynamics of survival,[139] a physiological approach to metabolism calls attention to the body's social reproduction, its openness and relationality. The ontological and epistemological space of metabolic circulation passes through the human body, so that is where geographical investigations should follow. These are the spatial politics that Josué de Castro inspires us to delineate.

Castro studied hunger as a dehumanizing force, unleashed by the historical geographies of colonialism and neocolonialism. It was dehumanizing in at least three ways: it forced people into suffering and indignity; it manifested the rupture of functioning social relations; and it manifested the rupture of a functioning human relationship with nature. Castro conceived of these all as political conditions, and the struggle against hunger was irreducibly a struggle against oppression, whether in its colonial, imperial, or fascist forms. Castro understood the starving as having been stripped of their humanity.

137 See, for example, Alex Loftus, *Everyday Environmentalism: Creating an Urban Political Ecology* (Minneapolis: University of Minnesota Press, 2012), x.

138 For example, Heynen, 'Bending the Bars of Empire'.

139 William W. Bunge, 'The Geography of Human Survival', *Annals of the Association of American Geographers* 63, no. 3 (1973): 275–95; Nik Heynen, '"But It's Alright, Ma, It's Life, and Life Only": Radicalism as Survival', *Antipode* 38, no. 5 (2006): 916–29.

Nevertheless, for all that Castro saw in global hunger the persistent failures of Western civilization, he wanted to revive, not abandon, humanism. This meant new conceptions of the human and society were needed.[140] His work can be put in dialogue with a tradition of reconstructing and reclaiming humanism advanced by many important anticolonial thinkers, notably Aimé Césaire, Frantz Fanon, and Sylvia Wynter.[141] Rekindling the geographical link between anticolonialism and humanism through Castro does involve contesting those elements of poststructuralist geography that question the humanist assumption that there are essential and irreducible facets of human being. It is to suggest that a dialectical, biophysical relationship with constantly changing socio-natural worlds is indeed at the basis of human subjectivity. This is not to propose a calculative kind of nutritional humanism; Castro directly opposes 'economic man', attempting 'to be a scientific account of the biological tragedy in which inummerable human groups died, and continue to die, of hunger, while this scabrous era of economic man draws to a close'.[142] In 1960, he wrote 'we aim, with […] [the geography of hunger], to make an infinitesimal contribution to the elaboration of a plan for the resurgence of our civilization, through appreciating anew the physiology of man'.[143] Castro brings a geographical, ecological, and physiological dimension to the central humanist problematic of anticolonial thought and praxis: to expand the subject of humanism into a new, truly universal category, on new grounds.[144]

In Aimé Césaire's *Cahiers d'un retour au pays natal* [Notebook of a Return to the Native Land], one of the most significant texts of anticolonial humanism, hunger returns again and again as a key trope. It marks the geography through which the poem circulates:

> vous savez que ce n'est point par haine des autres races
> que je m'exige bêcheur de cette unique race
> que ce que je veux
> c'est pour la faim universelle
> pour la soif universelle
>
> [you know that it is not from hatred of other races
> that I demand a digger for this unique race
> that what I want is for universal hunger
> for universal thirst].[145]

140 Josué de Castro, *A Estratégia Do Desenvolvimento* (Lisbon: Seara Nova, 1971), 11.

141 Scott, 'The Re-Enchantment of Humanism', 119–21.

142 Josué de Castro, *Geografia da Fome: O Dilema Brasileiro: Pão ou Aço*, 7th ed. (São Paulo: Editôra Brasiliense, 1961), 25.

143 Castro, *Geografia da Fome* (1961), 23.

144 Pithouse, '"That the Tool"', 110–11.

145 Aimé Césaire, *Aimé Césaire: The Collected Poetry*, trans. Clayton Eshleman and Annette Smith (Berkeley: University of California Press, 1983), 71.

Césaire's poetic vision ties universal hunger to a new humanist subject. This too is an inverse, a negative humanist premise. Césaire, of course, does not want a universal hunger, but he wants anyone's hunger to be universal. He reinserts the hungering subject as the premise of a truly universal humanism. This is the kind of hungry humanism that Castro shares, and it casts light on what is 'negative' in his geography, and what is radical about his vision of a world without hunger: that survival must be universal.

Castro's radical humanism needs to be put in the historical context of claims to universal humanism at the time. These emerged from many different fields in what Glenda Sluga calls 'that curiously utopian moment bracketed by the end of the Second World War and the onset of the cold war'.[146] As I will explore in chapter 4, Castro's position beyond Cold War binaries can be read in his 1946 argument that 'an interest in man and in the re-humanization of culture is the common denominator of both the great economic systems'[147] of capitalism and communism, and that in the post-war world there was 'a concentrated interest in biological man as a concrete entity'.[148] The concrete entity of the nutritional subject of his nutritional research lies behind his humanism's dual tenor as both deeply practical and politically utopian. Anticolonial and liberation thinkers at the time were developing new claims and forms of humanism. Fanon's revolutionary declarations – what Nick Nesbitt calls his 'revolutionary inhumanism'[149] – are a key part of this history, but debate over the status of the human as the universal subject was longstanding. These radical and revolutionary humanisms are 'context specific, and require [...] active struggle'.[150] I will return to the theoretical stakes of this humanism for political ecology in the conclusion.

Castro's work was mobilized within the wider field of anticolonialism, as revolutionary writers and film-makers used the spatial–ecological dynamics of the geography of hunger at significant junctures in their intellectual analysis of colonial oppression. The geography of hunger functioned as what Morton calls a kind of 'transgressive theory' connecting different sites and adapting to different needs.[151] Walter Rodney used Castro's *Geography of Hunger* as an empirical and historical source for colonialism's deleterious effect on African people's physical and mental well-being.[152] Paulo Freire used it to describe

146 Glenda Sluga, 'UNESCO and the (One) World of Julian Huxley', *Journal of World History* 21, no. 3 (2010): 393.

147 Castro, *Geography of Hunger*, 19.

148 Castro, *Geography of Hunger*, 18.

149 Nick Nesbitt, 'Revolutionary Inhumanism: Fanon's De La Violence', *International Journal of Francophone Studies* 15, nos 3–4 (2013): 395–413.

150 Rajeev Patel, 'Global Fascism Revolutionary Humanism and the Ethics of Food Sovereignty', *Development* 48, no. 2 (June 2005): 81, doi:10.1057/palgrave. development.1100148.

151 Morton, 'Traveling with Gramsci', 50.

152 Walter Rodney, *How Europe Underdeveloped Africa* (Nairobi: East African Publishers, 1972), 236.

a childhood similar to Castro's own: a geography of hunger articulating his own hungry home with the fertile fruit trees of his middle-class neighbours in Recife.[153] In the radical 1968 Argentine film *Hora de los Hornos* [The Hour of the Furnaces] the geography of hunger is placed amid scenes of street fighting between police and revolutionaries and deployed as a rallying cry for the revolutionary struggle against imperialism. In each context the work that the geography of hunger did was different, in political and in intellectual terms. For Frantz Fanon, for instance, the geography of hunger defines the Manichean separation between the settler town and the native town. In *The Wretched of the Earth*, in an important passage drawn on recently by Nik Heynen in his demand for an anticolonial, anti-racist 'abolition ecology',[154] Fanon wrote: 'the settler's town is a well fed town, an easygoing town[155]; its belly always full of good things. The settler's town is a town of white people, of foreigners. [...] The native town is a hungry town, starved of bread, of meat, of shoes, of coal, of light.'[156] Later he writes, 'the mass of the people struggle against the same poverty, flounder about making the same gestures and with their shrunken bellies outline what has been called the geography of hunger'.[157] Castro and Fanon met at least once,[158] and towards the end of his life the Brazilian was interested in Fanon's work, associating his own struggle against hunger with defending 'the wretched of the earth'.[159] What matters is the work Castro's concept did for Fanon, and for other anticolonial thinkers. What matters too is that through Castro we can place geography historically at the heart of these anticolonial ideas. Said contends that 'the issue for Lukács was the primacy of consciousness in history; for Fanon, it is the primacy of geography in history, and then the primacy of history over consciousness and subjectivity'.[160] Said discusses how Fanon, in *The Wretched of the Earth*, deployed Lukács to examine the dialectic between colonizer

153   Manuel Ouviña García, 'Josué de Castro (1908–1973). Biografía Intelectual, Científica y Política de Un Luchador Contra El Hambre', PhD thesis (Universitat Pompeu Fabra, 2017), 30.

154   Heynen, 'Urban Political Ecology II', 840.

155   'Easygoing' is a strange translation of Fanon's "paresseuse", which means lazy, implying that the settlers' bellies are full but they did not produce the food themselves.

156   Frantz Fanon, *Les damnés de la terre* (Paris: Gallimard, 2002), 42–43.

157   Fanon, *Les damnés de la terre*, 94.

158   Nancy Jachec, 'Léopold Sédar Senghor and the Cultures de l'Afrique Noire et de l'Occident (1960): Eurafricanism, Negritude and the Civilisation of the Universal', *Third Text* 24, no. 2 (March 2010): 198, doi:10.1080/09528821003722132.

159   Josué de Castro, 'Desarrollo, Ecologia, Desarme y Descolonización', in *America Latina y Los Problemas Del Desarrollo: La Encrucijada Del Presente y El Reto Del Futuro*, ed. Josué de Castro, 1st ed., Colección Estudios Especial (Caracas: Monte Avila Editores, 1974), 1–39.

160   Edward Said, 'Traveling Theory Reconsidered', in *Reflections on Exile and Other Essays* (London: Granta, 2001), 446.

and colonized. If, for Fanon, there is 'primacy' in 'geography', then it is certainly significant that he gets his geography from Castro. The spatialities of uneven development that Fanon (and indeed Rodney) explores in the settler and native towns are influenced by Castro's geographical thinking about hunger. This is less speculative than Said's suggestion that Fanon is deploying Lukács: Fanon's mobilization of Castro is concrete. Castro's militant geography travelled to become a framework for one of the single most important parts of anticolonial thinking.

Having changed and developed as it moved from the nutritional laboratories of Brazil in the 1930s to the stage of a global anticolonialism in the post-war period, the geography of hunger became part of the intellectual armoury of anticolonial thought in the 1960s and 1970s. Castro published, for instance, in the third edition of *Tricontinental* magazine launched following the seminal anticolonial conference in Havana in 1966.[161] He corresponded with the Organization for Solidarity with the Peoples of Africa, Asia and Latin America (OSPAAL)[162] and received newspapers from Cuba into the early 1970s. As Milton Santos wrote in 2001, thanks to Castro 'the discussion of the roots of the Third World gained new and decisive arguments', and at a time in which anticolonial solidarity was vital and growing, the theses of Josué de Castro 'gained followers on all continents'.[163]

In 1974 David Harvey wrote that

> although there is more of which to be ashamed than proud in the geographic tradition, there is a thread to geographic thinking which, at its best, produces an acute sensitivity to place and community, to the symbiotic relations between individuals, communities and environments. This sensitivity to locale and interaction produces a kind of parochial humanism – a humanism, that is, in certain senses deep and penetrating, but which is locked into the absolute spaces generated by the regional concept.[164]

Castro's metabolic, anticolonial humanism, and its part in his geography, is 'deep and penetrating', but in a different kind of way. His 'regional concept' is forged in a different flame to the imperialist history of geography Harvey has in mind. It moves outside 'absolute space' by beginning its geographical inquiry from the hungry body. Its humanism is parochial in another sense: not small-minded, but situated, metabolic, and from the margins.

161 Josué de Castro, 'The Significance of the Brazilian Economic Phenomenon', *Tricontinental Magazine*, December 1967.
162 Josué de Castro, 'Letters to OSPAAL: From Josué de Castro', *Tricontinental Bulletin*, August 1968.
163 Santos, 'Josué de Castro e a Geografia da Fome', 22.
164 David Harvey, *Spaces of Capital: Towards a Critical Geography* (New York: Routledge, 2001), 34.

CHAPTER 2

The Geography of Hunger and the Politics of Translation

Introduction

In 2001 Milton Santos wrote that the insight of *Geografia da Fome* underpinned *Geopolítica da Fome*, and became the 'site and inspiration for a great world debate about international injustices'.[1] As we will see, the true extent of the international public discussion that Santos refers to is somewhat in question, but the book that came out in English as *The Geography of Hunger* was certainly extremely prominent, both widely read and politically controversial. There are vanishingly few geographical works of the twentieth century which could be said to have had a greater public distribution and influence. This chapter will place Castro within the history of geography through a focus on the strange history of this book.

I do not seek to place Castro within a pre-existing disciplinary history, and suggest that such a history therefore has to be rewritten. This approach is rather different, for instance, to that captured in Barnes and Sheppard's *Spatial Histories of Radical Geography*. That book does an exemplary job of multiplying, repeopling, and expanding the historical geographies of radical geography. As the editors recognize, theirs is only one set of stories that could be told about radical geography, marked by the position from which the book begins, in particular a North American location, and a set of personal connections to the history of North American Marxist geography.[2] Throughout the book the content of radical geography remains clear: to only slightly over-simplify, its origin story is the Marxist coming-to-consciousness of David Harvey, and a concerted and multiple attempt to resist and overturn the fixities of the quantitative revolution and a conservative history of the discipline. That canon is put into dialogue with, for instance, francophone work in Quebec and histories of Mexican geography, but the end result of

---

1 Santos, 'Josué de Castro e a Geografia da Fome', 22.
2 A different, more global, historical geography of critical geography is traced by *Placing Critical Geography*, ed. Lawrence D. Berg, Ulrich Best, Mary Gilmartin and Henrik Gutzon Larsen (London and New York: Routledge, 2021).

what radical geography is remains relatively static, even if the journeys to get there are multiplied. My intention here is somewhat different. I want to place Castro alongside existing histories of geography without insisting that he can be folded into them, but suggesting that he offers an alternative to them. I do not, therefore, work to articulate Castro with histories of critical or radical geography, but attend instead to his life and his writing itself, and its itineraries. Those itineraries were only ever in very partial ways connected to the story of radical geography or of anglophone geography more broadly. Working outwards from the history of *The Geography of Hunger*, then, I will argue that translation helps expand and explode disciplinary history, and is a key dimension of the historical geography of ideas. Castro's understanding of what geography *is* (expansive, holistic, political) and what it should be *about* (hunger, underdevelopment) continues to challenge disciplinary thinking. How his ideas travelled does so too.

Castro's *Geografia da Fome* has never been translated into English. Yet a book published as *The Geography of Hunger* by Josué de Castro has. This is, in fact, a translation of a later work, *Geopolítica da Fome*. This book was written, though not in English, for an anglophone audience, so calling it a translation is only partly true. The two books contain very different arguments and structures. *Geografia da Fome* is a detailed and innovative analysis of the social biology of hunger in Brazil, tracking the relations between diet, space, and agriculture across the territory of Brazil. The *Geopolítica* is, ostensibly, an attempt to apply this approach to the scale of the globe, but it mutates into a different project, in which Castro tries to place hunger at the root of global politics. 'Few phenomena', Castro argued, 'have interfered so intensively in the political conduct of people as the alimentary phenomena, as the tragic necessity of eating; from this emerges the lively and cruel reality of a Geopolitics of Hunger'.[3] For Castro, the continuum between humans and nature mediated through the body's need to eat is a key driver of political organization and territorialization. This is the 'spatial reality' of the geography of hunger: not a determinist understanding of state form, but food as a vector by which the metabolic relation of humans and nature contribute to the construction and contestation of territory. In both works, hunger is a driving and foundational force at the root of the human relationship with nature. Yet the different scales create different kinds of analytical and political problems. These will be teased out later in this book. Read together, and within Castro's wider praxis, they constitute a new way of thinking about the political and spatial qualities of hunger. Read apart, they become dislocated.

Castro landed with a limited reputation in the anglophone world with the *Geography of Hunger* in 1952. By then, in Brazil and in France, he was already

---

3 Castro, *Geopolítica da Fome: Ensaio sôbre os Problemas de Alimentação e de População do Mundo*, 1:19.

an established author and public figure, with dozens of books and years of public roles behind him. I argue that the translation of only some of his work, alongside the non-translation of other parts of his work, is one of the major reasons why Castro has been overlooked in anglophone scholarship. Neither *Geopolítica da Fome*, published in 1951, nor *Geografia da Fome*, published in 1946, should be thought of as the beginning of Castro's career. On the contrary, they are the culmination of the first phase of Castro's work not only in geography but in the natural and social sciences and public health, the spatial relations of nutrition, ecology, agriculture, socio-economic structure, and historical geographies. *Geografia da Fome* sought a more literary style and wider audience than his previous work or much of his later writing: in writing it, Castro collaborated with Augusto Frederico Schmidt, a poet and influential publisher who also worked with key Brazilian intellectuals, particularly from the Northeast, such as Graciliano Ramos, Rachel de Queiroz, Jorge Amado, and Vinícius de Moraes. When published, it caused waves in Brazil and, in translation, in France. It is remarkable for its scope, intellectual breadth, and literary style. Five years later, in 1951, Castro released *Geopolítica da Fome* with the publisher Casa do Estudante do Brasil (another definitive edition was released slightly later with the bigger publishing house, Brasiliense[4]). Where *Geografia* focused on Brazil, this book covered the whole world. It was this second book that was published in the UK and the USA in 1952. To add to the confusion, a different, updated edition – also essentially a translation of *Geopolítica* – was later published, in 1977, by Monthly Review Press, in English, as *The Geopolitics of Hunger*. This edition included amendations in parantheses, reportedly from a manuscript edited by Castro in 1973. Castro added, for instance, an extended section on Brazilian economic development and industrialization.[5] In France, meanwhile, Castro's *Geografia da Fome* had already been translated and published as *Géographie de la Faim* by Les Editions Ouvrières and the geopolitics was published in 1952 as *Géopolitique de la Faim*.[6] (In this chapter, italicization is crucial!) I have examined editions in Portuguese, French, Spanish, and English, but a wider analysis would fruitfully consider the translation and reception of editions in Scandinavia, the USSR, Israel, China, Italy, and elsewhere.

The original *Geografia da Fome* had the subtitle 'Hunger in Brazil'. This subtitle later changed to *O Dilema Brasileiro: Pão ou Aço* – in the French translation, *Le Dilemme Brésilien: Pain ou Acier* [The Brazilian Dilemma:

---

4 Teresa Cristina Wanderley Neves, 'Josué de Castro: Cronologia' (Fundação Joaquim Nabuco, 2017), http://www.fundaj.gov.br/images/josue_castro/jc_cronologia_2017.pdf.

5 Josué de Castro, *The Geopolitics of Hunger* (New York and London: Monthly Review Press, 1977), 165–95.

6 It's worth noting the publishers are all left-wing bastions: Monthly Review Press, Gollancz, and Editions Ouvrières. The Brazilian edition also circulated in Portugal, as indicated by bookshop and library shelfmarks and contemporary Portuguese reviews.

Bread or Steel]. This second subtitle grounds the geography of hunger within very practical and political debates about national economic development, industrial strategy, and demography. Castro's role in the intellectual and political ferment over national development will be the subject of later chapters, but we can read it even in his books' changing subtitles. Most prominent in Brazil, Castro's place in these debates was also legible in France. The *Geopolítica da Fome* gained the subtitle *Ensaio sobre os problemas de Alimentação e de População do Mundo* [Essay on the problems of world diet and population], which placed the work in the field of demography. A new subtitle emerged on the cover of a 1972 edition of *Géographie de la Faim: Tragique, permanente, accusatrice: la faim'* [Tragic, permanent, accusatory: hunger].

Castro was deeply enthusiastic about publishing his work in Europe and North America.[7] He had different conceptions of his audience in different languages and used the architecture of his books to nuance ideas towards them. For instance, he characterizes his contribution to geopolitics in different terms for different audiences. In the introduction to the Brazilian edition of *Geopolítica da Fome* Castro explained that the book was written for the North American readership and is therefore different from his previous work. He registers his caution about the terminology of the Brazilian title and is wary of how '*geopolítica*' will be interpreted, but he explains it through his desire to reclaim geopolitics from its Nazi inheritances.[8] Castro positions the Brazilian edition as an intellectual intervention into the field of geopolitics. This contention is absent in English-language editions of *The Geography of Hunger*, in which not only is the word 'geopolitics' missing from the title but the framing intellectual, methodological reflections is also missing. In contrast, in the French edition of *Géographie de la Faim* (not the Geopolitics), Castro's intellectual contribution is established not only in the body of the text but in its prefaces, rubrics, and superstructure. On the inside cover a list appears – in French – of books by Castro, including all his early work. The list is somewhat misleading: though they are given French titles, many of the books had not been translated. However, the list figures Castro as the author of a long sequence of work on nutritional and geographical subjects, lending the Brazilian intellectual an intellectual gravitas through the endorsement of the publishing world. This disciplinary context is absent from the arrival of his work in the anglophone world.

Opening up disciplinary histories can mean wrenching his ideas from their context and abstracting from them. This necessarily follows the historical journeys of ideas themselves. As David Livingstone notes, 'as texts circulate, they transform': 'the movement of ideas from one site to another is never

7 Preface in Castro, *Geography of Hunger*; Josué de Castro, 'To Sanford Greenburger', Letter, February 1949, 290, CEHIBRA.JdC.
8 Ferretti, 'Geographies of Internationalism'.

simply relocation; migration always involves modification'.[9] Troubling the relationship between texts and ideas, this chapter dwells on the dissemination and reception of the geography and geopolitics of hunger as, in Said's terms, a 'travelling theory'. The history of Castro's ideas, particularly through the publication history of his books, is a 'fertile field' for research.[10] Rather than following the blood and sugar of metabolism, or the mud and crabs of Recife, like other chapters, this chapter's landscape is the myriad editions of these books – their prefaces, maps, rubrics, and footnotes. I explore the intellectual plasticity and political valency of the geography of hunger as it travelled through geography and geopolitics, demography, and radical and anticolonial politics. Castro's praxis and the reception of the geography of hunger speak to a post-war context in which humanitarianism and Third Worldism were molten and uncertain. I configure the geography of hunger not as a closed book but as an open membrane with many textual and discursive manifestations. I follow its construction less through the personal itinerary that constructed it[11] than by tracing its manifestation in the world through its publication and translation. Castro's own position – as a Brazilian intellectual and globally mobile diplomat – gave him a certain protean quality. This, however, was time-limited. The 1964 military coup saw to it that his counter-hegemonic position became unequivocal, as he took on the forced subjectivity of exile.

In 1983 Edward Said wrote that, 'like people and schools of criticism, ideas and theories travel'.[12] His idea of 'travelling theory' has become hugely influential in postcolonial studies, literary scholarship, the history of science, and the history of geographical ideas. David Livingstone argues that, for Said, 'theory is the *product* of time and place and for that very reason is always *appropriated* in time and place'.[13] Said suggests that 'there is [...] a discernible and recurrent pattern' to the movement of ideas, and identifies 'three or four stages common to the way any theory or idea travels'. These are the 'origin, or what seems like one', 'a distance transversed', 'a set of conditions – call them conditions of acceptance or, as an inevitable part of acceptance, resistances', and finally 'the now full (or partly) accommodated (or incorporated) idea is to some extent transformed by its new uses, its new position in a new time and place'.[14] Timothy Brennan has argued that the essay in which Said lays out the notion of 'Travelling Theory' 'is about the wilful appropriation of the

9 David N. Livingstone, 'The Geography of Darwinism', *Interdisciplinary Science Reviews* 31, no. 1 (2006): 34.

10 Amorim, 'Em Tempos', 61.

11 The approach, for instance, of Barnes in 'Lives Lived and Lives Told'.

12 Edward W. Said, 'Traveling Theory', in *The World, the Text, and the Critic* (Cambridge, MA: Harvard University Press, 1983), 226–47.

13 David N. Livingstone, 'The Spaces of Knowledge: Contributions towards a Historical Geography of Science', *Environment and Planning D: Society and Space* 13, no. 1 (1995): 7.

14 Said, 'Traveling Theory', 227.

past for reuse in the present: the distortion, not merely adaptation, of earlier moments of the chain of influence'.[15] Following theory as it travels is to pay 'critical attention to history and to situation' of ideas.[16] Travelling theory is a kind of method: how ideas travel – from origins, across distance, reformed under new conditions and settled in new formations – itself becomes a tool for thinking with.

In the original essay, Said follows György Lukàcs' 1923 book, *History and Class Consciousness*. Its 'particular voyage from Hungary to Paris, with all that entails, seems compelling enough, adequate enough for critical scrutiny, unless we want to give up critical consciousness for critical hermeticism'.[17] Said analyses how Lukàcs' ideas moved into the hands first of Lucien Goldmann, whose 'reading [...] mutes [Lukàcs'] almost apocalyptic version of consciousness'.[18] He then follows it into Raymond Williams's work. The Welsh critic's *The Country and the City* was a guiding star for Said's own *Orientalism*.[19] One of the things that Said took from Williams – as well as from Antonio Gramsci – was a profoundly geographical orientation. Following ideas is to follow them geographically, as well as historically. It is on the basis of his methodological analysis of how theory travels that he redoubles his commitment to an engaged dialectic between the world, the text, and the critic. The essay is less a denunciation of misappropriation than a commitment to how ideas' travels produce new intellectual alternatives and theoretico-political possibilities:

> to map the territory covered by all the techniques of dissemination, communication, and interpretation, to preserve some modest (perhaps shrinking) belief in noncoercive human community; if these are not imperatives, they do at least seem to be attractive alternatives. And what is critical consciousness at bottom if not an unstoppable predilection for alternatives?[20]

Josué de Castro is part of an alternative, multi-lingual tradition that multiplies the places and geographies that count in the history of geography. But, even more importantly, Castro's ideas are not fixed, but are constantly reforming and mobile. I want to return again to Gillian Rose's argument that it is the 'spatialization of tradition as a transparent territory that feminists need to displace'.[21] Simply adding the Northeast of Brazil to a static, coherent

---

15 Timothy Brennan, 'Edward Said as a Lukácsian Critic: Modernism and Empire', *College Literature* 40, no. 4 (October 2013): 17, doi:10.1353/lit.2013.0046.

16 Said, 'Traveling Theory', 227.

17 Said, 'Traveling Theory', 236.

18 Said, 'Traveling Theory', 236.

19 Timothy Brennan, 'Edward Said: American Theory and the Politics of Knowledge', *Atlantic Studies* 2, no. 1 (2005): 93–103.

20 Said, 'Traveling Theory', 247.

21 Gillian Rose, 'Tradition and Paternity: Same Difference?' *Transactions of the Institute of British Geographers* 20, no. 4 (1995): 414–16.

and taken-for-granted territory of disciplinary knowledge does not offer a true alternative. We need, rather, to bring together Said's idea that the movement of knowledge itself constructs theory with Donna Haraway's contention that (feminist) 'objectivity means quite simply *situated knowledges*'.[22] That is to say that, if objectivity is situated, it is also mobile. As Said, Livingstone, and others remind us, it is not simply a matter of knowledge coming from somewhere (and ending up somewhere else); we should also be concerned with how it moves and is shaped and reshaped as it does so. This movement is part of the essence of ideas, not merely something that follows from them. This is an important dimension of overcoming Eurocentric thought: not only to see that knowledge claims emerge from particular historical geographies, but that the movement of knowledge takes place along frictive channels and through patterns established by real and imaginary geographies. Eurocentrism functions not only at the source and in the object of knowledge, but through its mobility.

What necessarily follows from this, but has been under-emphasized in histories of geography, is a sustained interest in translation. We need to attend 'to the ways that discourses [...] *travel*, the ways they are translated, disseminated, reformulated in transnational contexts marked by difference'.[23] In the case of Castro, translations have been multiple, but incomplete and highly partial: some seeds of solidarity took root, while others fell on stony ground. Studying translation also turns our attention to the level of the sentence. Haraway writes: 'feminism loves another science: the sciences and politics of interpretation, translation, stuttering, and the partly understood. [...] Translation is always interpretive, critical, and partial. Here is a ground for conversation, rationality, and objectivity'.[24] Translations of Castro had multiple intentions, functions, itineraries, and destinations, one of which was to create networks of like-minded political thinkers, as well as to disseminate his ideas into the work of social movements. The production of international solidarities would be impossible without acts of translation.[25] Translation is one of the boundaries at which difference is constituted, which Gillian Rose suggests the feminist historiography of geography should attend to.[26] Translation is also critical to any attempt at multiplying the discipline of geography and its histories. The question of disciplinarity itself is at stake here. For Claudio Minca,

22 Donna Haraway, 'Situated Knowledge: The Science Question in Feminism as a Site of Discourse on the Privilege of Partial Perspective', *Feminist Studies* 14 (1998): 581.
23 Brent Hayes Edwards, *The Practice of Diaspora: Literature, Translation, and the Rise of Black Internationalism* (Cambridge, MA: Harvard University Press, 2009), 7.
24 Haraway, 'Situated Knowledge', 589.
25 Edwards, *The Practice of Diaspora*; David Featherstone, *Solidarity: Hidden Histories and Geographies of Internationalism* (London: Zed Books, 2012).
26 Rose, 'Tradition and Paternity'.

disciplines are, above all, the site of the production of a self-referential knowledge, an on-going elaboration of propositions, discussion, experimentation, and comparison which relies upon the existence of a community of scholars legitimated by reciprocal consideration, internal and external communication networks, these same scholars' social visibility, the accessibility of their propositions and their capacity for self-reproduction.[27]

Castro acted across all these practices, moving across and through various networks. Crucially, Minca emphasizes that 'it is exactly the interplay between diverse languages which constitutes a discipline'.[28] The history of geographical ideas requires more attention to the histories of translation, in the mould laid out by Hayes Edwards in his history of black internationalism.[29] Attention to translation, and translation histories, is essential to geographical disciplinarity itself. Lawrence Venuti argues that 'translation has always functioned as a method of introducing innovative materials and practices into academic institutions, but its success has inevitably been constrained by institutionalized values. Foreign scholarship can enter and influence the academy, although only in terms that are recognizable to it – at least initially.'[30]

Venuti and Minca help us to see translation as the theoretico-practical traffic of meaning across intelligibility and difference.[31] The passage between similarity and difference, between the new and the familiar, are essential liminal spaces in the history of geographical thinking.[32] Translation works at the level of the world, the text, and the critic, as well as the word, the institution, and the discipline. Following Castro's geography and geopolitics of hunger involves an exploration of the work that translation, non-translation and reception do in establishing both disciplinarity – what kind of discourse counts as geographical – and the object of the discipline – what that discourse is about. The co-ordinates of the discipline's ideas and their history are mystifying without incorporating translation into histories of publication and reception.

Innes Keighren's work on Ellen Semple's *Influences of Geographic Environment* (1911) approaches the reception of geographical knowledge in

27 Claudio Minca, 'Venetian Geographical Praxis', *Environment and Planning D: Society and Space* 18, no. 3 (2000): 288.

28 Minca, 'Venetian Geographical Praxis', 288.

29 Edwards, *The Practice of Diaspora*.

30 Lawrence Venuti, 'Translating Derrida on Translation: Relevance and Disciplinary Resistance', *The Yale Journal of Criticism* 16, no. 2 (2003): 238–39.

31 Venuti, 'Translating Derrida', 238–39.

32 See also Gayatri Chakravorty Spivak, 'Translation as Culture', *Parallax* 6, no. 1 (2000): 13–24; Gayatri Chakravorty Spivak, 'Translating into English', in *Nation, Language and the Ethics of Translation*, ed. Sandra Bermann and Michael Wood (Princeton, NJ: Princeton University Press, 2005), 93–110; Tariq Jazeel and Colin McFarlane, 'Responsible Learning: Cultures of Knowledge Production and the North–South Divide', *Antipode* 39, no. 5 (2007): 781–89.

highly specific geographical and scalar terms. He attends to the architecture, production, publishing, reviewing, and annotation of that book to explore the dense and uneven geography of geographical ideas.[33] Keighren grounds the history of ideas in the materiality of dissemination and exchange. In Robert Westman's words, 'books and letters, not 'isms, passed hands'.[34] Yet the notion that ideas circulate only through the passing of material (or indeed digital) texts is debatable. We can surmise that the work of many geographers – and others – has become canonical without necessarily having been read. However, a focus on the material transit of knowledge – in James Secord's terms – furnishes a historical emplacement of Donna Haraway's 'view from nowhere'.[35] Geographical knowledge emerged under particular conditions in particular spaces at particular times, and travelled unevenly and unreliably.[36]

This intersection between translation and the history of geography is empirical and historical, as well as theoretical. The translation and (re) publication of books illuminates the traffic of knowledge across language, but also its constitution and its politics. The intersecting and conflicting histories of Castro's books demonstrates that translation is more than another cog in the wheel of what Robert Danton called 'the Communications Circuit', an illustration of the material dynamics of the production and distribution of ideas.[37] This model has since been critiqued,[38] but provided an influential way of characterizing production and transmission in the history of the book. While Danton finds a place for publishers, purchasers, binders, and many others, he surprisingly ignores the process of translation. This is a common oversight in the field that has only recently begun to be systematically corrected. One exception in the history and geography of the book is Nicholas Rupke's investigation of how translations altered the meaning of Robert Chambers' *Vestiges of the Natural History of Creation* across European space. He noted in 2000 that 'the part played by translations of scientific texts in the development of science is as yet [...] largely neglected'.[39] Since then,

33 See Keighren, *Bringing Geography to Book*.

34 Cited in James A. Secord, 'Knowledge in Transit', *Isis* 95, no. 4 (2004): 665.

35 Steven Shapin, 'Placing the View from Nowhere: Historical and Sociological Problems in the Location of Science', *Transactions of the Institute of British Geographers* 23, no. 1 (1998): 5–12.

36 Livingstone, 'The Spaces of Knowledge'; see also Steven Shapin and Simon Schaffer, *Leviathan and the Air-Pump: Hobbes, Boyle, and the Experimental Life* (Princeton, NJ; Oxford: Princeton University Press, 2018); Keighren et al., 'Teaching the History of Geography'.

37 Robert Darnton, 'What Is the History of Books?', *Daedalus* 111, no. 3 (1982): 65–83; see also Robert Darnton, '"What Is the History of Books?" Revisited', *Modern Intellectual History* 4, no. 3 (2007): 495–508.

38 See Secord, 'Knowledge in Transit'.

39 Nicolaas Rupke, 'Translation Studies in the History of Science: The Example of Vestiges', *The British Journal for the History of Science* 33, no. 2 (2000): 209–22.

while there has been a great deal of work on the movement of knowledge,[40] and while translation has been given attention in recent work on historical geography,[41] more work remains to be done.[42]

As Rupke noted, the mechanisms by which processes of translation alter meanings are various, not only because translations are 'autochtonous cultural products' but also through 'new, additional prefaces, [...] footnote commentary [...] illustrations, [...] omissions and, most fundamentally, by the very act of cultural relocation'.[43] I would add editing and the fluid medium of language itself to this list. Furthermore, the geography of reception needs also to account for non-translation: 'translation has been an indispensable component of intellectual exchange and development throughout recorded history [...] the translation of a work of literature or scholarship – indeed, of any major cultural document – can have a significant impact on the intellectual community, while the absence of translations impedes the circulation of ideas'.[44] As we will see, this is key in Castro's case, in which non- and partial translation has not only 'impeded' but altered the circulation of his ideas.

Gaps and Maps

I want to turn here to some of the details of the differences between Castro's texts across languages. One such difference is in cartography, or the lack of it.

40 See, for example, Heike Jöns, Peter Meusburger, and Michael Heffernan, eds, *Mobilities of Knowledge*, Knowledge and Space (Cham: Springer International Publishing, 2017); Trevor J. Barnes and Carl Christian Abrahamsson, 'The Imprecise Wanderings of a Precise Idea: The Travels of Spatial Analysis', in *Mobilities of Knowledge*, ed. Heike Jöns, Peter Meusburger, and Michael Heffernan, Knowledge and Space (Cham: Springer International Publishing, 2017), 105–21, doi:10.1007/978-3-319-44654-7_6; Heike Jöns, 'Academic Travel from Cambridge University and the Formation of Centres of Knowledge, 1885–1954', *Journal of Historical Geography* 34, no. 2 (2008): 338–62.
41 Janice Monk, 'Canons, Classics, and Inclusion in the Histories of Geography', *Dialogues in Human Geography* 2, no. 3 (November 2012): 328–31, doi:10.1177/2043820612468550.
42 For exceptions see Karl S. Zimmerer, 'Retrospective on Nature–Society Geography: Tracing Trajectories (1911–2010) and Reflecting on Translations', *Annals of the Association of American Geographers* 100, no. 5 (October 2010): 1076–94, doi:10.1080/00045608.2010.523343; Federico Ferretti, 'Inventing Italy. Geography, *Risorgimento* and National Imagination: The International Circulation of Geographical Knowledge in the Nineteenth Century: Inventing Italy', *The Geographical Journal* 180, no. 4 (December 2014): 402–13, doi:10.1111/geoj.12068; Alison Martin, *Nature Translated: Alexander Von Humboldt's Works in Nineteenth-Century Britain* (Edinburgh: Edinburgh University Press, 2018).
43 Rupke, 'Translation Studies in the History of Science', 210.
44 Nicholas Harrison, 'Notes on Translation as Research', *Modern Languages Open* online (2015), accessed 16 June, DOI: http://doi.org/10.3828/mlo.v0i0.78.

Figure 2. Josué de Castro delivering a presentation in Santo Domingo, Dominican Republic, 1945. The maps are the same as those published in the 1946 *Geografia da Fome*. Source: Acervo Fundação Joaquim Nabuco – Ministério da Educação – Brasil

One of Castro's central intentions in *Geografia da Fome* was to map hunger in Brazil (Figure 2). This built on his longstanding work on Brazilian nutrition, and was one of the book's major political interventions.[45] The spatial analysis of hunger, connecting it with landscape, agriculture, social structure, culture, and historical geography, is one of the book's lasting political contributions. The early Brazilian editions contain elegant, full-colour maps of hunger, ecological regions, disease distribution, and alimentary traditions. In Brazilian editions these maps at times appear and at times do not – only one in the third, but all in the ninth editions, for instance. The *Geopolítica da Fome* largely did not include the same cartographic work. The French translations of *Geografia* include maps. Later editions of the *Geopolítica da Fome* – for instance, by *Brasília Editora* in Portugal – see different maps introduced, of world population according to calorie intake and malnutrition

45 Alves, 'A Contribuição de Josué de Castro'; Francisco Fransualdo de Azevedo, Fernanda Laize Silva de Lima, and Rafael Pereira da Silva, 'A Fome e a Escassez no Período Técnico-Científico-Informancional: Revistando o Pensamento de Josué de Castro em Relação ao Brasil e ao Nordeste', *Caminhos de Geografia* 13, no. 42 (June 2012), http://www.seer.ufu.br/index.php/caminhosdegeografia/article/view/16747; Andrade, *Josué de Castro e o Brasil*.

across the world. Polish- and English-language editions of his work do not include maps. In terms of reception, these are significant differences at the levels of aesthetics and interpretation. Cartography is an important part of the text's semantic totality; removing the maps fundamentally alters readers' access to what the geography of hunger is.

Indeed, Castro was concerned to avoid maps being published hastily in the English-language edition of *The Geography of Hunger*. His publisher wanted to do so, in order to 'illustrate' the text, but Castro wrote requesting that they did not. He noted that to produce maps of world hunger of similar value and accuracy to those in his Brazilian work would take 'some three months of work', which was not possible. He professes himself to '[not] feel enthusiastic about including illustrations in the text, especially if prepared in a hurry'. He agrees to compromise on some photographs: 'some good illustration suggesting a poor landscape – hunger area – such as Tanguy's paintings or a group of hungry people lost in a desert would be much more suggestive'.[46] This slightly dismissive tone perhaps cautions against reading too much into the final selection of the book's photographs. However, as we will see in the next chapter, it does show Castro's interest in the way that a landscape can depict the spatiality of hunger – a project of the aesthetics of hunger that was picked up and expanded both in his years of attempts to film the Geography of Hunger and in the films that he did make, including the *Drama das Secas* in Brazil and *O Grito*,[47] made for French television. The fact that he prefers the surrealist paintings of Yves Tanguy to maps reminds us of Castro's intent to confront hunger as a 'universal' problem, which will be explored in depth in the next two chapters. The key point here is that Castro's unwillingness to include maps, however, was 'because it may make [the book] look like a Geography, when it is actually rather a work on geo-politics or sociology'.[48] The irony that giving the book the title of 'The Geography ...' might perhaps make it seem 'like a Geography' seems somehow to have got lost. We can see the contrast, here, with his more directly regional geographical work on the city of Recife. His doctoral dissertation, which he later published as a monograph, included a number of maps, including relief maps and old charts and plans.[49] Though he doesn't specifically engage in a critique of cartography, given the importance of mapping to the regional tradition,[50] his growing caution about maps suggests the important shift that Castro makes in his deployment of regional geography.

46 Josué de Castro, 'To Ned Bradford', August 1951, 559, CEHIBRA.JdC.
47 Josué de Castro, 'O Grito: A Fome, Grande Descoberta Do Século XX' (unpublished, 1950s), 127, CEHIBRA.JdC.
48 Castro, 'To Ned Bradford'.
49 Josué de Castro, *A cidade do Recife: ensaio de geografia urbana* (Rio de Janeiro: Editôra da Casa do Estudante do Brasil, 1954).
50 Anssi Paasi, 'Regional Geography I', in *International Encyclopedia of Human Geography*, ed. R. Kitchin and N. Thrift, 9 (London: Elsevier, 2009), 214–27.

Prefaces

Prefaces can chart books' dynamic and multilingual trajectories as different editions reach different audiences. They can also be a way for authors to reframe their work. Castro used Brazilian prefaces to emphasize his international reception, to respond to critics, to suggest the ongoing and changing relevance of his arguments, and to clarify points of intellectual and political positioning.[51] He also used the commissioning of prefaces by other writers not only to burnish and enhance his own status through association but also to position the book within particular discourses. Furthermore, he selectively reprinted particular prefaces, in translation, in different editions.[52] The prefaces make substantial contributions to how the arguments of the books are to be understood. Sanford Greenburger, Castro's US editor, was keen that the *Geography of Hunger* have a preface by a 'great statesman', or no preface at all. He pushed back against Castro's suggestion of a preface by Norris Dodd, then the Director General of the FAO.[53] In the end, Lord John Boyd Orr agreed to write the preface for the first English edition of *The Geography of Hunger*. He wrote that the book should really be called 'Hunger and Politics'. This intervention immediately begins to unwrite the book's geography, and perhaps tells us something, too, about the wider understanding of the term, and the discipline, in the UK at the time. Both the geopolitical and the geographical are conferred secondary status to a broader positioning of the book as 'political', in a vague sense. While Castro appears to have been delighted with Boyd Orr's preface – he reprinted it in translation in other editions – it is revealing of the book's reception in English. A book called Hunger and Politics would be a very different thing. The English preface places the book squarely in the international humanitarian politics of food: Orr signed it as the former Director of the Food and Agriculture Organization. As chapter 4 will show, the institutional, internationalist politics of the books reward further attention.

For Said, traveling theories can 'shed their insurrectionary force [... be] tamed and domesticated somewhat, and [become] considerably less dramatic in their application and gist'.[54] Boyd Orr's preface does just this. The English-language *Geography of Hunger*, for its many merits, is a sweeping global tract that, while motivated by a burning sense of the injustice of hunger, lacks the more detailed, cartographic biosociology of *Geografia da Fome*. The way this idea travelled can be read in the material histories and geographies of the texts' new editions, formats, and languages. Boyd Orr's preface changes what

51 See Prefaces in Castro, *Geopolítica da Fome: Ensaio sôbre os Problemas de Alimentação e de População do Mundo*.

52 For example, including André Mayer's French preface in later Brazilian editions, Castro, *Geografia da Fome*.

53 Sanford Greenburger, 'To Josué de Castro', April 1950, 562, CEHIBRA.JdC.

54 Said, 'Traveling Theory Reconsidered', 437.

Castro's work means for an anglophone readership. In publishing it, Castro drew his own work's sting and altered his long-term intellectual legacy.

The ideas of the original *Geografia* remain potent because of the methodological proposition they contain.[55] In France, Castro's methodology is given centre stage in *Géographie de la Faim*'s editorial notes and the French geographer André Mayer's preface. Another influential French geographer, Maximillien Sorre, wrote the preface to the French translation of the *Geopolítica da Fome*, and argued that: 'Josué de Castro established in this book the principles and foundations of a new method of analysis of the alimentary phenomenon, that can be applied in other regions of the world.'[56] Castro drew on Sorre's work and Sorre wrote an article in the *Annales de Géographie*, 'La géographie de l'alimentation' [The geography of alimentation],[57] in response to Castro's work. The archive of the Musée de l'Homme in Paris holds a copy of the first edition of *Geografia da Fome* given to the influential anthropologist Roger Bastide by Castro. This relationship was part of the ecology of personal friendships that ensured that Castro's impact in France was greater than in the anglophone world. These exchanges amount to the kind of dialogue across languages and shared interests that, according to Minca, constitute disciplinarity. But they were a francophone and lusophone, not an anglophone phenomena.[58]

The architecture of *Geografia da Fome*'s various editions – prefaces, subtitles, cover flaps – give an insight into how, and with what baggage, the books and ideas of the geopolitics and geography of hunger travelled. The geography and geopolitics of hunger as 'methods of analysis' are largely lacking in the publication frameworks, rubrics, and footnotes of Castro's English-language publication history. The writers of the prefaces – the American novelist Pearl Buck in the USA and in the UK Boyd Orr – function as validating and valorizing chaperones for the Brazilian author. In contrast to the French and Brazilian editions, the texts' academic scaffolding, including some references, is largely removed in the English editions. The preface to the second edition of the *Géographie de la Faim* indicates the difference between the reception in France and the anglophone world, suggesting that the initial translation in 1949 'caused a profound emotional response in the French reading public and led to a great debate on the subject of hunger'.[59] Castro

55 Magda Zanoni, 'Josué de Castro: Actualité d'une Pensée', *Natures Sciences Sociétés* 18, no. 1 (2010): 36–41.

56 Preface in Castro, *Géographie de la faim*, 11.

57 Max Sorre, 'La Géographie de l'alimentation', *Annales de Géographie* 61 (1952): 184–99.

58 On questions of language, francophony, and Brazilian geography, see Mariana Lamego, 'How International Was the International Geographical Congress in Rio de Janeiro 1956? On Location and Language Politics', in *Decolonising and Internationalising Geography* (Cham: Springer, 2020), 113–26; and Silva, *French-Brazilian Geography*.

59 Preface in Castro, *Géographie de la faim*, 11.

later noted the success of the 1964 edition,[60] published with Seuil. This raises the importance of the publishing houses themselves. Seuil, for instance, was linked to leftist cultural intellectuals and secular humanism. Although they published Fanon's *Peau Noirs, masques blancs* (Black Skin, White Masks) in 1952, they were not the most radical of Paris' publishing houses, a role fulfilled by François Maspero.[61] In English, Castro has been published by notable leftist houses: Victor Gollancz in London and the Monthly Review Press in New York. The very different ways that publishers – in sometimes collaborative, and sometimes fractious relations with the author himself – brought these books to different publics had an inevitable, and important, impact on how these ideas have travelled. Part of these negotiations were precisely over translation.

Language and the Practice of Translation

Geopolítica da Fome appeared in English as *The Geography of Hunger* almost simultaneously with its publication in Portuguese. Castro wrote to Greenburger, on 14 February 1949, that he would provide him 'with a literal translation of the original as I write it', and that Greenburger would then be 'responsible for putting the text into English form acceptable to the American publishers'.[62] Translations multiplied quickly and by the time Castro was writing the preface for its second edition in Brazil, in December 1952, the book had already been translated into eight languages.[63] This led to immediate confusion and conflicting, overlapping reception in different language worlds. Castro's editor was keen to keep the original book down while promoting the new one. He wrote to Castro on 24 August 1950: 'I am sorry that you were unable to postpone the French publication as suggested. It may possibly interfere with the French publication of our book. I urge you *very, very* strongly to keep *the other* "Geographie de la Faim" away from publication everywhere until after the big book is published in *all languages*.'[64] Castro did not follow his urging. Greenburger elsewhere refers to the 'other' book in slightly dismissive terms as 'the scientific book'.[65] This ironic situation emerged principally because Greenburger and the anglophone publishers saw the *principal* sphere of reception and publication as the anglophone world. Others were secondary at best or interfering and problematic at worst. This

---

60 Josué de Castro, 'Letter to "Meus queridos, meu filho" from Josué de Castro', June 1964, 290, CEHIBRA.JdC.

61 Ruth Bush, *Publishing Africa in French: Literary Institutions and Decolonization 1945–1967* (Oxford: Oxford University Press, 2016), 43–45.

62 Castro, 'To Sanford Greenburger'.

63 See prefaces in Castro, *Geopolítica da Fome: Ensaio sôbre os Problemas de Alimentação e de População do Mundo.*

64 Greenburger, 'To Josué de Castro', August 1950, 562, CEHIBRA.JdC.

65 Greenburger, 'To Josué de Castro'.

primacy can be felt in the process of translation, in which the English text came to be the ur-text, over and above the original Portuguese. The Spanish and Polish translations were based on the English version by George Reed and G. Robert Stange.[66] The latter seems to have been the editor employed by Little Brown in Boston, and the former provided the original translation.[67]

Translation, of course, can yield gratuitous ideological emendations, as Ferretti finds in translations of Reclus.[68] This is not the story of the *Geopolítica*'s translation into the *Geography*, though important differences emerge and new passages appear. Indeed, as Castro notes with irritation to Greenburger, some of these appeared in the process of the revision of the translation by Robert Stange.[69] For example, Castro tried to lever into the English book some of the geographical methodology that his previous work had exhaustively expounded. In English a paragraph is added implying that geography can function as an 'accounting [...] of the mutual relations between the earth and its human inhabitants'[70] and new paragraphs are added giving an overview of his approach to geography.[71] Castro's letters with his editor also reveal the extent to which Greenburger and Robert Stange were involved in attempts to shift the book's emphasis. In an exchange in March 1951, just before the book is finalized, Greenburger writes to Castro asking him to 'rush some cuts'. He argues that 'the political examination of British imperial policy does not always give me an immediate connection with the hunger problem. Also, perhaps the use of the phrase the "English" by personalizing the imperial policy rather lets down the intensive convincingness of the facts.'[72] Castro's response, a fortnight later, is to ignore Greenburger's suggestions: 'the best thing to do [...] is to leave the book as it is. As a matter of fact, the political aspects which I describe are very much in the public eye at this moment, and this should give a certain impetus to the book.'[73] This shows translation as a negotiation across languages, but also across political positions.[74] Castro

---

66 For instance, the Spanish edition, *Geografía del Hambre*, published in Madrid by Ediciones Cid in 1961, translated by María Dolores López, and the Polish edition, *Geografia Glodu*, published by Pax in Warsaw in 1954, translated by Roman Kutyłowski.

67 Greenburger, 'To Josué de Castro', March 1950, 562, CEHIBRA.JdC.

68 Federico Ferretti, 'Political Geographies, "Unfaithful" Translations and Anticolonialism: Ireland in Élisée Reclus's Geography and Biography', *Political Geography* 59 (2017): 11–23.

69 Castro, 'To Sanford Greenburger', June 1950, 562, CEHIBRA.JdC.

70 Castro, *Geography of Hunger*, 13.

71 For example, Castro, 29; compare with Castro, *Geopolítica da Fome: Ensaio sôbre os Problemas de Alimentação e de População do Mundo*, 1:76–77.

72 Greenburger, 'To Josué de Castro', March 1951, 563, CEHIBRA.JdC.

73 Castro, 'To Sanford Greenburger 19th March', March 1951, 563, CEHIBRA.JdC.

74 Batchelor's analysis of the translations of Fanon shows this at work: Kathryn Batchelor, 'Fanon's Les Damnés de La Terre: Translation, de-Philosophization and the Intensification of Violence', *Nottingham French Studies* 54, no. 1 (2015): 7–22.

wanted to retain, not elide, both the anticolonial style and the immediate political charge of his work.

Some strange translations do appear: for instance Castro's '*as democracias ocidentais e o comunismo oriental*'[75] [the Western democracies and Eastern communism] is translated as 'capitalist democracy and Russian democracy'.[76] There are many other examples, but in analysing the significance of translation I want to dwell on the details of three crucial terms important not only to this book but to Castro's whole oeuvre: *fome, alimentação,* and *meio ambiente*. I focus on individual words not because translation is a process of word-for-word transcoding – on the contrary, translation functions at multiple scales, from word, to world, to text, to critic[77] – but rather because these three words are thresholds to broader questions of discipline, culture, meaning, context, and interpretation. This is not only to excavate how ideas mutate across languages but to suggest that in the interstices of translation lies new theoretical potential.

Fome

Translating is necessarily always a process of loss, but it can also be one of expansion, and the accrual of meaning across different systems of reference, lexicon, syntax, and poetics. To demonstrate this I want to examine Castro's use of the word *fome,* hunger, a keystone of his thought. Hunger is a complex carrier of meaning that opens onto philosophical, cultural, historical, and geographical concerns. Yet its translation is unstable. In *Geography of Hunger* '*fome*' is translated both as 'hunger' and, at other moments, as 'famine' (for example, Castro uses the plural '*fomes*' in relation to what are translated as 'famines' in Morocco[78]). *Fome,* largely unlike the English 'hunger', can refer to a temporally bound and spatially extended event: a hungering or, rather, a famine.[79] The English word 'hunger' derives from Germanic languages, while the word *fome* (as well as the French *faim* and the English 'famine') derives from the Latin *fames*. In fact, the English 'hunger' has a largely obsolete function as a noun with a similar meaning as famine. This was used in the context of the Irish famine, by, for example, the Irish poet Patrick Kavanagh in his extraordinary poem 'The Great Hunger'. The slippage between *fome* and hunger suggests that in Portuguese the difference between hunger (biophysical condition, sensation, individual lack, desire)

---

75 Castro, *Geopolítica da Fome: Ensaio sôbre os Problemas de Alimentação e de População do Mundo*, 1:55.

76 Castro, *Geography of Hunger*, 19.

77 See, for example, Spivak, 'Translation as Culture'.

78 Compare Castro, *Geopolítica da Fome: Ensaio sôbre os Problemas de Alimentação e de População do Mundo*, 1:273 and Castro, *Geography of Hunger*, 213.

79 See entries for 'hunger' and 'famine' in 'famine, n.', *OED Online*, accessed 13 May 2018, and *fome* in *Dicionário infopédia da Língua Portuguesa* [*em linha*], accessed 13 May 2018, 14:17:41, https://www.infopedia.pt/dicionarios/lingua-portuguesa/fome.

and famine (political and natural *event*) is ambiguous, or at least contextual. In Portuguese, the most common phrase for being hungry is *ter fome* – literally, to *have* hunger, usually associated with a prolonged condition, and almost synonymous with *passar fome* [to suffer/pass through/become hunger]. *Estar com fome* [to be with hunger], is also used, largely to indicate a more immediate or temporary state. In these forms, hunger is figured as something that accompanies, dominates, or is possessed. Unlike the English form – in which hunger infiltrates and determines a state of being (one *is* hungry) – these forms externalize hunger as an invader, duration, or experience. The two languages suppose different spatio-temporalities for hunger.

Castro discusses translation in the preface to *Geografia da Fome*, noting the difference between the English term 'starvation', with its suggestion of death from hunger, and his own interest in hunger more broadly conceived.[80] But an accurate translation of 'geography of famine' in Portuguese would be *geografia da fome*. Anglophone political ecology emerged in good part precisely through work on famine such as Michael Watts' seminal work *Silent Violence*, which has the subtitle *Food, Famine and Peasantry in Northern Nigeria*.[81] This continues in David Nally's work on the history of the Irish famine and Mike Davis' *Late Victorian Holocausts*. Castro's work is a precursor to this tradition: it could be called *The Geography of Famine*. This would not be a *better* translation, but it would be a different one and, in Lawrence Venuti's terms, a 'relevant' one.[82] The fact that Castro's work has been translated as a 'geography of hunger' – a phrase with a particular kind of built-in polemical charge – has played a role in establishing his position in, or external to, (anglophone) histories of the geographical study of *famine*. Nevertheless, in the interstices between languages we can see more clearly what Castro's work seeks to achieve. It is precisely through *fome*'s capacity to connote meanings that are simultaneously experiential, bodily, and phenomenological – that is, about *hunger* – and political, spatial, geographical, and historical – that is, about *famine* – that Castro's work has much to offer contemporary geography. The slippages of translation also help to explain – although clearly do not totally explain – why he has largely been overlooked in anglophone histories of hazards, drought, and famine.

Alimentação

Hunger – *fome* – in Castro's work is associated with territory and space as well as the body. This becomes clear when we analyse the translation of another key word of his bodily writing and practice, *alimentação*. The

80 Castro, *Geografia da Fome*, I:17.
81 See also Michael Watts, 'On the Poverty of Theory: Natural Hazards Research in Context', in *Environment: Critical Essays in Human Geography*, ed. Kay Anderson and Bruce Braun (London: Routledge, 2008), 57–88.
82 Venuti, 'Translating Derrida on Translation'.

translation of this Portuguese word – or the French *alimentation*[83] – into English is somewhat vexing. 'Alimentation', in its *Oxford English Dictionary* sense – 'the action or process of being nourished by or of ingesting and digesting food; the action or process of providing food or nutrients; nourishment; nutrition'[84] – gets exactly to the emphasis on praxis and process that underpins what we can learn from Castro's geographical approach to hunger, food, and famine. Yet 'alimentation' is relatively rare and technocratic in English[85] and, while 'the geography of alimentation', 'alimentary geography', or 'nutritional geography' are all useful phrases, they are compromised by being inadequately visceral, both literally and politically. In one of Castro's manuscripts a translation of the 'geography of nutrition' is proposed but discarded.[86] (It's worth noting that this has became a small interdisciplinary sub-field partly in the wake of Castro's work, and that of geographers such as Max Sorre and Jacques May.[87]) The English alternative 'feeding' loses the nutritional and somatic qualities of *'alimentação'*, as well as the agential, political, and social dimensions of the geography of hunger. Translating *'alimentação'*, therefore, is a subjective, literary judgement that has practical and theoretical significance. Castro deploys the word extensively, including in titles such as *Alimentação e Raça* [Diet and Race] and *A Alimentação Brasileira à Luz da Geografia Humana* [The Human Geography of the Brazilian Diet]. He uses the term *'alimentação'* alongside and distinct from both *'fome'* and *'nutrição'*. Yet *alimentação* emphasizes a crucial dimension of Castro's geographical humanist idea of hunger explored in the last chapter: that feeding is a bodily process that takes place between people, inside structures of social, spatial, and political relations. This meaning becomes legible only when we take seriously the intellectual and methodological depth behind Castro's geography of hunger – a possibility lost in the (non-) translation of his work into English. The processual quality of *'alimentação'*

---

83 For the distinction between these see Pierre Monbeig, 'Au Brésil: La «Géographie de La Faim» de Josué de Castro', *Annales. Histoire, Sciences Sociales* 3 (1948): 495–500.

84 'Alimentation, n.1', *OED Online*, accessed 11 December 2018, http://www.oed.com/view/Entry/5049.

85 The *OED* puts 'alimentation' in 'Band 4' of their Frequency Usage register, indicating that it 'occur[s] between 0.1 and 1.0 times per million words in typical modern English usage. Such words are marked by much greater specificity and a wider range of register, regionality, and subject domain than those found in bands 8–5.' 'Hunger', for instance, is in Band 6, which 'contains words which occur between 10 and 100 times per million words in typical modern English usage, including a wide range of descriptive vocabulary'. Portuguese and French equivalent dictionaries unfortunately don't provide equivalent metrics.

86 Josué de Castro, 'Geografia da Fome Translation Manuscripts' (manuscript, 1950s), 75, CEHIBRA.JdC.

87 Beal and Ervin, 'The Geography of Malnutrition'; Ben Wisner, Dan Weiner, and Phil O'Keefe, 'Hunger: A Polemical Review*', *Antipode* 14, no. 3 (December 1982): 1–16, doi:10.1111/j.1467-8330.1982.tb00034.x.

gets to what I analyse as the metabolic, rather than just the somatic. The difference between a geography of '*alimentação*' and one of 'food' is essential. Castro's thinking starts from negativity and lack, not from surfeit. Studying the necessary twists and turns of translation enables us to detail the object of Castro's enquiry: not just the spatial distribution or quality of food, but the spatial, social, political, and economic processes by which people come to eat, or are made hungry.

Meio Ambiente

Very late in life, Castro wrote a piece in Spanish calling for more research on the connection between environment and development. He reflects on the Spanish term '*medio ambiente*', usually translated into English as 'environment'. Apologizing for what he says is his poor grasp of Spanish, he notes that Spanish doesn't have a word for what in French is '*environnement*'. He likes the French *environnement* because, unlike *medio ambiente*, it 'includes man, who should be seen within the general context of the whole'.[88] The Spanish reads: '*porque incluye el hombre que se encuentra dentro del contexto general del conjunto*'. Translating this sentence is itself complex. '*Conjunto*' does not have an easy translation into English. It derives from *con+junto* – with+together – and suggests set, ensemble, and context, as well as whole. But the relationship between '*contexto general*' and '*conjunto*' is less hierarchical than the English words 'general context' and 'whole' suggest. My own choice of translation (above) embeds it in an interpretation of Castro's work that actively places it within a broader field of ecological thinking that understands humanity to be part of nature, not dominant over it. Yet this also potentially counteracts alternative interpretations of some of Castro's own earlier formulations, which at times had a productivist bent towards increasing food production that occasionally manifested in a discourse of dominating wild nature.[89] As his thinking moved towards the environmental, in the late 1960s and early 1970s, Castro himself struggled with translation in order to express his changing ideas. In a preface to the Brazilian edition of *Geopolítica da Fome* Castro uses the phrase '*o solo ambiente*' (literally 'the soil environment)'.[90] The phrase suggests a conception of the environment that prioritizes the soil as the determining feature of the relationship between nature and man. However, translating this into English loses some of the earthy textures of the phrase. These are necessarily subjective, interpretative choices: how such texts and words are translated emerges from a diachronic understanding of how Castro's thought developed. To think with Castro's work, therefore, it is most productive if we refute the two-sided coin of

88 Castro, 'Desarrollo, Ecologia, Desarme y Descolonización', 18.
89 Castro, *Geography of Hunger*, 13; for example, Castro, *Geografia da Fome: O Dilema Brasileiro: Pão Ou Aço* (1946), 102.
90 Castro, *Geopolítica da Fome: Ensaio sôbre os Problemas de Alimentação e de População do Mundo*, 27.

both direct and apolitical translation and moments of absolute impossibility of translation, and instead engage creatively in the productive field of translation itself.

Geographies of Reception

In arguing that the travels of the geography of hunger can yield important conclusions for the conceptualization of the history of geography and open new avenues for geographical theory, I have so far analysed publication and translation. I turn, now, to reception. Castro's ideas traversed places, from pages to fields, farms and factories, and from the Military Club of Rio de Janeiro to St Paul's Cathedral and Fanon's Algeria. His personal archive affords an analysis of the hundreds of newspaper clippings of reviews, comments, op-eds, and news articles that responded to his writing. Here I want to treat *Geografia da Fome* and *Geopolítica da Fome* together, as an extended contribution in two parts, or two volumes, as Castro often did. As noted at the beginning of this chapter, Milton Santos wrote in 2001 that the insight of the former underpinned the latter, which then became the 'site and inspiration for a great world debate about international injustices'.[91] To explore the geography of that 'great debate' means following the reception of Castro's work across contested national space, through academic disciplines, international politics, and anticolonialism. Castro was fascinated by the reception of his books and maintained a correspondence with his publishers asking that they retain copies of all reviews of his work.[92] The reviews of Castro's work in Brazil reveal him as a significant national intellectual. I will return to this question below, but his books elicited noteworthy public debate, at least among the elite. However, figuring reception through the national scale is very partial. National and international receptions affected one another. In Brazil itself reception was geographically divided, but its dominant fault lines were political, not geographical. Nevertheless, as Keighren argues, 'whilst location [does] not always *determine* how [...] [texts are] read, it [does] *facilitate* certain types of engagement'.[93]

There is a material continuity between publication, reception, and republication. Studying Castro's books makes a feedback loop clear: all later editions include on their dust sheets and inside flaps quotations from reviews of earlier work. The third Brazilian edition, for instance, has the back cover '*A Crítica Mundial Aplaude a* "Geografia da Fome"' [World Criticism applauds the *Geography of Hunger*]. This is, of course, entirely common. Yet it is worth noting for the oscillation it evidences between author and critics. Castro considered the book to be in active conversation with its reviewers. In the second edition he published a response to the national press, citing articles

91 Santos, 'Josué de Castro e a Geografia da Fome', 22.
92 Josué de Castro, 'To Victor Gollancz', July 1953, 88, CEHIBRA.JdC.
93 Keighren, *Bringing Geography to Book*, 4:88.

which he found useful in developing his critique and articulating points of disagreement with reviewers.[94] The breadth of opinion and comment, from the hagiographic to the vitriolic, shows that analysing hunger touched moral, political, and philosophical nerves in Brazil.[95] *Geografia da Fome* marked Castro's move into a fundamentally critical attitude towards Brazilian social reality. By 1946 Castro was directing a critique at the heart of Brazilian society.[96] Controversy, and ire from the right, centred on his analysis of the *latifundia*. The landowning elites were horrified.[97] This right-wing antipathy ultimately led Castro into political exile when his civil and political rights were cut off in April 1964. Indeed, as the diplomat José Constâncio de Athayde wrote in 1997, this reaction was both immediate and long-lasting: 'the plutocracy united with the most reactionary elements in the country and decreed the civil death of the writer who would still go on to write *Geopolitics of Hunger*'.[98] This civil death even led to the withdrawal of Castro's work from universities and libraries.[99] The oscillation between celebration and erasure is one of the curiosities of working on Castro's legacy.

Reading the reception of Castro's books, it is important not to draw too thick a line between his writing and other forms of praxis. Gramsci's notion of the intellectual, discussed further below, helps us fracture a simplistic understanding of intellectual work as not just book learning and writing but also much broader forms of practice. A dialectical mode of interpretation between text and action is necessary. If we are to appreciate the radical charge of the work – its ability to get to the roots of things – we should place it both in the political contexts in which it was written and those in which it was read. We can see how Castro's books were influential beyond

---

94 This appendix is also published in *Géographie de la Faim*, evidencing the close interconnections between French and Brazilian academic traditions. Castro also refers to the fact that he is working on a renewed investigation of hunger in Hispanic–American revolutions at the behest of Roger Bastide who he calls 'French-Brazilian', 'because few of our compatriots are identified and penetrated by the Brazilian spirit so much as Roger Bastide'; Appendix Castro, *Géographie de la faim*.

95 Formally, the response in the press was extremeley varied, from lengthy discussions, such as the seven-part series of articles published by Frederic Schwers in the *Diario de Carioco* in the first months of 1954, through to brief announcements, cartoons, captioned photographs of book signings, and formal reviews.

96 See Antonio Alfredo Teles de Carvalho, 'Josué de Castro Na Perspectiva Da Geografia Brasileira-1934–1956: Uma Contribuição à Historiografia Geográfica Nacional', Master's thesis (Dissertação de Mestrado. Orientador José Borzacchiello da Silva, 2001); Magalhães, *Fome: uma (re)leitura de Josué de Castro*.

97 For example, Hernani de Carvalho, 'Latifundios e Minifundios', *O Estado*, February 1952.

98 José Constâncio de Athayde Athayde, 'Problemas Fundiários [Basic Problems]', *Jornal Do Comercio*, February 1997.

99 Irineu Guimarães, 'Darcy Ribeiro: 1923–1997', *Jornal do Commercio*, February 1997.

the elite if we read them as intimately connected to his political practice.[100] In rural contexts of high illiteracy, vast distances, and only incipient political organization, evidence for Castro's impact is of course partial, but we can point to a number of threads. The first is the connection between Castro and the Northeast's *Ligas Camponesas*, the Peasant Leagues. He made practical contributions and was involved in some of the most significant moments of the Peasant Leagues' political existence. By the 1960s Castro was cautious about the achievements and radicalism of the Peasant Leagues,[101] but he has been lauded for decades by leaders of rural movements and was involved in the highpoint of the Peasant Leagues of the Northeast.[102] Castro's work on the geography of hunger was disseminated among Peasant Leagues. Francisco Julião, for instance, wrote a *cordel* poem (a popular form passed through troubadours) called '*Josué nosso profeta*', 'Josué our prophet', in response to *Geografia da Fome*.

Hunger was central to the politicization of the rural masses, and Castro was an important figure in the politics of hunger and agrarian reform in Brazil.[103] He straddled the worlds of parliamentary legislation, intellectual debate, and – to a lesser extent – mass politics. This expands the spatiality of his work's reception into rural space. The photograph in Figure 3 of Josué de Castro speaking at the Peasant Leagues' first ever land occupation, at Engenho Galileia, is thus not merely illustrative: it shows Castro – the intellectual – disseminating his ideas in a politicized rural space. This spatial crossing of borders from the rural to the urban is intrinsic to the interpretative frame of the geography of hunger itself. Like so much other important geographical work – from Antonio Gramsci, William Cronon, Raymond Williams, and Doreen Massey – Castro saw rural and urban places as deeply interconnected. His understanding of the geography of hunger was necessarily about connecting spaces of (non-/) consumption and spaces of (non-/) production in a single frame of analysis: the geography of hunger. Castro was also an urban thinker and throughout his career was associated with union and student interests.[104] In Recife, the dock workers founded the first union in the Northeast and were a significant political force from the

100 Bizzo, 'Ação política'.
101 Castro, *Death in the Northeast*.
102 Stédile, *A questão agrária no Brasil*; Clodomir, 'Josué de Castro: Brasileiro e Cidadão Do Mundo'; Tendler, *Josué de Castro – Cidadão do Mundo*.
103 Castro, *Semeador de Ideias*, 35–37; for a discussion of later Brazilian agrarian reforms see, for example, Anthony Pereira, 'Brazil's Agrarian Reform: Democratic Innovation or Oligarchic Exclusion Redux?', *Latin American Politics and Society* 45, no. 2 (2003): 41–65, doi:10.1111/j.1548-2456.2003.tb00240.x.
104 Melo and Neves, *Josué de Castro*, 93, 99–100. As a parliamentarian he was a key ally for student organizations, for instance promoting student positions in 1957, defending the student strike in Pernambuco in 1958 in the National Congress, and aligning himself with students and unions in August 1961 in defence of the constitution.

Figure 3. 5th June 1960. Josué de Castro (with microphone) speaking at the appropriation of the Engenho Galileia by the Peasant Leagues, alongside Francisco Julião (in white, to Castro's right). Rights: D.A. Press

1920s through to the 1960s;[105] Castro had longstanding relationships with both the Pernambuco Dock Workers' Union and dock workers in the state of São Paulo.[106] The spread of Castro's ideas in Brazil happened not only through his books' own travels, his personal relations, and his reputation among the country's elites, but also through a broad sweep of day-to-day engagement with political parties, urban workers, peasant organizations, and the student movement.

This continuity between writing and political action was folded into the materiality of his books' publication history, through reviews, prefaces, and back cover blurbs. For instance, it was a key tenet of the Brazilian critical response that Castro's books had been rapturously received in the international sphere. Innes Keighren notes a similar dynamic in his analysis of Ellen Semple's reception.[107] Castro's archives demonstrate assiduous attempts to gain allies and strengthen ties among sympathetic international readers. He proactively pursued translation projects as widely as possible, worrying over details of Lithuanian, Yugoslav, Japanese, Chinese,

---

105 Manoel Souza Barros, *A década 20 em Pernambuco: uma interpretação* (Rio de Janeiro: Graf. Edit. Acad., 1972).
106 See, for example, Fundaj.CEHIBRA.492; Fundaj.CEHIBRA.179. 12 August 1958.
107 Keighren, *Bringing Geography to Book*, 4:90.

German, Swedish, and other editions.[108] Positive international reviews were translated in Brazilian newspapers, including those originally published in *Le Monde* in Paris and *Pravda* in Moscow.[109] Reviews regularly trumpeted the growing number of translations of the book and argued that Castro's status was good for Brazilian national pride and helped promote Brazilian Portuguese as a language for intellectual advancement. In the other direction, Castro's agent Sanford Greenburger attempted to use Castro's national prominence as a tool for publicity for *The Geography of Hunger*, laying out a strategy of 'what we call making a person news in the United States' that involved attempting to secure coverage of Castro's activities by US foreign correspondents in order to help promote sales of the book.[110]

Underneath this promotional activity the international response was, in fact, quite uneven. The English response to *The Geography of Hunger* in the early 1950s was, in particular, muted. Some reviews were downright dismissive: 'confronted [...] by exaggerations and mis-statements that border on the grotesque, the reader is inclined not only to dismiss the book as nonsense, but to dismiss also from his mind the very real problems with which it is concerned'.[111] The reviewer, Eva Taylor, a specialist of early modern English geography, lands on the definition of hunger: 'does "hunger" in this sense [of lack of nutrients] demand to be described in intemperate language?'[112] Her review is enlightening with regard to the lack, in the anglophone sphere, of a contextual sense of Castro's broader work. Taylor launches a critique on the basis of Castro's inadequately geographical understanding of diet, arguing that he ignores the importance of local foodstuffs, and suggests that Castro wants a 'world-wide distribution of dried milk and eggs'.[113] A general knowledge – even a glance at the titles, as enabled by the French edition of the *Géographie de la Faim* in 1949 – of Castro's earlier work would show this to be a misreading. Castro's years of efforts to valorize the nutritional benefits of little-appreciated wild foodstuffs in the Northeast of Brazil,[114] for example, are obviously beyond

108 Josué de Castro, 'To Sanford Greenburger (Various)', Letter, 55 1949, 157, CEHIBRA. JdC.

109 Niedergang's review was republished in *Diario de Noticias*, and the editor of Pravda's review was in *Folha da Manhã* on 6 June 1955. A review by a North American professor, Earl Parker Hanson, was also translated and published, as was Joyce Butler's 'O colonialismo cria a fome'. Fundaj.CEHIBRA.6. See also *Noite Ilustrada*, 29 April 1952. 'Josué de Castro e a Crítica Inglesa'.

110 Greenburger, 'To Josué de Castro', March 1950, 562, CEHIBRA.JdC.

111 E.G.R. Taylor, 'An Under-Nourished World: Review', *The Geographical Journal* 118, no. 3 (1952): 348–50, doi:10.2307/1790323.

112 Taylor, 'An Under-Nourished World', 349.

113 Taylor, 'An Under-Nourished World', 350.

114 Josué de Castro et al., 'Os "Alimentos Bárbaros" Dos Sertões Do Nordeste', *Arquivos Brasileiros de Nutrição* 3, no. 2 (1947): 5–29.

the scope of Taylor's knowledge. The source of Taylor's ire becomes clearer, however, when she attacks Castro's emphasis on imperialism. Nevertheless, Taylor concludes oddly, '[if] we discount Dr de Castro's attitudes and opinions, and substitute such words as "deficiency," and "malnutrition" for the more sensational ones that he loves to employ, the book is worth reading'.[115] Taylor was not alone in her irritation with Castro. Paul Russell, an American scientist, noted in his diary that he found in Castro's work 'bad logic, false biology, historical dishonesty, self-righteousness, and even malice [... he] has a touch of hysteria in his blood'.[116] The reference to 'historical dishonesty' and hysteria is code for Castro's critique of colonialism. As readers, Taylor and Russell crystallize a central tenet of the reception of Castro – that his geography of hunger was too political to be scientific; too political to be 'true'.

Castro was highly self-conscious of the way in which his published work connected, and at times clashed, with his professional and political activities. In the preface to the second French edition of *Géopolitique de la Faim* Castro argued that 'the understanding and tolerance of criticism which the book has received – in response to its at times challenging perspectives and harsh accusations – seem to be precursors of a new era of better understanding between peoples'.[117] This is a somewhat vainglorious tone, but Castro, as a Brazilian and a diplomat, felt himself able to straddle the iron curtain. Throughout his political career in Brazil he had to resist characterizations of himself as a communist and a stooge of Soviet Russia. He never was such a thing, but the virulent, violent anti-communist Brazilian right picked him as one of their targets of loathing. He had friends and associates who were nationally and regionally significant communists – Luis Carlos Prestes and Caio Prado Júnior, for instance – but Castro resisted the Brazilian party's dogmatism, which never suited the independent cast of his own mind. One tradition in which we could place him, I think, is rather that of what he himself called, speaking about his friend Dom Hélder Câmara, the progressive, 'non-conformist Latin American spirit',[118] determined to disrupt the oligarchies and defined intellectually by a practised solidarity with the axis of Brazilian progressivism of the twentieth century: the alliance between rural peasants and the urban working classes. Castro saw the geography and geopolitics of hunger as a radical critique of existing power structures *and* a universalist, humanist programme relevant not only to both the USSR

115 Taylor, 'An Under-Nourished World', 350.

116 Cited in Socrates Litsios, 'Popular Education and Participation in Malaria Control: A Historical Overview 1', in *The Global Challenge of Malaria: Past Lessons and Future Prospects*, ed. F. Snowden (London: World Scientific, 2014), 92.

117 Preface in Josué de Castro, *Geopolitique de la faim* (Paris: Editions Economie et Humanisme, 1971).

118 Tulio Raúl Rosembuj, 'Josué de Castro: las dudas de un pacifista', *Cuadernos para el diálogo*, 1968, 62 edition.

and the West but also to the Third World. He wrote with both audiences in mind, and his work was received warmly on both sides of the intellectual fractures of the cold war.

Castro's books were received and interpreted among mid-century left-wing British parliamentarians and in the second edition of *Geopolítica da Fome* he wrote about exchanges with British parliamentarians in June of 1952, saying in particular that he used the book as a catalyst to muster agreement in the UK for an international food reserve.[119] Evidence for Castro's influence on British domestic politics is minimal, but his longstanding involvement in welfare politics in Brazil provides an interesting context for exchanges with crucial figures in the emergence of the welfare state and the National Health Service in the UK. Castro described, in English, these interlocutors' 'fair play': 'what surprised me – and I am very confused about it, was that I was very unfriendly with the British and they have been very friendly with me. They have been gentlemen as far as the book is concerned.'[120] His correspondence shows a warm personal relationship with Gilbert McAllister, Richard Acland, and Aneurin Bevan. All of them nominated him for the Nobel Peace Prize in 1963.[121] His nomination was seriously considered, and a dossier was prepared on his candidature.[122] Castro was in fact nominated for the prize a number of times, including in 1953 by the Soil Association, indicating his long history of entanglement with ecological concerns and institutions.[123] In 1963 the figures to publicly endorse him included the eclectic combination of the French priests Joseph Lebret and Abbé Pierre, the British communist scientist J.D. Bernal and the Pakistani pacifist Ahmed Jaffer.[124] In the end he never received the prize.

While he engaged with British politicians, he was less actively part of academic discourse in the United Kingdom during his lifetime. Castro did make attempts to intervene in anglophone academic geography. After visiting the United States he exchanged letters with the influential Michigan-based geographer Preston James[125] in the late 1930s and early 1940s. James spent significant periods of time doing research in Brazil from

119 Preface in Castro, *Geopolítica da Fome: Ensaio sôbre os Problemas de Alimentação e de População do Mundo.*

120 Rochelle Gibson, 'This Week's Personality: Josué de Castro', *Times of Roanoke*, undated, 9, CEHIBRA.JdC.

121 Gilbert McAllister and Lord Silkin, 'To The President, Nobel Committee', Letter, January 1963, 478, CEHIBRA.JdC.

122 Various, 'Nobel Prize Nomination Dossier: Josué de Castro' (Oslo: Nobel Peace Prize Centre, 65 1953), 1953 – Josué de Castro, Nobel.

123 Various, 'Nobel Prize Nomination Dossier'.

124 Anonymous, 'Genebra: Instituições Mundiais Lançam Pernambuco Josué Para o Nobel Da Paz', *Última Hora*, April 1963, Sexta-Feira edition.

125 Geoffrey J. Martin, 'Preston E. James, 1899–1986', *Annals of the Association of American Geographers* 78, no. 1 (1988): 164–75.

the 1930s onwards,[126] and it appears Castro assisted him during his trips. Indeed, Castro began a project of translating a book by James (presumably his 1935 *An Outline of Geography*), but what came of the project is unclear, and I have not been able to identify a published translation into Portuguese. James, for his part, encouraged Castro to attend the 1940 American Scientific Congress and to give a paper there.[127] Castro continued to attend later International Geographical Union (IGU) meetings, in Lisbon in 1949 and Washington in 1952, both while American Professor George Cressey was the President. It is difficult to say with precision the role that Castro took at the earlier IGU meetings. André Mayer suggests that his ideas were influential in 1949,[128] when one of the outcomes of the congress was the much wider agreement to produce an inventory of world land use.[129] In 1952 Castro and Cressey debated aspects of a geography of hunger, food, and agricultural production at the congress. Cressey was sceptical of some of Castro's connection between fertility and hunger, and about the specifics of Castro's cartographic approach, but he nevertheless invited the Brazilian to present a seminar on population at the Department of Geography at George Washington University,[130] and, as I discuss below, he consolidated a series of connections around medical geography in 1952. As discussed in chapter 4, during this period Castro was a member of the Standing Expert Committee on Nutrition at the FAO before being elected Chairman of the FAO Council in 1952. He was a conduit not only between American, French, and Brazilian geography but also (like his friend and interlocutor André Mayer) between the FAO and the IGU. The idea of the geography of hunger, however, went far beyond these institutional connections and Castro's limited access to mid-century disciplinary contexts was in many ways incidental both to him and to the history of his ideas.

Conclusion

The history of geography can be enriched by attending to questions of publication, translation, and reception. These are perhaps particularly acute, and particularly closely articulated with political change, in the post-war moment, when radical publishing was in its heyday. The way Castro's ideas

---

126 Preston E. James, 'The São Francisco Basin: A Brazilian Sertão', *Geographical Review* 38, no. 4 (1948): 658–61, doi:10.2307/211452; Preston E. James, 'Patterns of Land Use in Northeast Brazil', *Annals of the Association of American Geographers* 43, no. 2 (June 1953): 98–126, doi:10.1080/00045605309352107.

127 Preston James, 'To Josué de Castro. From Department of Geography, Ann Arbor', February 1940, 467, CEHIBRA.JdC.

128 André Mayer, Preface to first edition, Castro, *Géographie de la faim*.

129 Y.M. Goblet, 'De La Géographie de La Faim a La Géographie de l'Alimentation', *Le Monde*, August 1953.

130 George Cressey, 'To Josué de Castro', June 1952, 88, CEHIBRA.JdC.

moved and shifted are inseparable from their development, their influence, and their content. The history of the geography of hunger took place very largely outside the disciplinary constraints of Geography. What it meant differed according to audiences and contexts. The Castro of the American and British press was not the same as that of the French, Brazilian, or Pernambucan. As I will go on to explore, the geography of hunger meant different things, and worked in different ways, in the well-heeled and well-fed halls of the UN and the FAO. Its reach there was different from its manifestation in the British parliament, in the hungry streets of the outskirts of Recife or amid the rebellious fervour of land occupations in the *agreste*.

Yet the trajectory of his books' publication and reception have configured Castro's place in geographical thought. In Brazil, Castro's position as a figure of the left and a pioneer of Human Geography was enabled by an identifiable history of geographical, spatial, and scientific analysis. His Brazilian public, and to a lesser extent his French public, long had access to a Castro who was a doctor and geographer, but also an important figure in the political development of the Brazilian welfare state and arguments about national developmentalism. His *Geopolítica* was seen for what it was: an international excursion based on a long training in Brazilian political and social reality, and a deep exploration of the biosociological landscape of Brazilian hunger. To many of his anglophone recipients, however, Castro was either an international technocrat with powerful friends or a rabid anti-imperialist. He was cast as both a relatively exotic and a relatively obscure internationalist figure, cut loose from the political frictions that mark his Brazilian legacy. The emergence of the English version of *The Geography of Hunger*, without its cartographic, biosociological precursor, *Geografia da Fome*, compounds a reading of Castro as a liberal humanitarian, which runs counter to the critique of developmentalism,[131] aid, and imperialism that his anticolonial readership found in his work. This problematic will return in the chapters to come.

The non-translation of *Geografia da Fome* is a central part of this story. The history of geography can be enriched by attending to questions of translation, in terms of both the linguistic practice and the history of books. This analysis aims to add strings to the bows of travelling theory and situated knowledges by placing translation and material histories of publication at their heart. My interpretation of the history of geographical ideas sees geographical thought as forms of situated knowledge produced by the dialectic relationship between the production and reception of knowledge, and between the gaps of languages. The importance of the geography of hunger is found not as a fixed moment of pure thought but in its many contexts of location, locution, and situation, and through its many lives in motion and in translation. If the

---

131 For which see also Josué de Castro and Jorge Feio, *O drama do Terceiro Mundo* (Lisboa: Dom Quixote, 1968).

geography of hunger is a travelling theory then it is one that travels through translation. If the geography of hunger is a form of situated knowledge, in all its messiness, then its situation is always on the move. It is as both situated and mobile that geographical enquiry can still use the geography of hunger today. In the next chapter I continue to follow how this idea moved, but beyond the confines not only of the books themselves but also the written word, and into the politics of representation and the cultural worlds of Brazilian modernism. There the geography of hunger became transmuted and transformed into a political aesthetics of hunger.

CHAPTER 3

1946–1951: The Cry in the *Sertão*

Art and the Universal in
the Geography of Hunger

Introduction

This chapter argues that Josué de Castro's geography of hunger was linked to the production of a multi-faceted aesthetics of hunger in Brazilian visual art in the middle of the twentieth century. Josué de Castro had a broad, open, and humanistic conception of geography. It was not limited to spatial political economy, cartographic distribution, or hunger's persistence in, and propagation of, the relational production of space, bodies, and society. Rather, his conception of the geography of hunger also involved a set of cultural questions. In particular, this meant asking how art and literature could help us understand the spatial and social qualities of hunger. Throughout his writing, Castro used photographs and figurative and abstract art to illustrate his work, and his interpretation of the geography of hunger itself inspired art, film, and writing, particularly among a group of leading Brazilian writers and artists with whom Castro was in dialogue and who shared an interest in the political representation of hunger, and its aesthetic and artistic meanings. These correspondents included the Brazilians Rachel de Queiroz, Graciliano Ramos, and Antonio Callado (who all wrote about hunger and drought in the Northeast), as well as other Latin Americans such as Pablo Neruda, author of the great anti-hunger poem 'The Great Tablecloth', and Miguel Angel Asturias, whose masterpiece is named *Men of Maize*. But in this chapter I turn to the visual artists and filmmakers who refracted Castro's ideas. Through their efforts to represent hunger we can see more deeply the political stakes of the geography of hunger as a conceptual field.

Throughout his working life, Castro struggled with the problem of how, in its manifold senses, to represent the problem of hunger. He wanted to break with what he called the 'taboo' of hunger, in order to stimulate public action at many scales and in many sites. He also wanted to represent hunger by standing for it, politically. He declared himself to be the representative of the hungry not only in his public positions as an expert, an official, and a diplomat but also in his elected posts. Yet he was also concerned with aesthetic problems as such, with representation 'as a concept and a practice

– the key first 'moment' in the cultural circuit'.[1] I draw on Stuart Hall here not merely to place this discussion in the realm of cultural studies, but because the representation of hunger and the hungry always and indubitably runs the gamut of 'otherness': the hungry subject as distant, and marked by its difference from the viewer. Castro wrote about the art of hunger, used images of hunger in his many publications, spent years trying to make a major film of the geography of hunger, made television programmes about hunger, and was committed to the power of art and writing as a way of organizing moral campaigns against hunger, in particular at the global scale. Yet for him, and for all the artists and writers discussed here, the hungry subject remains an Other, accessible and representable through knowledge and imagination, but not through experience.

The problem of how to represent hungry people, and in particular hungry bodies, has been central to the politics of hunger, humanitarianism, and aid.[2] As I will show in the next chapter, Castro himself had a significant stake in the mid-twentieth-century emergence of international development and a fragile and contested international humanitarian consensus that stabilized in the 1960s. Analysing the history of this humanitarian attention to hunger, Jennifer Edkins argues that progressive waves of political understandings of hunger have become subsumed into a depoliticized, technologized vision of hunger thanks to its incorporation into discourses of modernity and progress.[3] This modern biopolitics of hunger is intimately connected to regimes of representation. How hunger is represented affects how it is understood and what is done, or not done, about it. The archetypical example, in the twentieth century, is the representation of the Ethiopian famine of the early 1980s and the ensuing bonanza of aid and charity responses.[4] We might think, too, of Don McCullin's photographs of the Biafran war,[5] or representations of the Irish famines of the nineteenth century in the British colonial metropole.[6] It is clear that *how* hungry bodies have been witnessed and represented has had a profound impact on the politicization and depoliticization of hunger.

1 Stuart Hall, 'The Spectacle of the "Other"', in *Representation: Cultural Representations and Signifying Practices*, ed. Stuart Hall, Jessica Evans, and Sean Nixon, 2nd ed. (London: Sage, 2001), 226.

2 Jenny Edkins, *Whose Hunger? Concepts of Famine, Practices of Aid*, NED-New edition, vol. 17 (Minneapolis: University of Minnesota Press, 2000), 1–24, https://www.jstor.org/stable/10.5749/j.ctttsxkq.

3 Edkins, *Whose Hunger?*, 17:129.

4 Edkins, *Whose Hunger?*, 17:3–4.

5 Lasse Heerten, *The Biafran War and Postcolonial Humanitarianism: Spectacles of Suffering* (Cambridge: Cambridge University Press, 2017).

6 Ian Bamford, 'Picturing Hunger: Photography and the Irish Famine 1945–50', PhD thesis (University of Ulster, 2013); Charlotte Boyce, 'Representing the "Hungry Forties" in Image and Verse: The Politics of Hunger in Early-Victorian Illustrated Periodicals', *Victorian Literature and Culture* 40, no. 2 (September 2012): 421–49, doi:10.1017/S1060150312000034; Nally, '"That Coming Storm"'.

But the representation of hungry, suffering bodies has also been a major concern in philosophy and the history of art. Elaine Scarry's *The Body in Pain* continues to be a sounding board for critiques of embodiment and representation.[7] Scarry explores how 'forcing *pain itself* into avenues of objectification is a project laden with practical and ethical consequence'.[8] Scarry argues that pain is distinct from other forms of feeling because it deprives its carrier of their extension into the world; it has no external referent, so resists representation. She writes:

> the interior states of physical hunger and psychological desire have nothing aversive, fearful or unpleasant about them if the person experiencing them inhabits a world where food is bountiful and a companion is near [...] in somatic and emotional states like hunger and desire, a person can continually modify the state itself – now minimizing it, now letting it occur, now intensifying and sustaining it, now eliminating it altogether – by continually modifying and adjusting his or her relation to the object.[9]

With acute hunger, the agency to 'continually modify the state itself' is absent, and as such 'the state itself' changes shape, becoming something altogether different. The representation of the achievable desire for food is a different question, which does not concern me here. At stake is the representation of the already hungry body, in a situation of continuing, acute lack. The additional dynamic is political: the collective and unevenly distributed human agency that determines who goes hungry, where, how, and when. Pain is in part, at times, inevitable, even natural; unlike hunger, it is not always the result of social and political structures. But it is inflicted pain – torture and war – that is the true subject of her account. Similarly, as has been clear throughout this book, hunger is inflicted, not just experienced.

Some artistic responses to hunger have attempted to address the interconnection between the representation and embodiment of hunger directly. As I will argue below, *cinema novo*, in particular, attempted to produce a mimetic–somatic aesthetics of hunger that emerged out of a reading of Josué de Castro and debates over the Brazilian Northeast.[10] The political and aesthetic problems of representing the hungry body are akin not just to representing the body in pain but to representing the body under torture or the body in war. This is where this chapter will conclude, considering a seminal representation of the geography of hunger by an artist who knew Josué de Castro's

---

7 Leila Dawney and Timothy J. Huzar, 'Introduction: The Legacies and Limits of The Body in Pain', *Body and Society* 25, no. 3 (2019): 3–21, doi:10.1177/1357034X19857133.

8 Elaine Scarry, *The Body in Pain: The Making and Unmaking of the World* (Oxford: Oxford University Press, 1985), 6.

9 Scarry, *The Body in Pain*, 166–68.

10 Paula Regina Siega, 'Violencia, fome e sonho: as estéticas do subdesenvolvimento no discurso de Glauber Rocha', *A Cor das Letras* 11, no. 1 (February 2017): 83–100, doi:10.13102/cl.v11i1.1504.

geography of hunger: Cândido Portinari. His *War* and *Peace* murals for the UN marks an apotheosis of the aesthetic problem Castro struggled with: how to represent hunger as *universal*.

Hunger in the Northeast: Expressionism and the Cry in the *Sertão*

For Josué de Castro, understanding and representing hunger through the relation between human bodies, cultural landscapes and migration had a resolute spatial correlative in the Brazilian Northeast. Castro became a source of inspiration for artists trying to articulate the politics and aesthetics of hunger in the context of Brazilian underdevelopment. His work was part of a broader project of intellectual and artistic work to find ways of representing poverty and underdevelopment in the Northeast. This manifested in radical regionalist politics and artistic and literary modernisms. Two visual artists whose work was used to illustrate Castro's writings, Abelardo da Hora and Candido Portinari, are significant here.

Abelardo was an important figure in mid-twentieth-century Northeastern modernism. His work was used to illustrate a number of Castro's books, including the significant 1964 French Seuil edition of *Géographie de la Faim*. Around 1960, as I will discuss below, Recife was the site of radical progressive political experiments, as a new coalition of rural and urban radicals managed to gain power at the level of both the mayoralty and the governorship of the state. In that context a series of cultural projects emerged under the umbrella of the *Movimento Cultura Popular* (MCP). Abelardo helped found the MCP, which was devoted not only to art and expression but also to literacy education. It hosted Paulo Freire's early experiments with cultural circles and adult literacy education in the poor, mangrove-lined communities of Recife. He helped found the *Sociedade de Arte Moderna do Recife* (SAMR) in 1946, and was a key figure in one of the city's focal points of creativity, the *Atelier Coletivo*. These were attempts to support and extend modern art in the city and to integrate it with educational, social, and political projects, with a particular focus on questions of regional identity and politics.[11] SAMR was the site of a new kind of political art in the city. Abelardo was at the forefront of a modern art that addressed the social inequality and poverty of the city itself in new aesthetic terms.[12] This movement also made itself felt in public space, as Abelardo was also – following the crucial figure of Brazilian tropical modernism, Roberto Burle Marx – the director of the Division of Parks and Gardens in the city.[13] Abelardo was a member of the Brazilian Communist Party and committed to making art in

---

11 Raissa Alves Colaço Paz, 'Preocupações Artisticas: O Caso Do Atelier Coletivo Da Sociedade de Arte Moderna Do Recife', Master's thesis (Universidade Estadual de Campinas, 2015).

12 Eduardo Dimitrov, 'Regional como opção, regional como prisão: trajetórias artísticas no modernismo pernambucano' (Universidade de São Paulo, 2013), 158–62.

13 Paz, 'Preocupações Artisticas', 52.

the cause of political projects orientated towards the most disadvantaged in society. This commitment led to censorship and repression, as well as to his involvement in radical politics.[14] Abelardo's art developed in connection with ongoing struggles in Recife and the wider Northeast: for instance, his drawing *Camponeses* [Peasants] (1952) captures the emerging political radicalism of the Northeastern peasant leagues. In 1962 Abelardo published an album of pen-and-ink drawings, *Meninos do Recife* [Children of Recife], of urban street children. Castro used these sketches in his books.

Abelardo had tackled hunger before *Meninos do Recife*. The sculpture *A Fome e o Brado* [Hunger and the Scream] (1947) references Edvard Munch's *Scream* (1893) through the striated round heads. When Abelardo's 1948 exhibition at SAMR caught the attention of Recife's press, he wrote an auto-critique about his approach:

> I explained to everyone that hunger does not have the same form as abundance, nor does pain have the same form as happiness. To express what poverty, hunger, desperation and revolt is in sculpture, the original elements of these misfortunes must dominate the whole. The movement towards death must dominate its characteristics. The muscles must seem to be bones, and become transformed into steel beams, so that everything is hard and sad. The opposite would be health, happiness, rest, love, fortune and stillness.[15]

This passage shows a fascination with the somatic manifestation of hunger as a key dynamic of its aesthetic representation. Hunger expresses poverty, desperation, and revolt in the bodily form of the human and the human collective. The transformation of society through hunger is to be shown through the transformation of the body, and its dehumanization: muscles become bone become steel. This dehumanization is paradoxical. As in Castro's work, hunger pushes the human to the extreme edge of being, but the *representation* of hunger-as-dehumanization operates through a recourse to a humanism that would save these figures from the very hunger which is stripping away their humanity. The body is the touchstone of a political humanism, captured in the *cry* of *A Fome e o Bardo*. The cry is central: it is the cry of the hungry configured as the demand for a political rejection of hunger. It is the same cry that names the television documentary, *Le Cri*, that Castro narrated, and for both he and Abelardo this was a specifically polemical political project.[16] But this is a displaced cry, made by the artist on behalf of an Other. Art is, here, a project to translate the cry of hunger into a moral demand.

14 Fernando da Silva Cardoso, Graciele Maria Coelho de Andrade Gomes, and Mário de Faria Carvalho, 'Memória, imaginário e subjetividade: notas a uma categoria estética à rememoração da história de horror brasileira', *Diálogos Latinoamericanos* 20, no. 28 (December 2019): 1–17.

15 My translation quoted Paz, 'Preocupações Artisticas', 81.

16 Paz, 'Preocupações Artisticas', 57.

Abelardo's work picks up themes of other Northeastern artists of hunger: a malnourished family group, distended stomachs, gaunt cheeks, wide eyes, and exposed ribs. The family group (repeated elsewhere in statues such as *Desamparados* [The forsaken] (1974) and the *Memorial aos Retirantes* [Memorial to the migrants] (2008)) – a male figure, a female figure, a baby, and two children – recalls the families of *retirantes*, migrants, of Portinari, discussed below, and the family in Graciliano Ramos' *Vidas Secas*. The original film poster of *Vidas Secas* similarly shows a cluster of figures against the scrubby landscape of the *sertão*. The ragged, disintegrating family group is a motif of the representation of the geography of hunger in all these works. It reinforces how hunger threatens social ties as well as creating individual suffering. (Such family groups are also reproduced in regional folk art, such as Manoel Eudócio's *Retirantes* (1995)).[17] There is a sense in these collectives that traditional gendered roles are becoming undone, as the masculine figures are unable to reproduce a role as provider, and destitution acts as a perverse kind of levelling. We can read a similar breakdown in Nelson Pereira dos Santos' cinematic interpretation of Graciliano Ramos' *Vidas Secas*, in which the almost mute male figure, Fabiano, has lost not only his social agency but also almost his entire capacity for communication. Sinhá Vitória, the main female protagonist, becomes the agential figure, for instance in the killing and eating of the family parrot. Elaine Scarry writes that 'physical pain does not simply resist language but actively destroys it, bringing about an immediate reversion to a state anterior to language, to the sounds and cries a human being makes before language is learned'.[18] In *Vidas Secas* the affective experience of hunger has rendered them almost silent. We can name, then, an irony between cry and silence that the form of painting itself captures, archetypically in *The Scream*. The cry of the hungry is silent in many senses; made by some for others, it is an appeal that tries to name a hunger that makes people mute, both politically and personally. The struggle to represent hunger is captured in this irony. As Marcel Niedergang's obituary of Josué de Castro in *Le Monde* had it, Josué de Castro was, for much of his life, a voice crying in the desert.[19]

The Somatic Aesthetics of Hunger: Portinari to *Cinema Novo*

In 1935 Castro wrote about Candido Portinari in *A Nação*. Illustrated by the canvas *O Café*, the article, 'Independencia Artistica do Brasil' [Brazilian Artistic Independence], praises Portinari and reflects on how Brazilian

17 Kimberly L. Cleveland, 'Coming and Going: Movement of Folk Art from Brazil's Backlands', *Review: Literature and Arts of the Americas* 49, no. 1–2 (July 2016): 65–71, doi:10.1080/08905762.2016.1257009.

18 Scarry, *The Body in Pain*, 4.

19 Marcel Niedergang, 'Josué de Castro avait longtemps crié dans le désert ...', *Le Monde*, 26 September 1973, https://www.lemonde.fr/archives/article/1973/09/26/josue-de-castro-avait-longtemps-crie-dans-le-desert_2564086_1819218.html.

education, intellectualism, and modern art is drenched in a knowledge of European, particularly French, intellectual culture. It is the Brazilian way, he writes, to appreciate Brazilian writers and artists only after they have been feted abroad. He correlates Brazilian artistic and intellectual excellence with its black inheritance, which saves it from the decadence of Europe and underpins the power of Brazilian modernism.[20] The next year, in 1936, Portinari drew a sketch of Josué de Castro.[21] Portinari was a prolific portraitist, sketching and painting hundreds of members of the Brazilian elite as well as working people and figures from history. The portrait of Castro is a delicate, quick sketch, not a major study such as those of Mário de Andrade or Carlos Drummond de Andrade. Castro probably sat for the portrait when they were both teachers at the short-lived Universidade do Distrito Federal, established by Anísio Teixeira in 1935. They were part of a modernizing, interconnected, leftist intellectual elite that was becoming institutionalized in the 1930s, partly through the short-lived UDF.[22] The UDF was closed, in part becoming incorporated into the University of Brazil, where Castro then taught for many years.

Castro and Portinari shared a subject in Brazilian hunger and underdevelopment. Across Portinari's work we can trace the outlines of an ecological sensibility of rurality and Brazilian space and a geographical interpretation of hunger drawing on Castro's influence. Portinari first took up migration as a social and political theme in his 1934 *Os Despejados* [The Expelled].[23] Those paintings coincided with a turn towards the Brazilian social subjects that would form the backbone of his oeuvre. A quarter of a century later, in 1958, he again took on the subject, in a new series of *retirantes* paintings responding to the growing drought and hunger that was ravaging Brazil.[24] In the same year the film by Rodolfo Nanni, *O Drama das Secas* [The Drama of Droughts], funded by ASCOFAM and based on Castro's work, appeared, with a frontispiece of Portinari's earlier paintings.[25] As one of the great artists of Brazilian rurality it is no surprise that Portinari returned to landlessness and migration, and that his interpretation of those questions was established in dialogue with Castro's writing. The nature of this dialogue needs to be made clear. There are limited archival traces of Portinari and Castro's

20 Josué de Castro, 'Independencia Artistica Do Brasil', *A Nação*, 1935, 306, Projeto Portinari.
21 João Candido Portinari, ed., *Candido Portinari: Catálogo Raisonné. Volume I: 1914–1938* (Rio de Janeiro: Projeto Portinari, 2004), 354.
22 Helena Isabel Mueller, 'Active Catholic Intellectuals in Brazil in the 1930s', *Revista Brasileira de História*, São Paulo 35, no. 69 (2015): 15.
23 Portinari, *Candido Portinari: Catálogo Raisonné*, Volume I: 1914–1938, 269–70.
24 Portinari, *Candido Portinari: Catálogo Raisonné*, Volume IV: 1955–1960, 352–55.
25 Augusto Lira, '"O Drama das Secas": Alegorias da Fome no Filme Documentário de Rodolfo Nanni', *Revista de História Bilros. História(s), Sociedade(s) e Cultura(s)* 6, no. 12 (September 2018): 33–56.

relationship, and I am not claiming that they collaborated or that Portinari was painting with Castro's words or political action directly in mind. It is hard to establish precisely how widespread Castro's influence was and, though it is reasonable to suspect some direct influence, it is more important to see them within a shared conjuncture, in which they were part of creating, in leftist intellectual and artistic practice in Brazil in the middle of the century, a concern with hunger that produced a distinctive interpretation of its politics and spatiality.

Portinari's 1944 *Os Retirantes* were first shown in Paris in 1946 and widely discussed in Brazil and Europe.[26] The emigrants' gaunt figures and hollow expressions are set against a no-man's landscape, their staff and packages emphasizing their transience. They will not reach their destination; the image is of hopelessness and death. The dissolution of bodies by hunger is manifested not just in familiar biological images of hunger but in the layering of figures who line up in front of one another, their thin bodies seeming to merge and fade as their bodies command less and less space. They have become airy; the wind that catches the old man's hair seems to blow him into non-existence, into the desolate landscape behind. His left arm is invisible; he turns away from us, disappearing. The flat smear that stands in for the mouth of the woman – his daughter? – in front of him returns us to the visual paradox of the silent/silenced mute/cry of hunger. The old man's disappearing left eye speaks of bodily disintegration. In *Geografia da Fome* Castro wrote:

> Hunger does not only annihilate the life of the *sertanejos* by ravaging their bodies, tearing at their guts and opening sores and blisters on their skin. It also disturbs their spirit, their mental structure and their social conduct. No other misfortune can so profoundly and poisonously disaggregate the human personality as hunger, when it reaches the limits of true starvation.[27]

Representing hunger is fraught not only with questions of human dignity and respect but with an attempt to develop an aesthetics of hunger – aesthetics, here, both in its broad sense of pertaining to the senses and in its more critical sense of an analysis of the field of the perceptible: in Rancière's terms, the 'distribution of the sensible'.[28] In the context of acute hunger, the senses' relationship to interpretation, selfhood, society, nature, and identity are not stable, but in flux and under extreme tension. The body exists in dynamic metabolic interdependence on socially produced natures,

26 Portinari, *Candido Portinari: Catálogo Raisonné*, Volume II: 1939–1944, 456–57; João Candido Portinari, ed., *Portinari et La France [Album]* (S.I.: Projeto Portinari, n.d.).

27 Josué de Castro, *Geografia da Fome: O Dilema Brasileiro: Pão Ou Aço*, 10th ed. (Rio de Janeiro: Edições Antares, 1984), 243.

28 Jacques Rancière, 'The Distribution of the Sensible', in *The Politics of Aesthetics* (London: Bloomsbury, 2004), 7–45.

and hunger is a manifestation of the breakdown of this interdependence. Furthermore, the hungry self is acutely, and differentially, sensitized to its human and physical environment. The somatic qualities of a metabolic humanism involve questions of sense perception and the experiential ruptures that hunger imposes on human being.

Castro wrote in *Geografia da Fome*:

> the sensation of hunger is not continuous. It is intermittent, periodically intensifying and receding. At first, hunger causes an unusual nervous excitement, extreme irritability and a great rapture of the senses. This leads to an extreme sensitivity, almost exclusively in relation to activities that lead to obtaining food and satisfying the mortifying drive of hunger.[29]

Representing this flagellated self is more than a question of painting skin and bones. Pain, Elaine Scarry contends, is uniquely resistant to representation in language because it has no external referent. The difference between hunger and pain is that hunger refers to something outside itself. Yet while hunger has a clear external referent, in the struggles over its representation we find a deep continuum with pain and a suggestion that the hungry person retracts from the world. This is one of the premises of Nancy Scheper-Hughes' anthropological understanding of hunger in the Brazilian Northeast, *Death Without Weeping*, which she herself declares to be a continuation of Josué de Castro's work. The cause of the silence that Scheper-Hughes identifies in the hungry mothers of hungry children in the Northeast is visceral, as well as social. The collapse of social mechanisms that manifest in the deaths of children from malnourishment eats away, in Scheper-Hughes' account, at the ability of these children's parents to grieve and to express their grief. While pain leads to the extra-verbal communications of cries, the representation of hunger is often, on the contrary, a representation of its muteness.

Critiques of Elaine Scarry have suggested that she perpetrates a mind–body dualism.[30] In the case of hunger such a dualism is psychologically and biologically untenable. Whether in Scheper-Hughes' anthropological work, our own individual experience, novelistic accounts such as Knut Hamsun's, neuroscience,[31] or clinical psychology,[32] the emotional, affective, metabolic, and psychological effects of hunger are interconnected in persistent and intractable ways. People do not communicate, feel, or see in the same way when they are hungry. There are, therefore, two interconnected sides of the *aesthetics* of

---

29 Castro, *Geografia da Fome: O Dilema Brasileiro: Pão Ou Aço* (1984), 235.

30 Dawney and Huzar, 'Introduction: The Legacies and Limits of The Body in Pain'.

31 P. Antonio Tataranni et al., 'Neuroanatomical Correlates of Hunger and Satiation in Humans Using Positron Emission Tomography', *Proceedings of the National Academy of Sciences* 96, no. 8 (April 1999): 4569–74, doi:10.1073/pnas.96.8.4569.

32 Alison Montagrin et al., 'Effects of Hunger on Emotional Arousal Responses and Attention/Memory Biases', *Emotion (Washington, D.C.)*, October 2019, doi:10.1037/emo0000680.

hunger: first, 'aesthetics', as relating to the senses, and, secondly, 'aesthetics', as the politics of representation. The sensory experience of hunger has both internal and external determinants. Even the individual lived experience of hunger is social and political, as it changes depending on whether hunger can be satiated. The politics of representing hunger in art or literature emerges in how it expresses the meaning of the experience of the hunger of another.

Castro drew a particular thread from the impact of hunger on sensory life: 'Of all the senses one is emphasised to the extreme, and gains astonishing keenness: sight. In the hungry person, while the rest of the living system seems to be gradually dying, the vision is increasingly sharp, with moments of deep intensity.'[33] In spite of increasing disassociation from social life, as starvation inhibits human drives and social interaction, vision seems to intensify. The narrator of Hamsun's *Hunger* focuses, too, on the effect of hunger on the act of seeing:

> I had remarked so plainly that, whenever I had been hungry for any length of time, it was just as if my brains ran quite gently out of my head and left me with a vacuum – my head grew light and far off, I no longer felt its weight on my shoulders, and I had a consciousness that my eyes stared far too widely open when I looked at anything.

Portinari's *Retirantes* series, too, has a particularly visceral interpretation of the eyes of his subjects. The paintings draw the viewer to the blank staring eyes of the migrants, and the dark centre of the painting is the eyes of the central figure, the small child whose face, in shadow, holds eyes that are black holes. '*Criança Morta*' [Dead Girl, 1944] (Figure 4) transforms and obscures the children's eyes, as they either pour tears or are closed, squinting against the same wind that blows across the first painting. The woman in pink – like a number of paintings of crying figures painted by Portinari around this time[34] – squeezes her own right eye, melting her face in tears. In spite of their intense gaze, the hungry *retirantes* do not seem, quite, to look back at us; there is a profound inequality of vision between viewer and subject. They look through us towards a void, or into themselves, or not at all. These crying figures, worked away at by Portinari through the 1940s and 1950s, recur in the UN murals *War* and *Peace*. The murals, measuring 34×46 feet, were installed in the south lobby of the UN General Assembly building in New York in 1957.[35] In the *War* mural there is a proliferation of crying figures, mainly female. There is a transition through Portinari's studies of crying figures, both specifically for the mural and before, in which the expressionist, almost cartoonish, pouring tears of the *retirantes* are supplemented

33 Castro, *Geografia da Fome: O Dilema Brasileiro: Pão Ou Aço* (1984), 235.
34 See, for example, Portinari, *Candido Portinari: Catálogo Raisonné*, Volume III: 1944–1955, 182–84, 204–05.
35 João Candido Portinari, ed., *Guerre et Paix de Portinari: Un Chef-d'Ouvre Brésilien Pour l'ONU* (Paris: Grand Palais, 2014).

Figure 4. Criança Morta, Candido Portinari, 1944. Source: https://masp.org. br/acervo/obra/crianca-morta, reproduced under Creative Commons Licence Creative Commons Attribution-Share Alike 4.0 International licence

by a repeated trope of faces with their eyes hidden, either with arms across the eyes in a gesture of woe or heads bowed slightly forward and the faces completely obscured by hair[36]. The blank suffering of the eyes of the *retirantes* has become a blankness of the face as a whole, retracted into itself. This trope has another form in the *War* mural, of faces tilted to the sky in a gesture of prayer, their faces contorted and semi-visible. The overall effect in War is to confront the viewer with a sea of obscured faces. *Peace*, meanwhile, is a flood of faces, looking outwards (see book cover). The denial of the face, as a way of representing hunger and suffering, can be interpreted in light of Scarry's argument about rupture. Instead of the possibility of identification

---

36 Portinari made dozens of these studies: see Portinari, *Candido Portinari: Catálogo Raisonné*, Volume IV: 1955–1960, 63–78.

with the other – the mutual recognition for which the face is a potent signifier – Portinari depicts suffering as a rupture with the world.

In the different artistic form of *cinema novo* we find another interpretation of the relationship between vision and hunger. The distinctive qualities of the *cinema novo* style included the use of natural lighting and an excess of bright light. In simple terms this captures the natural luminosity of the Brazilian *sertão*, but it has a more literal aesthetic quality too, which recalls the intensity of the hungry vision that Castro analyses. Castro was a research scientist with a particular interest in vitamin deficiencies. In a mid-1940s manuscript kept in Castro's archive, he writes in English about the history of the senses in the Northeast, and their connection to hunger. He is concerned, in particular, with discourses around night blindness – a condition that reduces vision in low light. When he wrote, this condition had been recently revealed to be related to a deficiency of Vitamin A. He applied this discovery to a reading of Euclides da Cunha's *Os Sertões*:

> This sharp-eyed observer of Brazilian natural phenomena was led to see excess of sunlight as the cause of night blindness precisely because it had been noted that this disease appeared only in prolonged dry spells, when the days were clear, day, and hot. At the beginning of this century, of course, when *Os Sertões* was written, nobody dreamed of the existence of vitamin A. It was only natural to attribute to excess sunlight what was in reality caused by a food deficiency. Because this deficiency always occurs during those days when the sun in [sic] an orgy of brightness – which are also times of misery and starvation.[37]

Castro discusses hunger blindness at some length in *Geografia da Fome*, particularly with reference to Rodolfo Teófilo's work on famine and hunger in Ceará.[38] The connection to *cinema novo*'s aesthetics of hunger is direct. The cinematic approach to natural lighting leads to over-exposure of the film and a blinding effect in the image. Glauber Rocha exacerbated the effect with the use of reflectors and long shots, recording 'the modalities and tonalities of the image and of light as captured by the camera'.[39] *A Idade de Terra* [The Age of the Earth] (1980), for instance, is a paradigmatic piece of *cinema novo*, its aesthetics constructed through 'over- and underexposure', incoherence, and chaos. Similarly, *A queda* [The Fall] (1976), by Ruy Guerra, uses 'long takes and one-shot sequences' and relies on 'ambient light (with no attempt to light even nighttime sequences artificially)'.[40] The 'aesthetics of hunger' of *cinema novo* does not, therefore, work only at the level of the political

37 Josué de Castro, 'Dietary Areas of Brazil' (unpublished, 1940s), 147, CEHIBRA.JdC.
38 Castro, *Geografia da Fome: O Dilema Brasileiro: Pão Ou Aço* (1984), 224–35.
39 Randal Johnson, *Cinema Novo X 5: Masters of Contemporary Brazilian Film* (Austin, University of Texas Press, 1984), 158.
40 Randal Johnson and Robert Stam, *Brazilian Cinema* (New York: Columbia University Press, 1995), 236.

economy of cinema and the political message of film, but is also a concerted technical attempt to make film see as the hungry see: over-exposed, sclerotic, over-sensitive, and confused. That *cinema novo* seems to achieve the kind of mimetic–somatic aesthetics of hunger that Castro reaches towards makes it ironic that, having seen the film in Paris in the 1960s, Castro was reported not to have liked Pereira dos Santos' *Vidas Secas*, finding it too bleak.[41] In these Brazilian artists we find hunger understood as a social rather than an individual condition. They do not figure hunger as a *metaphor* for artistic production – as, for example, Moody does in her discussion of modernism[42] – but as a technics of representation, part of the mechanism by which to bring the condition itself into what Ranciere calls the distribution of the sensible:[43] that which can be represented and, therefore, subject to critique.

The Aesthetics of Revelation: Art, Hunger, and Internationalism

Castro's books, articles, and television and film work are punctuated by photographs of starving people. Analysing these photographs, one could conclude that Castro was merely contributing to a humanitarian narrative, a process of 'documenting the tragic human scale of hunger, [...] making [...] reading publics bear witness to, and sentimentally connect with, the suffering of particular individuals', as Vernon argues about nineteenth-century Britain. Certainly, Castro does not shy away from photographic representations of extreme suffering. It is his conviction that the potential moral and political outrage incited by images of starving bodies is potent. He reproduces such images anonymously and repetitively. Through to the end of his life, even in the midst of emerging discourses of liberal humanitarianism and crisis journalism in the late 1960s,[44] he believed in these images' revelatory power. It is important not to read this visual language of hunger anachronistically. From a twenty-first-century perspective, images of hungry, often dark-skinned, children are over-coded by a neoimperialist humanitarian logic and the proliferation of patronizing and disempowering narratives of aid: a Band Aid aesthetics.[45] But it is important to place Castro's repeated use of these kinds of image in their appropriate context. As Eleanor Davey shows, the roots of post-Second World War humanitarianism – in particular,

---

41 Francisco Bandeira de Melo, 'Josué de Castro: Uma Certa Fome de Cinema', in *Josué de Castro, Perfis Parlamentar 52*, ed. Teresa Cristina Wanderley Neves (Brasília: Câmara dos Deputados: Coordenação de Publicações, 2007), 179–81.

42 Alys Moody, *The Art of Hunger: Aesthetic Autonomy and the Afterlives of Modernism*, 1st ed., Oxford English Monographs (Oxford; New York: Oxford University Press, 2018).

43 Rancière, 'The Distribution of the Sensible'.

44 Heerten, *The Biafran War and Postcolonial Humanitarianism*, 3–4.

45 On which, see Lilie Chouliaraki, *The Ironic Spectator: Solidarity in the Age of Post-Humanitarianism* (London: John Wiley & Sons, 2013).

French *sans frontiérisme* and its conflicts with *tiers-mondisme* – were deeply connected with a discourse of *témoignage*, witnessing. Debates over the success or failure of witnessing came to mark out what Davey calls 'radical humanitarianism'.[46] The FAO, the subject of the next chapter, was also part of this visual discourse of hunger. Wallace Aykroyd's 1964 *Food for Man*, for instance, uses images of starving people drawn directly from the FAO's information service, like Castro did before him,[47] and continued to do so in various formats throughout the 1950s and 1960s.[48] Little is to be gained from these horrific visions of suffering. Their repetition, in an archival perspective, serves to generalize human individuality into a banal abstraction of suffering. Nevertheless, we can see a more complex configuration of what these photographs do when we consider Castro's work as an open corpus of intertexts rather than as a series of conclusions. The crucial dynamic here is that of moral revelation.

I want to move away from the photographs as such to analyse the aesthetic dynamics of moral revelation more closely. Castro took forward his universalist project in the context of a multiple and fragmented global peace movement of intellectuals and civil society in the post-war years. Caught between the wings of the cold war, an internationalist field of prominent artists and writers, from Bertrand Russell to Pablo Picasso, sought to mobilize their practice and influence in campaigns against atomic armaments and the cold war. Castro moved in these circles – awarded the World Peace Council Peace Prize in 1955, for instance – and so did Cândido Portinari, who won a Gold Medal from the same institution in 1950. Both were members of a leftist modernizing elite in Brazil whose work took them beyond Latin America. Portinari's *War* and *Peace* murals sits in this milieu. The paintings are close intellectual and artistic cousins of Pablo Picasso's *Guernica*. Picasso's painting deeply influenced Portinari, as can be seen, for instance, in his 1943 paintings for the headquarters of Rádio Tupi in São Paulo.[49]

War and *Peace* was not the first time that Portinari had been involved in cultural diplomacy and internationalism. His 1940 exhibition at the Museum of Modern Art in New York was bound up with an attempt to reinvigorate a 'good neighbour' policy of cultural exchange by American elites, stung by an uncomfortable exchange with the Mexican painter Diego Rivera.[50] Portinari's work was often misunderstood. For instance, Portinari was commissioned to paint the murals for the Hispanic Foundation in the Library of Congress.

46 Eleanor Davey, *Idealism beyond Borders: The French Revolutionary Left and the Rise of Humanitarianism 1954–1988* (Cambridge: Cambridge University Press, 2015), 43–47.

47 Wallace Aykroyd, *Food for Man* (Oxford: Pergamon Press, 1964), 22–27.

48 For example, Josué de Castro and Odile Roullet, 'La Faim: Problème Universel', *Les Grands Enquêtes*, October 1961.

49 Portinari, *Candido Portinari: Catálogo Raisonné*, Volume II: 1939–1944, 345–50.

50 Niko Vicario, *Hemispheric Integration: Materiality, Mobility, and the Making of Latin American Art* (Oakland: University of California Press, 2020), 129–34.

The Assistant Director of the Foundation, Robert Smith, wrote that the paintings 'show the great American theme of pioneering, of the conquest of forests and the dominion of the land, the act of penetration which had gradually taken place all over Hispanic America from Patagonia to the Rio Grande'.[51] This is a naïve misreading of the paintings. Rather, we can look at them as putting an eco-critical lens on the spatial dynamics of colonialism. They show Portinari's geographical sensibility, through a ruptured but coherent interpretation of the ecological space of the forest. The foreshortened perspective, stripped of horizon, destabilizes the aesthetic norms of pioneering. The source of light, coming from within the forest, inverts a stereotypical colonial representation of the dark jungle, yet the inversion is unstable, and the boundary line between the foreground and the background – the blue stream – has been crossed. Human intrusion takes the arrow-like forms of the prone white figure and the felled tree. The painting recalls the nation-building narratives of Brazil in the early twentieth century,[52] but if nation building is a process of moving progress forward across a landscape, in which direction is this pioneering project happening? The four figures all look in different directions; none of their gazes meet. The lively eyes of the creatures challenge the blank gaze of the pioneer. The painting is full of unsettling details and spatial refractions. To the right of centre, in the foreground, the white pioneer holds what seems to be a kind of axe, but, in an uncanny corporealization, it blends into the muscular form of the calves of the man behind him. Why is that man barefoot, when the others are well shod in dark boots? What work does the triangular wedge around the base of the large tree on the left do? The enigmatic harlequin shirt gestures towards modernist tropes. Major Brazilian modernist poets such as Mário de Andrade[53] and Manuel Bandeira, as well as the novelist Murilo Rubião,[54] wrote about the tricksy figure of the harlequin, and the visual imagery recalls Picasso's famous harlequin paintings. The harlequin here brings in the evasive and uncertain qualities of the carnivalesque and the mercurial, at odds with the solid trees and the hulking shoulders of the pioneers. This is an unstable ecological space and an unstable set of human relationships with one another, and with that ecology.

Contrary to Vicario, who configures him as a broadly neutral artist, Portinari was repeatedly denied a visa to the United States because of his communist politics, and so was not able to be present at the unveiling of his

---

51 Smith, *Murals by Cândido Portinari in the Hispanic Foundation of the Library of Congress* (Washington: Library of Congress, 1943), 10.

52 Diacon, *Stringing Together a Nation*.

53 Roxana Inés Calvo, 'Olhar o Brasil. Cultura Popular y Vanguardia En Obras y Archivos Fotográficos de Mário de Andrade', PhD thesis (Universidad Nacional de La Plata, 2015), 43.

54 Marly Amarilha De Oliveira, 'The Harlequin of Murilo Rubião: The Silent Experience', *Portuguese Studies* 4 (1988): 196–205.

own mural at the UN headquarters.[55] His dissonant position was not merely biographical but can be read in his painting's geographical aesthetics. We can read these perspective-transforming canvasses through the words of the São Tomense geographer and poet José Francisco Tenreiro in his great poem 'De Coração em África' [From the heart in Africa]:

de coração em África com as mãos e os pés trambolhos disformes
e deformados como os quadros de Portinari dos estivadores do mar
e dos meninos ranhosos viciados pelas olheiras fundas das fomes de Pomar

[from the heart in Africa, with rambling, disformed hands and feet
and deformed like Portinari's paintings of the dockers of the sea
and the snotty boys hooked on the dark round depths of the hungers
    in Pomar].

Tenreiro's syntax connects Portinari and Júlio Pomar (1926–2018), a leading Portuguese neo-realist painter, and, like Portinari, also a communist and anti-fascist. The syntactical blurring also serves to suggest how Portinari's work seems to sidle alongside questions of hunger.

To return to Portinari's massive dual panels for the United Nations, *War* and *Peace*, then. They bring together questions of the aesthetics of hunger, the problem of universalism, and the didactic capacities of internationalist art to act through moral revelation. Portinari's expressionist forms and forthright use of colour sets up a clear set of dichotomies between the two panels, based on repeated figures. The four horsemen of the apocalypse give the painting a Christian overtone that is intimately connected to their discourse of revelation. The figures in *War*, or in the *retirantes* series, are retreated into themselves, beyond mutual recognition. Perhaps in response to its commission, *War* is a more hopeful vision than the *retirantes*: though not explicitly Christian, the suffering masses are turning towards a God located above, which, in the painting's dialogue in place with its partner, *Peace*, delivers them from their suffering into a land of play and plenty. This is the universal humanist mission of the UN configured as divine deliverance. Food is central to Portinari's universalist vision. The top third of the *Peace* panels are devoted to a joyful harvest: abundance has replaced the hunger that the *War* panel displays. This painting could illustrate both the foundational philosophy of the FAO – to produce an 'economy of abundance' – and any number of Josué de Castro's utopian visions of the geography of abundance that would follow if his calls for systematic political action against hunger were heeded.

Castro and Portinari both drew on progressive Catholic influences, and Portinari incorporated biblical reference points. Castro's later friendship with Dom Hélder Câmara and connection with the emergence of liberation

---

55 UNTV, *UN/Portinari Mural* (New York: UNTV/Portinari Project, 2010), accessed 16 June 2022, https://www.unmultimedia.org/avlibrary/asset/U101/U101120a/.

theology places this part of his influence and thought correctly. In both there is an implicitly Christian dimension to the revelatory qualities of their representations of hunger that is connected to the voluntarist dynamics of the early humanitarianism analysed by Davey. Indeed, the tropes, discussed above, of the emigrant crossing a hungry landscape has clear connections to Abrahamic religious traditions, not least to the biblical story of Exodus. This is a connection that has persisted into contemporary discourse in the language of the 'biblical famine'. In *War* and *Peace*, however, the Old Testament influence is not Exodus but the Revelation of St John. The painting includes the four horsemen of the apocalypse. By tradition, one of these horsemen, the white horse, is the figure of famine.

It is striking that Portinari does not illustrate war through violence, but through a representation of suffering that is clearly one of hunger. The connection between war and hunger is, of course, intimate, as the experience of Germany after the Second World War had recently made clear, and, at the time of writing, the different experiences of Afghanistan and the global implications of the war in Ukraine reiterate. But Portinari's project goes beyond this. We can see throughout the painting the traces of his previous work and his long engagement with the modality of representing suffering. For instance, prominent at the front and the bottom of *War* is the figure of a child seemingly dying of hunger. This is a painting Portinari had worked on not only in various studies for *War* and *Peace*[56] but, for instance, in *Criança Morta*. The significance of the horsemen of the apocalypse is precisely their connection with biblical ideas of revelation – the Greek root of the word is ἀποκαλύπτειν, to uncover, disclose, from the prefix ἀπό, 'off', and καλύπτειν 'to cover'. It is here that we can turn back to the photographs of the hungry, and the question of *témoignage*, to note what documentary photographs cannot do that the painting can. Where, for instance, Don McCullin's photographs of the Biafran War, taken and published over a decade later, reproduce the unfathomable suffering of starving children, they cannot abstract from it. They are blunt, anonymous, and absolute. In Portinari, on the other hand, there is a resistance to this nameless suffering through the artist's configuration of hope. We might connect witnessing, here, to a kind of bald empiricism, that presents the facts in the hope that they will speak for themselves, but they do not. In terms of the politics of hunger we might contrast the sequence witness–revelation–aid with a consciously political reconstitution of suffering that tries, in however flawed and impossible a way, to situate itself in solidarity, not in witness. Through its solidarity, this aesthetics of hunger surpasses the dehumanizing, othering dynamics of the aesthetics of aid. This works through its interpellation of the one who is looking. The impulse – at least, my own, from my own position – on seeing McCullin's photographs is to look away, and the fact that they remain seared

---

56 Portinari, *Portinari et La France* [Album].

on the visual memory is a cause of distress and remorse. As John Berger wrote of McCullin's photographs, 'it is not possible for anyone to look pensively at such a moment and to emerge stronger'.[57] The effect, Berger argues, is to make the viewer feel moral inadequacy, and to depoliticize the subject. For Portinari's paintings, meanwhile, the impulse is to look closer, to attempt to understand, and, perhaps, to recognize yourself. It is worth noting, here, that one of the largest contemporary projects against hunger in Brazil (a collaboration between major international NGOs including Oxfam and ActionAid, as well the Brazilian foundation Ibirapitanga) is called *Olhe para a fome*: 'Look at the hunger'.[58] The imperative, directional, additional preposition here, *para* – towards/onto/for – reasserts the potency of looking. Logics of seeing and revelation persist in contemporary anti-hunger discourses.

The didactic intent of internationalist, institutional art was clear from the beginning, and was part of the project of the international institutions. It was bound up in an attempt to create the scale of the globe as an arena of action. The UNESCO headquarters in Paris, for instance, was imagined as a synthesis of art, architecture, and modernist ideals, built and designed at the height of architectural modernism and theorized by UNESCO's first Director General, Julian Huxley. UNESCO's architecture, design, and furnishing was an attempt to reconcile scientific rationalism with universalist, idealist, humanist notions of art and culture.[59] At the FAO itself, the universalist claims of art as an embodiment of the universalist project to end hunger has its apogee in the Plenary Hall of the FAO Headquarters in Rome, opened in 1951. The ceiling is covered by a huge artwork by the Italian Mirko Basaldella called *The Universe*. Going beyond, even, the scale of the globe that the FAO aspires to act upon, the ceiling depicts in blue and gold a figurative representation of the expanse of the universe and the depths of the ocean.[60] Beneath this exponential scalar expanse governments and bureaucrats debated the global meaning of hunger and oversaw the failure of a world food policy to come into being.

Conclusion

Major Brazilian artists of the twentieth century, from Portinari and Rocha to Queiroz and Ramos, attempted to represent hunger in politically, morally, and aesthetically committed ways. Part of this commitment manifested through an insistence on hunger's geography. We can find this, in particular, in the ways in which their artistic projects juxtaposed

57 John Berger, *Uses of Photography* (New York: Pantheon, 1980), 39.
58 Olheparaafome.com.br, accessed 16 June 2022.
59 Christopher Pearson, *Designing UNESCO: Art, Architecture and International Politics at Mid-Century* (London: Routledge, 2010), xvi.
60 FAO, *Inside FAO – A Truly Global Forum* (Rome: FAO, 2019), 65–69.

bodies and landscapes. Their work opens up the spatial politics embedded in Castro's understanding of hunger, making the environmental and the somatic co-extensive and indivisible.

Castro frequently turned to the artistic, the literary, and the cinematic in his attempts to think through and represent the universality of hunger. He saw the aesthetic field as a key area of action in persuading the world that hunger was a universal problem that should be tackled globally. In Castro's work and writing we find the idea that the overcoming of hunger is a unifying and universal moral imperative. This assertion of a global moral economy of food and agriculture is captured in aesthetic form not, in a didactic sense, in the painting of Portinari itself, but in the insertion of his art into the concrete and modern spaces of internationalism. In Castro's conception, these two spheres were connected. He acted on the belief that it was through the revelatory power of representations of hunger that serious global action to eradicate it would emerge. It is to these practical efforts that the next chapter turns. But art is not performative. Guernica and Portinari could not will global change into being just by representing suffering. This is perhaps why the UN is a uniquely inappropriate place for a painting such as Portinari's. Its location suggests a misapprehension of its possibilities, positing that art is capable of direct action and moral transformation. Whether it ever is is open to vigorous debate;[61] my argument here is that this art, at that time and in that place, was not. The notion that putting representations of hunger inside or in front of the workings of global institutionalism would somehow imbue those workings with moral focus was a deeply idealist interpretation of the power of aesthetics that came up against the profoundly materialist realities of the post-war politics of hunger and food.

On the unveiling of Portinari's murals on 6 September 1957 Dag Hammarskjöld, the then Secretary General of the UN and leading voice of internationalism, said:

> we do well to be thus reminded that all our labours in this building have for their ultimate aim the security and enrichment of the lives of individual men, women and children. The 'peoples of the United Nations' have in the Charter made their choice between war and peace; these murals illustrate for us the meaning of that choice.[62]

Portinari wanted UN delegates to first be confronted by the mural of war, and be inspired by its moral clarity, before seeing the mural of peace on their exit from the room, as a 'symbolic wish', to remind them of their duties. His son, João Portinari, argues that you would need to be 'completely insensitive'

61 For reference points on the wider debate on this question see, for example, Karen van den Berg, Cara M. Jordan, and Philipp Kleinmichel, eds, *The Art of Direct Action: Social Sculpture and Beyond* (Berlin: Sternberg Press, 2019).

62 Dag Hammarskjold Secretary General, 'Secretary-General's Press Releases' (United Nations, 1957), S-0928-0001-05-00001, UN Archives.

to resist the moral appeal to love of the vast murals. 'All you need is love', he says.[63] As the UN Secretary General U Thant wrote on the death of Portinari in 1961, the murals 'lend their inspiring message to the purposes of the world organization'.[64] This cannot be gainsaid, but nor can it be evidenced, other than in the actual workings of such organizations. It is these that the next chapter addresses.

63 'War and Peace' Panels Reinstalled at UN, 2015, accessed 16 June 2022, https://news. un.org/en/audio/2015/09/604152.
64 U Thant, Secretary General, 'Notes to Correspondents – February 1962, Notes #2495, 2510' (United Nations, 1962), S-0891-0002-55-00001, UN Archives.

CHAPTER 4

1952–1956: Castro at the FAO

Hunger and Technocratic Utopianism

'The marriage of agriculture and health.'

Stanley Bruce

Introduction

'The archives of the UN are full of sentences that sound like sighs', wrote historian Emma Rothschild in 2008, 'but so too is the real world of internationalism'.[1] The sound of a sigh, of course, is ambivalent; it can evoke disappointment, but also passion. For Josué de Castro, internationalism was the object of both. In the last chapter a related passion can be seen in the earnest, fervent attempts of artists to capture a utopian vision of humanity and to compel a just internationalism through art. The morally committed political aesthetics that represented hunger as contingent and reparable, and food as an ethical pathway to the realization of human equality, is the expression of a sigh of passion. The worldly achievements of art, when set against such impossible standards, must elicit a sigh of disappointment.

Castro saw hunger as universal, underpinned by the fact that eating is a primary, bodily connection between the individual and the social and natural environment, and that hunger is a primary, existential rupture between the human subject and its social and natural context. In an anti-Malthusian understanding of hunger, in which the problem of feeding people is displaced from a fallacy of natural limitations, the failure to feed one another becomes the most basic breakdown of social life and mutual human solidarity. This translates into an understanding of hunger as the first, universal problem of global society. For Castro, and other advocates against hunger, this seems like an obvious logic, and the basic premise for political action, but it comes up, of course, against an overwhelming set of scalar and political problems.

---

1 Emma Rothschild, 'The Archives of Universal History', *Journal of World History* 19, no. 3 (2008): 393.

In this chapter I turn to the more prosaic side of Castro's attempt to make the problem of hunger a meaningful kind of universal. Castro was not content to assert the universality of hunger; he wanted to address it *as* a universal human problem. He sought to do this through the new internationalist, apparently universalist, institutions of the post-war moment. I analyse Castro's time at the UN's Food and Agricultural Organization (FAO) through nutrition, world food policy, and an international food reserve. These areas constitute a frontier between Castro's ideas and his practice. They map how his intellectual projects and commitments manifested in attempts to make policy and create institutions.

Castro saw the FAO as capable of raising the problem of hunger to a planetary status. He thought it could come up with solutions that would reach every corner of the globe and create an 'economy of abundance'.[2] In analysing Castro at the FAO we can see the culture of technocratic utopianism which briefly flourished in the international institutions of the post-war moment. As Mark Mazower argues, one of the significant features of the emergence of the post-war international institutions was the rise of a 'model of universalism, based [...] on deploying science across the ideological boundaries of the Cold War in the service of mankind'.[3] The appointment of the biologist Julian Huxley to be the chair of UNESCO embedded a particular vision of a cosmopolitan, scientific internationalism and of world citizenship at the heart of the international organizations.[4] For Huxley, the philosophy of UNESCO was to be 'a scientific world humanism, global in extent and evolutionary in background'.[5] This version of internationalist humanism was, as Mazower shows, in tension with other visions of what the United Nations and its associated institutions were for; a tension between an imperial internationalism and more transformative forms of universal projects. What emerged, however, was a set of bodies that, rather than opening the possibilities for deeper transnationalism, had at their core a commitment to the form of the nation state. Nevertheless, embedded within the international institutions themselves, more radically transnational projects briefly flourished. We can see this by reading the history of the FAO from a new perspective: that of the global Third Worldist diplomat. Because, though largely overlooked by mainstream histories of the FAO – Amy Staples, for example, does not refer to him or cite any of his writing in her densely referenced 2006 work *The Birth of Development: How the World Bank, Food and Agriculture Organization, and*

2 FAO, *Towards a World of Plenty* (London: United Nations Information Organisation, 1945), 19.

3 Mark Mazower, *No Enchanted Palace: The End of Empire and the Ideological Origins of the United Nations* (Princeton, NJ, and Oxford: Princeton University Press, 2009), 23.

4 Sluga, 'UNESCO and the (One) World of Julian Huxley'.

5 Julian Huxley, 'UNESCO: Its Purpose and Philosophy', *Free World* 12 (December 1946): 28.

World Health Organization Changed the World, 1945–1965 – Castro was at the heart of this project. For him the international was a vital sphere of action, and he saw international tools as powerful levers to drive change at other scales. The perspective adopted here can add to historical understandings of hunger within the post-war food regime and extend histories of international institutions by attending not just to the policies that emerged from them but the machinations within them as sites at which discourses of value and humanism were contested.

For James Vernon, hunger, in late nineteenth-century Britain, 'gained new significance as a social problem and – because the hunger of one was now the concern of all – demanded a new mentality of government to act on it in the interests of society as a whole'.[6] In the post-war moment, with its roots in the 1930s, we can see how hunger emerged in a similar way at the scale of the international. Struggles over nutritional measurement and world food reserves were arenas for intractable meetings of opposing scales: the bodily and the global. A world food policy was an attempt to manage global nutritional metabolism, to create a holistic and governable system that could hold production and consumption in dynamic equilibrium at the scales of the globe and the individual body, and in the temporalities of everyday life and global agricultural cycles. The inner workings of the FAO show an international attempt to modulate what Friedmann called the post-war international food order, a 'stable set of international arrangements [...] that operated in ways that maintained grain surpluses, especially American grain surpluses, well above effective world demand'.[7] These were not inevitable arrangements, and attending to the actual processes by which international norms were made – or not – can help emphasize the historical contingencies of powerful analytical frameworks such as the food regime and modulate nation-state centric, and US-centric, histories of global food.

The FAO sought, in the words of its first Chairman, Stanley Bruce, to marry agriculture and health. This marriage began with a flirtation, ended with an ugly divorce, and was decidedly patriarchal and unequal. A vision of food as a global right, subject to global distribution, ceded to a food regime that operated on the basis that food was a commodity. In the midst of this process, visions of world government and international responsibility very different from contemporary discourses of governance and humanitarianism rose and faded away. Lucy Jarosz sees the failures of the FAO across its first six decades as down to the fundamental tension between an argument 'that world trade and the ability to buy food on the world market

6 James Vernon, 'The Ethics of Hunger and the Assembly of Society: The Techno-Politics of the School Meal in Modern Britain', *The American Historical Review* 110, no. 3 (June) (2005): 695.

7 Harriet Friedmann, 'The Political Economy of Food: The Rise and Fall of the Postwar International Food Order', *American Journal of Sociology* 88, Marxist Inquiries: Studies of Labor, Class, and States (January 1982): S248–S286.

as an individual or a nation is the most effective way to reduce the numbers of hungry people in the world' and the idea 'that reducing world hunger is a collective moral, ethical, and social responsibility, and that people have a right to food', which would lead to a world food policy that managed prices, democratically allocated food reserves and intervened to avoid dependency on imported grains.[8] This tension does tell the key story of the FAO. It reveals hunger as an epistemic problem that gets to the foundational building blocks of political economy: scarcity.

Castro and the FAO

Given that it was one of the key international institutions of the post-Second World War settlement, there has been comparatively little attention paid to the history of the FAO, whose archives are a rich resource of a kind arguably undervalued in transnational historical research.[9] Castro's own archive contains important documents from the FAO in this period – verbatim records of meetings, speeches, and research papers – not all of which are present in institutional archives and have been overlooked by histories of the institution. A biographical approach through these histories can help draw out counter-hegemonic intellectual geographies of the international.

In the post-war period the FAO had transnational legitimacy to reconfigure global food and agriculture, though its reach was more limited than its rhetoric. Yet Anne Hardy was right in 1995 that 'the story of the FAO's policies and of its work remains to be written'.[10] Since then, the FAO has also been approached from the perspective of the history of humanitarianism,[11] global governmentality,[12] food regimes, international institutions, and histories of nutrition and rural development.[13] Biographical approaches have addressed nutritionist and ethnographer Emma Reh,[14] the scientist Ancel

8 Lucy Jarosz, 'The Political Economy of Global Governance and the World Food Crisis: The Case of the FAO', *Review (Fernand Braudel Centre)*, Political Economic Perspectives on the World Food Crisis, 32, no. 1 (2009): 38.

9 Glenda Sluga, 'Editorial – the Transnational History of International Institutions', *Journal of Global History* 6, no. 2 (2011): 220, doi:10.1017/S1740022811000234.

10 Anne Hardy, 'Beriberi, Vitamin B1 and World Food Policy, 1925–1970', *Medical History* 39 (1995): 61–77.

11 John Shaw, *World Food Security: A History since 1945* (London: Palgrave Macmillan, 2007).

12 Phillips and Ilcan, '"A World Free From Hunger"', 436.

13 Corinne A. Pernet and Amalia Ribi Forclaz, 'Revisiting the Food and Agriculture Organization (FAO): International Histories of Agriculture, Nutrition, and Development', *The International History Review* 41, no. 2 (2019): 346.

14 Corinne A. Pernet, 'FAO from the Field and from Below: Emma Reh and the Challenges of Doing Nutrition Work in Central America', *The International History Review* 41, no. 2 (2019): 391–406.

Keys,[15] the nutritionist and FAO administrator Wallace Aykroyd,[16] and John Boyd Orr.[17] My reading of Castro's involvements can contribute both to this recent resurgence of interest in the FAO and to recent work on Castro that sees his life and work as continuing to offer a path for radical approaches to the international politics of hunger.[18]

In the aftermath of Hot Springs, John Boyd Orr had proposed a World Food Board. It was an ambitious project. It would support world agricultural production by intervening to stabilize prices at a global scale and hold a world food reserve, based on buying and storing buffer stocks amounting to up to a year of world trade in agricultural products. In periods of high prices the World Food Board would release some of this stock onto the market, and would purchase stocks when the price was low.[19] It would provide long-term credit for agricultural development and connect repayment to economic growth. It would increase producers' purchasing power and help stimulate industrial development. It aimed to assuage social unrest, increase supply, distribute surpluses, establish unprecedented levels of global cooperation, eliminate world hunger, and support world peace.[20] In spite of enthusiasm from many quarters, Boyd Orr's plans were dead on arrival. The United States and the United Kingdom would neither countenance radical and interventionist proposals nor cede power to international bodies.[21] Orr's power was quickly limited and, instead of nutrition and health coming first, economic development became the ultimate priority. As he reported it later to Castro, 'As you know I submitted to all governments a World Food Policy in 1947 and when it was not accepted I resigned, saying that events would

15 Sarah Tracy, 'A Global Journey – Ancel Keys, the FAO, and the Rise of Transnational Heart Disease Epidemiology, 1949–1958', *The International History Review* 41, no. 2 (2019): 372–90.

16 Kenneth Carpenter, 'The Work of Wallace Aykroyd: International Nutritionist and Author', *The Journal of Nutrition* 137, no. 4 (2007): 873–78.

17 Amy L.S. Staples, 'To Win the Peace: The Food and Agriculture Organization, Sir John Boyd Orr, and the World Food Board Proposals', *Peace & Change* 28, no. 4 (2003): 495–523.

18 Federico Ferretti, 'A Coffin for Malthusianism: Josué De Castro's Subaltern Geopolitics', *Geopolitics* 26, no. 2 (2021): 589–614; Alain Bué and Magda Zanoni, 'L'oeuvre de Josué de Castro: Une Penseé Globale et Géopolitique de La Faim et l'ecologie Politique', *Bué A, Plet F. Alimentation, Environment et Sauté*. Paris: Ellipses, 2010, 17–35; Sirlandia Schappo, 'Josué de Castro por uma agricultura de susten-tação', Tese de Doutorado. Programa de Pós-graduação em Sociologia. Universidade Es-tadual de Campinas – Unicamp, 2008.

19 See Amy L.S. Staples, *The Birth of Development: How the World Bank, Food and Agriculture Organization and World Health Organization Changed the World, 1945–1965* (Kent, OH: The Kent State University Press, 2006), 84–96.

20 Jarosz, 'The Political Economy of Global Governance', 41–42.

21 Michel Cépède, 'The Fight against Hunger: Its History on the International Agenda', *Food Policy* (November 1984): 285.

prove that such a policy was inevitable and would be approved in some form within the next few years.'[22] This was, in fact, hardly inevitable.

Though the FAO was not administering a World Food Board, the hopes for the agency remained high in its early years. Castro's first involvement was as a member of the Standing Advisory Committee on Nutrition just after the Second World War, probably through his connections with André Mayer, the French nutritionist who was the first Chair of the Executive Committee of FAO and wrote the preface to the first French edition of the *Géographie de la Faim*. This Committee helped establish the programme of the FAO Nutrition Division and later morphed into the FAO–WHO Joint Expert Committee responsible for, for instance, the Codex Alimentarius in the early 1960s. Initially the Joint Committee had ten members, including other scientists from the Third World, Dr V.N. Patwardhan from India and Dr J. Salcedo from the Philippines. It produced reports on nutritional minimums, technical assistance, childhood nutrition, and more. The Committee's reports are jointly authored but they pick up on some of Castro's particular concerns – for instance, a project on synthetic vitamins in underdeveloped countries[23] – and we can see his involvement in long-term projects, such as that on Kwashiorkor.[24] The formalization and distribution of nutritional knowledge was one of Castro's key concerns throughout the 1940s, particularly through the tellingly named *Arquivos Brasileiros de Nutrição* that he had founded in 1944, discussed in chapter 1.

Castro was a pivotal figure at a series of early FAO Latin American regional conferences held in 1948 in Montevideo, Uruguay, in 1950 in Rio de Janeiro, Brazil, and in 1953 in Caracas, Venezuela. With varying success, these conferences sought to set the agenda for nutritional politics in Latin America, often informed by the FAO–WHO Joint Committee on Nutrition.[25] The influence fed in both directions, with Castro as a mediator; the FAO's Standing Advisory Committee on Nutrition considered the findings of the Montevideo conference in their annual 1948 report.[26] In his archive, Castro's personal papers from the October 1949 Joint FAO–WHO Nutrition

22 Lord Boyd Orr, 'Letter to Josué de Castro' (unpublished, February 1954), 557, CEHIBRA.JdC.
23 Various, 'Joint FAO/WHO Expert Committee on Nutrition 1949: Manufacture of Synthetic Vitamins in Underdeveloped Nations', Provisional Agenda Item Number 14, WHO/NJT/1. Add.9 (Geneva: Palais des Nations, FAO/WHO, October 1949), RG 57.0.I7, FAO.
24 Various, 'Joint FAO/WHO Expert Committee on Nutrition: Report on the First Session', World Health Organization Technical Report Series (Geneva: WHO, June 1950), RG.0.57.0.I3, FAO.
25 FAO, 'Conferencia de Nutricion, Agenda Provisional, June 5–13', 1950, 613, CEHIBRA.JdC.
26 FAO, 'Conference on Nutrition Problems in Latin America: Final Report. Montevideo, Uruguay' (unpublished, July 1948), 591, CEHIBRA.JdC.

Committee meeting in Geneva are adjacent to the papers preparing for the Rio conference of 1950.[27] As Castro was the only Latin American on the FAO–WHO Joint Committee, he and Wallace Aykroyd, the director of the Nutrition Division of the FAO, were probably the only two people who attended all of these meetings. Castro organized the 1950 follow-up in Rio de Janeiro, although a bout of ill health stopped him doing as much as he would have liked. At these conferences Castro was part of the FAO's attempt to institutionalize Latin American scientific knowledge through leveraging the power of the international, shoring up national institutions, and increasing the training of nutritionists in Latin America.

On the basis of this international networking, Castro set out to become President of the Executive Council of the FAO in 1951. He wanted to be a new Boyd Orr, and wrote to the Glaswegian to secure his support. Orr replied wishing him success and trusting that he would 'be able to put more drive into F.A.O'.[28] Although he proclaimed his appointment widely, including in the Brazilian press and in Brazilian government propaganda,[29] he was in fact elected in a somewhat contentious manner. Rather than the expected unanimous nomination by the members of the Council, Castro won a vote to replace Stanley Bruce in November 1951 that pitted him against a prominent Justice Party politician as the Indian nominee, Ramaswami Mudaliar.[30] He chaired his first session just a month later, in December 1951.

Castro took his role as a roving international diplomat seriously, arranging meetings and flying around the world to advocate for more action on nutrition, agrarian reform, and more.[31] However, his appointment quickly led to controversy and he was accused of being too political an appointment. In 1952 *The Geography of Hunger* was published, and the book's political message was seen as a reputational risk for the organization. While the book received welcoming reviews[32] and assessments of the state

27 It is interesting to note that these papers include discussions of a 'codex' for analysing the contents of foodstuffs, indicating an earlier history inside the FAO and WHO of the emergence of the Codex Alimentarius which was formalized over a decade later FAO, 'Joint FAO/WHO Expert Committee on Nutrition, 24–29 October 1949, Geneva', 1949, 613, CEHIBRA.JdC.

28 John Boyd Orr, 'To Josué de Castro', September 1951, 559, CEHIBRA.JdC.

29 João Cleophas, 'Do Ministro Da Agricultura Ao Ministro Das Relações Exteriores: Assunto: Posição Do Brasil Em Relação a F.A.O.', Memo, March 1953, 288 Pasta OPQ, Fundaj.JdC.

30 FAO Council Papers, 'Report of the Council of FAO, Thirteenth Session', November 1951, CL 13, FAO Council Reports.

31 For example, Reginald Franklin, 'To Josué de Castro (From UK Ministry of Agriculture and Fisheries)', December 1951, 559, CEHIBRA.JdC.

32 For example, R.K. Hazari, 'Review: Josué de Castro: Geography of Hunger', *Indian Economic Journal* 1, no. 4 (1954): 418.

of the debate,[33] it was also subject to virulent attacks from Malthusians. 'This is one of those horrid twisted books ...' began a review of *The Geography of Hunger* in *Eugenics Review* by G.C.L. Bertram in 1952.[34] The book came out at the peak of what Alison Bashford has called the United States' 'Malthusian moment'.[35] Oswald de Andrade put the controversy down to the connections between neoMalthusianism and US Imperialism.[36] Castro's writing was important in wider Latin American resistance to Malthusianism and the ebbs and flows of population discourse in Latin America during the Cold War.[37] At this moment, one of the world's leading Malthusians, William Vogt, took issue with Castro's role at the FAO. The Director General, Norris Dodd, and his deputy Herbert Broadley were berated by Vogt's pressure group, The Population Reference Bureau, over the institution's association with Castro. Broadley tersely defended both the FAO and Castro and insisted that the two could not be elided.[38] Castro himself defended his right to publish the book, but was concerned that the dispute could undermine his diplomatic projects. He wrote increasingly urgent letters to his US agent to organize ways to reassure the FAO and attempted to distance his official role from his writing.[39] These were highly consequential political debates at the moment of the emergence of the international aid industry, and Castro's intellectual work can be seen at the root of an alternative tradition of critical development studies.[40] He often contested that true social and human development would render drastic interventions in population control unnecessary.[41]

At the FAO, Castro was happy to position his work in politically ambitious terms. He arrived as President of the Council after a period of significant change at the organization. In 1950 and 1951 there had been mounting confusion over its goals and significant changes in organizational structure, as well as growth in the organization's budget and the major move of the

---

33 For example, Paul Arqué, 'Le Monde Est-Il Menacé de Famine?' *Les Cahiers d'Outre Mer* 7, no. 25 (1954): 95–98.

34 G.C.L. Bertram, 'Geography of Hunger', *The Eugenics Review* 44, no. 3 (1952): 163.

35 Alison Bashford, *Global Population: History, Geopolitics, and Life on Earth* (New York: Columbia University Press, 2014), 277–80.

36 Oswald de Andrade, 'A Atualidade da Fome' (Draft, undated), 374, CEHIBRA. JdC.

37 Carter, 'Population Control'; Eve Buckley, 'Overpopulation Debates in Latin America during the Cold War', *Oxford Research Encyclopedia of Latin American History [Online]*, February 2018, doi:10.1093/acrefore/9780199366439.013.338.

38 Herbert Broadley, 'To and From Population Bureau, Washington', Letters, May 1952, RG 0.2.2.A.1, FAO.

39 Josué de Castro, 'Letters to Sanford Greenburger', 1952, 157, CEHIBRA.JdC; Josué de Castro, 'Letters to Herbert Broadley', 1952, 157, CEHIBRA.JdC.

40 Ferretti and Viotto Pedrosa, 'Inventing Critical Development'.

41 For example, Anonymous, 'Josué Sustenta Em Paris: Desenvolvimento Racional Eliminará a Fome e a Subnutrição', *Última Hora*, January 1963, Terça-Feira edition.

headquarters to Rome. At the beginning of the 1950s the FAO's focus shifted from 'a holistic, socio-cultural and long-term approach to rural change to a practical program of circumscribed and short-term interventions'.[42] The Council discussions themselves were always cornered by a lack of definite agency. Castro, however, was full of an almost utopian sense of its possibilities. In his opening address to the 15th Council of the FAO, in June 1952, Castro called, in French – the language he generally used in international contexts – for an *'esprit de large synthèse'* – 'a great synthesizing spirit'.[43] His call for synthesis was to ring through the next four years of his speeches and contributions on the council.

A World Food Reserve

Castro's work at the Council had many branches, but I want to follow just one, because it is a particularly revealing episode in the history of world food policy. Castro was involved, as President, in a long-running debate that brought together discourses of value, geo-biopolitics, and fraught efforts to construct calculative bridges between the scales of the nutritional body and the global institutions. In particular, this turned on the question of a world food reserve.

Since Hot Springs, this key part of a global mechanism to end hunger had hardly advanced. But in response to ongoing food shortages in various parts of the world, Resolution No. 16 of the 1951 Sixth Session of the FAO Conference – the decision-making body, made up of national representatives – had tasked the Council with exploring the question of an international food reserve.[44] In the details of what a global food reserve could be is the kernel of a struggle over the status of the international and over the seminal question of whether food was a global commodity or a global right. Utopian visions of world food policy were caught up in the emergence of a discourse of value that ran counter to the possibility of a truly global anti-hunger project driven by international institutions. Food and hunger were reduced to the calculative logics of agricultural expansionism. Competing discourses of value confronted the establishment of a manageable, dynamic metabolic equilibrium that a world food policy aspired to.

The FAO's machinations over an international food reserve were underpinned by a nutritional logic. The attempt to instil nutritional thinking into international institutions had begun in the mid-1930s through the

---

42 Amalia Ribi Forclaz, 'From Reconstruction to Development: The Early Years of the Food and Agriculture Organization (FAO) and the Conceptualization of Rural Welfare, 1945–1955', *The International History Review* 41, no. 2 (2019): 354.

43 Josué de Castro, 'Discours d'Ouverture de M. de Castro à la Quinzième Session du Conseil' (unpublished, June 1952), 95, CEHIBRA.JdC.

44 FAO Council Papers, 'Report of the Council of FAO, Sixteenth Session', November 1952, CL 16, FAO Council Reports.

League of Nations. As Alexander Loveday, the Director of the Financial and Economic Department at the League, put it:

> The nutrition campaign changes our whole economic outlook. Ever since the time of Adam Smith, economic thought has centred around the art of production or the conditions of citizens as producers. The nutrition movement reflects the first serious attempt on an international scale, to consider the economics not of production but of consumption.[45]

If this was a new economics of consumption it faced major challenges, not least in terms of defining its object. The creation of a nutritional subject was a complex process of scientific and political knowledge-making. At the international scale:

> the problem of definition resolved itself into one of measurement – of how to translate knowledge of an adequate diet into a practical assessment of the malnourished. By 1935, the League of Nations had catalogued three basic systems of measurement – the anthropometric, the clinical, and the physiological – each with its own competing standards, techniques, and problems.[46]

In the mid-twentieth century technologies of nutritional measurement emerged that became critical to understandings of food and bodies. The calorie is perhaps the archetypal example; as Nick Cullather has shown, it even expanded to become a tool of US foreign policy.[47] The question of measurement came to underpin global discourses of hunger and malnutrition. In this sense, as well as others, the UN and its various bodies continued the ideological work of the League of Nations.[48] In terms of food and hunger too, the League was the key precursor, as the interwar period saw the emergence of international cooperation and debate on agriculture and nutrition.[49] As the first two chapters showed, how much people ate, and how much they needed to eat, was intrinsically political at the national scale. With the advent of the League of Nations, that political dimension of hunger grew an international body.[50] The League of Nations, and then the FAO, worried not only about measurement but about nutritional standards. For instance, should they

---

45 Quoted Lamartine Yates, *So Bold an Aim: Ten Years of International Cooperation toward Freedom from Want* (Rome: FAO, 1955), 41.

46 Vernon, 'The Ethics of Hunger and the Assembly of Society', 705.

47 Nick Cullather, 'The Foreign Policy of the Calorie', *American Historical Review* (April 2007).

48 Mazower, *No Enchanted Palace*, passim.

49 Staples, *The Birth of Development*, 64–81.

50 Wallace Aykroyd, 'Nutrition, International and National', *Current Science* 4, no. 9 (March 1936): 639–42; Iris Borowy, *Coming to Terms with World Health: The League of Nations Health Organisation 1921–1946* (Frankfurt am Main: Peter Lang, 2009); Bizzo, 'Latin America and International Nutrition'.

concern 'normal', minimal, or optimal levels of nutrition? As Vernon notes, the process of technologizing hunger didn't necessarily take away its moral and political dimensions, but the project of measurement was a project of universalization. It sought to make hunger globally comparable, and therefore subject to global intervention.[51] Rationalist science aimed to underpin rationalist nutritional and agricultural policies for food production and distribution, and measurement and definition would constitute an imagined scale of international action. Recent scholarship has characterized the FAO as a new scale of governmentality, constructing a 'global imagination' of food and food governance that brought disparate geographies and contexts into the universalizing comparative framework of a scientific understanding of food and agriculture.[52]

Castro was committed to a form of anticolonial humanism, but operated within hegemonic discourses of Western scientific calculation. His internationalist nutritional humanism shows how nutrition moved away from its colonial roots. Warwick Anderson argues that 'colonial medicine was a sociospatial discourse that becomes reframed as a discourse on human rights and governmentality during the twentieth century'.[53] Castro was working around a liminal point in this process, struggling with both sides of the shift. First, he attempted to redeploy the socio-spatial discourse of colonial ideas of nutrition into a socio-spatial discourse of hunger that specifically contested the colonial, to show how the map of the colonial world overlay the map of world hunger. Secondly, he engaged in debates that centred on whether food should be treated as a right or as a commodity. In international debates over food and hunger, discourses of rights came into conflict with those of capitalist value. Capitalism relies on scarcity both at an ontological level and at the multiple scales through which the functioning of markets is transformed into the priority for all forms of governmental action. A rights-based anti-hunger politics necessarily runs counter to a project in which food is understood as another commodity. This contradiction lurks constantly inside the FAO's debates on emergency food reserves and world food policy.

In part, this tension underpinned the marginalization of the nutritional discourse as a whole, not just its dissonant or anticolonial features. Inside the FAO, nutrition was disempowered. The Expert Committee, in 1948, raised concerns that nutrition was becoming less prominent in the FAO, particularly in the Conference – the inter-governmental decision-making body of the organization[54] – while the Nutrition Division was underfunded in relation to

51 Vernon, 'The Ethics of Hunger and the Assembly of Society', 710.
52 Phillips and Ilcan, '"A World Free From Hunger"'.
53 Warwick Anderson, 'The Third-World Body', in *Medicine in the Twentieth Century*, ed. Roger Cooter and John Pickstone (London and New York: Routledge, 2000), 235.
54 FAO, 'Standing Advisory Committee on Nutrition, Third Meeting, 29 November – 7 December 1948. Report to the Director General. N/N3/10' (Washington: FAO, 1948), 613, CEHIBRA.JdC.

the other divisions. (In preparing for a conference in Rio, it couldn't even afford to print articles on food composition.[55]) It was later incorporated into the Technical Department and then the Economics and Social Department.[56]

Partly in response to this, the nutritional approach became increasingly medicalized in the 1950s, with biochemical analysis prioritized, as a more politically palatable suite of interventions.[57] Castro's own understanding of nutrition – as eminently political, all the way down – diverged from the increasingly medically orientated logics of the FAO's Nutrition Division. These shifts reflected changing historical understandings of malnutrition and the function of protein,[58] but also longstanding internal tension between technical and structural approaches to malnutrition.[59] Castro stopped taking part in the advisory committee as a formal member in 1951, though the head of the Nutrition Section of the WHO, F.W. Clements, continued to solicit Castro's advice, including on Nutritional Assessment and training in underdeveloped areas.[60]

The 'marriage of agriculture and health' was often also a story of commercial and national self-interest. So, in terms of nutrition, while Castro entered the FAO's various institutional organs with enthusiasm, and while the project of calculation was not homogeneous, neither was nutrition destined to become the lever by which the right to food became enshrined in a global project to end hunger. Biopolitics were generally subsumed not by what Castro called the geopolitics of hunger, but by geopolitics tout court, and increasingly by the demands of agricultural capital. The attempt to construct a global nutritional subject at the FAO was all very well, but national and international politics on the one hand (the emerging cold war) and the emerging capitalist food regime on the other prevented the application of much of the rational, biopolitical international governmentality that post-war technocrats and globalist scientists imagined for the FAO.

While Wallace Aykroyd may have seen the FAO as 'a child of the science of nutrition',[61] questions of production were increasingly favoured over those of consumption and distribution. Attempts to use the FAO's institutional power

55 Anonymous, 'Comments on the Second Conference on Nutrition Problems in Latin America: Confidential' (Hotel Quitandinha, Petrópolis: FAO, June 1950), Uncoded Files. Nutrition Division. 12ESN543, FAO.

56 Tracy, 'A Global Journey – Ancel Keys, the FAO, and the Rise of Transnational Heart Disease Epidemiology, 1949–1958', 378–81.

57 Forclaz, 'From Reconstruction to Development'.

58 Pernet, 'FAO from the Field and from Below', 400.

59 Donald Mclaren, 'The Great Protein Fiasco', The Lancet 204, no. 7872 (1974): 93–96; Kenneth Carpenter, Protein and Energy: A Study of Changing Ideas in Nutrition (Cambridge: Cambridge University Press, 1994); Nott, '"How Little Progress"?'

60 F.W. Clements, 'To Josué de Castro [On Behalf of WHO]', February 1951, 563, CEHIBRA.JdC.

61 Aykroyd, Food for Man, 84.

to focus on consumption came up against opposition from rich producer states who insisted upon the role of the technical division of the FAO as a means for increasing productivity of agriculture around the world. During the 1950s the focus on 'technical assistance' was felt across the UN.[62] The FAO followed a similar trend to the World Health Organization, which, in the post-war period, was 'moving away from discussions about the social and economic roots of ill health and the structure of health services' towards technical assistance and economic productivity.[63] Nutrition was not only sidelined to production but harnessed to it, and 'translated into the need for an extensive development program for agriculture which emphasized protecting land from depletion and encouraging the poorly nourished vegetarian Africans to acquire animal protein in the form of milk and meat'.[64] Nutritional policy and nutritional science had long been linked to surplus disposal and agricultural priorities, whether in Boyd Orr's promotion of the British dairy industry or Escudero's of the Argentina beef industry, and this linkage began to have an international dimension in this period.[65]

The issue of surpluses brings me back to the question of an international food reserve. While the possibilities for a world food policy were at least partly still molten in the early 1950s, the FAO was still attempting to construct an international food reserve on the basis of an understanding of the nutritional body. We can see the tensions between the global and the somatic scales in the calculative logics attempted in the analytical work by the FAO, particularly in the proposal for a new way of calculating global food: the 'Emergency Food Reserve Unit' (EFRU). A report written by FAO staff for the council, responding to the Conference Resolution No. 16, sought to outline possible paths towards a food reserve. It was submitted to the Executive Council for discussion under Castro's Presidency. It began from a calculation: 'One Emergency Food Reserve Unit is defined as the quantity of food required for supplementing the diet of one million people at the rate of 1200 calories per day for one month.'[66] The definition crystallizes many decades of nutritional debate and a politics of globally differentiated bodies. We might compare it to the geographer L. Dudley Stamp's attempts, later in

62 David Webster, 'Development Advisors in a Time of Cold War and Decolonization: The United Nations Technical Assistance Administration, 1950–59', *Journal of Global History* 6 (2011): 250, doi:10.1017/S1740022811000258.

63 Hardy, 'Beriberi, Vitamin B1 and World Food Policy, 1925–1970', 70; on technical assistance at the FAO see Staples, *The Birth of Development*, 96–104.

64 Cynthia Brantley, 'Kikuyu-Maasai Nutrition and Colonial Science: The Orr and Gilks Study in Late 1920s', *The International Journal of African Historical Studies* 30, no. 1 (1997): 77.

65 Escudero, *Los Requerimientos Alimentarios Del Hombre Sano y Normal y Las Encuestas de Alimentacion*.

66 FAO Council Papers, 'Council of FAO, Fifteenth Session (9–14 June 1952), Item 6, Emergency Food Reserve' (FAO, April 1952), 3, CL 15/10, FAO.

the 1950s, to define 'A Standard Nutrition Unit', connecting the consumption of calories with land use.[67] Stamp concludes that 1,000,000 calories are needed per person per year for basic health. This amounts to significantly more than the FAO's assessment:

'Emergency subsistence calorie intake' per person has been assessed [by a previous 1946 FAO report] at 1900 calories per caput per diem [...] This figure relates, however, to total intake and even under famine conditions some food is usually available locally. Further, it was intended to apply to western populations and the needs of populations in the areas most likely to be affected by famine are somewhat less (Report of Committee on Calorie Requirements, FAO 1950). The figure of 1200 calories is put forward with these considerations in mind.[68]

The FAO paper relies on a geography of nutritional minimum that suggests that non-Western populations need less food. It is worth recalling here that Josué de Castro had shown some years earlier that the average consumption of Brazilians between 1920 and 1946 had never reached more than 1800 calories per person, lower than the *regiões famintos* – hungry regions – of Europe.[69] The FAO's comparative metric, in which famished populations need less food in the first place, embeds a geobiopolitics that emerges out of a nutritional science that, in spite of the presence of scholars such as Josué de Castro, remained a Northern, colonial science.

The report argues that 'experience shows that serious food shortages are most likely to occur among rice-eating populations'.[70] The socio-political reasons for this are not analysed, but underpin a discussion of the make-up of the reserve between different crops. The reserve, they emphasize, is not a total solution to famine. It does, though, embed the idea of acting against the free market in food: 'relatively small supplies, which are made available rapidly when danger of food shortage and famine arises, can do much to prevent hoarding, panic and rise in food prices which, if unchecked, may greatly aggravate the effect of the shortage itself'.[71] This recognizes the damaging effects of a 'free' market in food during famines.

The EFRU is deployed as a mode of global biopolitical calculation, declaring that '100 EFRUs = 1,000,000 m.t. – 10 million people for 10 months'. This utopian calculative logic is a kind of global Saint-Simonianism, showing the calculations of flawed, but radical, technocrats attempting to figure the end of hunger in terms of a geobiopolitics. The report emphasizes

---

67 L. Dudley Stamp, 'The Measurement of Land Resources', *Geographical Review* 48, no. 1 (1958): 1–15.
68 FAO Council Papers, 'Emergency Food Reserve Report', 3.
69 Josué de Castro, 'Política Alimentar', *Arquivos Brasileiros de Nutrição* 3, no. 4 (1947): 1–2.
70 FAO Council Papers, 'Emergency Food Reserve Report', 5.
71 FAO Council Papers, 'Emergency Food Reserve Report', 6.

quite how small such utopianism is: 'even a quantity of say fifteen EFRUs [...] would still be very small indeed in relation to world production and generally very small also in relation to world trade of the commodities composing it'.[72] The speculative terms of the discourse here – 'say', 'indeed' – give a sense of these projections' projected failure. We can hear the sigh Emma Rothschild writes about.

The report sees two key problems. The first is explicit: currency. The second is implicit: geopolitics. Currency – whether stocks could be bought and sold in local currencies – was the threshold at which emergency food met the emerging hegemony of the dollar. It became impossible to separate a system of international food governance from the international financial system. This was in part why the World Food Policy itself included ambitious plans for agricultural credit organized at the scale of the international, and was in part why these ideas were rejected. The functioning of an international system to obviate hunger was rendered almost impossible by the dominance of the dollar. Disempowered countries with disempowered money were unable to exercise agency at the scale of the international, or even take part in international exchanges. Between the lines of this FAO report we can see why the international food regime cannot be understood outside the broader context of the post-war global economic disposition and the centrality of the dollar.[73]

Around the time of the report, between the fifteenth and the sixteenth councils, Castro tried to take the problem of geopolitics into his own hands. He travelled to the United States and visited President Truman in the late summer of 1952 to convince him of the benefits of an international food reserve (Figure 5).[74] It seemed to have little effect, but, back in the FAO, as Chairman, Castro attempted to move things forward. Reading the 1952 Council papers captures in miniature Castro's experience at the FAO. It begins with his impassioned call for synthesis and action, framed in moral terms. Progress stalls, and Castro attempts to intervene to at least establish a working group of the Council, but fails, as the Canadians, UK, and USA want a purely technical group that cannot advance any of the crucial political issues. National representatives resist any technical work on political aspects of the food reserve. They use an insistence on the technical to steer clear of substantive debates over funding or the distribution of authority. The matter is left for the following council with the FAO Director General tasked with further internal exploratory work. This led to a proposal for an Internationally Owned Emergency Relief Fund rather than a food reserve or emergency stocks. But, again, at the November 1952 Council the UK were unhappy with the FAO proposals and announced that they would not commit money in its current form. The matter was deferred once more.[75]

72 FAO Council Papers, 'Emergency Food Reserve Report', 6.
73 Friedmann, 'The Political Economy of Food'.
74 Anon., 'De Castro to See Truman', *The New York Times*, August 1952, sec. UN.
75 FAO Council Papers, 'Report of the Council of FAO, Sixteenth Session'.

Figure 5. Josué de Castro with President Truman at the White House, Washington D.C., 1952. Source: Imagem do Fundo Correio da Manhã, Public domain/Arquivo Nacional do Brasil

The next Council minutes elicit another sigh:

> In general, it was felt that in the further development of the plan it would be wise to aim at simplicity and not to start off on too ambitious a scale, while at the same time keeping in mind the minimum requirements for meeting the essential purpose underlying the Conference Resolution on an 'Emergency Food Reserve'.[76]

We could locate the impossibility of a *world* food policy in the context of an *international* politics in the contradiction between the two halves of this sentence. The scale of a global food reserve could not be anything other than ambitious, if it was to be meaningful; but, as so often in internationalist projects, the conflicting interests of national actors in international policy made such ambition untenable. By June of 1953 the Council passed the question back to the decision-making body, the Conference. Resolution No. 21 of the 7th Conference of the FAO, in November 1953, crystallizes this impasse in the history of world food. The Conference

---

76 FAO Council Papers, 'Report of the Council of FAO, Sixteenth Session'.

[r]ecognizes, *notwithstanding a difference of opinion as to whether the creation of an international emergency food reserve or fund is necessary, that in any case a pre-requisite to the creation of such a reserve or fund would be evidence that Member Nations would be in a position to provide the necessary stocks or money resources; and that in the absence of such evidence it is impracticable to create an international reserve or fund as contemplated by the Sixth Session of the Conference.*[77]

So the question is moot. The road turns away from structural solutions to famine and towards humanitarianism. The Conference resolves that:

ad-hoc measures to relieve famine conditions are useful and necessary [and] notes with warm approval and commends to the favourable attention of Member Nations the action of the United States Congress in author-izing the President to use for emergency famine relief up to $100 million of government held stocks.[78]

The celebration of US aid decisively shifts the discourse of world food away from a globally recognizable right to food, met by some measure of permanent distribution of surpluses at an international scale, to an ad hoc liberal humanitarianism. In this pivot we can see that the emergence of international humanitarian food aid was co-extensive with the death of world food policy.

Yet it was a slow death and, in spite of the headwinds of national govern-ments, work on food reserves continued.[79] Indeed – from the perspective of the history of geography – it is worth remembering that throughout these years Castro was also deepening his engagement with the international geograph-ical community. In 1952 he was invited by the National Research Council of the United States of America to take part in the Washington meeting of the International Geographic Union. He was to be on a panel with Theodore Schultz, the influential Chicago economist, on World Food Supply. After the meeting, which Castro attended, he was invited by Jacques May, the medical geographer and Chairman of the Commission on Medical Geography, to be part of a reformed IGU Commision on the Ecology of Health and Disease, alongside Max Sorre and Arthur Geddes, the Scottish geographer who was the son of Patrick Geddes and an expert on Bengal.[80] This commission met again in 1954 in New York, and various projects were initiated, including with the Australian geographer Griffith Taylor, and a possible collaboration with the Soil Association, led by Lady Eve Balfour, a long-term correspondent

77 FAO Conference Papers, 'Report of the Conference of the FAO, Seventh Session, Rome' (Food and Agriculture Organisation, December 1953) emphasis in original.
78 FAO Conference Papers, 'Report of the Conference of the FAO, Seventh Session, Rome'.
79 Shaw, *World Food Security*, 41–48.
80 Jacques May, 'To Josué de Castro', September 1952, 575, CEHIBRA.JdC.

and friend of Castro's.[81] The point of this brief return to the history of geography is to reiterate that in this period Castro's geographic practice and his practice as an international diplomat went hand in glove. In his archive the documents from the FAO are interspersed with his correspondence with geographers, as well as with projects such as the Parliamentary Group for World Government, led by British Labour MPs Henry Usborne and Gilbert McAllister. Indeed, his relations with an internationalist, British parliamentary left were longstanding (Figure 6). In 1954 Castro was re-elected, and again committed himself to reviving the world food plan. Again, he sought Boyd Orr's advice, who wrote to congratulate him on the 'great success of [his] book, and wish [him] all success for [his] leadership in a world food plan which has the approval of the vast majority of the people of the world'.[82] But by the end of Castro's two-year tenure the proposal for a world food policy was no nearer to fruition. Indeed, the prospects were relatively bleak. Herbert Broadley, the FAO Deputy Director General, wrote warmly to Castro at the end of 1955, noting that under his leadership 'the Council has increased its authority and influence in FAO affairs'. But it is possible that the institution of the independent council itself was under threat, implying that that threat had emerged precisely because the Council's role was growing. Broadley's tone, like Castro's, is ambivalent at best: 'what the future holds, we do not know'.[83]

The Council did survive, but by 1956 Castro was profoundly disillusioned. Like many of those involved in the first years of the FAO he saw it as a failure. By the end of the 1950s the FAO had become a hybrid: a body of technical expertise on the one hand and the facilitator of global advocacy on the other. The latter converged around a new attempt to carve out a global movement against hunger. As the organization attempted to address its own incapacity to act, it turned, under the Director General B.R. Sen, to international civil society, through the Freedom From Hunger Campaign (FFHC),[84] endorsed by the UN, ECOSOC, and FAO in 1959. Sen has been seen as attempting both to depoliticize the FAO[85] and to transform it from a technical to a development agency.[86] Dwarfed in material terms by

---

81 Jacques May, 'To Josué de Castro', June 1954, 557, CEHIBRA.JdC.

82 Orr, 'Letter to Josué de Castro'.

83 Herbert Broadley, 'To Josué de Castro' (unpublished, December 1955), 566, CEHIBRA.JdC.

84 See Shaw, *World Food Security*.

85 Margaret Rose Biswas, 'FAO: Its History and Achievements during the First Four Decades, 19451985', DPhil thesis (University of Oxford, 2007), 40–44; Ruth Jachertz, '"To Keep Food Out of Politics": The UN Food and Agriculture Organization, 1945–1965', in *International Organizations and Development, 1945–1990* (London: Palgrave Macmillan, 2014), 75–100.

86 Benjamin Siegel, '"The Claims of Asia and the Far East": India and the FAO in the Age of Ambivalent Internationalism', *The International History Review* 41, no. 2 (2019): 428, 440.

Figure 6. Josué de Castro with John Boyd Orr and Clement Attlee, British
Labour Prime Minister, 1945–51. Photograph undated. Source: Acervo
Fundação Joaquim Nabuco – Ministério da Educação – Brasil

the US Food for Peace projects, the FFHC sought to 'reanimate the moral
mission' of the FAO.[87]

In spite of his disappointment as a result of his experience at the FAO as a
whole, Castro was always a willing participant in anti-hunger advocacy, and
wrote in the *Black Book of Hunger* that the FFHC 'would serve to create such
a climate in world opinion that the problems of hunger and need would be
viewed in a realistic fashion, that their causes would be analysed objectively,
and that the appropriate remedies would be sought with determination and
courage'.[88] Castro engaged extensively with the campaign through his NGO,
ASCOFAM. It had chapters in a number of countries and was most active
in Brazil and France, where it facilitated Castro's work with an influential
generation of French humanitarians, notably Abbé Pierre, whose legacy is
still alive in the French third sector today. Castro's practice in the campaign
was transnational, operating through a global civil society manifesting in the

87 FAO, Development through Food: A Strategy for Surplus Utilization (Rome: FAO,
 1961), v.
88 Josué de Castro, *The Black Book of Hunger* (Boston: Beacon Books, 1969), 112.

wide range of newspaper and magazine articles he wrote and interviews he gave, repeating the same set of arguments and soundbites across languages and geographies. The systematic inclusion of civil society actors in the FFHC and the attempt to bring into being an international civil society through the alliance between civil society and international institutions was striking, though not without its internal conflicts.

In 1961, the *UN General Assembly Resolution No. 1496 (XV) on the Provision of Food Surpluses to Food Deficient Peoples through the UN System* was greeted by the FAO Director General, B.R. Sen, as 'a fresh chapter in the history of international relations'. Seeing 'past international efforts' as 'a history of frustration', this new start would change the landscape of global food policy.[89] At this time Sen proposed an international mechanism for emergency food supplies that recalled elements of the earlier vision espoused by Boyd Orr and Castro. Sen claimed that this would lead to food being used in the pursuit of development, not just as humanitarian aid. However, contrary to Sen's claims, it overwhelmingly proved to be the latter and the Resolution was largely greeted with disappointment.[90] Instead, the early 1960s saw the beginning of the World Food Programme, when humanitarian action became enshrined as a global institutional project, and the continuation of the advocacy of the FFHC. Ultimately these were international humanitarian projects, not a world food policy. While the World Food Programme was at least partially successful, it and the FFHC demonstrated the flaws of international voluntarist humanitarianism and the coalitional world of international humanitarian NGOs. Ironically, international humanitarianism's very success closed the door on fifteen years of attempts to structurally end hunger through rigorous and far-reaching food policy constructed at the scale of the international, based on the idea that food was a universal right. The 1960s were named the UN Decade for Development, but the discourse of food as a human right fell foul of the coalition between strengthening global agri-business and the drive to establish grain dependency in the global south as a tool of US foreign policy. In 1964, Wallace Aykroyd wrote of the FAO that 'this is not a success story'.[91] As the 1960s ended, the prospect of a genuine World Food Policy that would challenge the commoditization of food at the global scale had long since expired. Instead, FAO debate centred on the management of prices and surpluses, as this had become the priority of the USA. These discussions were far from the utopian possibilities of the World Food Policy, or even the alternative calculative logics of Emergency Food Reserve Units. Castro was deeply critical of the destruction of surplus in the pursuit of maintaining prices: in unfinished edits to *The Geopolitics of Hunger* in the early 1970s he wrote of these as deliberate 'policies of hunger'. The United States, he observed, housed at least 10 million people suffering

89 FAO, *Development through Food*, v, 13.
90 Staples, 'To Win the Peace', 511.
91 Aykroyd, *Food for Man*, 9.

undernutrition, yet continued to destroy food. He laments that, by the early 1970s, 'in terms of the struggle against hunger, we are still, unhappily, in the domain of paternalism, charity, aid, and humanitarianism, when we should be moving toward international economic solidarity and toward a human solidarity that would aim at security for all the world'.[92] His sometime collaborator, and later Independent Chairman of the FAO Council, Michel Cépède, noted acerbically in the early 1980s that in the FAO in the 1950s 'putting a brake on "overproduction" in the rich countries soon seemed a more effective course of action than responding to calls to step up production to feed the poor'.[93]

Conclusion: Deepening Internationalism

In spite of the failure of the FAO, Castro was not put off universalist projects. Indeed, he became committed to even more ambitious and unlikely projects for world federalism and world government, particularly through the World Parliament Association. As Gilbert McAllister wrote to Castro in 1961, the aim of that body was to 'present world problems from the point of view of a world solution which would make even Berlin, Laos, Korea and the like, fade into their proper perspective'.[94] There was no shortage of ambition, but most of these projects for world federalism became little more than talking shops.

Castro's attempts to make hunger understood as a universal problem and to practise a geopolitics of hunger at the FAO came up against insurmountable problems of scale. The universality of hunger exists in a divided world and within a capitalist system in which scarcity is an underpinning necessity. Once the struggle over whether food is a right or a commodity was lost, moral and aesthetic arguments about hunger come to a dead end against the realpolitik of global capitalism. Castro's frustrations need to be seen in this light, but also in the light of his only partially materialist understanding of what was at stake. His appeals to morality and goodwill inside global institutions, whether in association with artistic work or in the nitty gritty of geopolitics and international technocracy, were necessarily doomed.

By the end of the 1950s Castro had retired his belief in technocratic utopianism at the FAO. His major work of this period was, after all, called the *Black Book of Hunger*. Its darkness is also inside Castro: the loss of idealism, the loss of faith in a global vision of humanity, run by 'men of good will' who will align their misaligned interests in the service of ending the great scourge of hunger. The dream of deracinated international technocrats rationally ending hunger was stillborn. The realization that this post-war utopia of a world free of hunger would never emerge was a personal, as well as a global, tragedy.

92 Castro, *The Geopolitics of Hunger*, 73.
93 Cépède, 'The Fight against Hunger', 285.
94 Gilbert McAllister, 'To Josué de Castro [On Behalf of World Parliament Association]', August 1961, 560, CEHIBRA.JdC.

However, his experience at the FAO did not lead Castro to resign himself to abstraction or to turn away from the struggle against hunger; rather it led him to redouble his efforts to overcome underdevelopment at home, in the Northeast. It is back to the Northeast that I now turn.

CHAPTER 5

1955–1964: The Northeastern Question

'Each place will have its own science, because science is not universal, it is local, it is a science of the region.'

Josué de Castro[1]

'The whole of Brazil is one immense Northeast.'

Francisco de Oliveira[2]

Introduction

Having followed Castro's work as it travelled along its global itineraries, in this chapter I return again to the site of its origins: Recife, in the Northeast. In the late 1950s and early 1960s Recife was a thriving hubbub of political and creative life, and in this chapter I listen to some of what was bubbling there.[3] While conducting archival research in Recife I was a visiting member of a research group at the *Universidade Federal de Pernambuco* (UFPE). The campus is west of the centre of Recife, where the state archives live, and between the neighbourhoods of Várzea and Apipucos which house the former home of Gilberto Freyre and the *Fundação Joaquim Nabuco*, where I worked through Castro's papers. Friends at UFPE helped me find a studio flat in the neighbourhood of Iputinga, near the university. A few hundred metres from my flat in one direction, towards the university, was the tropical modernist brutalism of Glauce Campello's headquarters for

---

1 Josué de Castro, 'Développement et Environnement', May 1972, 28, 92, CEHIBRA. JdC.
2 Francisco de Oliveira, *Elegia para uma Re(li)gião: SUDENE, Nordeste. Planejamento e Conflitos de Classes*, 3rd ed., Estudos Sobre o Nordeste 1 (Rio de Janeiro: Paz e Terra, 1977), 14.
3 Francisco de Oliveira, *Noiva da revolução/Elegia para uma re(li)gião* (São Paulo: Boitempo Editorial, 2008), 21–80.

the *Superintendencia do Nordeste*, the powerful regional planning agency more commonly known as SUDENE.[4] Just past the seat of SUDENE is a radio mast of the University Radio station, whose '*Serviço de Extensão Cultural*' [Cultural Extension Service], a radio literacy project, was directed by a young Paulo Freire in the early 1960s, during the radical municipal experiments of the government of Miguel Arraes.[5] Somewhere in Iputinga, too, was the unrecorded site where the first Peasant League in Brazil was founded on 3 January 1946.[6] The leader of that group, José dos Prazeres, working alongside Francisco Julião and Josué de Castro, was to become a crucial figure in the appropriation of the Engenho Galileia, a key moment in Brazilian rural political history.

Among their other social, political, and natural effects, droughts reminded national governments of the existence of the Northeast, and in 1958 an aggressive dry spell hit the region. The drought brought to the forefront of national political consciousness the spatial and regional dynamics of economic development. The 1958 crisis helped trigger[7] attempts to end a mode of infrastructural politics that had long dominated responses to crisis in the region, what novelist and journalist Antonio Callado influentially called the 'industries of drought'.[8] This involved public expenditure on reservoir construction being captured by large landowners for private benefit and entrenching oligarchic social relations.[9] The state provided aid and work to migrants fleeing drought, but most was seized by large landowners to employ what was essentially *corvée* labour to enhance the value of their own land by building reservoirs (recalling the Franco regime in Spain's use of political prisoners to build reservoirs[10]). As Josué de Castro put it, such reservoirs 'serve for nothing more than to reflect the sky of the Northeast: the most futile of all futilities'.[11] This was a form of

4   Sudene was founded in 1959 but its massive concrete base was not completed until 1968. During my first visit it had recently been redesignated as the home of a revitalized Sudene by Dilma Rousseff, but its future was uncertain after the coup and Jair Bolsonaro's election in 2018.

5   Germano Coelho, 'Paulo Freire e o Movimento de Cultura Popular', in *Paulo Freire: Educação e Transformação Social* (Recife: Universitária da UFPE, 2002), 31–96.

6   Elide Rugai Bastos, *As Ligas Camponesas* (Petrópolis: Vozes Petrópolis, 1984), 139.

7   Anthony L. Hall, *Drought and Irrigation in North-East Brazil* (Cambridge: Cambridge University Press, 1978), 7.

8   Antônio Callado, *Os industriais da sêca e os 'Galileus' de Pernambuco: aspectos da luta pela reforma agrária no Brasil* (Rio de Janeiro: Editôra Civilização Brasileira, 1960).

9   Ronald H. Chilcote, *Power and the Ruling Classes in Northeast Brazil: Juazeiro and Petrolina in Transition* (Cambridge: Cambridge University Press, 1990).

10 Erik Swyngedouw, 'Technonatural Revolutions: The Scalar Politics of Franco's Hydro-Social Dream for Spain, 1939–1975', *Transactions of the Institute of British Geographers* 32, no. 1 (January 2007): 22–23, doi:10.1111/j.1475-5661.2007.00233.x.

11 Josué de Castro and Celso Furtado, 'Operação Nordeste: Dois Nomes e Duas Opinões', *O Observador Economico e Financeiro*, April 1959, 278 edition, 33.

hydro-statecraft,[12] in which the state was captured by a particular section of capital: the *latifundia* that Castro had so long struggled against. The state in the Northeast functioned as a kind of socio-ecological relation, through an infrastructural production of nature – spatially controlled irrigation – organized around the crises of droughts. As Swyngedouw put it, the "'production of nature" is an integral part of a process of "producing scale"'.[13]

In 1958, driven by a constellation of national developmentalist political forces, the President, Juscelino Kubitschek, declared the region a national priority. After his stint at the FAO came to an end Castro had returned to Brazilian politics full time, being elected as a Federal Deputy for Pernambuco. He was among those, in early 1958, allying with and lobbying Kubitschek about the Northeast and its food supplies.[14] Kubitschek's solution was to create SUDENE, headed by the charismatic young economist Celso Furtado. Furtado became one of the most significant Brazilian thinkers of the twentieth century and a key exponent of dependency theory. Under his leadership, by 1959 SUDENE had accrued massive, but nevertheless crucially limited, powers to influence the economic development of the Northeast. The SUDENE project attempted to integrate the Northeast into a newly conceived national polity and to overcome regional underdevelopment.

Establishing SUDENE was a complex and contested process of struggle between urban, rural, regional, national, and international interests. The cold war pitted Pernambucan radicals in Recife and in the sugar plantations against the weight of North American cold war paranoia, covert operations, and the politics of humanitarian aid. The US increasingly regarded the Northeast's Peasant Leagues, and the radical municipal, and later regional, government of Miguel Arraes and the *Frente do Recife* [The Recife Front] as a revolutionary threat.[15] The vexed space of the Northeast was tense: its deeply entrenched plantation-owning rural élites, a nascent industrial sector, and an export-focused economy were increasingly being challenged by leftist political thought and organization and a spreading rural radicalism. Miguel Arraes argued in 1972 that the political struggle in Brazil in this period, and particularly in the Northeast, could be understood centrally as a question of anti-imperialism: a struggle between a section of the bourgeoisie intent on

12 Erik Swyngedouw, 'Modernity and Hybridity: Nature, Regeneracionismo, and the Production of the Spanish Waterscape, 1890–1930', *Annals of the Association of American Geographers* 89, no. 3 (1999): 443–65; Katie Meehan and Olivia C. Molden, 'Political Ecologies of the State', in *The Wiley-Blackwell Companion to Political Geography*, ed. John Agnew, Virginie Mamadouh, Anna J. Secor, and Joanne Sharp (Chichester: Wiley-Blackwell, 2015), 438–50, doi:10.1002/9781118725771.ch32.

13 Swyngedouw, 'Technonatural Revolutions', 10.

14 Juscelino Kubitschek, 'Telegram to Josué de Castro' (unpublished, April 1958), 559, CEHIBRA.JdC.

15 Stefan Robock, *Brazil's Developing Northeast : A Study of Regional Planning and Foreign Aid* (Washington: The Brookings Institution, 1963).

aligning the Brazilian economy with foreign capital, particularly from the USA, and a section of the bourgeoisie in tenuous and often fractious alliance with workers and peasant movements.[16] In the end, it was land reform that triggered the rupture of April 1964. President João Goulart tried to 'play both sides', announcing a radical, national agrarian reform that he did not have the power to enact.[17] It was this that precipitated the coup, and Josué de Castro's own exile.

In the rest of this chapter I explore the place of the region in this political history in order to think through how it can inform political ecology and contribute to understandings of the intellectual history of the Northeast. I begin by suggesting that the region has an important place in political ecology, before returning to Castro's own writing on the Northeast and the transformation from regional geography to a proto-regional political ecology. I then situate this development within *dependentista* debates on regional underdevelopment, in particular through analysing Castro's debates with Celso Furtado over the making of SUDENE. I argue that the Northeast itself played an important and under-acknowledged role in the history of dependency theory and, further, that Josué de Castro, put in the proper context of a nexus of intellectual and political struggles over the Northeast, can provide a bridge between the development of critical geography and political ecology on the one hand and dependency theory on the other.

The Region and Political Ecology

Asked, in 1998, about how to approach drought in the Northeast of Brazil, the Bahian geographer Milton Santos replied: 'the first thing is, this question is social, not natural. Once again, it's Josué de Castro first, and then Celso Furtado.'[18] Santos figures Castro as a bridge between schools of thought with apparently distinct intellectual histories: regional geography on Castro's part and underdevelopment and dependency theory on Furtado's. Recent work in English by scholars including Kevin Carter and Federico Ferretti has shown Castro's influence on geographical thinking about population and underdevelopment in the second half of the twentieth century.[19] As they recognize, this has long been clear to Latin American geographers such as Milton Santos,[20] Enrique Leff and Carlos

---

16 Miguel Arraes, *Brazil: The People and the Power* (London: Penguin, 1972).

17 Shepard Forman, 'Disunity and Discontent: A Study of Peasant Political Movements in Brazil*', *Journal of Latin American Studies* 3, no. 1 (May 1971): 3–24, doi:10.1017/S0022216X00001139.

18 Milton Santos, 'Entrevista explosiva com Milton Santos', *Geledés* (blog), December 2016, accessed 17 June 2022, https://www.geledes.org.br/entrevista-explosiva-com-milton-santos/.

19 Carter, 'Population Control'.

20 Tendler, *Josué de Castro – Cidadão do Mundo*.

Walter Porto Gonçalves,[21] and Manuel Correia de Andrade.[22] However, how exactly his influence can be felt not only in critical geography but in studies of underdevelopment and dependency remains under-determined. This chapter aims to address this question and, like the previous chapter, rectify what Ferretti calls Castro's '(neglected) roles in shaping international scholarly and political debates'.[23] Reinserting Castro into a regional prehistory of dependency theory does two important things. First, it animates dependency theory's scalar problematic by insisting that the question of the underdeveloped region was important to its intellectual history. Secondly, it insists on the ecological dimensions of underdevelopment and dependency theory, by articulating them with Castro's geography of hunger.

Understanding the historical geography of Brazil in the middle of the twentieth century – or indeed the historical geography of Recife, transatlantic trade relations, rural social movements, the reproduction of everyday life, or Latin American politics – all require confronting the question of the region. This is not to reify or fix the scale of the region, but to address its formation and function as a material and imagined space that had real political, social, cultural, economic, and ecological consequences. The region was both cause and effect. In the anglophone discipline, regional geography has been declared dead and resuscitated more than once. So has regional political ecology. This in spite of the fact that the influential Blaikie and Brookfield, often cited as at the root of anglophone political ecology, in the 1980s explicitly had in mind a 'regional political ecology'.[24] However, for a regional political ecology to be worth pursuing – indeed, Enrique Leff has recently reiterated the epistemological importance of the regional for the field[25] – what we mean by 'region' must be further explored.

Joel Wainwright, writing in the shadow of the death of Edward Said, asks 'what precisely constitutes a "context" of, and for, political ecology? How does something come to be a space or region that calls for political ecology? How

21 Carlos Walter Porto-Gonçalves and Enrique Leff, 'Political Ecology in Latin America: The Social Re-Appropriation of Nature, the Reinvention of Territories and the Construction of an Environmental Rationality', *Desenvolvimento e Meio Ambiente* 35 (2015), doi:info:doi/10.5380/dma.v35i0.43543.

22 Andrade, 'Josué de Castro'.

23 Federico Ferretti, 'Geographies of Internationalism: Radical Development and Critical Geopolitics from the Northeast of Brazil', *Political Geography* 63 (March 2018): 10–19, doi:10.1016/j.polgeo.2017.11.004.

24 Peter A. Walker, 'Reconsidering "Regional" Political Ecologies: Toward a Political Ecology of the Rural American West', *Progress in Human Geography* 27, no. 1 (February 2003): 7–24, doi:10.1191/0309132503ph410oa; on the connection with French rural geographers see, for example, Denis Gautier and Baptiste Hautdidier, 'Connecting Political Ecology and French Geography: On Tropicality and Radical Thought', in *International Handbook of Political Ecology*, ed. Raymond Bryant, 1st ed. (Cheltenham: Edward Elgar Publishing, 2015), 57–69.

25 Leff, 'Power–Knowledge Relations in the Field of Political Ecology', 232–33.

do we know where the context of our research lies? Is the inquiry into this knowledge itself part of doing political ecology?'[26] If the region is to constitute such a context for political ecology, then its conceptualization needs to be relational and open. The region is a scale that is constantly the subject of struggle over its own constitution, extent, and description. It needs to be both discursively and materially defined. It needs to be articulated with and distinguished from other spatial terms, such as place, territory, and scale. It has something to do with an area of socio-cultural and political ecological identity, and the relationships between these two things. It is a product of natural history and political history. For contemporary political ecology to be regional, then, requires some further thought.

While the question of the region has been around as long as modern geography, Edward Said's *Orientalism*, Sidaway suggests, precipitated debates within geographical thought about 'metageographical categories'[27] and the substantive role of 'imaginative geographies' in organizing space, nature, and politics. In reopening the question of a regional political ecology I follow Wainwright and others to draw from and contribute to Gramscian approaches in political ecology. My contribution, in part, responds to Anssi Paasi's blunt statement in 2011 that 'the theoretical dialogue between English-speaking geographers and scholars working elsewhere over key spatial categories has largely disappeared'.[28] What follows is an effort – necessarily highly selective – to re-establish some of this missing dialogue.

In particular, I draw on Rogério Haesbaert's conception of 'the region as an arte-fact (always with the hyphen), caught in the imbrication between fact and artifice and, as such, as a piece of political hardware'.[29] Haesbaert is influenced by the regional thinking of both Milton Santos – whose ideas shifted significantly over his career[30] – and his post-doctoral mentor, Doreen Massey. I put the notion of arte-fact to work to give order and form to the enormous proliferation of possible ways of thinking spatially and ecologically about the region. Haesbaert's concept brings together discourse and representation with more materialist concerns around the production of space.

26 Wainwright, 'The Geographies of Political Ecology', 1034.

27 James D. Sidaway, 'Geography, Globalization, and the Problematic of Area Studies', *Annals of the Association of American Geographers* 103, no. 4 (July 2013): 984–1002, doi:10.1080/00045608.2012.660397.

28 Anssi Paasi, 'From Region to Space, Part II', in *The Wiley-Blackwell Companion to Human Geography*, ed. John A. Agnew and James S. Duncan (Oxford: Wiley-Blackwell, 2011), 173.

29 Rogério Haesbaert, 'Região, regionalização e regionalidade: questões contemporâneas', *Revista Antares: Letras e Humanidades* 3 (2010): 7.

30 Ines E. de Castro, 'A Região Como Problema Para Milton Santos', *Scripta Nova. Revista Electrónica de Geografía y Ciencias Sociales* vi, no. 124 (September 2002), http://www.ub.edu/geocrit/sn/sn-124e.htm.

In 2015 McKinnon and Hiner, following Walker[31] and Zimmerer,[32] reconsidered whether political ecology ought to be regional. They asked, 'should political ecologists participate as active agents in the construction and reconstruction of regions?' They answer a 'cautious "yes"'.[33] Josué de Castro was much less cautious. It was precisely as a political ecologist – an activist scholar committed to analysing and disrupting the hierarchical, structural relations of power, colony, and capital that configured social and ecological life in particular places – that he threw himself into the socio-political and economic production of the space and nature of the Northeast of Brazil. In the rest of this chapter I follow him doing so, in order to find new ways of thinking the region in political ecology. I first turn back to Castro's own writing on the region, and on the Northeast.

Josué de Castro Thinking the Region

In the 1930s Marcus Power and James Sidaway suggested that

> an interest in regional geography was reinforced by the long crisis [...] and the attendant sociospatial disparities, codified as 'regional problems' [...] and contrasted with 'congestion' [...] as well as through the dissemination of Vidal de la Blache's (1845–1918) methodologies of regional synthesis, with their focus on national and regional questions in the metropole rather than the global (which meant colonial) frames of reference.[34]

There were certainly exceptions to this characterization, and we should both recognize the diversity of work that falls under the Vidalian heading[35] and the multiplicity within disciplinary histories of regional or tropical geography.[36] Yet what is significant here is to place the processes of geographical theorization in the conjunctures in which they emerge and in which they intervene. Castro wrote against the backdrop of a different form of regional

---

31 Walker, 'Reconsidering "Regional" Political Ecologies'.

32 Karl S. Zimmerer, 'Wetland Production and Smallholder Persistence: Agricultural Change in a Highland Peruvian Region', *Annals of the Association of American Geographers* 81, no. 3 (September 1991): 443–63, doi:10.1111/j.1467-8306.1991.tb01704.x.

33 Innisfree McKinnon and Colleen C. Hiner, 'Does the Region Still Have Relevance? (Re)Considering "Regional" Political Ecology', *Journal of Political Ecology* 23, no. 1 (2016): 116, doi:10.2458/v23i1.20182.

34 Marcus Power and James D. Sidaway, 'The Degeneration of Tropical Geography', *Annals of the Association of American Geographers* 94, no. 3 (September 2004): 587, doi:10.1111/j.1467-8306.2004.00415.x.

35 Guilherme Ribeiro, 'Paul Vidal de La Blache – Para Além Da Ingenuidade: Releituras Vidalianas', *GEOgraphia* 10, no. 20 (2008): 124–44.

36 J.K. Gibson-Graham, 'Reading for Difference in the Archives of Tropical Geography: Imagining an (Other) Economic Geography for beyond the Anthropocene', *Antipode* 52, no. 1 (2020): 12–35.

uneven development, a social context that made its way into his own regional geography. As Andrade argued, his geography was always heterodox:[37] what his daughter Ana Maria called his 'strange geography'.[38] Nevertheless, Mateus Litwin Prestes has suggested that Castro's rejuvenation of regional geography itself was his greatest contribution to the discipline.[39]

Castro wrote that he wanted to deploy 'not the descriptive method of the geography of the past, but the interpretative method of the modern science of geography, embodied by the rich intellectual work of Ritter, Humboldt, Jean Brunhes, Vidal de la Blache, Griffith Taylor and others'.[40] Castro's influences included regional geographers of different stripes, languages, and backgrounds, exemplified by his intellectual exchanges with American regional geographers, in particular Preston James[41] and George Cressey.[42] Castro understood geographical disciplinary history as an open field: he was rigorously non-systematic in drawing influences from across schools of thought and academic disciplines. This emerged from his own practice, with its blend of natural science, medicine, nutritional experimentation, urban social fieldwork, political theory, and a wide reading in literature and art. Nevertheless, in his explicitly geographical texts, French regional geography was his starting point. Here we can see his approach to disciplinary history clearly: having laid out this school of influence, Castro makes his movement beyond it clear. He writes in *Geografia da Fome* that his work is not a regional monograph in 'strict terms [...] which would leave aside [the] biological, medical and public health aspects of the problem'. Rather, it is

> always oriented by the fundamental principles of geographical science, [...] within these geographical principles, of localization, extension, causality, correlation and terrestrial unity that we will try to face the phenomenon of hunger. In other words, we will try to undertake an ecological overview, in the broad sense of 'Ecology' as the study of the actions and reactions of living beings in relation to their environment.[43]

Castro was perhaps overly respectful of European geography, but we can see how far he diverged. He took the tools of regional geography – its emphasis on area, place, and modes of life – in order to deal with a new subject: hunger. This is a simple, but radical, manoeuvre that displaces the neutrality of regional geography – its interest in regions for their own sake – and turned it to distinctively political ends. Elsewhere he describes this move as a turn from the 'positive' concerns of geography – a set of

37 Andrade, 'Josué de Castro e Uma Geografia Combatente'.
38 Castro, *Semeador de Ideias*, 22.
39 Prestes, 'O Pensamento de Josué de Castro'.
40 Castro, *Geografia da Fome* (1963), 1:19.
41 James, 'To Josué de Castro. From Department of Geography, Ann Arbor'.
42 Cressey, 'To Josué de Castro'.
43 Castro, *Geografia da Fome* (1963), 1:19.

descriptions and interpretations of man's transformations of the surface of the earth – to a 'negative', sceptical geography that sees the failure of society and its transformations of nature to reproduce life, health, and sustenance.[44] Castro sought to turn geography towards the service of oppressed groups, against the depoliticized geography of La Blache and the French regional school.[45] We might redeploy the Gramscian cliché to see the optimism of Castro's geographical method tempered by the pessimism of his geographical subject.

Yet even as it is surpassed, the region remains important. *Geografia da Fome* moves according to regional logics, demarcating spatial areas with geographical features of diet, landscape, and agriculture and correlating them with types and extents of hunger. This carries over from regional geography a conception of regions as relatively stable figurations that are knowable and examinable.[46] But Castro's thought moved on: twenty years later he made explicit that 'society must be understood as a developing process, not as a set piece. I do not expect, nor would I wish, the social process to hold still while I photograph it.'[47] This surpasses regional geography's static view of the humanized landscape as a 'medal struck in the image of a people'.[48] In the 1960s Castro was developing an 'ecological' attention to the relationship between social processes and environmental transformation. I will explore Castro's later work – his growing interests in relativity, knowledge, and environmentalism – in the final chapter, but it is important that his grounding in regional geography, and his transformation of it, continued until his last years. Regional geography in its Vidalian form is a single science to be applied to many places. Castro came to endorse a quite different thing. In exploring the epistemology of science he held onto both the ecological and the regional, but proposed a reconstructed, regional 'ecology' as a more situated, local structure of knowledge: 'ecology is the science of the future [...] the science of the "eco," of place [...] each place will have its own science, because science is not universal, it is local, it is a science of the region'.[49] This constitutes a different connecting thread between the history of regional geography and the history of political ecology.

Throughout Castro's life the Northeast cropped up as a formative subject, example, and inspiration. His relationship with the place was simultaneously emotional, political, and intellectual. He declared: 'what I write, I owe to

44 Castro, *Geography of Hunger*, 32.
45 Manuel Correia de Andrade, *Poder político e produção do espaço* (Recife: Massangana, 1984); Arruda, 'The Geography of Hunger'.
46 Wainwright, 'The Geographies of Political Ecology', 1035.
47 Castro, *Death in the Northeast*, 4.
48 Cosgrove, 'Towards a Radical Cultural Geography', 2; Anne Buttimer, 'Geography, Humanism, and Global Concern', *Annals of the Association of American Geographers* 80, no. 1 (1990): 17.
49 Castro, 'Développement et Environnement', 28.

the Northeast'.[50] This meant he always stood – as E.M. Forster said of his sometime partner, the Greek modernist poet Constantine Cavafy – at a slight angle to the universe.[51] He was, like Antonio Gramsci, from the backwoods.[52] In Pernambuco's Legislative Assembly in 1958 he said:

> I never forget that this is the place where I first formed a sense of life, that it was here I first understood the meaning of the world, in such a way that, however universal may be the pretension of my achievements, they are always marked by this sense of the earth, by something in essence regional.[53]

Castro's writing about the Northeast was very varied. From what Ferretti has described as the 'geopoetics' of his fiction[54] and his engagement with 'non-European heritages',[55] to his nutritional and ecological exploration of Northeastern flora and fauna, habits of life, and diets, to his urban geography with its tropes of resistance and humanism, Castro's thinking about hunger, space, and nature is profoundly regional. Both his monograph on the city of Recife and his book on the conditions of the working classes in the city are deeply political reflections on the human geography of the Northeast.[56] His two most explicit engagements were *Documentario do Nordeste* (1959), never published in English, and *Sete Palmas de Terra e Uma Caixão* (1965), published as *Death in the Northeast* in 1966. The former is a republication of diverse writings, in particular short works from the 1930s, including *Condições*. That these were republished by Castro in the late 1950s, as the region was in turmoil, shows him shoring up his intellectual credentials as a voice on the Northeastern question, alongside his political activities. *Death in the Northeast*, meanwhile, is a considered reflection on the region in this period. As I return to in the next chapter, it is poignant that this book

50 José Augusto Guerra, 'Um Nome em Evidência: Josué de Castro: Geógrafo da Fome', *O Observador Economico e Financeiro*, August 1958, 270 edition.

51 E.M. Forster, 'The Poetry of C.P. Cavafy', in *Pharos and Pharillon* (London: Hogarth Press, 1923).

52 Michael Ekers et al., '"A Barbed Gift of the Backwoods": Gramsci's Sardinian Beginnings', in *Gramsci: Space, Nature, Praxis*, ed. Alex Loftus et al., 1st ed. (London: John Wiley & Sons, 2013), 3–5.

53 Josué de Castro, 'Speech in Legislative Assembly of Pernambuco', May 1958, 529, CEHIBRA.JdC.

54 Federico Ferretti, 'From the Drought to the Mud: Rediscovering Geopoetics and Cultural Hybridity from the Global South', *Cultural Geographies* 27, no. 4 (2020), doi:1474474020911181.

55 Ferretti, 'Decolonizing the Northeast'.

56 Archie Davies, 'Landscape Semaphore: Seeing Mud and Mangroves in the Brazilian Northeast', *Transactions of the Institute of British Geographers* 46, no. 3 (2021); Archie Davies, 'The Racial Division of Nature: Making Land in Recife', *Transactions of the Institute of British Geographers* 46, no. 2 (November 2020): 270–83, doi:https://doi.org/10.1111/tran.12426.

was written largely from Europe, but prior to 1964 and Castro's exile. The book, written in a late style that was to remain undeveloped in longer works, in which geographical and biosociological methodological strictures are loosened, marks something of a departure for Castro. *Death in the Northeast* gives the impression of a man at an intimate unease with his subject. These books, however, are not Castro's last word on the Northeast. We need to see his broader theory and praxis of underdevelopment as deeply regional itself.

Castro's writings on the Northeast are part of a long tradition in Brazilian studies.[57] Yet discussions of region and nation in Brazilian studies have been at times disconnected from the history of Brazilian geographical ideas. Castro is one of the crucial missing links here. The Northeast itself has a vibrant regionalist tradition – of literature, folklore studies, anthropology, and social sciences – whose twentieth-century figurehead was Gilberto Freyre. Freyre produced a critical understanding of the history of Brazil and an endorsement of a multi-racial conception of society in the Northeast. However, his work relied upon a historical myth of a benign Brazilian form of slavery and a consequent presentist myth of Brazilian racial democracy that manifested in an increasingly conservative, supremacist, and imperialist tenor of thought.[58] But Freyre is only one figure in a much richer tradition. Ironically, the most influential recent work on the Northeast – Durval Muniz de Albuquerque Júnior's *The Invention of the Brazilian Northeast*, published in English in 2014 – denounces or, in spite of the book's impressive scope, ignores a large part of the Northeast's intellectual and political output. As Ronald Chilcote puts it, Albuquerque Júnior 'makes a case that politicians, intellectuals, writers, and artists "invented" the Northeast as a region and calls upon historians to abandon the static categories of regionalism in favour of national unity'.[59] Rogério Haesbaert critiques Albuquerque Júnior's post-modernist notion of 'invention', in which the Northeast is 'less [...] a place than a topos'.[60] Albuquerque Júnior himself dismisses what he calls 'diverse "leftist" intellectuals' for failing to 'invert the official image of the region'.[61] But he has little interest in the actual material forces that produce the region as a space to be negotiated: precisely that which those '"leftist"' intellectuals were interested in themselves. He does not deal with the content or complexities

57 Courtney J. Campbell, 'The Invention of the Brazilian Northeast – by Albuquerque Jr., Durval Muniz De', *Bulletin of Latin American Research* 36, no. 2 (April 2017): 247–48, doi:10.1111/blar.12608.

58 Jessé Souza, *A Modernização Seletiva: Uma Reinterpretação Do Dilema Brasileiro* (Brasília: Universidade de Brasília, 2000), 211.

59 Ronald H. Chilcote, 'Mystifying the Brazilian Northeast', *Latin American Perspectives* 43, no. 2 (March 2016): 238–42, doi:10.1177/0094582X15606885.

60 Rogério Haesbaert, 'Região, regionalização e regionalidade: questões contemporâneas. *Antares* 3 (January–June 2010): 8.

61 Durval Muniz de Albuquerque Jr, *The Invention of the Brazilian Northeast* (Durham, NC, and London: Duke University Press, 1999), 223.

of the modernizing forces and radical political agendas that did emerge in the Northeast in the middle of the twentieth century. He disregards the efflorescence of radical thought and action that sought to remake the region materially and iconographically in thoroughly modern terms.[62] He makes a single reference each to SUDENE and Castro. Though studying imaginary and real geographies, he makes no reference to actual geography or geographers. His bibliography does not include a reference to the most important Brazilian thinker of space and the region (and a Northeasterner) in the twentieth century: Milton Santos.

Similarly, Sarah Sarzynski's recent history of the Northeast around 1964 mentions Castro once, but does not classify him as a geographer – a common feature of his legacy[63] – or cite any work, not even *Death in the Northeast*, a monograph on the agrarian and political movements Sarzynski studies.[64] She gets a number of things wrong about Castro's work: she identifies 'crab people' – referring to Castro's *homem caranguejo* – as a 'new catchphrase' in the early 1960s when Castro first wrote about the cycle of the crab around 1930. This is more than a point of pedantry: both Sarzynski and Albuquerque Júnior proceed through discourse analysis, seeing Northeastern social scientific and political work merely in terms of the propagation of, or resistance to, certain 'tropes', rather than as integral to political projects, or as agential theoretical and political analysis. Their consequent lack of interest in geographical thought – even where their research deals with space – is limiting. It curtails their interest in the actual content of ideas about space and nature that emerged in the Northeast itself. This reproduces the Northeast – as Kirkendall wrote of the 1964 coup – as 'more [...] a problem than [...] a generator of possible solutions'.[65] Albuquerque Júnior argues that the 'invention' of the Northeast 'as a region completely defined by lack and need' is down to the victimhood of Northeastern intellectuals: 'arguments regarding Brazil's dependency and colonial roots of exploitation [...] have little of merit to offer since they share the premise that victimization defines us, that others are always to blame for every aspect of our primitivity, hunger, and misery'.[66] As the historian and Black militant Beatriz Nascimento argued many decades ago, a history of the Northeast told from the perspective of Afro-Brazilian movements and subaltern groups tells a very different story of

---

62 Milton Santos, 'O Futuro Do Nordeste: Da Racionalidade à Contrafinalidade', in *Era Da Esperança: Teoria e Política No Pensamento de Celso Furtado*, ed. Francisco de Sales Gaudencio and Marcos Formiga (Rio de Janeiro: Paz e Terra, 1995), 99–107.

63 Ferretti, 'Geographies of Internationalism'.

64 Sarah Sarzynski, *Revolution in the Terra Do Sol: The Cold War in Brazil* (Stanford, CA: Stanford University Press, 2018).

65 Andrew J. Kirkendall, 'Entering History: Paulo Freire and the Politics of the Brazilian Northeast, 1958–1964', *Luso-Brazilian Review* 41, no. 1 (January 2004): 184, doi:10.3368/lbr.41.1.168.

66 Albuquerque Jr, *The Invention of the Brazilian Northeast*, 224.

conquest and the construction and defence of an imperial, white supremacist Brazilian state project.[67] Albuquerque Júnior's vision fails to account for the actual arguments of dependency analysis or the relational mode of thinking that underscores it. It also disregards the political possibilities of a regional anti-imperialism. I understand Northeastern intellectuals, and the idea of the region, in a very different way. Rather – as per Rogério Haesbaert's couplet of the region as 'arte-fact' – I understand them as dialectically connected to the region as material form and to international movements of thought and politics. I therefore now turn to two key ways in which the geography of the Northeast has been imagined: firstly as *both* the most Brazilian of regions *and* as its most backward and dependent; secondly as a natural space, associated with the Nation, the divine, and the messianic.

Castro writes of the Northeast as 'this piece of our territory so characteristically Brazilian'.[68] 'It is commonly said', wrote Francisco Julião, the Peasant League leader, 'that the roots of Brazilian nationality lie in the North-East, with their origins and focus in Pernambuco'.[69] Julião describes the Northeast's *sertão*, rugged *sertanejos*, landlessness, deep inequality, migratory peoples, and hunger and insists 'this Brazil, or rather this North-East, is the true face of Brazil'.[70] For Julião this is a critique of the nation that emphasizes its divisions and inequality. A similar rhetorical strategy is to describe other regions in Brazil as 'Northeasts'.[71] The Northeast is a potent imaginative geography as much as a material one. In the twentieth century it emerged under two contradictory somatic signs as the most foundationally Brazilian of regions, the heartland, and as subordinate, extraneous, backward, and dependent: the appendix. The notion of the Northeast as backward can be illustrated in culturally and socio-ecologically derived southern superiority complexes, with political and economic correlates and consequences. It also has a racial connotation, with the Northeast associated with racialized Afro-Brazilians, *caboclos*, and *sertanejos*, often couched as inferior to a putatively 'white' South.[72] Being Black and Northeastern in Brazil is to be subject to manifold kinds

---

67 Beatriz Nascimento, 'O Negro Visto Por Ele Mesmo', *Revista Manchete* (Setembro 1976): 130–31; Beatriz Nascimento, 'O Movimento de Antônio Conselheiro e o Abolicionismo: Uma Visão de História Regional', unpublished thesis (1979), 80, Código 2D. Caixa 21, Arquivo Nacional. Fundo Maria Beatriz Nascimento.

68 Castro, *Documentário do Nordeste*, 7.

69 Julião, *Cambão – The Yoke*, 87.

70 Julião, *Cambão – The Yoke*, 90.

71 For example, Franklin de Oliveira, *Rio Grande do Sul: um novo Nordeste* (Rio de Janeiro: Editôra Civilização Brasileira, 1960).

72 Barbara Weinstein, *The Color of Modernity: São Paulo and the Making of Race and Nation in Brazil* (Durham, NC: Duke University Press, 2015); Stanley E. Blake, *The Vigorous Core of Our Nationality* (Pittsburgh, PA: University of Pittsburgh Press, 2011).

of discrimination and disadvantage.[73] When Castro argued against racial anthropology in the 1930s – '*não é mal da raça, é mal da fome*' ('not a flaw of race, but of hunger') – this was also an argument against a regionally inflected racial discourse. As Courtney Campbell has argued, outside the region Northeastern racial identities were mobilized to define a regional identity precisely in order to reproduce the idea that they do not constitute a national identity.[74] The political and economic sides of these tropes can have either regressive or progressive political potential, depending on how they are mobilized and addressed in material terms.

Questions of regional underdevelopment are built on distinctly geographic problems: land, soil, irrigation, landscape, climate, and energy. Albuquerque Júnior argues that the term 'Northeast' 'as a regional designation originated [...] to describe a space specifically related to droughts, and the need for federal aid'.[75] Certainly the way in which the region came to be understood was intimately associated with its climate and ecology. The 1920s and 1930s saw the rise and fall of regional separatism among the Northeastern sugar élites, associated in particular with Gilberto Freyre's thought. This interacted with ebbs and flows of national state aid and intervention targeted at alleviating drought.[76] Amélia Cohn, in 1976, argued that 'the problem presented by the Northeast for the nation is configured, up to now, as a *regional* problem, represented by droughts':[77] that is, an ecological space determined by the dynamics of drought in the *sertão*. But the Brazilian Northeast was a site of geographical contention. It came into being, as a region and as a place (the distinction between the two not being hierarchical, but hermeneutic[78]), through an often contradictory set of processes, deeply entangling ideas of place with those of ecology. The geographical demarcation of the Northeast employed by the state, in

73 Sueli Carneiro, *Racismo, sexismo e desigualdade no Brasil* (São Paulo: Selo Negro, 2015); Maria Beatriz Nascimento, 'O Conceito de Quilombo e a Resistência Cultural Negra', *Revista Afrodiáspora* 3, nos 6–7 (1985): 41–49; Lélia Gonzalez, 'Racismo e sexismo na cultura brasileira', in *Pensamento Feminista Brasileiro*, ed. Heloisa Buarque de Holanda, 1st ed. (Rio de Janeiro: Bazar do Tempo, 2019).

74 Courtney J. Campbell, 'Four Fishermen, Orson Welles, and the Making of the Brazilian Northeast', *Past & Present* 234, no. 1 (February 2017): 173–212, doi:10.1093/pastj/gtw052.

75 Albuquerque Jr, *The Invention of the Brazilian Northeast*, 38; Campbell, 'Four Fishermen'.

76 Eve Buckley, 'Drought in the Sertão as a Natural or Social Phenomenon: Establishing the Inspetoria Federal de Obras Contra as Secas, 1909–1923', *Boletim Do Museu Paraense Emílio Goeldi. Ciências Humanas* 5, no. 2 (August 2010): 379–98, doi:10.1590/S1981-81222010000200011.

77 Amélia Cohn, *Crise Regional e Planejamento* (São Paulo: Perspectiva, 1976), 56.

78 Milton Santos, *A natureza do espaço: técnica e tempo, razão e emoção*, 4th ed. (São Paulo: Universidade de São Paulo, 2009), 108.

various forms, fluctuated,[79] but it was always associated with a set of socio-natural relations particular to the region.[80] As Breno Viotto Pedrosa's work has shown, the ecology, infrastructure, and space of the region was also the subject not only of Milton Santos' work in this period but of that of visiting left-wing French geographers, including Jean Tricart, Jean Dresch, and Pierre George. These engagements between Brazilian and French geography led to work on planning, regionalization, and geomorphology, as well as becoming the basis for Santos' influential output over the longer term. Indeed, the connections established at this time led to collaborative development of ideas about the region in geography, for instance in the 1968 seminar 'La régionalisation de l'espace au Brésil' [The regionalization of space in Brazil] held at the Centre of Studies of Tropical Geography at the University of Bordeaux, where Santos worked in exile.[81] Castro, and the debates I analyse below, were key precursors of this work.

One essential tenet of the region's artifice, art, and factuality is drought. Drought was the most important initial correlate of Castro's central argument that hunger was a social, not a natural, phenomenon. He debunked the idea – like many later political ecologists and political economists[82] – that climatic conditions were the direct cause of hunger in the Northeast: 'the most important problem of the Northeast is far from being that of drought. Drought is just the drop of water that makes the pool of suffering of the Northeast overflow. Drought is absolutely secondary.'[83] Picking up on chapter 2, translation, here, is theoretically productive. Drought, in Castro's original Portuguese here, is 'a sêca'. This term can also mean a permanently dry place[84]: it is partly a spatial as well as a temporal concept. For Castro 'the problem of water is important in the Northeast, but much more important is the problem of man'.[85] Drought raises the question of who is to blame and who is going to do something about it, but also raises questions about the spatial, social, political, and ecological constitution of the region itself. This leads to the deeply political issues of the state and of infrastructure. All of

79 Buckley, 'Drought'; Eve Buckley, *Technocrats and the Politics of Drought and Development in Twentieth-Century Brazil* (Chapel Hill, NC: UNC Press Books, 2017).

80 Campbell, 'Four Fishermen'.

81 Breno Viotto Pedrosa, 'O Périplo Do Exílio de Milton Santos e a Formação de Sua Rede de Cooperação', *História, Ciências, Saúde-Manguinhos* 25, no. 2 (June 2018): 429–48, doi:10.1590/s0104-59702018000200008; see also Gavin P. Bowd and Daniel W. Clayton, 'Geographical Warfare in the Tropics: Yves Lacoste and the Vietnam War', *Annals of the Association of American Geographers* 103, no. 3 (May 2013): 639–41, doi:10.1080/00045608.2011.653729.

82 Amartya Sen, *The Political Economy of Hunger: Volume 1: Entitlement and Well-Being*, (Oxford: Oxford University Press, 1991); Davis, *Late Victorian Holocausts*.

83 Castro and Furtado, 'Operação Nordeste: Dois Nomes e Duas Opiniões', 33.

84 *Dicionária Priberam da Língua Portuguesa*, 'Consulte o significado/definição de seca', accessed 12 October 2018, https://dicionario.priberam.org/seca.

85 Josué de Castro, 'Interview Typescript' (draft, 58 1952), 76, CEHIBRA.JdC.

this suggests the political ecology of the region itself: that is, the region is produced as a territorially demarcated, active part of space whose existence as such depends on a politicized conception of nature.

Marilena Chauí's work helps us understand the philosophical, historical, and political stakes of nature here. It can help identify the stakes of nature here, and of Castro's geographical intervention into understandings of the Brazilian Northeast. In a seminal essay recently translated by Maite Conde, Chauí associates the Brazilian 'foundation myth' with a renaissance Portuguese conflation of Nature and Brazil rooted in Catholic legal doctrine and medieval European myths of the Fortunate Islands to be found in the West. This produced the image of Brazil–Nature, captured in the Brazilian flag, whose four colours

> do not express politics or relate to the country's history. It is a symbol of nature. It is Brazil as garden, Brazil-paradise. Any Brazilian child knows very well that the green represents our forests, the yellow our mineral wealth, the blue the perfection of our sky, the white the kindness of our good natured hearts.[86]

This foundation myth required extraordinary contortions by the colonizing Portuguese in order to justify the plantation economic system based on slavery: 'the enslavement of Indians and Blacks shows us that God and the Devil do battle in the Land of the Sun. It could be no different, since the serpent inhabited paradise.'[87] Chauí further defines the spatiality of this profoundly political and ecological 'image of Brazil-Nature' as associated with the Northeast's internal divisions. 'The cosmic battle between God and the Devil that appears in the colonial period [is not due to] social divisions, but to divisions of and in nature itself: the New World is divided between the coast and the backlands.'[88] Chauí's analysis dissolves Albuquerque's more simplistic notion that 'the Northeast is a child of the ruins of an older conceptual geography of Brazil that posited a national segmentation into North and South'.[89] For Chauí, a more precise ideology of space and nature was at stake. If 'Said [...] drew from Gramsci a sensitivity for the ways in which imperial geographies come to be accepted as natural',[90] then we can draw from Chauí a specific idea of such imperial geographies in the Brazilian context, the work that 'natural' did, and the work that such imaginative geographies of nature have since done.

The *sertão* – the dry inland of the Northeast – is, as a kind of place, relational: it exists in terms of a coast, or a centre. The English translation reveals this: backlands are the back of somewhere.[91] Castro drew his

---

86 Chauí, *Between Conformity and Resistance*, 117.

87 Chauí, *Between Conformity and Resistance*, 120.

88 Chauí, *Between Conformity and Resistance*, 120.

89 Albuquerque Jr, *The Invention of the Brazilian Northeast*, 15.

90 Wainwright, 'The Geographies of Political Ecology', 1036.

91 Tayguara Torres Cardoso, 'Josué de Castro e os sertões nordestinos de Geografia da Fome', in *Memória Do Saber: Josué De Castro*, vol. 1 (Rio de Janeiro: Conselho

understanding of the *sertões* not only from research and personal experience but from the regional literature of the Northeast, in particular Graciliano Ramos and Rachel de Queiroz. He wrote about these novelists as truly disruptive, even 'proletarian' voices against the complacencies of Brazilian literature's intellectualism.[92] A key precursor for Castro in geographical study of the Northeast was Euclides da Cunha. For Chauí, Euclides' description 'substitut[es] God and the Devil for science, that is, a study of the climate, geology, and geography' of the *sertão*.

> Euclides describes a land tortured by the fury of the elements. He describes a rape. Feminized, the land is assaulted, tormented; its intimate texture is martyred, beaten by the heat and degraded by the rain. Yet, this tragic vision of a tortured nature is counterposed with epic descriptions of its inhabitant – the *sertanejo* [...] establishing a contrast between the land's feminine pain with his courageous masculine force.[93]

Chauí argues that this conception of nature underwrites narratives of natural, racial destiny critical to the spatial conquest of the interior and the west of the country. This 'geography of power'[94] drove integralist and fascistic national imaginaries in the first half of the twentieth century and relates not only to the concentrations of force in the Centre–South but also to how that force was reliant on spaces imagined to be subservient. Reliant in two ways: first as the material conditions of the possibility for power, with the West and the Northeast functioning as sites of primitive accumulation and expansion, and secondly as discursive resources for nation-building.[95] Exploring the ideologies of nature and nation that underpinned such projects, Chauí returns to the prophecy of the messianic figure of the *sertão*, Antônio Conselheiro: 'the backlands will become the sea and the sea will become the backlands', a prophecy repeated and reimagined in popular music and *cinema novo* in the 1960s.[96] In a stylish turn of phrase, elegantly translated by Conde, Chauí writes that, 'intoxicated by nature, we entered history'. 'Brazil, a Portuguese discovery, entered history through the gates of paradise. This idea will become the dominant class's version of this country, according to which our history has already been written.'[97] The gendered, colonial concept of nature can be seen in productivist narratives of modernist economic development and infrastructure in the arid Northeast, conceptualized, as Chauí describes, as passive, inert, and

---

Nacional de Desenvolvimento Científico e Tecnológico: Fundação Miguel de Cervantes, 2012), 524.

92 Josué de Castro, 'O Nordeste e o Romance Brasileiro', in *Documentário do Nordeste*, 2nd ed. (São Paulo: Editôra Brasiliense, 1959), 59–68.

93 Chauí, *Between Conformity and Resistance*, 121.

94 Chauí, *Between Conformity and Resistance*, 122.

95 Diacon, *Stringing Together a Nation*.

96 Sarzynski, *Revolution in the Terra Do Sol*, 1–3.

97 Chauí, *Between Conformity and Resistance*, 131.

inferior.[98] The intoxication with nature relies on a profound semantic division, by which the natural landscape of the Northeast is associated with the nation, the divine, and the messianic. Chauí therefore helps us locate the importance of Castro's intervention into the political natures of the Northeast. Castro at times wrote in masculinist and conquistorial terms about the colonization of land,[99] but, contrary to intoxication, he recasts the Northeast's landscape as already and continually a product of human intervention and socio-economic forces, and configures messianic politics as driven by the injustice of endemic hunger. Nature–Nation is no longer earthly paradise and natural racial destiny, but the exploitative landscapes of colonial social relations. As black Brazilian Brazilian scholars have long shown, these relations remain woven deeply into Brazil's social structure to today.[100] Castro's fundamental geographical analysis – that drought is not a 'natural' but a social phenomenon – is therefore a powerful intervention in the epistemology of nature and the spatial politics of the Northeast.

The Struggle for SUDENE: Praxis and Theory of the Underdeveloped Region

Haesbaert's notion of the dialectically connected quality of the region as arte-fact requires moving from geographical imaginaries to the material transformations that produced the region as a space to be negotiated. These transformations were a hot political topic between 1955 and 1964. Different groups were trying to produce the Northeast as a region in opposing ways. Conflicting assessments of the economic, political, and ecological drivers of the Northeast's problems were also epistemological debates over scale: over what it meant to define the Northeast's problems as predominately local, national, or international.

To prioritize the region as a scale here is to say two things. First, that we can't understand Brazilian thought or politics in this period – whether in terms of the cold war, agrarian social relations, or national developmentalism – without thinking about the region. Secondly, it is to dwell on those radical projects that sought to materially transform the region. This praxis of radical regionalism included SUDENE, but also attempts at agrarian and land reform and the radical governments of Miguel Arraes in Recife and Pernambuco. In various ways these were practical attempts to remake the region by unpicking

98 James Scott, *Seeing Like a State: How Certain Schemes to Improve the Human Condition Have Failed*, new ed. (New Haven, CT: Yale University Press, 1999).

99 For example, Josué de Castro, 'Regionalismo e Paisagem Cultural' (notes, undated), 76, CEHIBRA.JdC.

100 Beatriz Nascimento, 'Por Uma História Do Homem Negro', in *Eu Sou Atlântica: Sobre a Trajetória de Vida de Beatriz Nascimento. São Paulo: Instituto Kuanza*, by Alex Ratts (São Paulo: Imprensa Oficial, 2006), 93–97; Lélia Gonzalez, *Por um feminismo afro-latino-americano* (São Paulo: Editora Schwarcz – Companhia das Letras, 2020).

and reconstituting the material drivers of regional underdevelopment. That required, therefore, a theory of regional underdevelopment in the first place. While enlightened technocrats figure heavily in this discussion, radical regionalism emerges through not only intellectuals but also peasant leagues, grassroots movements, films, institutions, and public debates. This was praxis as theory. That SUDENE was a patrician project is significant – it is one of the reasons that it ultimately failed – but must be placed in context. There were observable connections not only between technocrats and peasants but across the intellectual worlds of dependency theory and agrarian movements. For instance, in February 1964, there appeared, in the newspaper of the Peasant Leagues, *Liga*, distributed directly to peasants and organizers in the *sertão*, a translation of Andre Gunder Frank's *Monthly Review* article on the 'development of underdevelopment' of July 1963. This translation, writes the journalist in *Liga*, has as its original a translation of Frank's work published by the *Movimento de Izquierda Revolucionária* [The Movement of the Revolutionary Left] in Cuzco, Peru.[101] This flow of knowledge is worth emphasizing for its intimations of divisions between the rural Northeast and the rest of the country. At the time that *Liga* published Frank's first major foray into what became dependency theory he was working at the University of Brasília.[102] Yet the article did not reach *Liga* through the backlands of Brazil but via the highlands of Peru. The wider anticolonial project – in the context of which I am suggesting the struggles of the radical Northeast should be seen – was peppered with elite, enlightened technocrats, often attempting to align themselves with grassroots movements.

Third Worldist intellectuals were critical to the largest emancipatory movement of the twentieth century: decolonization. The technocratic tenor of SUDENE can be read in this key. This might seem an unusual extension, but it was not only in Third World contexts that the idea of rational planning had a radical, even anti-imperialist tenor. As David Harvey noted of the 1960s in British geography, 'you need to remember that for many of us who had some political ambitions for the discipline, rational planning was not a bad word in the sixties [...] the efficiency of regional and urban planning was going to be a lever of social betterment for the whole population'.[103] In exploring economic planning, though, in the Northeast we cannot ignore agrarian reform. In the 1950s 'the problem of agrarian reform, hitherto avoided as being too explosive to touch, became an obligatory item in all political discussions'.[104] Castro had been arguing for agrarian reform since

101 Anonymous, 'Liga, 2nd February 1964', in *Ligas Camponesas Outubro 1962 – Abril 1964*, ed. Francisco Julião, CIDOC Cuaderno 27 (Cuernavaca: Centro Intercultural de Documentación, 1969), 493.

102 Anonymous, 'Anders Gunder Frank, Biography', Personal, *AG Frank Personal Website* (blog), accessed 11 January 2018, http://rrojasdatabank.info/agfrank/personal.html#short.

103 Harvey, *Spaces of Capital*, 5.

104 Arraes, *Brazil*, 152.

the 1930s, but reform efforts had failed and the state of tension increased throughout the 1950s. Rural organizers and peasants were subject to incessant violence and repression amid accusations of communist activity and rumours of violent revolt.[105] In September 1955 Castro hosted the first meeting of rural workers in Pernambuco, with thousands of peasants marching through Recife. As Featherstone argues, with Gramsci, it is important to be 'attentive to the spatial practices through which solidarities are constructed'[106] and this movement of rural workers into urban Recife was a key moment in building Northeastern solidarities in this period. It can be seen as prefiguring the alliances of Arraes and the *Frente do Recife* [Recife Front] that would emerge at the end of the decade.[107] In a speech at the march in 1955, Castro compared the struggle over Engenho Galileia with Jesus's struggle in Galilee.[108] Arguably the high point of the Peasant Leagues' movement was the Congress in Belo Horizonte in 1961, which marked a victory for more radical elements of the rural movements. Celso Furtado thought the agrarian movement had the characteristics of classic pre-revolutionary formations[109] and Antonio Callado called Pernambuco a 'pilot revolution' under Miguel Arraes.[110] Much of this discussion is laced with a hope many on the left in Brazil felt in the years before the coup.[111] They certainly played a part in raising the political stakes of the time: Vânia Bambirra, for example, argued that rural unrest in the Northeast was critical to the rupture of 1964, citing large strikes in May 1963.[112]

Castro had longstanding political and personal relationships with peasant leaders – including the divisive Francisco Julião[113] – but was himself not

---

105 Vandeck Santiago, Pernambuco em chamas: a intervenção dos EUA e o Golpe de 1964 (Recife: CePe Editora, 2016); Sarzynski, Revolution in the Terra Do Sol, 20–40; Luciana de Barros Jaccoud, *Movimentos sociais e crise política em Pernambuco, 1955–1968* (Recife: Fundação Joaquim Nabuco, Editora Massangana, 1990).

106 David Featherstone, '"Gramsci in Action": Space, Politics, and the Making of Solidarities', in *Gramsci: Space, Nature, Politics*, ed. Alex Loftus et al., 1st ed. (London: John Wiley & Sons, 2013), 68.

107 José Arlindo Soares, *A frente do Recife e o governo do Arraes: nacionalismo em crise, 1955–1964* (Rio de Janeiro, RJ: Paz e Terra, 1982); Pereira, *The End of the Peasantry*, 121–22.

108 Sarzynski, *Revolution in the Terra Do Sol*, 36.

109 Santos de Morais Clodomir, 'Entrevista: Clodomir Morais – Os camponeses e suas Ligas combatentes', March 2003, accessed 17 June 2022, https://anovademocracia. br/no-7/1233-entrevista-clodomir-morais-os-camponeses-e-suas-ligas-combatentes.

110 Callado, *Industriais da sêca*.

111 Rogers, *The Deepest Wounds*, 133–35.

112 Vania Bambirra, 'Exodo Rural y Exodo Urbano: La Lucha Por La Reforma Agraria En Brasil', in *Los Retos de La Globalización, Ensayos En Homenaje a Theotonio Dos Santos*, vol. 1 (Caracas: UNESCO, 1998); Forman, 'Disunity and Discontent'.

113 Forman, 'Disunity and Discontent'; Anthony Pereira, 'Profeta no exílio: o retorno no mito de Francisco Julião', *Cadernos de Estudos Sociais* 7, no. 1 (1991), https://

convinced of the Peasant Leagues' revolutionary potential, and his relationship with Julião was also somewhat fraught.[114] Castro emphasized that the Leagues were a manifestation of desperation: their initial demand was not even for the rights of the living, but for a decent funeral.[115] His relationship with the communist pedagogue Clodomir Santos de Morais – another key Peasant League leader – was more important: they remained in epistolary contact in the late 1960s, and in 1968 Castro discussed with Morais the possibility of writing a further analysis of the Peasant Leagues and their role in the Northeast.[116]

Castro had long argued that agrarian reform was about not only appropriation and redistribution of land but also 'a process of revision of the legal and economic relations between those who hold ownership of agricultural land and those work it'.[117] In the early 1950s he was part of a National Commission on Agrarian Policy. He had sought advice and support from the FAO, requesting experts 'with experience in the problem of land division as such, as well as to the classification of land with regard to its agricultural possibilities'.[118] The commission did not achieve meaningful reform. The Brazilian constitution required compensation for expropriated land, so the key question became whether land should be given 'just value', 'historical value', or 'attributed value'. Clashes between the *latifundia* and reformers crystallized around these questions and reform efforts stalled. SUDENE emerged in part as a way around the fact that a large part of the state – particularly the lower house of Parliament[119] – was an extension of the interests of landed capital, from whom it faced strong resistance.[120] As Haesbaert suggests, the region is a piece of 'political hardware': in the absence of structural reform, it was to be put to new uses.

Castro was sympathetic to the SUDENE project, but keen to debate and influence its make-up. Here, I come back to Milton Santos' contention: when

fundaj.emnuvens.com.br/CAD/article/view/1095; Pereira, 'O Declínio das Ligas Camponesas', 253–55.

114 An article mildly critiquing Castro by Julião is acerbically annotated in Castro's archive. See Francisco Julião, 'Encuentro con América', *El Dia*, December 1969, sec. Fía y Política, 25, CEHIBRA.JdC; Josué de Castro, 'Annotations on article "Encuentro con América" by Franciscio Julião' (Annotations, December 1969), 25, CEHIBRA.JdC.

115 Castro, *Death in the Northeast*, 7.

116 Letter to Morais, published in Clodomir, 'Josué de Castro: Brasileiro e Cidadão Do Mundo'.

117 Josué de Castro, 'A Reforma Agrária – Um Imperative Nacional', *Revista do Clube Militar*, 1957, 220, CEHIBRA.JdC.

118 Castro, 'Letters to Herbert Broadley'.

119 Oliveira, *Elegia para uma Re(li)gião*, 47–53.

120 Valdênio Freitas Meneses, 'Um "Macarthismo Hidráulico" Contra a Sudene: Notas Sobre a Disputa Entre o Senador Argemiro de Figueiredo e Celso Furtado (1959–1963)', *Cadernos Do Desenvolvimento* 11, no. 19 (2016): 83–102.

thinking about drought in the Northeast it is Castro first, Furtado second. In April 1959 Furtado and Castro directly debated this question on the radio programme 'Cartas na Mesa' [Cards on the Table].[121] A transcript was published by the magazine *O Observador Econômico e Financiero*: 'Operação Nordeste: Dois Nomes e Duas Opinões' [Operation Northeast: Two Names and Two Opinions]. This provides us with a key source for analysing Castro's geographical mode of thinking about the Northeast and the emerging Weberian approach of Celso Furtado.[122] Furtado had just published *Operação Nordeste*, commissioned by President Kubitschek, which laid out not only the political and economic philosophy of what was to become SUDENE but also its core plan of action.

The two men's initial statements of position reveal distinct interpretations of the spatial and ecological dimensions of regional underdevelopment.[123] In *Operação Nordeste* Furtado proposed moving tens of thousands of people to Maranhão for agricultural colonization. Defending this displacement, he said the problem of where the workforce was located, 'for us economists, [...] seems very simple'.[124] Castro's humanist geography is opposed to such forced movement. Furtado's response is illuminating: the combination of factors of production is a question of '*técnica*' [technics] and technology. The debate therefore prefigures concerns of theoretical and critical geographers in following decades. I'll return to this in the next chapter, but *técnica* was to become central to Milton Santos' work on spatial theory,[125] as it was to Castro's critique of 'progress' and 'development'.[126] Debates over technology were also significant at the time to the emerging Prebisch–Singer hypothesis of declining terms of trade, which underpinned much of dependency theory's work. Furtado and Castro debated precisely the spatial division of labour and the relationship between labour, land, and territory. The structuralist economics of Furtado here came into contact with the proto-political ecology, and human geography, of Castro. While Furtado's solution appears radical, Castro argued that it was fundamentally aimed at an effect not a cause. The

121 See also other public debates between Furtado and Castro in December 1962. 'Celso Presta Contas ao Conselho: "SUDENE Cumpriu as Suas Tarefas'. *Última Hora*. Recife. Terça-Feira, 4 December 1962, 3.

122 This is how Oliveira characterises Furtado's thought. Though a Marxist by instinct, Oliveira sees his old colleague above all as a Weberian. See Francisco de Oliveira, 'A criação da Sudene', *Cadernos do Desenvolvimento* 5, no. 7 (October 2010): 17–22.

123 Tayguara Torres Cardoso, 'Sertão Nordestino, Desenvolvimento e População –Josué de Castro, Celso Furtado e o debate em torno da "Operação Nordeste"', in *Encontro Nacional de Estudos Populacionais* (Campinas: Campinas, 2008), 17; Magno, *Memória Do Saber*.

124 Castro and Furtado, 'Operação Nordeste: Dois Nomes e Duas Opinões', 29.

125 Archie Davies, 'Milton Santos: The Conceptual Geographer and the Philosophy of Technics', *Progress in Human Geography* 43, no. 3 (January 2018), 1–8, doi:10.1177/0309132517753809.

126 Castro, *Ensaios de biologia social*, 183–85.

avowed dialectician, Furtado, stood accused by the erstwhile regional geographer, Castro, of being insufficiently dialectical: 'it does not seem to me that a structural excess of work-force is sufficient to authorize this displacement [of people]. Structure is in movement. It is dynamic. It is exactly upon this structure that we must act.'[127] Furtado defended his plan, saying capital is a limiting factor, so the movement of people was necessary. Castro retorted that moving thousands of people to new lands is surely expensive.

Castro then turned to Recife and the cycle of the crab. By referring to the *mocambópolis* – city of mocambos –, Castro was connecting urban poverty directly to the macro-economic policy debates of underdevelopment and dependency. In bringing the socio-natural conditions of urban life into discussions over the regional production of space he was ahead of his time. Fifty-one years later, in 2010, Francisco de Oliveira, the political and economic theorist who worked with Furtado as a young man at SUDENE,[128] wrote that returning to the original problem – the poverty of the Northeast as a *rural* region – was not adequate. 'The greatest destitution today is urban. It is in this context that the question of the Northeast must be confronted, if not, it will have no resolution.'[129] It was central, too, to Oliveira's broader theorization of Brazilian political economy[130] and the upsurge of work on Brazilian urbanism and inequality. In 1959, Castro was already exploring these questions.

A key point of differentiation emerged in the debate when Castro suggested that natural conditions can be changed. Furtado, meanwhile, promoted the Northeast's 'pastoral vocation'. Castro's longstanding geographical argument was in play: social outcomes are not determined by natural conditions, but by their interplay with political and economic structure. Furtado was more willing to propose solutions that ran with the grain of existing rural structures. Covering land reform, irrigation, institutional structures, agricultural incentives, and the pricing of water, Castro critiqued Furtado for failing to make a clear statement in favour of agrarian reform. The latter's position is ambiguous and cautious, and Castro insisted that he had skipped over the most important factor in the Northeast's economic problems: the structure of agrarian social relations.[131] Furtado seems on the back foot: 'I hope to be able to create an irrigated agriculture in the Northeast with a social purpose. And I hope that with Dr Josué, in the Parliament, with his prestige, with his dialectical power, will contribute to giving us the necessary instruments.'[132] While the 'necessary instruments' (i.e. meaningful legislative agrarian reform) are

127 Castro and Furtado, 'Operação Nordeste: Dois Nomes e Duas Opiniões', 29.
128 Roberto Schwarz, 'Preface with Questions', *New Left Review* II, no. 24 (2003): 31–39.
129 Oliveira, 'A criação da Sudene', 18.
130 Francisco de Oliveira, 'The Duckbilled Platypus', *New Left Review* II, no. 24 (2003): 43–44.
131 Castro and Furtado, 'Operação Nordeste: Dois Nomes e Duas Opiniões'.
132 'Operação Nordeste', in Magno, *Memória Do Saber*.

elusive, Furtado staked out the ground of the enlightened technocrat as a means to manage Castro's political commitment.

This political difference is connected to differing conceptions of nature. As Doreen Massey put it, 'a lot of thinking about place has nature as the stable backdrop, as the eternal',[133] and Castro's role in this debate – specifically here, and more broadly – was to unsettle that conception. Castro resisted Furtado's characterization of rural poverty as a consequence of the quality of the soil: the quality of the soil, Castro insisted, was a historical, political, and economic problem itself:

> Castro – Sugar cane exhausted the soil by deeply unsuitable forms of cultivation [...] I want to insist that we are not dealing with a physical problem. It is not a problem of the richness or poorness of the soil. It is an economic problem.

> Furtado – It is a physical problem: the problem of the quantity of land per person working in agriculture, land that, as I said, is a little more than half as good as that which we see in the centre-south of Brazil.

> Castro – But I consider this ratio to be a human, economic problem and not a physical problem. Physical problems are the type of the soil, its fertility, its biotic potential [...] the volume of population that rely on it cannot be considered as part of its physical condition. The population is a human condition, not physical.[134]

Castro was not alone in identifying sugar as a despoiling crop that transformed the environment,[135] a position that has since become received wisdom,[136] but it seems he did not convince Furtado. In 1964 the latter wrote that 'the agricultural pattern that predominates throughout the country, based on rudimentary techniques, has been increasing its costs as a result of the *natural exhaustion* of soil and the moving of farms further inland from the principal consumption centres along the coast' (my emphasis).[137] Furtado's analysis, unlike Castro's, sees environmental exploitation as a stable factor of production, not a dynamic moment in the expansion of colonialism and capitalism. This point is intrinsic to practical political problems: whether to directly intervene in agrarian social relations or hope they will resolve themselves by industrial investment, what Castro called the choice between 'bread and steel'. This choice has spatial

---

133 Doreen Massey et al., 'The Possibilities of a Politics of Place Beyond Place? A Conversation with Doreen Massey', *Scottish Geographical Journal* 125, nos 3–4 (September 2009): 412, doi:10.1080/14702540903364443.
134 Castro and Furtado, 'Operação Nordeste: Dois Nomes e Duas Opiniões'.
135 Julião, *Cambão – The Yoke*, 31.
136 Andrade, *Land and People*.
137 Celso Furtado, *Diagnosis of the Brazilian Crisis* (Berkeley and Los Angeles: University of California Press, 1965), xxi.

implications. Castro criticized the post-1964 government for directing investment to already industrialized areas: without balanced development through structural reform and geographically distributed state investment in agrarian and industrial sectors the fundamental contradictions in the Brazilian economy would remain.[138]

In spite of Castro's critiques and Furtado's caution, the founding of SUDENE was a seminal moment that 'divide[d] the history of the Northeast into a before and an after'.[139] The idea to use economic planning produced the Northeast as an experimental site of developmental economics, just as it was a pre-revolutionary rural tinder-box. From the expansion of reservoirs through to the relocation of workers to distant parts of Maranhão, the developmentalist regional planning deepened and broadened a politics of state intervention in rural economies. SUDENE was not the only instance of such attempts, which also extended to the *Companhia do Vale do São Francisco* [The San Francisco Valley Company], a project enacted in collaboration with the United States and modelled on the Tennessee Valley Authority. Breno Viotto Pedrosa sees this organization as also influenced by ongoing debates over geography and planning. Milton Santos was involved in an economic planning commission in Bahia, just south of Pernambuco.[140] Not least through Santos this was closely tied to the development and application of Brazilian geography at the University of Bahia's Laboratory of Geomorphology and Regional Studies.[141] SUDENE was a very different kind of approach, however, with the direct intention of altering the balance of class power in the region. This was a new vision for the regional state. The shifting beneficiaries of intervention were no longer venal landowners who controlled federal agencies but new agents of developmentalist policy: the progressive state, the regional commercial farmer, the mid-scale industrialist, and external capital, all coordinated in the public interest by the radical technocrat.

The plan for SUDENE amounted to the production of a new scale and form of the region. Treating the Northeast as a whole for economic purposes was still controversial, with many arguing that it was too diverse for such an approach.[142] This rescaling was attempted through a material reinterpretation of the area that the regional state could act upon: for instance, the state of Maranhão was incorporated into SUDENE's remit, even though it

138 Castro, *The Geopolitics of Hunger*, 165–95.

139 Paul Singer, 'Crítica e Rememoração', in *Francisco de Oliveira: A Tarefa Da Crítica*, ed. Cibele Saliba Rizek and Wagner de Melo Romão (Belo Horizonte: Editora UFMG, 2006), 15.

140 Pedrosa, 'O Périplo Do Exílio de Milton Santos e a Formação de Sua Rede de Cooperação'.

141 Milton Santos and Ana Carvalho, *A Geografia Aplicada* (Salvador: Universidade da Bahia, 1960).

142 Hans Singer, *Estudo Sôbre o Desenvolvimento Econômico Do Nordeste* (Recife: Comissão de Desenvolvimento Econômico de Pernambuco, 1962), 124.

was not normally considered part of the Northeast.[143] SUDENE also tried to alter investment flows as tax incentives encouraged investment from the Centre–South into the Northeast (tellingly, after 1964, the same mechanisms encouraged foreign investment in the Northeast[144]). These approaches altered the region's relationship with the nation, but also with the global and the local. In 1961 Castro was still an important spokesman for the need for radical regional reform as a prerequisite for national development.[145] He was optimistic about SUDENE's early achievements[146] and wrote later that, following the debates of SUDENE's early years, outlined above, in the years up to 1964 Furtado 'began to see the situation in its totality and to pay attention not only to industrialization but to the much more serious and immediate agricultural problems'.[147] In 1964, in Castro's analysis, the 'people and movements [...] represent a variety of forces which are all going in the same general direction – toward emancipation [...] the problems, desires and movements sprang spontaneously from the social structure of the region and were charged emotionally by a climate of despair'.[148] He wrote this just prior to the military coup of 1964. The region was the site of both political hope and socio-political risk.

Like in Swyngedouw's analysis of Spain's early twentieth-century hydraulic mission, SUDENE sought to construct new political spatialities.[149] Reconsidering 'regional political ecology', Peter Walker argues that 'the meso-scale of regional and especially county-level political institutions [... are] key arenas of environmental politics'.[150] This was certainly the case for SUDENE. However, state interventions in 'environmental politics' are themselves efforts to construct scale: here, the region. Conceptualizing the regional state through its manifestation as infrastructure or land reform treats it not as a fixed entity, object, or thing but as 'produced through – and help[ing to] reproduce – historically and geographically specific socioecological processes. When the state is de-fetishized in this way [...] we can introduce a helpful distinction between the state *qua* apparatus and *qua* relation.'[151]

143 Laurindo Mékie Pereira, 'A Questão Regional No Pensamento de Antonio Gramsci e Celso Furtado', *Topoi (Rio de Janeiro)* 10, no. 18 (June 2009): 48–66, doi:10.1590/2237-101X010018005; Oliveira, *Elegia para uma Re(li)gião*, 37.
144 Oliveira, *Noiva da revolução/Elegia para uma re(li)gião*, 263–70.
145 Josué de Castro, 'Problema Regional e Problema Nacional', *Diario de São Paulo*, April 1961, sec. Suplemento espacial – A Integração do Nordeste, 5, CEHIBRA.JdC.
146 Various, 'Newspaper Clippings 1961: Northeast' (1961), 5, CEHIBRA.JdC.
147 Castro, *Death in the Northeast*, 184.
148 Castro, *Death in the Northeast*, 168.
149 Swyngedouw, 'Technonatural Revolutions', 11.
150 Walker, 'Reconsidering "Regional" Political Ecologies', 25.
151 James Angel, 'Towards an Energy Politics In-Against-and-Beyond the State: Berlin's Struggle for Energy Democracy', *Antipode* 49, no. 3 (June 2017): 557–76, doi:10.1111/anti.12289.

Thinking of SUDENE as a relational actor helps to understand the debates about nature and space that attended its creation. These debates were not simply about economic policy but about the existence of the Northeast in relation to the local, the national, and the international. They were debates, too, about the region in relation to contested, specific, spatially defined socio-natures – the polygon of droughts, the *sertão*, and the *mocambópolis* – which, as the discussion of Chauí and Euclides above demonstrates, were profoundly important geographical imaginaries.

The Northeast, Castro, and Dependency Theory

SUDENE emerged from prior attempts 'to identify the new nature of the "regional" relations of Brazil under the aegis of the capitalist expansion radiating from the Centre-South'.[152] In other words, it emerged amid the beginnings of dependency theory. Hans Singer, one of the authors of a key tenet of dependency theory – the Prebisch–Singer hypothesis of declining terms of trade – visited the Northeast in 1953 while working for the UN. Another, Paul Baran, visited SUDENE in the early 1960s to give a seminar.[153] Hans Singer, in 1953, wrote a report analysing the Northeastern economy, which argued in part that agrarian structure was a key factor in the Northeast's underdevelopment,[154] and helped establish regional development institutions.[155] Mainstream accounts of dependency theory's history describe the emerging argument in this period as aiming 'to change the unequal international division of labour they believed was responsible for decreasing the bargaining power of Latin American countries in their commercial relations with Europe and the United States'.[156] They do not address how this argument was being worked through also at the scale of the region itself. The question of whether the exchanges between the Northeast and the rest of the country were unequal was not new. The core tenets of the Prebisch–Singer hypothesis had already been established in 1949–50, but they were developed in important ways in the Northeast into what became a theory of internal colonialism.[157]

152 Oliveira, *Elegia para uma Re(li)gião*, 99.
153 Oliveira, *Noiva da revolução/Elegia para uma re(li)gião*, 69.
154 Singer, *Estudo Sôbre o Desenvolvimento Econômico Do Nordeste*, 95–96.
155 Buckley, *Technocrats*, 183–86.
156 Ana Saggorio Garcia, Maria Luisa Mendonça, and Miguel Borba de Sá, 'International Political in Latin America: Redefining the Periphery', in *The Palgrave Handbook of Critical International Political Economy*, ed. Alan Cafruny, Leila Simona Talani, and Gonzalo Pozo Martin (London: Palgrave Macmillan, 2016), 436.
157 Joseph Love, *Crafting the Third World: Theorizing Underdevelopment in Rumania and Brazil* (Stanford, CA: Stanford University Press, 1996), 165–70; Joseph Love, 'Modeling Internal Colonialism: History and Prospect', *World Development* 17, no. 6 (June 1989): 905–22, doi:10.1016/0305-750X(89)90011-9.

In this period, not just Celso Furtado but also Fernando Henrique Cardoso, Vânia Bambirra, and Milton Santos were all beginning to address the question of uneven regional development in the Northeast. David Slater argued that 'the radical *dependencia* perspective of the 1960s and early 1970s cannot be separated either from the geopolitical impact of the Cuban Revolution, or from the perceived need on the part of critical Latin American intellectuals to confront and challenge the relevance of modernization theory at the periphery'.[158] I would argue, further, that the 'radical *dependencia* perspective' cannot be separated from the history of the Northeast. Slater recognized the influence of studies of Brazil – and of Josué de Castro – in his papers on the geography of underdevelopment in 1973 in *Antipode* and referred, in particular, to Castro's work on the Northeast.[159] The breadth of Latin American work on underdevelopment expanded after the Cuban revolution,[160] but already in the 1950s Castro and a Brazilian group of early *dependentistas* were developing and debating their ideas and attempting to put them into action at the scale of the region. Dependency theory has long been a key tool for theorizing the expansion of capital into and through the underdeveloped world.[161] Although more closely associated with the scales of the nation and the world system and the centre and periphery,[162] in its early stages its Brazilian theorists developed their ideas in the context of a struggle over the question of the region. Attention to the region can help to fracture what David Featherstone has called the 'unthinking centrality' accorded to the nation-state 'as the privileged arena for the construction of hegemonic and counterhegemonic politics'.[163] Right in the middle of these machinations – intellectually and politically – was Josué de Castro.

It is important not to oversimplify the intellectual history involved here. Inside analyses of the Northeast we can observe the fracturing of dependency theory,[164] with Furtado's structuralist approach splitting off from Ruy

158 David Slater, 'The Geopolitical Imagination and the Enframing of Development Theory', *Transactions of the Institute of British Geographers* 18, no. 4 (1993): 422, doi:10.2307/622559.

159 David Slater, 'Geography and Underdevelopment', *Antipode* 5, no. 3 (December 1973): 23, doi:10.1111/j.1467-8330.1973.tb00568.x.

160 Joseph Love, 'Raul Prébisch and the Origins of the Doctrine of Unequal Exchange', *Latin American Research Review* 15, no. 3 (1980): 45–72.

161 Slater, 'Geography and Underdevelopment'; David Slater, 'Geography and Underdevelopment – Part II*', *Antipode* 9, no. 3 (December 1977): 1–31, doi:10.1111/j.1467-8330.1977.tb00089.x.

162 Fouad Makki, 'Reframing Development Theory: The Significance of the Idea of Uneven and Combined Development', *Theory and Society* 44, no. 5 (2015): 471–97, doi:10.1007/s11186-015-9252-9.

163 Featherstone, '"Gramsci in Action"', 66.

164 Fernando Correa Prado, 'História de um não-debate: a trajetória da teoria marxista da dependência no Brasil', *Comunicação e Política* 29, no. 2 (2011): 68–94; Cristóbal Kay, *Latin American Theories of Development and Underdevelopment* (London and New

Mauro Marini's concept of 'underdevelopment as super-exploitation'.[165] Marini connected the export of primary raw materials with further suppression of wages in the dependent context, a theory that has potentially fruitful connections with Castro's geography of hunger, in particular through Dussel's development and clarification of Marini's claims.[166] Contrary to Furtado, Marini embraced revolutionary politics: at this time – alongside other dependency theorists Vânia Bambirra and Theotônio dos Santos – he was involved in militant Marxist movements in Brazil. Yet Castro's own work cannot be placed simply across a Marxist/structuralist divide.

Dependency theorists themselves often cited him. Beyond the exchanges with Furtado, Theotônio dos Santos put Castro's 'extremely modern' work within a group of Brazilian scholars who influenced him, and even organized an 'international year of Josué de Castro'.[167] Paul refers to Castro in his *Political Economy of Growth*,[168] and Argentinian Raúl Prebisch, author of dependency's 'manifesto',[169] was in contact with Castro from the 1950s to the 1970s, and they collaborated on various projects.[170] As early as 1953, Castro wrote to the Secretary General of the FAO in May 1953 about a meeting of the UN Economic Commission for Latin America (CEPAL) in Brazil, the core of dependency thinking, where Furtado and Prebisch were working. Castro wrote that he was encouraged that 'the lines of economic policy laid out for Latin America were closer to the FAO point of view than was ever possible before. Problems of agriculture were brought out more than previously, when it sometimes seemed as though industry and commerce were the only things worth considering.'[171] We can see that the fault-lines of his debate with Furtado and his geographical evaluation of dependency theory had been laid for a number of years. Placing Castro in this context draws out the political content and context of his work and

York: Routledge, 2010), doi:10.4324/9780203835418; Love, 'Raul Prébisch and the Origins of the Doctrine of Unequal Exchange'.

165 Higginbottom, 'Underdevelopment as Super-Exploitation'; Marini, *Subdesarrollo y Revolución*.

166 Enrique Dussel, *Towards an Unknown Marx: A Commentary on the Manuscripts of 1861–63*, trans. Fred Moseley (London: Routledge, 2002), 209–12, https://ebookcentral.proquest.com/lib/uqac-ebooks/detail.action?docID=166177.

167 Theotônio dos Santos, *Teoria de La Dependencia: Balance y Perspectivas* (México: Plaza y Janés, 2002); Theotônio dos Santos, 'O grito que não foi ouvido', *Jornal do Brasil*, September 1993, Domingo edition, sec. Caderno Fome.

168 Paul A. Baran, *The Political Economy of Growth* (New York: Monthly Review Press, 1957), 279.

169 Kay, *Latin American Theories of Development and Underdevelopment*.

170 For example, Josué de Castro, ed., *America Latina y Los Problemas Del Desarrollo: La Encrucijada Del Presente y El Reto Del Futuro*, 1st ed., Colección Estudios Especial (Caracas: Monte Avila Editores, 1974).

171 Josué de Castro, 'To FAO Secretary General from Josué de Castro', May 1953, 401, CEHIBRA.JdC.

emphasizes the geographical content of dependency theory itself. It does so, in particular, through the question of the region. By the early 1970s the Northeast was an important point of debate in the emergence of critical geography, meriting a long discussion, which references Castro, in the first of David Slater's two papers on 'Geography and Underdevelopment' in 1973.[172] Slater falls short of integrating Northeastern thought into geography, but does use it to expose the fallacies of then mainstream theories of regional underdevelopment.

Various figures from dependency theory, such as Aníbal Quijano, have flitted in and out of anglophone geography. More deserve to be reconsidered, such as Celso Furtado, Vânia Bambirra,[173] and Ruy Mauro Marini.[174] Other critical thinkers of the Northeast do not fall into the *dependentista* tendency but, likewise, have an enormous amount to offer anglophone geographical thought: I have only been able to scratch the surface here. This chapter suggests that the genesis of underdevelopment and dependency theory played out in the Northeast of Brazil. Castro largely has no place in intellectual histories of dependency theory,[175] in spite of the role outlined here in debates over the region, national developmentalism, and underdevelopment.[176] If, as Power and Sidaway suggest, Milton Santos is one agent through which dependency ideas entered geography,[177] Castro, on the other hand, was an agent through which geographical ideas entered dependency theory.

How, then, might this intellectual history point towards ways of understanding the region afresh in political ecology? First, it returns to Haesbaert's notion of the region as an arte-fact: a dialectical combination of imaginary and material geographies. Regional political ecologies need to take into account how that scale is itself arte-factually produced. The region is produced, in part, by the infrastructure politics of the state, understood as an outcome of struggle. Regional dynamics are both relational and specific. Understanding agrarian reform in the Northeast, for example, requires accounting for the mediating power of the idea of the region itself. The way in which space and nature is divided up and struggled over,

---

172 Slater, 'Geography and Underdevelopment'.

173 Fernando Correa Prado, 'Vânia Bambirra e o marxismo crítico latino-americano', *REBELA – Revista Brasileira de Estudos Latino-Americanos* 1, no. 1 (June 2011), https://www.rebela.emnuvens.com.br/pc/article/view/24.

174 Andy Higginbottom, 'The Political Economy of Foreign Investment in Latin America: Dependency Revisited', *Latin American Perspectives* 40, no. 3 (May 2013): 184–206; Higginbottom, 'Underdevelopment as Super-Exploitation'; Sotelo Valencia, 'Latin America'.

175 Kay, *Latin American Theories of Development and Underdevelopment*.

176 Maria José de Rezende, 'Colonialismo, subdesenvolvimento e fome em Josué de Castro', *Cadernos de Estudos Sociais* 19, no. 2 (2003): 227–46; Andrade, 'Josué de Castro'; Magalhães, *Fome: uma (re)leitura de Josué de Castro*.

177 Power and Sidaway, 'The Degeneration of Tropical Geography'.

and how that manifests in people's bodies – the geography of hunger – is the product not only of colonial histories of land and nature but of the extended, relational, arte-factual region itself. The Northeast as a form of periphery to the Centre–South – the dependency paradigm at another scale – forged the political ecologies and metabolic geographies of everyday life for Northeasterners.

The region is an important and powerful part of scalar strategies and also – in the case of the Northeast, certainly – not merely reducible to them. Milton Santos wrote that what we might call a radical regionalism 'endures [...] as a seed for our thought and our action; a seed for our anguish, but also for our hope'.[178] There can be something special about regions. Calling for a Gramscian approach to political ecology, Joel Wainwright insists that there is a responsibility to engage with the colonial experience. This chapter has attempted to present an alternative intellectual history for political ecology populated by scholars, in this case from the Brazilian Northeast, who have long thought deeply about the colonial experience, the imperialist expansion of capitalism, and uneven development. Many of them became exiles, forced to think about their own region, the Northeast, from afar. In the next chapter I will think through the personal and public geographies of this intellectual condition. I suggest that how this period in the Northeast was later interpreted has something to offer critical geographical thought. As Milton Santos put it, writing in the late 1990s, 'the region still exists, it's just more complex than ever'.[179]

Conclusion: SUDENE and the Coup

The idea of the underdeveloped region was fought over in a particularly molten period of Brazilian political and intellectual life between 1955 and 1964. The Northeast was deployed as a piece of 'political hardware' by counter-acting forces, just as it was being retheorized and reconstructed by others. The Northeast was not a settled bundle of space and nature but a profoundly significant geography over which radical, national developmentalist and international imperialist forces did battle. The vision of the region that emerges here is one based in struggle, that is conflictual and political. This conceptualization is distinct from Northern regional geography. Though far from Castro's own set of references, this version of the region has more in common with Gramsci than it does with Vidal.

SUDENE's own attempt to refound material relations between the Northeast and the Centre–South came across resistance. In Parliament this resistance was, in Oliveira's analysis, 'an admirable reflection of the different social classes'.[180] It did not line up in straightforward spatial terms:

178 Santos, 'O Futuro Do Nordeste', 100.
179 Santos, *A natureza do espaço*, 166.
180 Oliveira, *Elegia para uma Re(li)gião*, 115–16.

the most fervent opposition to SUDENE was from Northeastern politicians who had long had a conflictual relationship with national, infrastructure-driven drought agencies.[181] These agencies' capacity to bridge state lines and invest in large-scale reservoir, irrigation, and transport projects challenged state-level authorities, and their support from politicians fluctuated.[182] In the mid-1950s Castro sought to bring together a unified Northeastern voice in the national Parliament but little came of the project as regional unity was always partial (his role in a Nationalist grouping of deputies was more lasting).[183] One of SUDENE's tools in overcoming parliamentary opposition was its Council, which included governors from across the Northeast. It was a political tool (again in Haesbaert's terms) for a new kind of state project, integrating functions of the federal and state governments.[184] In Oliveira's analysis, SUDENE attempted to make the state a productive force in the Northeast through novel combinations of capital underpinned by the coercive power of the state.[185] Oliveira was inspired by Gramsci, and his spatial understanding of class and state relations recalls recent political ecological approaches, deploying a Gramscian understanding of the state apparatus as 'a material form that condenses the balance of social forces and, as such, is the outcome of struggle'.[186] Miguel Arraes – with whom Oliveira was in correspondence over political strategy in exile[187] – saw in this a national political struggle between two sections of the bourgeoisie: one orientated towards international capital, the other towards national popular movements. The regional question was one factor in a conjuncture with uneven effects across national territory. But Castro insisted that the problem of the Northeast was precisely about scale. The problem must be confronted not 'in its regional aspect, in its local singularity, but [...] in its correlation with the problem of the cost of living and the social and economic crisis of the whole country'.[188] Regional underdevelopment had to be overcome through a national project that redistributed incomes, corrected regional inequality, increased productivity, reformed agriculture and land ownership, and rebalanced agricultural and industrial production.[189]

But while these debates played out in the 1950s, the Northeast was also becoming a locus for cold war politics. The region was being inserted into an international scale. Thanks to anti-communist fervour, breathless

181 Buckley, 'Drought'.
182 Buckley, *Technocrats*.
183 Melo and Neves, *Josué de Castro*, 89–90.
184 Cohn, *Crise Regional e Planejamento*, 151.
185 Oliveira, *Elegia para uma Re(li)gião*, 116.
186 Angel, 'Towards an Energy Politics In-Against-and-Beyond the State', 561.
187 Miguel Arraes, 'Caro Chico | Letter to Francisco de Oliveira', letter, undated (1960s), CRp 1 doc 7, CEHIBRA.FJ.
188 Castro, *Documentário do Nordeste*, 93–94.
189 Rezende, 'Colonialismo, subdesenvolvimento e fome em Josué de Castro', 240.

foreign correspondents, Brazilian military machinations, and cold war obsessions, an atmosphere of trepidation about the Northeast grew in Washington D.C.[190] To some limited extent their assessment of the Peasant Leagues as a communist, or at least Castroist, threat was justified: Alexina Crespo, an important militant leader in the Leagues, described a visit to China to petition Mao Tse Tung for arms, and she and her husband Francisco Julião visited Cuba to get Castro's support[191] and used the Cuban revolution to rally support for the Peasant Leagues.[192] But the paranoia was vastly overblown. American interventionism enabled the Brazilian right to concoct the need for a military coup.

Even prior to this, the US had engaged in a battle of aid vs development with SUDENE. Celso Furtado was invited to the White House to meet President John F. Kennedy, Henry Kissinger visited the Northeast and Kennedy sent his own brother, Ted, to visit in 1961.[193] This visit was a remarkable moment: he was escorted to the Engenho Galileia by Celso Furtado, who translated between him and the peasants who had only recently expropriated their land. The clean-cut symbol of American empire met the bare-footed peasant, mediated by the emerging Third World intellectual and Marxist technocrat. Furtado's translation, in this moment, is much more than linguistic. If there is a moment in which translation is both partial and political it was this. What did Kennedy understand of these peasants, recently organized, still desperately poor? What did the peasants, on their liberated land, make of this American, with his promises of a generator – a promise delivered, and then, symbolically, left to rust as there was no fuel to run it? (Sarah Sarzynski's new book reports that it is still there, though the gift is attributed to the wrong Kennedy.[194]) What did they make, indeed, of the sharp-suited Furtado? They were used to visiting intellectuals from the capital, not far distant: Josué de Castro had been there, with Francisco Julião, just a few months before. In any case, the cold war played out in a cane field, and translation took place. In spite of these American shows of friendliness in the Northeast, a few months later Teddy's brother, Bobby, visited Rio de Janeiro to insist, unsuccessfully, that Goulart purge the leftists from his government. One of the American demands was that Celso Furtado be removed as head of SUDENE.[195] On this Goulart demurred.

190 Santiago, *Pernambuco em chamas*; Anthony Pereira, 'God, the Devil, and Development in Northeast Brazil', *Praxis: The Fletcher Journal of Development Studies* XV (1999): 1–3.

191 Flávio José Gomes Cabral, Maria da Glória Dias Medeiros, and A.H. da Silva Araújo, 'Lugar de mulher é na revolução: confissões de uma clandestina', *V Colóquio de História. Perspectivas Históricas*, November 2011, 1207–08; Stédile, *A questão agrária no Brasil*.

192 Pereira, 'O Declínio das Ligas Camponesas', 249.

193 Oliveira, *Elegia para uma Re(li)gião*, 120.

194 Sarzynski, *Revolution in the Terra Do Sol*.

195 Santiago, *Pernambuco em chamas*, 147.

In spite of protestations in favour of dialogue and support, the Americans' aid plans – devised by economist Merwin Bohan – sat uncomfortably alongside SUDENE's, and relations soured.[196] Bohan, claiming to be a neutral economist, proposed American-sponsored militias to combat the Peasant Leagues.[197] The Americans sought to enrol the Northeast in broader international struggles in particular ways. Both USAID and the CIA established large presences in Recife.[198] The city was a vibrant political and cultural centre at the time under the jurisdiction of the radical Arraes government. It hosted Paulo Freire's radical plans to mobilize and educate the Northeastern masses.[199] Germano Coelho, the head of the city's Popular Cultural Movement, hyperbolically called the American presence 'a silent invasion'[200] and reportedly licensed an exhibition of anti-American cartoons in February 1963, to the consternation of the Americans in Recife.[201] The task of these deployments was to halt the advance of leftist politics in the Northeast. The vehicle for this project – as well as directly funding Arraes' political opponents[202] – was the Alliance for Progress. The US targeted aid at the scale of the region. Up until the coup these competing visions of aid and economic development co-existed alongside and underneath the turbulent motions of national politics. In 1964 the nationalist left emphatically lost, as the military gathered outside Recife's Governor's palace, and Miguel Arraes was deposed and arrested.

In 1965, after the coup, another Kennedy – Bobby, this time – landed in Recife. He visited the *Zona da Mata* (though not with the exiled Furtado) and declared that the Northeast was the 'region [that] symbolized the embodiment of the Alliance for Progress as a whole'.[203] This kind of vernacular regional imagination tells us more about cold war politics than about the geographical construction of the region as a socio-natural territory. However, these multiple scales of political thought and action – international forces of US development politics, translated through local aid interventions – functioned, too, to produce the region as region. The Northeast was not only the field of

196 US Department of State, 'Report on SUDENE Policy of Non-Cooperation with USAID' (Brown Digital Repository, July 1963), Opening the Archives: Documenting U.S.–Brazil Relations, 1960s–80s. Brown University Library.

197 Oliveira, *Noiva da revolução/Elegia para uma re(li)gião*, 27.

198 Joseph A. Page, *The Revolution That Never Was: Northeast Brazil* (New York: Grossman, 1972).

199 Kirkendall, 'Entering History'.

200 Santiago, *Pernambuco em chamas*, 155.

201 US Department of State, 'Anti-American Art Exhibit Draws Numerous Visitors, Reportedly Sponsored by Recife Department of Culture and Documentation' (Brown Digital Repository, February 1963), Brown University Library: Opening the Archives: Documenting U.S.–Brazil Relations, 1960s–80s.

202 Page, *The Revolution That Never Was*; Santiago, *Pernambuco em chamas*.

203 Quoted in Santiago, *Pernambuco em chamas*, 187.

intervention for SUDENE's enlightened technocrats, but it was also a space that Cold War grand strategists could think with. The arid Northeast was a convenience of mind for Kennedy to articulate how US power could be projected through international aid. For the generals of the Brazilian military the Northeast was a bridgehead against communism and a key site of national defence in alliance with North American military allies.[204] The region, in these modes of thought, is a kind of laboratory. Kennedy was speaking in 1965. The coup had not brought an end to SUDENE's work – developmentalism and authoritarianism are familiar bedfellows – but it aligned it with the US politics of aid and skinned it of radical potential for meaningful changes for the people of the Northeast. By 1970 Castro argued that the Northeast continued to be the key point of extraction for foreign, particularly US, capital. The tax incentives SUDENE had planned had been turned towards inciting foreign investment and deepening the Northeast's economic dependency both in terms of the national and international economies.[205] Castro had initially greeted the Alliance for Progress signed in Punta del Este in 1961 with cautious open-mindedness. Soon, though, he was one of the most trenchant critics of the type of international development the Alliance stood for. In a public debate in October 1964 (shortly before Bobby Kennedy's visit) he joked that Brazil was the only Latin American country in which the Alliance actually did what its name suggested. In Portuguese the 'Aliança para o Progresso' has a double meaning: para means both 'for' and 'stops': 'the Alliance stops Progress'.[206] Castro's critique is excoriating: the Alliance leads to a 'colonial type' of progress, propping up elites and the very structures that cause the continent's underdevelopment. This critique was part of Castro's broader anticolonial censure of the development industry, which would come to fruition, as the last chapter will show, as an intervention into international environmental politics. It was a critique founded, once again, at the scale of the region and in the light of the Northeast.

204 Josué de Castro, 'Draft Note for French edition of Death in the Northeast' (notes, 1970), 284, CEHIBRA.JdC.
205 Castro, 'Draft Note for French edition of Death in the Northeast'.
206 Yves Jouffa, Claude Julien, Mario Vargas Llosa, Juan Arcocha, and Josué de Castro, *Ou En Est La Révolution En Amérique Latine? Débat Publique* (Paris: Cahiers du Centre d'Etudes Socialistes, 1965).

CHAPTER 6

1960–1968: The Geographical Intellectual

Region, Nation, Exile

'The point of theory is to travel, always to move beyond its confinements, to emigrate, to remain in a sense in exile.'

Edward Said[1]

Introduction

As the last two chapters have shown, Castro was engaged in the machinations of political life at many scales. Indeed, in this book I only lightly touch upon his party-political life in Brazil, which would be worthy of a monograph of its own. But in this chapter I directly address Castro's self-fashioning as an intellectual. It was first and foremost as an intellectual that Josué de Castro conducted his political militancy. He was a particular kind of intellectual at a particular moment: a regional thinker, a radical utopian, and an anti-imperialist, but with a modernist faith in the redemptive power of international institutions and the possibilities of global civil society. He lived out a particular trajectory available only in a precise historical moment: a Third Worldist anticolonial and a militant institutional intellectual. In this chapter I want to think through the geographies of Castro's intellectualism, to explore the valences of geography's political possibilities. This is a concern that underpins the whole of this book, but here I want to bring it explicitly onto centre stage.

I approach critical analysis of the question of the intellectual in twentieth-century Western thought as having two prevailing dimensions: analysis of their role in society and their position as a class; and analysis of the individual characteristics of intellectual work and the responsibility, interpretation, and engagement that it implies. For Edward Said, the intellectual is committed to human freedom and aligned with popular movements, and the true intellectual nevertheless holds to the dictum: never solidarity before

---

1 Edward W. Said, *Reflections on Exile and Other Literary and Cultural Essays* (London: Granta, 2001), 451.

critique.[2] Marilena Chauí has a slightly different understanding, seeing the 'two fundamental characteristics' of the intellectual as the 'defence of *universal causes*, namely those separate from personal interests, and the *transgression* of the dominant order'.[3] The question of the nature of commitment will underpin this chapter. Castro himself was clear that the intellectual must be committed: 'I don't believe', he wrote 'in any science independent from reality and the social context'.[4] Castro spoke in gendered terms of the intellectual: 'I don't believe in non-engaged sociology. The sociologist is a man, so he is irremediably engaged.'[5] This gendered language is in spite of the female public intellectuals – Pearl Buck, Rachel de Queiroz, and Simone de Beauvoir,[6] for instance – whom he saw as mentors and interlocutors. Castro was also more than happy to call himself economist, doctor, or sociologist depending on the circumstances. Paying attention to his at times vain (in both senses of the word) efforts to be a public geographical intellectual can help us modulate received understandings of the geographies of intellectual life. By geographies here I mean two things: firstly, the spaces through which engaged intellectual practice takes place and, secondly, the role of intellectual practice in producing particular kinds of space. In Gramscian terms, intellectuals are important elements in the elaboration of hegemony. As Joel Wainwright puts it, hegemony is 'doubly geographical [...] constituted on the basis of spatial relations, and such relations become hegemonic as geographies are naturalized as common sense through political and cultural practices'.[7] I will explore Castro's geographical intellectual practice firstly through continuing to investigate the question of the region and the intellectual as a conductor of scalar politics; secondly, through the articulations of commitment at the national and international scale; and finally in terms of the spatial distention of exile.

'No-one has any idea, today, of the importance of Josué. In the fifties and the sixties [...] Josué was one of the five most important people in all of humanity', and the most prominent intellectual figure in the country, pronounced Darcy Ribeiro, the anthropologist, politician, and founder of the University of Brasília, in 1995.[8] Ribeiro's comment, made in a film concerned to re-establish Castro's legacy in Brazil as part of a wider reclamation of left intellectual history, should not be taken as a statement of fact, but it reiterates why Castro's lack of incorporation into 'global' histories of geography

---

2 Edward W. Said, *Representations of the Intellectual: The 1993 Reith Lectures*, new title ed. (New York: Vintage Books, 1996).

3 Chauí, *Between Conformity and Resistance*, 15.

4 Josué de Castro, 'Panorama Socio-Economique de l'Amerique Latine' (speech, June 1964), 230, CEHIBRA.JdC.

5 Castro, 'Panorama Socio-Economique de l'Amerique Latine'.

6 Signed edition.

7 Wainwright, 'The Geographies of Political Ecology', 1037.

8 Tendler, *Josué de Castro – Cidadão do Mundo*.

remains a conundrum. As this book has shown, though Castro has had some renown in Brazilian and French geography, it hardly matches Ribeiro's assessment. Castro is one of a relatively small group of geographers with such a prominent, inter-disciplinary, public role in Western intellectual life in the twentieth century. Indeed, if we are to take Chauí's definition – that the true intellectual is both dissonant and committed to human freedom – then he is in a much smaller group. Comparable public geographers before him – we might list Richard Hartshorne, Ellen Semple, Friedrich Ratzel, Isaiah Bowman, or Vidal de la Blache – did not perform such humanist dissonance. Castro disowned and counteracted the long-established association between geography and imperial power. In an inverse way to Neil Smith's work on Isaiah Bowman, Castro's career tells an important story about the twentieth century, as well as about the discipline of geography.[9] The question of the intellectual has been fiercely debated in the fields of cultural studies and social theory,[10] but relatively little theorizing of the formation, role, and antinomies of the public intellectual exists in geography.[11] Noel Castree has argued, cautiously, that 'the (Left) geographer as public intellectual is not [...] infeasible'.[12] Castro enacted the role of the leftist, critical geographer as public intellectual, with all of the compromise, incoherence, achievement, hypocrisy, and vanity performing it involved, but this seems not to have enhanced his standing in geography.

From an early age Castro sought out public platforms. His institutional and political roles were often vehicles for a process of self-fashioning as a public intellectual that was contingent upon contested access to mobility, audiences, and institutions. His star waxed and waned. After the different kinds of prominence analysed in the last two chapters, exile led to exclusion from both specialized and popular publics in Brazil and formal international roles as a national representative. This did not, however, lead him to abdicate the path of public intellectual. On the contrary, in the last period of his life

9 Neil Smith, 'Geography, Empire and Social Theory', *Progress in Human Geography* 18, no. 4 (December 1994): 491–500, doi:10.1177/030913259401800404; Livingstone, *The Geographical Tradition*; Smith, *American Empire*.

10 See, for example, Stefan Collini, '"Every Fruit-Juice Drinker, Nudist, Sandal-Wearer ...": Intellectuals as Other People', in *The Public Intellectual*, ed. Helen Small (Oxford and Malden, MA: Blackwell, 2002), 203–23; Pierre Bourdieu, 'The Intellectual Field: A World Apart', in *In Other Words: Essays towards a Reflexive Sociology* (Stanford, CA: Stanford University Press, 1990), 140–49.

11 For exceptions see Kevin Ward, '"Public Intellectuals", Geography, Its Representations and Its Publics', *Geoforum* 38, no. 6 (November 2007): 1058–64, doi:10.1016/j.geoforum.2006.11.021; Kevin Ward, 'Geography and Public Policy: Towards Public Geographies', *Progress in Human Geography* 30, no. 4 (2006): 495–503; Noel Castree, 'Geography's New Public Intellectuals?' *Antipode* 38, no. 2 (March 2006): 396–412, doi:10.1111/j.1467-8330.2006.00585.x; Duncan Fuller, 'Public Geographies: Taking Stock', *Progress in Human Geography* 32, no. 6 (2008): 834–44.

12 Castree, 'Geography's New Public Intellectuals?' 408.

Castro fought against exclusion and strategically opened new audiences, and exile did enable some kinds of intellectual freedom for Castro. In many ways these were the most prolific years of his writing and speaking. Though his academic practice always remained geographical, it was geography as a means, not as an end. That is, he was less interested in the institutional frameworks of disciplinary geography than in what geographical method could do for his ideas.

Castro moved in the same circles as some of the most influential intellectuals of the twentieth century, not only in Brazil, as previous chapters have outlined, but in Europe, including Jean-Paul Sartre and Simone de Beauvoir.[13] These were also key figures in a self-reflexive moment interrogating the role of the intellectual in anti-imperialist struggles.[14] Castro himself explored the question of intellectual responsibility frequently and one of Sartre's important reflections on the question – revolving around the Bertrand Russel Peace Tribunal – was published in the anticolonial *Tricontinental* magazine alongside Castro's own article, 'The Significance of the Brazilian Economic Phenomenon'.[15] For a time, Castro was written about in breathless terms by newspapers and magazines. He was interviewed for television programmes and radio broadcasts and invited to speak all over the world. He was published by leading publishing houses and was bound into prominent left-wing Catholic circles in France and beyond through friendships and collaborations with men such as Abbé Pierre, Joseph Lebret, and Jean-Marie Domenach, his publisher at *Esprit*. In the UK he was friends with J.D. Bernal, the British communist scientist, with whom he corresponded over ideas and sources in their respective books[16] and who contributed to an unsuccessful project to film the geography of hunger in the late 1950s.[17] He made programmes for French National Television. He was friends with the most internationally prominent writers and intellectuals from across Latin America, including the Brazilian novelist Guimarães Rosa[18] and the Guatemalan Nobel Laureate Miguel Angel Asturias,[19] for instance. His name was regularly discussed in relation to the Nobel Prize and he was invited to sit

13 Josué de Castro, 'Une Zone Explosive: Le Nordeste Du Brésil, First Edition, Signed Copy Dedicated to Simone de Beauvoir' (signed book, 1965), accessed 18 June 2022, https://www.edition-originale.com/en/literature/first-and-precious-books/beauvoir-une-zone-explosive-le-nordeste-du-1965-59664.

14 Said, Representations, 13.

15 Castro, 'Significance'; Jean-Paul Sartre, 'De Nuremberg a Estocolmo', *Tricontinental*, December 1967.

16 Josué de Castro, 'To J. D. Bernal (4th March)', 1959, 564, CEHIBRA.JdC.

17 Michael Altman, 'To Josué de Castro (28th February)', 1959, 564, CEHIBRA.JdC.

18 Guimarães Rosa, 'To Josué de Castro: "meu caro Embaixador e querido Amigo"', handwritten letter, April 1963, 478, CEHIBRA.JdC.

19 Miguel Angel Asturias, *Latino America y otros ensayos* (Madrid: Guadiana de Publicaciones, 1970).

on groups such as Bertrand Russell's International Tribunal to investigate US war crimes in Vietnam[20] and a nuclear Disarmament Committee including Albert Schweitzer, Russell, Sartre, Eleanor Roosevelt, Ilia Ehrenbourg, and others.[21] He was the subject of hundreds of profiles and interviews in newspapers and magazines throughout Latin America, Europe, the Soviet Union and beyond from the late 1940s through to the early 1970s. These often took on a hagiographic tone, casting Castro as a 'universal' figure and a 'citizen of the world'.[22]

He used public platforms to campaign against hunger[23] and, as explored in previous chapters, had what Edward Said called the intellectual's 'vocation for the art of representing'.[24] Not only was he an effective communicator in both written and spoken forms but he thought deeply about his audiences, for example seeking to bring the 'geography of hunger' to cinema through abortive attempts to work first with Charlie Chaplin and then Roberto Rossellini and Cesare Zavattini. He wrote to Chaplin asking him to film the geography of hunger 'both for his creative genius and for the interest he has always shown [in] the artistic representation of the tragedy of hunger'.[25] Notwithstanding the force of Chaplin's bodily performance, Castro wrote to him, Chaplin had nevertheless 'never entirely penetrated [hunger's] essence to show, through his human substance, all the social implications which this tragedy contains'.[26] Castro proposed that they worked together to provide Chaplin with a vector for expressing his own conception of hunger.[27] Castro's interest in the dumb power of Chaplin's art reiterates the Brazilian's attention to this duality and to the representation of suffering. The film never came off, and nor did the long and tortuous negotiations with Rossellini – including a trip to Brazil by the Italian and years of scripts, letters, and fundraising.[28] Nevertheless, Castro had a significant power to convene not only powerful political and scientific but also cultural figures.

20 For which Yves Lacoste also worked: Bowd and Clayton, 'Geographical Warfare in the Tropics', 631.

21 For example, Anonymous, 'Josué de Castro voltou de Londres: um "Comité" pró-desarmamento nuclear', *Jornal do Comercio*, July 1960, 5, CEHIBRA.JdC.

22 See, for example, 'Conversacion con Josué de Castro', *El Dia*, Mexico, 23 July 1965, or 'Josué de Castro, un Brasileño Universal', *El Nacional*, Caracas, 16 August 1965 or 'Une Jeunesse "Revolutionnaire"', *Témoignage Chrétien*, 27 May 1965.

23 The files of newspaper clippings in his archive show this over and over again, for example, Various, 'Newspaper Clippings 1959 (i)', 1959, 27, CEHIBRA.JdC; Various, 'Newspaper Clippings 1961: Northeast'.

24 Said, *Representations*, 10.

25 Reprinted in Magno, *Memória Do Saber*, 149.

26 Reprinted in Magno, *Memória Do Saber*, 149.

27 See also Josué de Castro, 'Letter from Josué de Castro to Charlie Chaplin', November 1957, 478, CEHIBRA.JdC.

28 Maria Carla Cassarini, *Miraggio di un film: carteggio De Castro-Rossellini-Zavattini* (Livorno: Erasmo, 2017).

Despite this, he wrote that he always felt provincial. Underpinning his self-conception as an intellectual was his own personal geography, and the Northeast. It is to the oscillation between his different geographical scales of practice and vectors of commitment that I now turn.

The Regional–National Intellectual

As the previous chapter outlined, Castro was one of many politically engaged Northeastern intellectuals working in the mid-twentieth century, and had important debates with Celso Furtado. To unpick the dynamics of commitment at work here, I want to return to an earlier chapter's concerns through reading prefaces – here not only of Castro's books but of other intellectual confrontations with the question of the region. In a preface written in 1964, writing about the Northeast in particular, and Brazil in general, Furtado deployed a classical set of ideas about the role of intellectuals to argue that

> the intellectual has a particular social responsibility, being, as he is, the only element in society who not only can, but should, place himself above the more immediate social conditioners of individual behaviour. This permits him to move on a higher plane of rationality and invests him with a very special responsibility: the responsibility of intelligence [...] Because he has this responsibility, the intellectual cannot refuse to see further than group loyalties or cultural ties allow. [He has a] supreme commitment [...] to the dignity of the human being – an inalienable attribute of the intellectual's very being.[29]

Furtado wrote that he was publishing his works on the Northeast 'with the intention of promoting an intellectual mobilization of the Left'.[30] Furtado's economistic and technocratic tendencies are balanced by a commitment to universal principles. But Castro took a stronger position in the preface of his own book published in 1964. He declared himself 'committed to a partisan and progressive point of view. I deplore things as they are, and my deepest desire is to see them changed and improved.'[31] Writing on the Northeast, and about this moment, has a particular tenor of commitment. I will return to both of these prefaces in the last section of this chapter, written in the traumatic months of 1964.

Another preface, to Francisco de Oliveira's *Elegia para uma Re(li)gião*, published in 1977, recalls that he wrote about the period: 'under the sign of passion: passion for Orieta, for the Northeast, passion for the workers, labourers and peasants of the Northeast. Passion in the broadest and narrowest senses.' Oliveira's analytical drive is a 'passion in the sense of Gramsci: of putting

---

29 Furtado, *Diagnosis*, xiii.
30 Furtado, *Diagnosis*, xiii.
31 Castro, *Death in the Northeast*, 4.

oneself in the way of things, and through this positioning, and because of this positioning, to try to understand a tragedy'.[32] Here we can recall Gramsci's connection of the region to the question of intellectuals. The parallels between the Mezzogiorno and the Northeast are profound.[33] Oliveira goes on: 'neutrality does not exist in the social sciences, for which reason I prefer to follow Gramsci's advice: to take a position and, adopting it as a point of departure, to set in motion the theoretical-analytical elements of an interpretation'.[34] This expresses Castro's own intellectual commitment, beginning from the Northeast and a humanist position radically opposed to hunger. The representation of hunger constituted the pith of his political struggle.

The problem of the intellectual has overwhelmingly been figured as national. Questions of commitment, dissonance, and engagement address the scale of the nation.[35] But, as the quotations above suggest, the nation was not the only scale that Castro (and others) navigated as an intellectual, and it is not the only scale that he helped to produce. In order to explore this dual question – the space of the intellectual and the space intellectuals produce – I turn to Antonio Gramsci.[36] It is in the context of investigating the region and the socio-spatial dimensions of hegemony that some of Gramsci's most important reflections on the intellectual emerge. The essay 'Some Aspects of the Southern Question' 'emphasis[es] the rootedness (or otherwise) of social classes and political and intellectual forces in specific places, spaces and scales of economic and social life'.[37] As David Featherstone argues, Gramsci 'situates the formation of solidarities and identities in relation to dynamic, ongoing, uneven development of northern and southern Italy and engages with both the cultural and political character of that inequality'.[38] Solidarity is geographical in Gramsci's work. This – as I attempted to show in chapter 2 – is also a question of following theories as they travel and become new forms of solidarity, rearticulating contexts in relation to one another – in particular, historical geographies. Gramsci configures the intellectual as key to how regions are constructed as such, and how they act as conduits

---

32 Oliveira, *Elegia para uma Re(li)gião*, 13.

33 See, for example, Nivalter Aires Santos, 'Questão Nordestina: Esboço de Uma Interpretação a Partir Da Questão Meridional de Gramsci', *MovimentAção* 4, no. 7 (2017): 108–30; Pereira, 'A Questão Regional No Pensamento de Antonio Gramsci e Celso Furtado'.

34 Francisco de Oliveira, 'The Lenin Moment', *Meditations* 23, no. 1 (2007): 109.

35 For example, the influential Homi K. Bhabha, *Nation and Narration* (Abingdon: Routledge, 2013).

36 See Alex Loftus et al., *Gramsci: Space, Nature, Politics* (Chichester: Wiley-Blackwell, 2012); Bob Jessop, 'Gramsci as a Spatial Theorist', *Critical Review of International Social and Political Philosophy* 8, no. 4 (December 2005): 421–37, doi:10.1080/13698230500204931.

37 Jessop, 'Gramsci as a Spatial Theorist', 424.

38 Featherstone, '"Gramsci in Action"', 68.

through which historical blocs are continually in formation. Linking the regional question and the question of intellectuals engages the geographies of knowledge production with the geographies that knowledge produces. Intellectual practice takes place within and through particular geographies and plays a part in producing space. Where Said emphasizes the consistently problematic negotiations of national commitment,[39] Gramsci also opens out the question of the intellectual's regional commitment. This is significant not least because of the reams of intellectual work that have unwound from the bobbin of Gramsci's essay, which sits at the base of subaltern studies.[40] Nevertheless, while the questions of the nation and the intellectual have been resolutely woven together, the question of the region and the intellectual have been less tightly spun.

The spatiality of Castro's intellectual practice was distinctive: not a metropolitan urbanity, but a provincial globalism. For Castro, the Northeast was the defining geography of his intellectual practice:

> travelling all over the world, always seeking to refresh my spirit with currents of thought that flow in all directions [...] I never stopped feeling like a provincial, my spirit and sentiment impregnated with the substance of the earth of the province [...] It is always possible, if you scrape back the superficial crust of appearances, to see the same substance appear: the human landscape of the Northeast.[41]

The region, therefore, is a key territory of identity, but not a fixed scale. It is also internally differentiated. Gramsci at once thinks about the South as a whole and emphasizes how different parts of the South relate to one another, and to the national.[42] As Jessop notes, 'Gramsci distinguished between the social functions of northern (industrial, technical) and southern (rural, organic) intellectuals in building different types of hegemony.'[43] For instance, Gramsci wrote that Benedetto Croce 'fulfilled an extremely important "national" function. He has detached the radical intellectuals of the South from the peasant masses, forcing them to take part in national and European culture; and through this culture, he has secured their absorption by the national bourgeoisie and hence by the agrarian bloc.'[44] Meanwhile, for Gramsci, 'the Southern peasant is tied to

39 See, for example, Edward W. Said, *Nationalism, Colonialism and Literature: Yeats and Decolonization*, vol. 15 (Minneapolis: University of Minnesota Press, 1988).

40 Gayatri Chakravorty Spivak, 'Scattered Speculations on the Subaltern and the Popular', *Postcolonial Studies* 8, no. 4 (November 2005): 475–86, doi:10.1080/13688790500375132.

41 Castro, *Documentário do Nordeste*, 7–8.

42 See Morton, 'Traveling with Gramsci', 47–48.

43 Jessop, 'Gramsci as a Spatial Theorist', 428.

44 Antonio Gramsci, 'Some Aspects of the Southern Question', in *Antonio Gramsci: Selections from Political Writings (1921–1926)*, ed. and trans. Quentin Hoare (London: Lawrence and Wishart, 1978), 460.

the big landowner through the mediation of the intellectual [...] it creates a monstrous agrarian bloc which, as a whole, functions as the intermediary and the overseer of Northern capitalism and the big banks. Its single aim is to preserve the *status quo*.'[45] In addition, he wrote, 'the South can be defined as a great social disintegration [...] Southern society is a great agrarian bloc, made up of three social layers: the great amorphous disintegrated mass of the peasantry; the intellectuals of the petty and medium rural bourgeoisie; and the big landowners and great intellectuals.'[46] It was the role of intellectuals – 'the few intelligent bourgeois' – to 'pose the Southern problem as a national problem'.[47] This figures the regional intellectual as a conductor of scalar politics.

As outlined in the last chapter, in mid-twentieth-century Brazil a few Northeastern intellectuals, including Castro, took up the role of posing the Northeast as a national problem. In his earlier thinking on development, Castro also drew on work on cultural landscapes and regional geography to argue that any projects for development needed to take not only national but *regional* cultural and economic characteristics into account.[48] He navigated between regional and national analysis. In 1955 he was part of the founding group of the influential progressive Paulista journal the *Revista Brasiliense*, which asserted the need to address 'national, not regional problems'.[49] Between 1955 and 1960 his political activity inside Brazil was intense. He did not publish any major original works in the period addressed in the last chapter: he released *Geopolítica da Fome* in 1951, and *Death in the Northeast* would not emerge until 1965. He did publish collections of essays, and substantially updated *A Geografia da Fome* in 1959–60 to publish what he called a 'definitive' edition,[50] but, as extracts from his 1957 diary show, he felt he had no time to write, as he was constantly subject to political demands. He was profoundly disenchanted by domestic politics, and what he saw as the dishonesty and vaingloriousness of political life in Brazil.[51] These personal struggles came up against a public profile. Castro had appeared to be hand-picked by João Goulart – the head of Castro's own *Partido Trabalhista do Brasil* and candidate for the vice-Presidency – to run for mayor of Recife. This prospect had first arisen in 1955, when Goulart publicly supported Castro for the post, and in 1958 there was talk of a Castro–Julião slate in

45 Gramsci, 'Some Aspects of the Southern Question', 457.
46 Gramsci, 'Some Aspects of the Southern Question', 454.
47 Gramsci, 'Some Aspects of the Southern Question', 457.
48 Castro, 'Regionalismo e Paisagem Cultural'.
49 Ronald H. Chilcote, *Intellectuals and the Search for National Identity in Twentieth-Century Brazil* (Cambridge: Cambridge University Press, 2014), 127, doi:10.1017/CBO9781107785298.
50 Josué de Castro, *Geografia da Fome: O Dilema Brasileiro: Pão Ou Aço*, 9th ed., vol. 1 (São Paulo: Editôra Brasiliense, 1965), 29.
51 Silva, 'Josué por ele mesmo: o diário', 39–40.

Recife, a prospect that grew more serious in 1959–60. Castro also considered running for Governor of Pernambuco. In 1960 this would have meant Castro running against Miguel Arraes. Conflicting reports surmised that Castro was toying with the candidacy in order to help Arraes by muddying the waters of his rivals. In the end, to much public surprise, he withdrew.[52]

Castro was moved to justify his involvement in party machinations. He declared in the Northeastern press that he withdrew because he had no political desire for the post and did not believe that the mayoralty had the necessary power to fundamentally change conditions in Recife. Describing himself as a servant of the Northeast but also as a public intellectual, he preferred, he said, to stay in the national parliament.[53] Indeed, the political situation in 1960 in Brazil was somewhat confused. There was a vicious competition to take over the mantle of Juscelino Kubitschek. The populist Jânio Quadros, who had risen from being mayor of São Paulo, stood for election at the head of a coalition against the PTB's ill-fated candidate Marshal Henrique Lott. João Goulart, meanwhile, stood for the vice-Presidency on behalf of the PTB, the two posts being elected separately at the time. Castro was vice-President of the PTB, but decided to support Quadros. In a sign of both his influence and his vanity, after this decision Castro published an explanation of his actions as his 'Carta ao Povo do Nordeste' [Letter to the People of the Northeast]. In addressing the povo Castro imagines his capacity to represent a particular public, and an accountability to it. Newspaper clippings of the time collected in his archive attest to a rolling daily interest in Castro's political positions, and he was something of an intellectual and political celebrity in the region. But the Carta was also a strategic document, in party political terms, addressed to his interlocutors, rivals, and friends inside the party itself, justifying his decision to abandon loyalty.

In this moment Castro was navigating the scales of the city, region, and nation as well as the role of public intellectual. The backdrop, Castro wrote in 1960, to his 'preaching' as a 'political militant' was always to denounce hunger.[54] National attempts to tackle hunger had failed, he declared, and amounted to little more than paternalist assistencialism. 'As a man of study, concerned above all by our social problems, I have for some time sought to examine the candidates [...], their ideologies, their experience of social problems, how they address our sad reality, and the solutions that they are putting forward.'[55] In the middle of his political ruminations, Castro

---

52 On these various machinations see Various, 'Newspaper Clippings 1955' (Various, 1955), 76, CEHIBRA.JdC; Clóvis Melo, 'Josué Admite ser Candidate ao Govêrno', *Diario da Noite*, February 1960, 5, CEHIBRA.JdC; Various, 'Newspaper Clippings 1959 (i)''Josué Aceitou candidatura'; Various: 'Jango no Recife: Josué o Candidate'.

53 Various, 'Newspaper Clippings 1959 (i)': Diario de Pernambuco, 16 June, 1.

54 Josué de Castro, 'Carta ao Povo do Nordeste' (Article Draft, 60 1959), 314, CEHIBRA.JdC.

55 Castro, 'Carta ao Povo do Nordeste'.

wrote, Quadros made overtures to him and announced a true anti-hunger politics, with a focus on the Northeast. Indeed, Castro's archive includes letters between them discussing the contents of this plan.[56] Castro declared that he would support Quadros 'to serve the Northeast in order to better serve Brazil'.[57] He noted that, while some may be annoyed by his choice to abandon party commitment, he himself was driven by a higher purpose. In the trilogy of party, nation, and region, region is first, nation second, and party a relatively distant last.

In the end, Quadros was elected. His principal achievements were in foreign policy, aligning Brazil with Cuba. As President of the Brazilian Commission for Solidarity with the Cuban People, Castro influenced Quadros along these anti-imperialist lines.[58] While supportive, particularly of Quadros' foreign policy, Castro continued to critique Quadros while he was in power.[59] After a brief term, Quadros abruptly resigned. His intention may have been to shore up his authority, but it spectacularly backfired and João Goulart became President. In 1959 Goulart intended to appoint Castro as Minister of Agriculture, a post Castro had long desired. He was stopped by members of his own party in the Northeast, as recalled by Darcy Ribeiro, at the time Goulart's Chief of Staff. They resented Castro's international profile and argued that he was too often absent from the Northeast in the capital or on international trips.[60] The regional, the national, and the international could not productively coexist as much in political practice as they did in political theory, and intellectual and political practice came into conflict at the scale of personal life.

This was a turbulent time in intellectual life in Brazil. Marilena Chauí explains the social function of the intellectual in Brazil in the earlier twentieth century as consisting of three roles: 'the formulation of power, as theologians and lawyers; the exercise of power, as members of a vast state bureaucracy and university hierarchy; and benefactors of the favours of power, as graduates and prestigious writers'.[61] In Francisco de Oliveira's account of the Northeast, *Elegia para uma Re(li)gião*, the political role of the *latifundia* and their regional bourgeois allies have echoes of Gramsci's account of the *mezzogiorno*. But things changed as intellectuals played an important role in political ructions between 1956 and 1964. A class of leftist intellectuals gave themselves the role of the 'advanced conscience' of the people: *o povo*. The appeal to the *povo* was a geographically specific instance of the perennial idea of the intellectual as vanguard, or as true representative of the unrepresented masses. Appealing

---

56 Josué de Castro, 'To Deputado Jânio Quadros', 1960, 478, CEHIBRA.JdC.

57 Castro, 'Carta ao Povo do Nordeste'.

58 Josué de Castro, 'To Jânio Quadros: Cuba', Draft Letter, April 1961, 196, CEHIBRA. JdC.

59 Various, 'Newspaper Clippings 1961: Northeast', 79.

60 Tendler, *Josué de Castro – Cidadão do Mundo*.

61 Chauí, *Between Conformity and Resistance*, 35.

to 'the people', as Castro himself had done in his 'carta', was a widespread penchant of Latin American radicals in the period,[62] and emphatically present in the Brazilian Northeast, where populist pomposity was brutally satirized, for instance, in Glauber Rocha's *Terra em Transe* [Entranced Earth] (1967). The *'povo'* was used as a marker of a rhetorical commitment to the apparently awakening masses. The risks and failures of such associations in emancipatory and decolonization struggles are analysed by Frantz Fanon in 'The Pitfalls of National Consciousness', written in 1961: 'the unpreparedness of the educated classes, the lack of practical links between them and the mass of the people, their laziness, and, let it be said, their cowardice at the decisive moment of the struggle will give rise to tragical mishaps'.[63]

This indictment of traditional intellectuals could describe Brazil in the period up to 1964. It recalls the weakness of some of the claims of Miguel Arraes' 1969 *Brazil: The People and the Power*, which overstates plausible links between 'the mass of the people' and the intellectual class.[64] Fanon's own 'messianism' has itself been accused of giving a 'problematical' and 'impossible' account of the mobilization of the Algerian people.[65] In the Brazilian context, while there were attempts to build 'practical links' across class and the kind of bottom-to-top democracy Fanon espouses – Freire's practised theory of the pedagogy of the oppressed, for example – they were clearly not strong enough to resist the rupture of 1964.

The role of the Brazilian intellectual in this period has been the subject of much enquiry,[66] and it is important not to hold up these leftist intellectuals to a standard they did not themselves seek to meet. Those Chauí refers to were not all – Castro was not – avowing their loyalty to the masses on the basis of revolutionary solidarity. On the contrary, they were producing 'political, economic, and governmental plans for the state' and 'possess[ed] a vision of the demiurgic role of the state to solve class struggle'.[67] Many

---

62 Enrique Dussel, 'Transmodernity and Interculturality: An Interpretation from the Perspective of Philosophy of Liberation', *TRANSMODERNITY: Journal of Peripheral Cultural Production of the Luso-Hispanic World* 1, no. 3 (2012): 28–59; Dussel, *Politics of liberation*, 467–97, 528–40.

63 Frantz Fanon, *Wretched of the Earth*, trans. Constance Farrington (New York: Grove Press, 1963), 119.

64 Arraes, *Brazil: The People and the Power*; see also Misael José de Santana, 'Elementos Para Uma Análise Ideológica Do Discurso de Posse Do Primeiro Mandato Do Ex-Governador Miguel Arraes', in *Língua Portuguesa: Ultrapassar Fronteiras, Juntar Culturas*, ed. João Marçalo et al. (Évora: Universidade de Évora, 2010), 111–21.

65 Neil Lazarus, 'National Consciousness and the Specificity of (Post)Colonial Intellectualism', in *Colonial Discourse/Postcolonial Theory*, ed. Francis Barker, Peter Hulme, and Margeret Iverson (Manchester and New York: Manchester University Press, 1994), 200.

66 For example, Chilcote, *Intellectuals*; Rafael R. Ioris, *Transforming Brazil: A History of National Development in the Postwar Era* (New York: Routledge, 2014).

67 Chauí, *Between Conformity and Resistance*, 36.

different strands of thought competed, on both the right and the left,[68] but in the 1950s and early 1960s the question of the nation, and of national economic development, drew intellectuals like moths to the institutional flames of the Economic Commission for Latin America (CEPAL) and the Instituto Superior de Estudos Brasileiros (ISEB). Both housed distinct and shifting approaches. Characterizing them as respectively structuralist and national developmentalist is schematically useful, though reductive. ISEB included important Brazilian intellectuals such as the sociologist Alberto Guerreiro Ramos and the political theorist Hélio Jaguaribe. The dependency theorists of the last chapter gathered at CEPAL. Holding them together was a shared concern with how to describe, define, practice, and theorize national development, but their approaches to the problem were radically different and changed quite dramatically.[69] Jaguaribe, for instance, moved from a revolutionary socialist position in 1953 to endorsing a capitalist developmentalism led by the national industrial bourgeoisie by 1958.[70] This was one of many dividing lines among left intellectuals that saw 'antagonisms [...] between localism and cosmopolitanism, nationalism and internationalism'.[71] Castro was part of a broad field of debate about modes of development, consistently flying the flag for agrarian reform and the priority of addressing social deprivation in the Northeast. He argued in 1962 in the *Revista Brasileira de Ciências Sociais* [Brazilian Journal of the Social Sciences] that the Brazilian left was 'politically conservative and economically revolutionary':[72] conservative in defending representative democracy and the structure of congress and executive, and in its obsession with anti-communism, and economically revolutionary because of the tenets of underdevelopment theory and because true agrarian reform would really be revolution.[73]

Castro's concept of revolution is important. His position recalls Enrique Dussel's analysis, outlined in the first chapter. Specifically, though, in the early 1950s Castro defined revolution through José Ortega y Gasset's concept of 'historical crisis', as 'a process of transformation of the whole, a historical transmutation which replaces one world of social beliefs by another in which the former social values no longer have meaning'.[74] By 1966, on the other

---

68 Chilcote, *Intellectuals*.
69 Ricardo Bielschowsky, *Pensamento Econômico Brasileiro: O Ciclo Ideológico Do Desenvolvimentismo*, vol. 19 (Rio de Janeiro: Ipea/Inpes, 1988).
70 Caio Navarro de Toledo, 'ISEB Intellectuals, the Left, and Marxism', trans. Laurence Hallewell, *Latin American Perspectives* 25, no. 1 (1998): 111–13.
71 Chilcote, *Intellectuals*, 108 quoting Marilena Chauí.
72 Josué de Castro, 'A revolução social brasileira', *Revista Brasileira de Ciências Sociais* 2, no. 2 (1962): 209.
73 See also Irving Louis Horowitz, Josué de Castro, and John Gerassi, *Latin American Radicalism* (New York: Vintage Books, 1969), 245.
74 Castro, *Geography of Hunger*, 18.

hand, lecturing in Peru, Castro drew on Hegel's idea that revolution was the passage from the quantitative to the qualitative. He described Hegel's thought as obscure – like the clouds that wrap the city of Lima for months at a time – but seeks to apply the idea of the historical accumulation of quantity, leading to a social explosion through transmutation to the atomic world. For Castro, the post-war period was increasingly defined by this atomic transformation.[75] Importantly, in the 1950s Castro shared a common trope with many other left-wing intellectuals: that the Brazilian people were awakening and accruing their own destiny. Paulo Freire argued later that

> culture, the arts, literature, and science showed new tendencies towards research, identification with Brazilian reality, and the planning of solutions rather than their importation. ([SUDENE], directed by the economist Celso Furtado before the military *coup*, was an example of such planning.) The country had begun to find itself. The people emerged and began to participate in the historical process.[76]

In part, this is a classical trope of nationalism. As Terry Eagleton wrote in 1988, 'the metaphysics of nationalism speak of the entry into full self-realiza-tion of a unitary subject known as the people. As with all such philosophies of the subject from Hegel to the present, this monadic subject must somehow curiously preexist its own process of materialization'.[77] Eagleton's analysis exposes some of the pathologies inherent in intellectuals' appeals to the *povo*, but it is important to put this into historical and geographical context. For Fanon, 'the anticolonial struggle for national independence was inseparable from a distinctly transnational struggle for liberation from imperialism on a global scale'.[78] Or, as Neil Lazarus puts it, there is an important distinction between 'bourgeois nationalism [and] liberationist, anti-imperialist, nationalist internationalism'.[79] However, these commitments must be geographically nuanced: Fanon also observes deep regional distinc-tions that are articulated with the emergence of national consciousness.[80] Emancipatory consciousness – both the rhetorical insistence on it and actually existing popular movements – took place unevenly across national territory and, as Gramsci emphasizes, in particular spatial formations.

---

75 Castro, *Adónde va?* 26–27.
76 Paulo Freire, *Education for Critical Consciousness* (London and New York: Continuum, 2005), 26.
77 Terry Eagleton, 'Nationalism, Irony and Commitment', in *Nationalism, Colonialism and Literature*, by Edward Said, Terry Eagleton, and Frederic Jameson, ed. Seamus Deane, vol. 13 (Minneapolis: Field Day, University of Minnesota, 1988), 28.
78 Cesare Casarino, 'The Southern Answer: Pasolini, Universalism, Decolonization', *Critical Inquiry* 36, no. 4 (June 2010): 683, doi:10.1086/655208.
79 Lazarus, 'National Consciousness and the Specificity of (Post)Colonial Intellectualism', 197.
80 Fanon, *Wretched of the Earth*.

Many – not least the United States government – saw the Northeast as a new Cuba. As the last chapter outlined, this was somewhat tendentious. But I want to pick this thread up again to argue that the Cuban experience was key in establishing new models for Northestern radicalism for intellectuals connected to the internationalist nationalism encapsulated by the Tricontinental conference. The idea of the Northeast as a new Cuba suggests a new conception and scale of the region that was not the tribalist regionalism that Fanon excoriates: 'African unity, that vague formula [...] takes off the mask, and crumbles into regionalism inside the hollow shell of nationality itself.'[81] Radical Northeastern regionalism was tied to national developmentalism, anti-imperialism, and internationalism. This is to follow Featherstone's argument that 'subaltern articulations of cosmopolitanism can become constitutive of internationalism allowing a more generous account of who matters in shaping internationalist politics and broadens agency beyond national left leaderships'.[82] Brazilian nationalism and Northeastern regionalism are emancipatory positions when considered in these particular historical and geographical terms. Indeed, as the previous chapter argued, the regional identity of the Northeast and regional thinking on underdevelopment were connected with a global movement for economic emancipation of which Castro was a part. It was a Third Worldist commitment to the nation articulated through the Northeast. These tensions marked both the geographies of Castro's intellectualism and the geography that his intellectual work put forward. Represented by the countervailing pulls of Recife, Rio, and Brasília, this period was marked by competing, fraying loyalties to national and regional parties, and twin external desires: to engage in internationalist projects and to pursue an intellectual life of writing and academic practice.

The National–International Intellectual: Subaltern Geopolitics and Globalisms

How, then, did this regionalist internationalism play out in Castro's own public intellectual practice? After not appointing Castro as Minister of Agriculture, Goulart decided to make him Ambassador to the United Nations. This allowed Castro to build on the networks he had established at the FAO and to continue to make a name for himself in international circles, but withdrew him from the turf wars of regional politics at an important juncture in the Northeast's modern history between 1960 and 1964. The UN post gave him the opportunity to enact deeply held positions on internationalism. His hopes – as they had been at the FAO – were in various ways to be dashed and his navigation of affiliation and independence tested. Like Ferretti, I understand Castro's work in this period as a kind of 'subaltern geopolitics'.[83] Here, I focus

81 Fanon, *Wretched of the Earth*.
82 Featherstone, '"Gramsci in Action"', 75.
83 Ferretti, 'A Coffin for Malthusianism'.

on the scalar dynamics of his geopolitical praxis. Developing Joanne Sharp's work, Ruth Craggs has recently conceptualized a subaltern geopolitics, in which she uses subaltern to mean 'neither in charge, nor excluded entirely', and given a sense of the 'mundane, messy and sometimes contradictory' practices that subaltern geopolitics can consist of.[84] My analysis of Castro's work in the FAO, above, and in the UN and multiple spaces of informal or liminal geopolitics[85] responds to Craggs' call for postcolonial geographers to 'look more carefully at the mid-twentieth century era during which people, institutions and states negotiated, performed and experienced becoming postcolonial'.[86] Ferretti's work on Castro's later international organization in Paris develops some similar dimensions of Castro's work.[87] It is important, in Castro's case, to understand that we are dealing with a philosophy of praxis: he both theorized and practised geopolitics. In *Geopolítica da Fome* Castro declared that he wanted to reclaim geopolitics from its Nazi heritage. He sought to 'demonstrate that political drivers make no sense outside geograph- ical parameters, that is, disassociated from reality and from the contingencies of the natural and cultural environment'.[88] Castro's work constitutes an important strand of critical geopolitics, later developed by other critical geographers in the Northeast of Brazil, including Milton Santos and Manuel Correia De Andrade.[89] Articulated in the early 1950s, it emerged before the growth of schools of critical geopolitics in France – notably that associated with Yves Lacoste and Beatrice Giblin – and elsewhere.

Castro's geopolitical theory and praxis went beyond the formulations in *Geopolítica da Fome*. He saw himself as having a role both inside and outside institutions. For instance, in notes for a presentation on the geopolitical significance of Brasília, seemingly to be given at the influential ISEB in 1960,[90] Castro wrote that geopolitics involved the 'relations between the environment or the geographical context and the political process' and the relations 'between the State and the ecological framework in which it sits.

84 Ruth Craggs, 'Subaltern Geopolitics and the Post-Colonial Commonwealth, 1965–1990', *Political Geography* 65 (July 2018): 47, doi:10.1016/j.polgeo.2018.04.003.

85 Fiona McConnell, 'Liminal Geopolitics: The Subjectivity and Spatiality of Diplomacy at the Margins', *Transactions of the Institute of British Geographers* 42, no. 1 (November 2016): 139–52, doi:10.1111/tran.12156.

86 Ruth Craggs, 'Postcolonial Geographies, Decolonization, and the Performance of Geopolitics at Commonwealth Conferences', *Singapore Journal of Tropical Geography* 35, no. 1 (March 2014): 39–55, doi:10.1111/sjtg.12050.

87 Federico Ferretti, 'Decentring the Lettered City: Exile, Transnational Networks and Josué de Castro's Centre International Pour Le Développement (1964–1973)', *Antipode* 54.2 (2022): 397–417.

88 Castro, *Geopolítica da Fome: Ensaio sôbre os Problemas de Alimentação e de População do Mundo*, 1:27.

89 Ferretti and Viotto Pedrosa, 'Inventing Critical Development'.

90 Neves, 'Josué de Castro: Cronologia'.

Geographical phase in time. It is geography in movement.'[91] These gnomic fragments show how Castro's thought continued to develop. A sophisticated approach to the relations between historical time, space, and the state appears to be emerging. The phrase 'geographical phase in time' gestures towards the periodization of history through geography that Milton Santos would later formalize.[92] We see these hints developed in the later chapters of *Death in the Northeast*, and in the work that emerges from his time at Vincennes. I will return to these (and the methodological question of reading such fragments) in the next chapter.

It was as a public intellectual that Castro traversed academic, pedagogical, governmental, popular, and radical spaces. He used the same arguments and analysis in his theoretical writing as in his political praxis.[93] For instance, opening a session as the Brazilian Chair of the 'Committee of Eighteen Powers' under the auspices of the UN conferences on disarmament in February 1964, Castro began by reflecting on Einstein. He admits to his audience of Geneva diplomats that 'this manner of approaching the subject – that is to say, getting to practical realities by the paths of theory – might seem strange to members of the Committee', but it is because of the theoretical work of Einstein that they are there at all: 'there is no essential difference between practice and theory, since the theory of today transforms into the practice of tomorrow'.[94] His distinctive approach to geopolitics constituted a concerted effort to engage in meaningful political conversations in geopolitical spaces and to leverage (what he saw as) his intellectual, and consequently moral, prestige.

Moving in and out of state circles, Castro took on a particular form of subjectivity. As ambassador, his formulations are those of traditional geopolitics – 'Brazil thinks', 'Brazil desires' – but bear the marks of his own political and intellectual project; as, for example, when he claimed that 'the politics of my country are based on a trilogy: that of the three 'ds': development, decolonization and disarmament'.[95] His claims to representation oscillated but his formal geopolitical interventions were dissonant also because the geopolitical

91 Josué de Castro, 'Significação Geopolítica de Brasília: Notes' (manuscript, undated), 309, CEHIBRA.JdC.

92 Lucas Melgaço and Carolyn Prouse, 'Milton Santos and the Centrality of the Periphery', in *Milton Santos: A Pioneer in Critical Geography from the Global South* (Cham: Springer, 2017), 1–24.

93 See, for example, Josué de Castro, 'Discurso do Delegado do Brasil, Embaixador Josué de Castro: Sétima Conferência Regional da FAO Para a América Latina', November 1962, 218, CEHIBRA.JdC.

94 Josué de Castro, 'Conférence du Comité des dix-huit puissances sur le désarmement. Discours prononcé par l'ambassadeur Josué de Castro, Chef de la Délégation du Brésil', February 1964, 1–2, 224, CEHIBRA.JdC.

95 FAO, 'Proceedings of Conference of the FAO. 12th Session. Commission III' (FAO, November 1963), 9, 224, CEHIBRA.JdC.

position of Brazil (particularly up to 1964) was itself dissonant. Formulating the 'geopolitics of knowledge', Walter Mignolo points out that 'dependency theory [ran] parallel to decolonization in Africa and Asia and suggested a course of action for Latin American countries some 150 years after their decolonization'.[96] This theory and course of action was one Castro helped formulate intellectually and was involved in through geopolitical practice.

Yet, unlike Mignolo's formulation of the 'decolonial', which proposes a form of delinking between Eurocentric thought and Latin American ideas, Castro's geopolitics was not and never had been exterior to the entanglements of power and knowledge it appraised and intervened in. His geopolitical critique emerged within 'Western civilization' both geographically and philosophically. He was formed intellectually under the conditions Enrique Dussel lays out of Latin American intellectuals' 'transmodernity'. He wrote that when he was a child he 'had no idea of the existence of a country called Venezuela, but knew of France, England, Portugal, Spain, of which we spoke every day at school'.[97] Like Dussel, under the influence of European thinkers such as Oswald Spengler, José Ortega y Gassett, and Arnold Toynbee, he was also part of the generation of Latin American critical scholars who negotiated this inheritance in new ways. Dussell discussed taking part with Castro in a 'Latin American Week' in Paris in December 1964, during which Latin American intellectuals proposed formulations for the cultural and intellectual identity of Latin America. Movement and geography are again key to this narrative: 'we discovered ourselves to be "Latin Americans," or at least no longer "Europeans," from the moment that we disembarked in Lisbon or Barcelona'.[98]

The framework of 'transmodernity' therefore offers a way to understand Castro's own biography. Castro was among those who argued that Brazil should configure itself as a 'leader' of the Third World. In 1963 he wrote a piece for the anticolonial journal *Présence Africaine*, itself a site of great debate over the role of intellectuals and *hommes de cultures* [men of culture] in the political revolutions of decolonization. This was not his only association with the journal: in 1960 he had been a 'leading participant'[99] in a meeting in Rome of the *Société Européene de Culture* [European Society of Culture] organized in part by *Présence Africaine*. This places him in a significant 'epistemic community':[100] the conference was attended by key thinkers of

96 W.D. Mignolo, 'The Geopolitics of Knowledge and the Colonial Difference', *South Atlantic Quarterly* 101, no. 1 (January 2002): 62, doi:10.1215/00382876-101-1-57.

97 Castro, 'A La Recherche de l'Amérique Latine', 67.

98 Dussel, 'Transmodernity and Interculturality', 28.

99 Nancy Jachec, *Europe's Intellectuals and the Cold War: The European Society of Culture, Post-War Politics and International Relations* (London: IB Tauris, 2015).

100 Ruth Craggs and Martin Mahony, 'The Geographies of the Conference: Knowledge, Performance and Protest', *Geography Compass* 8, no. 6 (June 2014): 414–30, doi:10.1111/gec3.12137.

decolonization and independence such as Frantz Fanon, Aimé Césaire, and Léopold Senghor. Castro constituted a Brazilian (and geographical) link with African intellectual and political projects in this critical moment of decolonization. However, these were not smooth relationships. The Rome conference had been marked by divisions and Castro's piece for *Présence Africaine* itself seems clumsily formulated, arguing that Brazil could be the 'parent' of the Afro-Asiatic world.[101] Castro suggests Brazil's place in the world is tied to its intellectual life: 'today, we are a politically mature nation, with our own thought, with well defined aspirations, crystallized above all in the central tenet of economic development and the desire for wholesale political and economic emancipation, free of all foreign interference'.[102]

Castro asserts an emancipatory nationalism and positions himself, and Brazil, firmly in the non-aligned movement, arguing, as he had elsewhere, that the 1955 Bandung conference was the most significant geopolitical event of recent decades.[103] Castro was an important part of bringing the discourse of 'Third Worldism' into Brazil and Latin America in the 1960s.[104] He spoke in the Brazilian parliament in favour of an anticolonial foreign policy for Brazil, sharply criticizing the Brazilian government's failure to support Algerian independence, calling it 'a position in support of slavery, colonialism and imperialism'.[105] Here it is worth dwelling on translation again. Castro's words were: '*orientação escravagista, colonialista e imperialista*'. The word '*escravagista*' means a position in favour of slavery – a slavist politics. Castro's tripartite description insists on the necessary interconnectedness of slavery, colonialism, and imperialism, and emerges from the particular economic, social, and ecological forms of extractivism and oppression in the Brazilian Northeast.

Castro's anticolonialism was particularly dogged in support of the Cuban revolution. He was the president of the Brazilian Cuban Solidarity Commission in the early 1960s and travelled there in the late 1950s.[106] On 17 April 1961 Cuban exiles supported by the US government invaded Cuba at the Bay of Pigs. At 9am on 18 April Josué de Castro received a telegram from the Cuban government, through the *Instituto Cubana de Amistad Con Los Pueblos* [The Cuban Institute of Friendship with the Peoples, ICAP], announcing that the attack had been repelled. The telegram urgently

101 Josué de Castro, 'Le Brésil Parent Du Monde Afro-Asiatique Dans l'unité et Le Neutralisme', *Présence Africaine*, Le Brésil, no. 48 (1963): 187–92.
102 Castro, 'Le Brésil', 187.
103 Castro, 'De Bandung a Nova Dehli'.
104 Alburquerque, 'Tercer Mundo y Tercermundismo En Brasil'.
105 'essa orientação escravagista, colonialista e imperialista'. *Diario de Congresso Nacional*, 1960, Quinta-feira 17 November.
106 Josué de Castro, 'Notes for interview with Jornal do Comercio' (Manuscript, 59 1957), 464, CEHIBRA.JdC; See also Josué de Castro, 'To Students Union of Pernambuco', Letter, April 1961, 478, CEHIBRA.JdC.

appealed to Cuba's friends – Castro received it in his role as a principle defender of Cuba in Brazil – to help co-ordinate Latin American solidarity in the face of this imperialist attack. Castro immediately wrote in an official capacity to President Quadros,[107] co-ordinated a parliamentary appeal to the US government to desist,[108] and went, alongside the communist leader Luis Carlos Prestes, to the US Embassy in Brazil to denounce the US's action.[109] He drew a broad anticolonial conclusion from this historical moment. For Castro, the Cuban revolution was the most important event in twentieth-century Latin American history, tied to American imperialism and economic dependency, in particular through the plantation system.[110] Unsurprisingly, but importantly, he attributed some importance to the prevalence of hunger in Cuba prior to the revolution, which he called a 'War Against Hunger'.[111] It prefaced the next stage in anticolonial emancipation: 'it is human and just that a people revolt against a colonial state of things and, through herculean effort, emancipate themselves and organize a government that cleanses the nation of the opprobrium of colonial oppression'.[112] This is an important moment at which we can see Castro articulating in praxis a geopolitical critique, the geography of hunger, and an increasingly strident anticolonialism.

In geopolitical terms, decolonization altered the frameworks of possibility and the conditions of subaltern praxis. At meetings of the UN a new discourse of the international was possible. Castro's archive shows his own role in this new kind of geopolitical discourse. The *Présence Africaine* piece was published at the very end of 1963. In November of that year Castro had taken part in the FAO annual conference in Rome as chair of the Brazilian delegation. A transcript of the meeting survives. A controversy arose when the Ghanaian delegation, supported by all the African delegations, sought to alter FAO rules to enable the expulsion of member states if they violated fundamental principles. Their target was apartheid South Africa. European countries and the United States opposed the motion on the basis that the FAO was a specialized agency that should address 'technical' issues, and this was a 'political' intervention. Castro emerged as a central figure in the dispute. He used his intervention to make a theoretical point: he had long disputed the separation between 'technical' and 'political' questions. This was why he

107 Castro, 'To Jânio Quadros: Cuba'.
108 Josué de Castro and Frente Parlamentar Nacionalista, 'Apelo ao Presidente Kennedy dos Estados Unidos da América do Norte' (April 1961), 196, CEHIBRA.JdC; Various, 'Newspaper Clippings 1961: Cuba' (clippings, 1961), 5, CEHIBRA.JdC.
109 Various, 'Newspaper Clippings 1961: Cuba'.
110 Josué de Castro, 'Significação Política Da Revolução Cubana' (notes, 1960), 244, CEHIBRA.JdC.
111 Anonymous, 'Josué de Castro: "Revolução em Cuba é Guerra Contra a Fome"', *Última Hora*, February 1960, 5, CEHIBRA.JdC.
112 *Diario de Congresso Nacional*, 1960, Terça-feira 6 December.

always refused to refer to hunger as 'under-nutrition'. Speaking in French, Castro said, '*la technique* is nothing other than the instrument which is applied to resolve economic and social problems in the the world, thus: political problems'.[113] I have touched on this debate earlier, in discussing the FAO, and I want to dwell, here, on how to translate '*technique*'.[114] Normally '*technique*', like the Portuguese '*técnica*', would be translated as 'technology', but neither this nor the English word 'technique', which has accrued a different emphasis, capture Castro's meaning. The English 'technics' is much closer to '*technique*' in French and '*técnica*' in Portuguese. Both refer to a mediating concept: the mode of doing that sits between theory and practice; the Greek 'têchne' that bridges episteme and praxis. This was to become an important point in Milton Santos' geographical theory.[115] In his use of *technique* Castro is resisting the reification of the pragmatic that resides in the English terms 'technology' and in the Anglo-Saxon politics of abstracting 'technical' from 'political' questions. This is precisely the politics of knowledge and practice that Timothy Mitchell and others would later go on to theorize in the history of development.[116] This detour into technics is important because it demonstrates Castro's attempt to overcome the distinction between theory and praxis. He did so in part by insisting on the political qualities of the spaces of geopolitical practice. Castro saw intellectual work as taking place within and through institutions, not against them.

In the conference room in Rome, Castro declared, sylphishly, that he had waited two days to speak, hoping that the experienced hands of international diplomacy, the 'well-developed nations', would come up with a solution to the impasse. But he had waited in vain. He was unwilling, he said, to expel members, believing that international bodies should be spaces of dialogue and challenge. Nevertheless, the actions of the apartheid government constituted a betrayal of human conscience. He was interrupted by the Chairman, and told not to attack individual countries. He responded that he was not: he was defending principles.[117] He declared Brazil to be in favour of the Ghanaian proposal and was interrupted by applause. Having set out this stall of non-aligned solidarity, Castro suggested that a sub-committee be established to find a negotiated solution. Castro's suggestion was unanimously accepted, and a tragi-comic bickering ensued on the make-up of the sub-committee (the Algerians tried to nominate the Yugoslavians to the European group, which somewhat irritated the English and French), where it should meet

113 FAO, 'Proceedings of Conference of the FAO. 12th Session. Commission III', 5.
114 See Davies, 'Milton Santos'.
115 Davies, 'Milton Santos'.
116 Timothy Mitchell, *Rule of Experts: Egypt, Techno-Politics, Modernity* (Berkeley: University of California Press, 2002); James Ferguson, *Anti-Politics Machine: Development, Depoliticization, and Bureaucratic Power in Lesotho*, new ed. (Minneapolis: University of Minnesota Press, 1994).
117 FAO, 'Proceedings of Conference of the FAO. 12th Session. Commission III', 8.

(there wasn't a room with simultaneous translation available), and how it should report. Attending to the micro-geographies of this meeting reveals the disruption to 'normal' practice stirred up by the new geopolitical reality of decolonization.[118] It shows Castro's approach to international politics; his speech is peppered with references to his longstanding in international institutions[119] and to his friendships across the organization.[120] It is based on defending universal principles while attempting to reconcile this with a continuing belief in the potential of international institutions.

Writing as ambassador to the UN, in his *Présence Africaine* article Castro lays out a new direction for Brazilian foreign policy. Recognizing previous failures, Brazil will now enact its 'anti-imperialist vocation', be a friend to proletarian and formerly colonized people around the world, and 'throw a bridge of comprehension, mutual aid and political solidarity across the Atlantic', driving peace and neutrality.[121] Brazil is part of the world of people of colour, linked to underdeveloped countries in the 'four corners of the world'.[122] Castro was sent by the Brazilian President on a diplomatic mission to sub-Saharan Africa in 1960, in pursuit of an emerging Africa-orientated foreign policy at the time.[123] This emphasis on an Atlantic vocation, Africa, southern solidarity, and multilateralism were to re-emerge as the key discursive tenets of Brazilian foreign policy under the Lula governments of the early twenty-first century.[124] In the early 1960s Castro was actively involved in laying the groundwork for enhanced relations between Brazil and newly independent countries.[125]

In 1964, as well as serving a geopolitical function, publishing in the hugely influential *Présence Africaine* was part of Castro's intellectual self-fashioning. The edition in which he published included poetry by the

118 Craggs and Mahony, 'The Geographies of the Conference'.

119 FAO, 'Proceedings of Conference of the FAO. 12th Session. Commission III.'

120 See also remarks about Castro made by various delegates at Final Session as Chairman of the Executive Council of the FAO: FAO Council, 'Council of FAO: Twenty-Second Session: Fourth Plenary Meeting: Verbatim Record', November 1955, 29–32, 381, CEHIBRA.JdC.

121 Castro, 'Le Brésil', 190.

122 Castro, 'Le Brésil', 189.

123 Ministério das relações exteriores, 'Decreto de Josué de Castro', July 1960, 610, CEHIBRA.JdC.

124 Emir Sader and Pablo Gentili, 'The Lula Government's Foreign Policy: An Interview With Emir Sader', *NACLA Report on the Americas* 44, no. 2 (April 2011): 32–33; José Flávio Sombra Saraiva, 'The New Africa and Brazil in the Lula Era: The Rebirth of Brazilian Atlantic Policy', *Revista Brasileira de Política Internacional* 53, no. SPE (December 2010): 169–82, doi:10.1590/S0034-73292010000300010; Sean W. Burges, 'Auto-Estima in Brazil: The Logic of Lula's South-South Foreign Policy', *International Journal* (Autumn 2005): 1133–52.

125 Anonymous, 'O Brasil Quer Estreitar Relações com os Novos Países Africanos', *O Globo*, June 1960, 5, CEHIBRA.JdC.

Haitian revolutionary René Depestre, the American Marxist humanist Raya Dunayevskaya on African socialism, and a report on the struggle for independence in Mozambique by Eduardo Mondlane. This is not to claim a unity of purpose among these pieces – *Présence Africaine* itself, though committed to radical humanism and liberation, was in Alexandra Reza's terms, an 'unstable compound'[126] – but this company reveals Castro's self-fashioning as a radical, anticolonial intellectual. He was not the only Brazilian geographer in these circles: Milton Santos, having travelled with Quadros to Cuba, also engaged with anticolonial movements in the early 1960s.[127] However, in Castro's piece a familiar theme pops up. In the small print, his biography reads: 'Josué de Castro: Brazilian Economist. Specialist in the problems of hunger in the world. Author of Geopolitics of Hunger. Permanent Representative of his country to the UN. Geneva'.[128] Nowhere does it say 'geographer'. Being a public intellectual had always come before being a geographer. As argued above, he mobilized geography as a means, not an end. Nevertheless, placing Castro in Rome at the FAO, as a diplomat in newly independent Africa, and in the pages of *Présence Africaine* at the end of 1963, sees the history of geography not only, as we familiarly have it, by the side and in the hands of imperialists and colonialists, but alongside and in solidarity with movements for liberation. In late 1963 and early 1964 Castro was in militant company, circulating in international spaces, and politically enabled by the increasingly radical scope of Brazil's regional, national, and international politics. It turned out, however, that this would shortly come to an abrupt end.

The Exiled Intellectual, 1964–1968: Peace and Internationalism

The events of spring 1964 fundamentally changed the calculus of the anti-imperialist Brazilian left and altered the personal political circumstances of its intellectuals and activists. Any consideration of the impacts of the coup on intellectuals should not forget their relative privilege: violence and immiseration was enforced on many in Brazil not only immediately after the coup but for the decades of military rule. Castro and his intellectual colleagues' situation was to a great extent one of safety, security, and good fortune in comparison with the majority of Brazilians. Castro's own name was one of the first on the military coup's lists for exile. Yet he was already in Geneva, which, Jean Ziegler argues, may have 'saved his life'[129] and allowed him to avoid the imprisonment that Miguel Arraes, Francisco Julião, and

---

126 Alexandra Reza, 'African Literary Journals in French and Portuguese, 1947–1968: Politics, Culture and Form', DPhil thesis (University of Oxford, 2018).

127 Pedrosa, 'O Périplo Do Exílio de Milton Santos e a Formação de Sua Rede de Cooperação'.

128 Castro, 'Le Brésil', 192.

129 Jean Ziegler, *Betting on Famine: Why the World Still Goes Hungry* (New York: The New Press, 2013), 97.

others suffered at the hands of the military. Castro was aware of how his own circumstances of exile opened out onto the common experiences of all Brazilians. Speaking in May 1965 in Peru, as an honorary professor, he said, 'apparently they have stripped me of my so-called political rights. They have stripped me of nothing because no-one in my country has political rights in this moment. They have stripped me of nothing because everyone living there lives without political rights.'[130]

Many scholars were forced into exile or imprisoned. Some went to Europe, like Castro. Others went to the cities of the non-aligned world: Miguel Arraes made a home in Algeria, Francisco Julião in Cuernavaca in Mexico, Anna Montenegro in Mexico and Cuba. The key Peasant League activist Elizabeth Teixeira went into internal hiding. She lived as a schoolteacher in the *sertão* until she was located in 1984 by a film crew completing a documentary about the Peasant Leagues begun, and abandoned, in the spring of 1964.[131] Vânia Bambirra initially went into hiding in São Paulo before escaping to Chile. The coup made the further institutional development of dependency theory in Brazil impossible, and the site of intellectual activity moved – initially to Santiago de Chile, and then to Mexico City.[132] Yet émigrés, as they were for world literature[133] or area studies,[134] then became significant to the project of underdevelopment and dependency thought. One of the functions of intellectual networks at this time was precisely to protect those forced into exile. Alberto Guerreiro Ramos, for instance, secured a post at the University of Southern California through intellectual networks,[135] and Milton Santos and his brother Nailton similarly drew on scholarly connections.[136] Exile was the 'dividing of the waters' of Milton Santos' life, leading to new and distinct combinations of interlocutors, influences, and institutions.[137] Santos' and Castro's lives in exile overlapped: Maria Adélia Aparecida de Souza, an influential Brazilian geographer who worked with Santos, describes having

130 Castro, *Adónde va?*, 21.
131 Eduardo Coutinho, *Cabra Marcado Para Morrer* (New York: Cinema Guild, 1984), https://www.youtube.com/watch?v=KUYlBosaXJ8.
132 Vania Bambirra, *Teoria de La Dependencia: Una Anticritica*, Serie Popular Era/68 (México: Ediciones Era, 1978); Prado, 'Vânia Bambirra', 20–22.
133 Emily Apter, 'Global Translatio: The "Invention" of Comparative Literature, Istanbul, 1933', *Critical Inquiry* 29, no. 2 (2003): 253–81, doi:10.1086/374027.
134 Sidaway, 'Geography, Globalization, and the Problematic of Area Studies', 995–96.
135 Diana De Groat Brown, 'Guerreiro Ramos in the United States: His Life through the Lens of Political Exile', *Ilha Revista de Antropologia* 18, no. 1 (October 2016): 207, doi:10.5007/2175-8034.2016v18n1p207.
136 Pedrosa, 'O Périplo Do Exílio de Milton Santos e a Formação de Sua Rede de Cooperação'; Adriana Bernardes, 'Milton Santos: Breve Relato Da Trajetória Científica e Intelectual de Um Grande Geógrafo', *Boletim Paulista de Geografia* 78 (2017): 139–52.
137 Pedrosa, 'O Périplo Do Exílio de Milton Santos e a Formação de Sua Rede de Cooperação', 444.

lunch with him and Castro at UNESCO in Paris in 1971.[138] In Santos' case, this network was part of an under-appreciated role in the formation of radical geography, which Pedrosa and Ferretti have begun to establish in recent research.

As the next chapter explores, Castro's own exile led to new intellectual opportunities. Yet it also took its toll on him. We can trace its effects in both public and private spheres. When the coup took place, Castro had just finished writing a book about the Northeast. So too had Celso Furtado. Both were published in translation almost immediately: Castro's *Sete Palmos de Terra e Uma Caixão* (1964) as *Death in the Northeast* (1965) and Furtado's *Dialética do Desenvolvimento* (1964) as *Diagnosis of the Brazilian Crisis* (1965). The translation of the titles tells its own story of travelling theory: Castro's translates as 'Seven Feet of Earth and a Coffin' and Furtado's as 'Dialectic of Development'. Castro's Brazilian title refers directly to the Peasant Leagues' demand for burial rights. In Furtado's it is explicit that the word 'dialectic' was a red flag for North American audiences, and the emphasis on crisis seemed more palatable. The translations attempted to create particular lexicons with which to tell the story of the Northeast to Anglo-Saxon audiences. As well as new titles, both were given new prefaces, cited in the introduction to this chapter. These prefaces are dispatches from the heat of a profoundly disturbing and molten moment in Brazilian history. Furtado's book has two: the first, for the Brazilian edition, written in Recife, in January 1964, begins with a grandiose tone, leavened by deep political commitment: 'at no time has the responsibility of intellectuals been as great as it is now. And this responsibility has been betrayed by the commissions of some intellectuals and the omissions of others.'[139] Castro's *Death in the Northeast*, meanwhile, has one preface that is one page long, signed 'Geneva, May, 1964':

> When a military junta brought down the administration of President João Goulart in the spring of 1964 and set up a new Brazilian government, this book was already being translated into English. My first impulse was to recall the manuscript and add a chapter on the downfall of Goulart and his land reform programs [...] to describe [...] still another setback to the progressive forces of Brazil at the hands of the reactionary minority [...] On reflection, however, I decided to let the book stand as it was, since the historical and sociological interpretation I had already provided adequately covered, and indeed anticipated, the incident.[140]

There is a certain poignancy and coolness here that belies the personal and political upheaval that 'Geneva, May 1964' stands for in Castro's life. His exile

138 Maria Adélia Aparecida de Souza, 'As geografias da desigualdade: relendo a Geografia da fome', in *Josué de Castro: memória do saber*, ed. Tânia Elias Magno da Silva, 1st ed. (Rio de Janeiro: Fundação Miguel de Cervantes, 2012), 430.
139 Furtado, *Diagnosis*.
140 Castro, *Death in the Northeast*.

was less than a month old. He was unable to return to Brazil, isolated from his wider family and friends and uncertain where he would be able to live and work. His letters at the time illustrate the trauma this engendered in a man who suffered from extensive and profound periods of depression, which he referred to in French as *surmenage*, overstrain.[141] Said suggests, cautiously, that there is a certain kind of pleasure in exile. Such pleasure was not in Castro's experience of the condition. Personally, the pain of exile was profound. He wrote to his children in mid-1964: 'I received a telegram from an Arnaldo – I suppose it must be Arnoldo Nisker – but whose text did little to clarify its subject. I enclose it here. In it, as you can see, I'm asked to urgently send photos. What photos? I don't know. Why urgent? I don't know.'[142]

Many things rendered the early months of exile bewildering. The political situation remained opaque: he talks about the 'confusing Brazilian reality', and his astonishment at the paradox of Franco-ist Spanish newspapers condemning the right-wing Brazilian 'revolution'. With the coup he lost his employment and position, and he had to reflect on what path to take: 'of my activities the one that seems most promising, and with most of a future, is being a writer'.[143] Paulo Cavalcanti – a fellow exile and former communist leader in Pernambuco – wrote 'if you had asked me, before the coup of 1964, who, in my opinion would have the capacity to best bear political exile, I would have responded without hesitation: Josué de Castro'. A polyglot, well travelled, and incredibly well connected, he would be fine. Cavalcanti admitted, though, that he had been wrong, and that Castro 'died from the anguish of exile',[144] struck down by episodes of depression.

In a letter to his children, Castro notes that *Geografia da Fome* was eliciting attention from more publishers precisely because of his exile and Brazilian upheaval.[145] (Amusingly, the tangling up of titles means he needs to gloss this even to his own children as '(the study of Brazil)'.[146]) Exile marked a shift in the form of Castro's intellectual work. The preface of *Death in the Northeast* is one of the earliest of his writings that registers his exile. It also raises questions about the book's authorship. Castro notes that, 'in preparing this book, [he] enjoyed the invaluable collaboration of the Brazilian sociologist Alberto Passos Guimarães, who supplied background material for the chapters on the feudalistic Brazilian agrarian system'.[147] Elsewhere he also noted that his wife, Glauce, was indispensable to continuing his work under the condition of exile, as he had acknowledged her to be to his early work, writing in 1946

---

141 See, for instance, Silva, 'Josué por ele mesmo: o diário', 35–38, 42–43.
142 Castro, '"Meus queridos"'.
143 Castro, '"Meus queridos"'.
144 Paulo Cavalcanti, *A luta clandestina: Memórias Políticas* (Recife: Companhia Editora de Pernambuco (CEPE), 2015).
145 Castro, '"Meus queridos"'.
146 Castro, '"Meus queridos"'.
147 Castro, *Death in the Northeast.*

that her name should be associated with *A Geografia da Fome*.[148] Castro wrote to his children from Paris in June 1964 and told them he was struggling under the pressures of commitments and thanks to 'the weight of age and accumulated fatigue'. He asked them to consider Alberto Guimarães' political standing and his position in relation to the coup and, if they approve, to approach Guimarães for agreement to reuse material published in a book called *Quatro séculos de Latifundio* [Four Centuries of the Latifundio] in return for a third or a quarter of the rights to the completed work.[149] Guimarães was a Northeasterner, from Alagoas. A communist and self-taught intellectual, he was part of a group based in Maceió that included Castro's friends Rachel de Queiroz and Graciliano Ramos. In the early 1960s he worked for the *Instituto Brasileiro de Geografia e Estatística* [Brazilian Institute for Geography and Statistics] (IBGE). Guimarães did more than provide background material. Chapters 3 and 4 of *Death in the Northeast* are written by him. Castro added some sections – on the foundation of Recife and Olinda, for example[150] – but the large majority is effectively identical to the opening chapters of Guimarães' *Quatro Séculos* [Four Centuries].[151] Presumably – although I haven't found further letters pertaining to it – Castro's children came to an agreement with Guimarães. The texts diverge when Castro begins to draw on Gunnar Myrdal on the economics of underdevelopment. But the sections written by Guimarães provide the historical analysis for Castro's argument that the *latifundio* is a hybrid, feudal–capitalist formation. This informs Castro's theory of underdevelopment and his understanding of the political dynamics of the Northeast in the mid-twentieth century. The timings of the preface and the letter raise some questions. Either Castro had already 'written' these sections on the history of the *latifundia* prior to getting Guimarães' consent, or the preface is dated May but is actually written later. It is no coincidence that *Death in the Northeast*, his most explicitly regional work, not only coincided with Castro identifying himself principally as a writer but bears the marks of exile in its very language.

In exile Castro stayed in close contact with political and cultural developments in Brazil. As Ferretti points out, he was indeed able to travel to the country briefly in the later 1960s, under a diplomatic passport, but could not work or proceed with any of his professional activities. Ferretti shows how this ambivalent status was tied in to the frustrations and limitations of his project to create and run a *Centre International de Development* from Paris.[152] In March 1969 he wrote to his friend André Chamson at the *Archives Nationales* in Paris enclosing a record from the Northeast, noting how the songs are

148 Castro, *Geografia da Fome: O Dilema Brasileiro: Pão Ou Aço* (1965), 1:32.
149 Castro, '"Meus queridos"'.
150 Castro, *Death in the Northeast*, 74–75.
151 Alberto Passos Guimarães, *Quatro Séculos de Latifúndio*, Fulgor Biblioteca de Estudos Brasileiros (São Paulo: Fulgor, 1964), 9–70.
152 Ferretti, 'Decentring the Lettered City'.

engaged in the dramatic political struggle in the country. (Which record, sadly, he does not say.[153]) But he also travelled extensively, to Russia, China, the Middle East, the Caribbean, the United States, and Latin America. There was a self-imposed limit to his mobility – he noted in a letter in 1964 that he had been invited on an all-expenses paid trip to Australia. He wasn't planning to go, because, ever the geographer, he 'had a quick look at a map and Australia really is at the end of the world'.[154] Indeed, such travelling often cost him in terms of his health and consequent ability to work. There are many references to breaks in his schedule thanks to fatigue and usually unspecified ill health.[155]

Another consequence of exile was Castro's subsequent muted reception in Brazilian geography. His books were banned in Pernambuco[156] and he fell out of university courses and public education.[157] He lost both of what Ward calls the 'bounded' and 'relational' publics for his work: those within his discipline and those beyond it.[158] Exile skewed the academic impact of his work beyond his death.[159] As Milton Santos put it, he 'died at the wrong time' and in the wrong place.[160] Nevertheless, as for Santos, exile opened up extraordinary opportunities for Castro that were to take his work and politics in new directions. He became an active participant in many international networks, from the Brazilian and Latin American exile community to the World Government network and others. I want to draw attention, here, to his place in a global network of anticolonialists.[161] (Whereas Daniel Clayton lays out the appearance of decolonization in geography, what is at stake here is the appearance of a geographer in decolonization.[162]) In 1960 he

153 Josué de Castro, 'To André Chamson', March 1969, 290, CEHIBRA.JdC.

154 Castro, '"Meus queridos"'.

155 For example, Josué de Castro, 'Letter to Raja Gabaglia', August 1944, 165, CEHIBRA.JdC; Josué de Castro, 'Letter to Gilbert McAllister', August 1960, 544, CEHIBRA.JdC.

156 Comissão Estadual da Memória e Verdade Dom Hélder Câmara, '67 – Movimento Estudantil', n.d., Série TD – Transcrições de Depoimentos – 67, Arquivo Público Pernambuco Jordão Emerenciano.

157 Santos, 'Entrevista explosiva'.

158 Ward, '"Public Intellectuals"', 1041–42.

159 Campos, 'A Presença Na Geografia de Josué de Castro'.

160 Armen Mamigonian et al., 'Entrevista Com o Professor Milton Santos', Geosul 6, no. 12 (1991): 116–47.

161 See also Federico Ferretti, 'Geopolitics of Decolonisation: The Subaltern Diplomacies of Lusophone Africa (1961–1974)', Political Geography 85 (March 2021): 102326, doi:10.1016/j.polgeo.2020.102326; Ferretti, 'A Coffin for Malthusianism'; Ferretti, 'Subaltern Connections: Brazilian Critical Geographers, Development and African Decolonisation', Third World Quarterly 41, no. 5 (2020): 822–41.

162 Daniel Clayton, 'The Passing of "Geography's Empire" and Question of Geography in Decolonization, 1945–1980', Annals of the American Association of Geographers 110, no. 5 (2020): 1540–58.

met with Benyoucef Benkhedda, a Minister of the Algerian *Front de libéra-tion nationale*, in Brazil,[163] and Clodomir Morais claimed that Castro's flat in Paris was used as a late-night safe house by African National Congress militants en route between secret missions.[164] Clodomir suggested that Castro had personal friendships with quite an extraordinary list of famous men: 'Sukarno, Nyerere, Nehru, Nasser, Sekou Touré, Chu En-lai, N'Krumah. [...] BenBella, Lumumba, Mandela etc. [...] general Cárdenas, of México; Perón, of Argentina; the Generals Torrijos, of Panamá; Alvarado, of Peru, and his friends Fidel and Allende, respectively, of Cuba and of Chile'.[165] We would do well to take this list with some caution. Not because Castro did not know many of them: in his archive there are epistolary exchanges with Nehru, Léopold Senghor, Juán Peron, and Salvador Allende, and he certainly met Fidel Castro, who read *Geografía da Fome* and invited him to Cuba when he was visiting Brazil in 1959.[166] These lists and letters are important for putting the history of geography into unfamiliar company. But they don't demonstrate the extent of his involvement in clandestine struggle, or his influence, or that of geographical thought, on the anticolonial movement.

When the ex- (and future) President of Argentina, Juan Perón, was in exile in Madrid in December 1968 he wrote to Castro: 'here we work in the most absolute secrecy, for now, because one way of not exposing ourselves to the actions of our enemies (and we have powerful enemies) is to work in the greatest clandestinity, at least until we have organization and means enough to resist in the struggle'.[167] Perón wrote that Castro and he will meet, either in Paris or in Madrid in the coming months, to see one another's organi-zations. Castro's organization that Perón is referring to was not a secret (in Perón's case, ultimately successful) project to return to power but the rather more run-of-the-mill Centre for International Development. Further research in other archives could contribute to a deeper understanding of these networks. The evidence available here precipitates interesting questions about what Castro contributed – intellectually and practically – to various kinds of political struggle, and what these relationships mean for the history of geography.

In 1969 Castro co-edited a collection of essays called *Latin American Radicalism*. The book ties Castro to a later generation of critical Latin

---

163 Rodrigo Nabuco de Araujo Araujo, 'A Voz Da Argélia. A Propaganda Revolucionária Da Frente de Libertação Nacional Argelina No Brasil. Independência Nacional e Revolução Socialista (1954–1962)', *Estudus Históricos (Rio de Janeiro) May/Aug. 2017* 30, no. 16 (August 2017).

164 Clodomir, 'Josué de Castro: Brasileiro e Cidadão Do Mundo'.

165 Clodomir, 'Josué de Castro: Brasileiro e Cidadão Do Mundo'.

166 Unknown, 'Fidel Castro e Josué de Castro' (unknown, May 1959), 27, CEHIBRA. JdC.

167 Juan Perón, 'Juan Perón to Josué de Castro', December 1968, 115, CEHIBRA.JdC; see also Juan Perón, 'Juan Perón to Josué de Castro', May 1972, 115, CEHIBRA.JdC.

American thought, including Rodolfo Stavenhagen and Régis Debray. It also situates him within anglophone social science and Latin American studies. On the other hand, the book is marked by the ambivalence of its political positioning. As a contemporary review by Robert F. Smith in *The Nation* noted, 'it is apparent that [the editors] agreed to disagree as to the nature of radicalism [...] Are nationalist movements invariably radical? Is there a line, however dim, which separates a radical from a liberal?'[168] These questions were of crucial importance as revolutionary movements bubbled across Latin America, and the vagueness of the collection can apply to Castro's own writings. The apparent apotheosis of Castro's own late radicalism can be seen in Eduardo Galeano's *Open Veins of Latin America*, in which Galeano wrote, in 1973: 'says Josué de Castro: "I who have received an international peace prize, think that, unhappily, there is no other solution than violence for Latin America."'[169] Galeano does not give a reference for this statement, but the source of the quotation seems to be an interview with the Spanish magazine, *Cuadernos para el Diálogo* [Notebooks for Dialogue], in 1968, in which Castro said 'the ideal solution for the world would be peaceful. During periods of violence a great deal of lucidity and and consciousness of circumstances is lost. However, I believe that for Latin America there is now no other possibility than violent revolution. I am a desperate pacifist.' Castro refuted the possibility of gradualism and reform, saying 'all efforts at reform have failed'.[170]

It is worth dwelling on how Castro's thought became more radical as he grew older. By the late 1960s he is explicit that truly satiating the hunger of the oppressed would require a massive rupture of the existing order. A comparison with Gilberto Freyre shows Castro's radical ageing (a recovery of his radical youth). In 1950, in his first ever run for election, Castro put his name forward under the banner of the same coalition as Gilberto Freyre.[171] By 1968, Freyre was championing the Portuguese Salazar regime's lusotropical fascism and Castro was admiring the May '68 graffiti on his Parisian classroom walls and declaring that hopes for peaceful reform in Latin America were over.[172] As his own biography led him to new places, his intellectual work increasingly placed Latin American struggle deeper in tricontinental, revolutionary contexts. This movement was tied not only to the changing political situation in Latin America and his own exile in 1964 but also to his pedagogical and research

168 Robert F. Smith, 'Latin American Radicalism (Review)', *The Nation*, March 1969, 526, CEHIBRA.JdC.

169 Eduardo Galeano, *Open Veins of Latin America: Five Centuries of the Pillage of a Continent* (New York: NYU Press, 1997), 4.

170 Rosembuj, 'Josué de Castro: las dudas de un pacifista'.

171 Marcelo Mário de Melo, 'Josué de Castro: Um Intelectual-Político', in *O Brasil Em Evidência: A Utopia Do Desenvolvimento* (Rio de Janeiro: Fundação Getúlio Vargas, 2012), 30–45.

172 Castro, 'Desarrollo, Ecologia, Desarme y Descolonización'.

experiences in the radical spaces of the Parisian universities during the 1968 uprisings. It is to these that I turn in the final chapter.

Conclusion

Thinking about the question of the public geographical intellectual through Castro's work and life might suggest that public prominence is a pre-condition of intellectual praxis. This is not what I want to argue: Castro is an exception, not the rule. Edward Said emphasizes that the role of the intellectual is not contingent on the scale of audience. Converging on Gramsci's conception, Said argues that intellectuals are not a select few but a larger group who conduct various kinds of intervention in many different settings. This opens up more space for considering contemporary geographers to be public intellectuals.[173] It renders more immediate and less high-flown the questions of solidarity and critique that are the fault lines of intellectualism. Solidarity, as David Featherstone has drawn out, has everyday geographies and relies on practices of exchange, communication, translation, and generosity that constitute historically and geographically specific webs of solidarity.[174] Nevertheless, there is necessarily a negotiation to be undertaken between solidarity and commitment. This chapter has shown that Castro navigated different kinds of intellectual commitment and responsibility.

These fault lines continue to mark the relationship between intellectual, movement, party, region, nation, and universal causes today. In Brazil they are particularly keenly delineated, not least in the rise of neo-fascism in the late 2010s. Brazil's *Partido Trabalhista* (PT) was the inheritor of the PTB. Many intellectuals have had close ties to the party. Its 2018 Presidential candidate against Jair Bolsonaro was Fernando Haddad, a Professor of Political Science at the University of São Paulo. Marilena Chauí and Francisco de Oliveira were both involved in founding the PT in the 1980s. By 2005, however, they were in the midst of a negotiation over how to position themselves, and intellectual work, in relation to the first Lula government. Both were to establish a profound critique of that government.[175] They engaged in a public dialogue over what the role of the intellectual was. Chauí addressed Oliviera:

> Look, Chico. They asked what I was going to say. I told them that there was something that I'd said to you, privately, that I was going to say in public. It is that you are the light of our eyes. Whenever some explanation

173 Castree, 'Geography's New Public Intellectuals?'
174 Featherstone, '"Gramsci in Action"'; David Featherstone, 'Maritime Labour and Subaltern Geographies of Internationalism: Black Internationalist Seafarers' Organising in the Interwar Period', *Political Geography* 49 (2015): 7–16, doi:10.1016/j.polgeo.2015.08.004.
175 Francisco de Oliveira, 'Lula in the Labyrinth', *New Left Review* II, no. 42 (2006): 5–22; Oliveira, 'The Lenin Moment'.

about Brazil crystallizes – a historical, sociological or economic explanation – we can rely on your work to break it down, to give us another explanation, another understanding. Not any old understanding, a materialist understanding – but a serious one. There is also always the sense [...] that you always arrive at just the right time. Whenever there is the feeling that there is an explanation out there, but that it doesn't really account for its object, a work of yours arrives which helps us understand our time [...] This is why you are the light of our eyes.[176]

Chauí describes not only the task of the intellectual but also the key role of friendship in intellectual life, which is a recurrent feature of Castro's own biography.[177] Chauí's words offer a good starting point, too, for where to look for light, and new explanations, in pitch-black times in Brazil's contemporary history. Chauí picks up some of Said's conceptions of the role of the intellectual: timing, publicness, and a resolute contrariness of critique. She defines the 'radicalism of critique' as that which is immanent to the object it studies (a definition similar to Labriola's of the philosophy of praxis[178]). It is precisely in terms of struggle that such work lives and breathes. Not in the sense of being aligned, or not, on particular forms of policy or political strategy, but in the sense that the struggle is contiguous with its own representation and interpretation. Speaking in 2009 about her work in the 1970s, Doreen Massey made a similar case: 'we *were* the struggle. We didn't have to go out and link up with the struggle. We were the struggle. [...] You know it is not like we find the nice people to help. We *were* the women's movement or whatever.'[179] Affiliation and commitment is intimate and complete: the intellectual is not autonomous because they are separate or independent. On the contrary, intellectual autonomy, Chauí argues, can exist 'only if it is supported by the stance of taking a position within class struggle against the dominant classes, and in the redefinition of universals, comprehended as concrete universals'.[180] Massey, Oliveira, and Chauí sublate the criteria that Said proposes: 'never solidarity before critique'. Like Priyamvada Gopal, they ask, 'why not both?'[181]

---

176 Marilena Chauí, 'Radicalidade Da Crítica', in *Francisco de Oliveira: A Tarefa Da Crítica*, ed. Cibele Saliba Rizek and Wagner de Melo Romão (Belo Horizonte: Editora UFMG, 2006), 25.

177 On his relationships in Paris, see Ferretti, 'Decentring the Lettered City'.

178 Wolfgang Fritz Haug, 'Gramsci's "Philosophy of Praxis"', *Socialism and Democracy* 14, no. 1 (January 2000): 3, 14, doi:10.1080/08854300008428251.

179 Massey et al., 'The Possibilities of a Politics of Place Beyond Place?' 418.

180 Chauí, *Between Conformity and Resistance*, 25.

181 Cambridge Critical Theory and Practice Seminars, *Priyamvada Gopal: 'What Are Intellectuals for? Edward Said and the Question of Representation'*, Cambridge Critical Theory and Practice Seminars (Cambridge: Mill Lane Lecture Theatre, 2015), accessed 18 June 2022, https://www.youtube.com/watch?v=B3rp4nFKT_0.

This modality of commitment is challenging for academic practice. Yet before getting carried away with the grandiosity of its claims, it is crucial to reiterate Said's insistence on the many scales of intellectual work. Its audience is not pre-ordained as national or global. Intellectuals are a broad group conducting many kinds of work at many kinds of scale. Furthermore, it is by no means to claim that the intellectual is the *whole* of the struggle, but that intellectuals should seek to establish an immanent connection between intellectual work and political practice. It suggests less that intellectual work should be the preface to, threshold of, or guilty pleasure after the real work of political commitment. It doesn't require the intellectual to stop writing and get on with real politics. As Paulo Freire wrote, 'the radical, [...] rejects activism and submits his actions to reflection'.[182] Freire's concept of 'activism' here is not the same as that in common usage now: he means a kind of action-ism, which excessively prioritizes doing over theorized practice.[183] The task of the radical intellectual necessitates profound reflections on Said's 'vocation for representation'. It requires orientating the intellectual process and methodology with the speaking voice of the intellectual. The vocation for representation is also the duty of representation. How, what, who, and on what terms to represent is therefore the pith of intellectual work. This means holding to the almost wistful, utopian humanism of Said's nevertheless resolutely grounded political insistence on fundamental principles – or Chauí's 'universal causes' – and the pursuit of human freedom. From within the neoliberal institutions of contemporary academia there is something almost embarrassing about the audacity of this definition, but it nevertheless remains a crucial political starting point for radical geographical thought.

182 Freire, *Education for Critical Consciousness*, 9.
183 On the question of political ecology and praxis see Alex Loftus, 'Political Ecology as Praxis', in *The Routledge Handbook of Political Ecology*, ed. Tom Perreault, Gavin Bridge, and James McCarthy (London and New York: Routledge, 2015), 179–87.

CHAPTER 7

1968–1973: Reading Fragments

Vincennes, the International Environment, and Anticolonialism

Introduction

The *Casa dos Estudantes do Imperio* [House of the Students of Empire] in Lisbon was a key site of anticolonial resistance to the Portuguese empire, in terms of both intellectual production and political organization.[1] From its inception in 1948 the *Casa* had published a literary and political journal, *Mensagem*. In February of 1964, at the back of *Mensagem*, they published a pamphlet, called '*Fome ou Abundancia*'[2] [Hunger or Abundance]. The pamphlet was an overview of world hunger and, to all intents and purposes, a précis of Josué de Castro's *Geopolítica da Fome*. It was the last thing the *Casa* ever published: they were shut down by the Portuguese imperial authorities shortly after. For twenty years its writers and activists had undergone the constant threat of repression, arrest, violence, and censorship. *Fome ou Abundância* was part of a crescendo of political radicalism that led to the *Casa*'s closure.[3]

It is not surprising that anticolonialists used the geography and geopolitics of hunger as a rallying cry. It is the counterpart political history to Enrique Dussel's recourse to hunger as the negative foundation of the philosophy of liberation, and the visceral premise of Fanon's *Wretched of the Earth*. Castro's was always a geography of colonialism, and the geography of the resistance to hunger was that of the resistance to the 'slavocratic, colonialist and imperialist orientation' of European (and North American) states.[4] His anticolonialism went back to 1928, when he wrote an article called 'America

---

1 Inocência Mata, 'O Singular Enfrentamento à Ideologia Colonial Da Colecção "Autores Ultramarinos" Da Casa Dos Estudantes Do Império', *ABRH: Revista Do NEPA/UFF* 10 (June 2018): 15, doi:10.22409/abriluff.2018n20a495.

2 Álvaro Mateus, 'Fome Ou Abundancia?' (Lisbon: Casa dos Estudantes do Império, February 1964), 11123.002.004, Fundação Mario Soares.

3 Alexandra Reza, 'African Anti-Colonialism and the Ultramarinos of the Casa Dos Estudantes Do Império', *Journal of Lusophone Studies* 1, no. 1 (2016).

4 *Diario de Congresso Nacional*, 1960, Quinta-feira 17 November.

Libre' [Free America]: 'we will reach this future slowly, like those who seek perfection. Stage by stage. From individualism to socialism. Throwing down first the preconceptions of class. Second, those of race. Third, those of nationality. Always tending towards total brotherhood.'[5] His language here is full of broad, youthful revolutionary overtones, and Castro rarely wrote in this pan-Americanist, Marxist tone later in his career, but his early radicalism was always only restrained and repurposed, not abandoned.

At the back of *Fome ou Abundancia?* alongside Castro, the author Álvaro Mateus cites Yves Lacoste's *Os Países Sub-desenvolvidas* [Underdeveloped Countries].[6] In the late 1960s and early 1970s Castro and Lacoste both worked at a place widely lauded in the history of radical thought but not considered in anglophone histories of radical geography: the University of Vincennes, Paris VIII.[7] As Power and Sidaway argue, 'attention to seemingly obscure branches of twentieth-century academic geography has the capacity to enrich and disturb wider understandings of paradigm shifts in the discipline'.[8] What is 'obscure' and what is not is a question of standpoint, and their formulation risks reiterating a pre-ordained linguistic and hegemonic centrality, but Power and Sidaway are right in other ways. The broader question of why francophone radical geography, and more specifically the experimental avenues opened at Vincennes, has been largely ignored within anglo-North American radical geography remains an open question. I do not close that down here, but rather take geography in the first five years of Vincennes' existence on its own terms, and from the perspective of Castro's Third Worldist radicalism, rather than from the perspective of Vincennes' place in the history of the French discipline of geography.[9] Nevertheless, I consider first Paris, and then more specifically Vincennes, between 1968 and 1973, as important places in a global history of critical geographical ideas.[10]

In the early 1970s, in the Bois de Vincennes, in temporary university buildings hastily thrown up after May 1968, a distinctive political critique of human ecology was established. In this chapter I follow the paraphernalia of intellectual practice and the history of geography: inscriptions, course notes, dissertations, and syllabi. Castro's work at Vincennes is an important

5 Melo and Neves, *Josué de Castro*, 19.
6 Mateus, 'Fome Ou Abundancia?'
7 See, for instance, Jean-Michel Dijan, ed., *Vincennes: Une Aventure de la Pensée Critique* (Paris: Flammarion, 2009).
8 Power and Sidaway, 'The Degeneration of Tropical Geography', 587.
9 On which see Yann Calbérac, 'Close Reading Michel Foucault's and Yves Lacoste's Concepts of Space Through Spatial Metaphors', *Le Foucauldien* 7, no. 1 (2021) and Béatrice Giblin, 'Vincennes's Fiftieth Anniversary. What Hérodote Owes to Vincennes', *Hérodote* 1 (2018): 151–56.
10 Gavin Bridge, James McCarthy, and Tom Perreault, 'Editors' Introduction', in *The Routledge Handbook of Political Ecology*, ed. Gavin Bridge, James McCarthy, and Tom Perreault (London and New York: Routledge, 2015), 3–18.

episode in the history of critical geography, as a scholar from the south embedded in a northern institution. But, as so much of Castro's work and life demonstrates, it is impossible to distil the southern from the northern here. There is no miraculous conception of knowledge from either north or south. This necessarily complicates the way in which we position post and decolonial critiques of the epistemology of geography: figuring European geography as hermetic in the first place is a false start. This is not to establish a straw man argument: clearly the issue at stake is the relative power of discourses. While postcolonial theory has never conceptualized traditions as distinct,[11] 'decolonial' approaches increasingly appear to do so.[12] Therefore it is vital to insist that the tangled and relational histories of geographical knowledge remain important. Castro's trans-modern biography shows us a Brazilian thinker addressing Brazilian and global social reality through a commitment to pan-Americanism and liberation movements, but profoundly formed by deep readings of European and American philosophy and French geography.[13] If we are to place Castro in, or against, a tradition – or a canon[14] – then it must be a canon that is already his own. Milton Santos' trajectory is similar: moving between the north and south and engaging across and through this relationship, not relocating from one side to another.[15] That these scholars have been listened to less by northern interlocutors than they themselves listened to European traditions is to northern geography's detriment, because these are histories not of absence but of unequal epistemic exchange.[16] This is to offer a relational history of geography that contributes a sustained attention to a set of positions – more precisely, as I outlined in chapter 3, a continuous situated mobility – that are all already both in and outside European histories of thought. This elicits new objects of study, new empirical sources and interlocutors, and competing universalisms.

This chapter places critical geographies of environment and development in an important place and time in the history of European leftist thought: Paris, 1968, and the University of Vincennes. Placing Castro more firmly within the history of Vincennes complicates French-centric accounts of the impact of May '68 and Vincennes in French universities. The story of

11 Achille Mbembe et al., 'What Is Postcolonial Thinking?' *Esprit* December, no. 12 (2006): 117–33.

12 Archie Davies, 'Review: On Decoloniality, Walter Mignolo and Catherine Walsh', *Journal of Latin American Studies* 53.2 (2021): 399–402.

13 Dussel, 'Transmodernity and Interculturality'.

14 Keighren, Abrahamsson, and della Dora, 'On Canonical Geographies'.

15 This is a related, but slightly different argument to that of Lucas Melgaço, 'Thinking Outside the Bubble of the Global North: Introducing Milton Santos and "The Active Role of Geography" Symposium: Introducing Milton Santos and "The Active Role of Geography" Organisers: Lucas Melgaço and Tim Clarke', *Antipode* 49, no. 4 (2017): 946–51.

16 Halvorsen, 'Cartographies of Epistemic Expropriation'.

Vincennes has been well told, and I do not seek to rewrite it here or to try to make geography central to that story. French historians of geography, in particular revolving around the hugely influential of Yves Lacoste, and various revisions of his role, have already done that work.[17] I want, rather, to place Castro alongside these histories – I use the term *alongside* deliberately in order precisely to avoid subsuming Castro to a pre-established history of geography (critical, radical or otherwise) in which an end result of geography's disciplinary and contemporary manifestation is already known.

Castro's appointment to Vincennes in 1968 filled him with enthusiasm for new plans, and he saw the conditions of the new university as an opportunity to develop his academic work in new and stimulating directions.[18] His presence, pedagogy, and practice in Paris brought a distinct set of influences – dependency theory, Latin American radicalism, French regional geography, ecological politics, Northeastern thought, and anti-imperialist histories – into distinctive forms and forums. These existed within an institutional and disciplinary frame different from those more often associated with radical geography's origin stories, and outside the normalized trajectory of political ecology. I offer this history alongside what Power and Sidaway describe as the 'degeneration' of tropical geography into development geography, and its 'refraction' 'into differing channels of modernization theory and a radical development geography of dependency'.[19] This chapter is also part of the history of the latter, but these subsections themselves 'have splintered'.[20] The history of critical geography is a multi-lingual, multi-sited story. Existing histories are too quick to delimit their scope according to linguistic boundaries. The moment analysed here belies such separations. Taking Castro's career at Vincennes as a starting point allows us to tie the history of geography more closely to wider radical intellectual movements and to anticolonial thought and practice. This, of course, constitutes a major departure from geography's colonial past.[21] It is, as Manuel Correia de Andrade pronounced Josué de Castro's work, 'Geography Combatant': the ally of anticolonial praxis.[22]

I read the partial and fragmentary texts of a geographer's archive to access

17 Yves Lacoste, 'Vincennes et Le Département de Géographie', *Hérodote* 168, no. 1 (2018): 157–63; Yann Calbérac, '"Can These Words, Commonly Applied to the Anglo-Saxon Social Sciences, Fit the French?" Circulation, Translation, and Reception of Radical Geography in the French Academic Context', in *Spatial Histories of Radical Geography*, ed. Trevor Barnes and Eric Sheppard (Hoboken, NJ: Wiley-Blackwell, 2019).

18 Josué de Castro, 'To Francisco Bandeira de Melo', Letter, December 1968, 169, CEHIBRA.JdC.

19 Power and Sidaway, 'The Degeneration of Tropical Geography', 592.

20 Power and Sidaway, 'The Degeneration of Tropical Geography', 592.

21 Felix Driver, 'Geography's Empire: Histories of Geographical Knowledge', *Environment and Planning D: Society and Space* 10, no. 1 (1992): 23–40.

22 Andrade, 'Josué de Castro e Uma Geografia Combatente'.

this counter-history. What remains from the five years he stayed at Vincennes is a distinctive corpus of largely unpublished and fragmentary late work of enormous interest to a multilingual history of political ecology and critical geography. In it we can hear, perhaps, the kinds of intransigent radicalism that Said terms 'late style'.[23] Picking up and twisting this idea of Said's, I use it less to insist on a homogeneity of form in Castro's own late writing than to reflect in a more meta-textual vein on working with the archive that survives of this period. Castro's late style is felt in the fragmentary and generative qualities of the sources used here. He did not write a great late work: his last completed full-length book was the novel *Homem e Caranguejos* [Of Men and Crabs]. But this was a time full of emendations, updates, articles, teaching, essay collections, and, above all, uncompleted works. Book projects such as *The Geography of Despair*, a study on hunger in the United States, and a study of the Amazon all remained unfulfilled in the last decade of his life.

Places matter: Paris in the late 1960s and Stockholm in June 1972 provided the conditions of possibility for the exchange of ideas and the criss-crossings of biographical trajectories of not only French radicals but Latin American exiles, African anticolonialists, and emerging coalitions of radical ecologists and international environmentalists. Here the biographical approach – despite its limitations – opens a chink in the door to see complicated, contingent, and multi-lingual histories of ideas. This is not to simply add another fixed institutional site to the history of critical geography or political ecology: Vincennes+Berkeley=x – not least because the networks are wider: see for instance how João Sarmento's recent work shows how the Portuguese secret police were suspicious of critically minded geographers teaching with *Geografia da Fome* in Mozambique in the early 1970s.[24] Recent work has begun to explore the role of geographers in decolonization and various geographers' response to decolonization.[25] There is further work to be done to explore how these histories of thought are connected, and multiple, at the levels of network and place as well as at the levels of political and intellectual commitment and innovation. My work attempts to extend and complicate the history of political ecology laid out by Michael Watts, for instance, which – while an open, transnational, and multi-sited account – nevertheless prioritizes North American universities in the 1980s.[26]

23 Edward W. Said, *On Late Style: Music and Literature against the Grain* (New York: Pantheon, 2006).

24 João Sarmento, 'Portuguese Tropical Geography and Decolonization in Africa: The Case of Mozambique', *Journal of Historical Geography* 66 (October 2019): 20–30, doi:10.1016/j.jhg.2018.11.002.

25 Daniel Clayton, 'The Passing of "Geography's Empire" and Question of Geography in Decolonization, 1945–1980', *Annals of the American Association of Geographers* 110, no. 5 (2020): 1540–58.

26 Michael Watts, 'Now and Then: The Origins of Political Ecology and the Rebirth of Adaptation as a Form of Thought', in *The Routledge Handbook of Political Ecology*,

Recent work has begun to broaden these histories.[27] In terms of radical geography – in particular the narrative David Harvey gives of the anti-imperialist tendencies of young geographers in the early 1970s both around the journal *Antipode* and Doreen Massey and colleagues[28] – it is perhaps to be regretted that there were not connections made between Castro in his last years and anglophone radical geography in its first. But what links Vincennes, Clark, Milton Keynes, and Berkeley is not so much a set of academic citations or personal networks as a set of shared, but open and contingent, understandings of the relationship between space, nature, history, environment, and development.

Vincennes 1968–1973: Pedagogy and Practice

Castro arrived at Vincennes in the autumn of 1968, just at the same time that David Harvey joined the faculty of John Hopkins. Unlike Harvey, in the early 1960s Castro had not been writing a *magnum opus* of geographical theory, to awake to find that politics had changed around him,[29] but had been continuing to be involved in Third Worldist politics, while teaching at the Sorbonne and elsewhere.[30] Jean Dresch, the communist French geographer, who was then head of the *Institut de Géographie* [Institute of Geography] in Paris, and was at the time a vice-President of the International Geographical Union, had been tasked with appointing staff to the new experimental centre at Vincennes.[31] Castro was, at least as far as his French secret police handlers were aware, the only foreign professor at the new institution.[32] Notwithstanding the global geography of ''68',[33] this puts Castro at one of its most important sites, and one the radicalism of which should itself be understood as multilingual, transnational, and global. Castro's personal archive suggests a lively interest in new social movements and the radical branches of European politics.[34] He was inspired by student radicals'

ed. Tom Perreault, Gavin Bridge, and James McCarthy (London and New York: Routledge, 2015), 29–36; see also Leff, 'Power–Knowledge Relations in the Field of Political Ecology', 226–28.

27 Barnes and Sheppard, *Spatial Histories of Radical Geography*.

28 Harvey, *Spaces of Capital*, 8–10.

29 Harvey, *Spaces of Capital*, 5–7.

30 Castro, 'Desarrollo, Ecologia, Desarme y Descolonización'.

31 Lacoste, 'Vincennes et Le Département de Géographie', 157.

32 Ferretti, 'Decentring the Lettered City'.

33 Michael Watts, '1968 and All That …', *Progress in Human Geography* 25, no. 2 (2001): 157–88; see also Beatriz Nascimento's *For a New Territory*, translated in Christen Smith, Archie Davies, and Bethânia Gomes, '"In Front of the World": Translating Beatriz Nascimento', *Antipode* 53, no. 1 (January 2021): 279–316, doi:10.1111/anti.12690.

34 There are extensive newspaper and magazine clippings, for example, about May 1968 in Paris, including a number of articles about Marcuse, Sartre, and the student movement. For example, file CEHIBRA.JdC.43.

rejection of authority over the truth, admiring the graffiti on the Sorbonne's walls: '*Vous, propriétaires de la Vérité, abstenez-vous*' [You, the proprietors of Truth, give it a rest]'.[35] This fracturing of authority aligned with his own reassessment of ecological and philosophical thought.[36] Castro never stopped working on hunger, and never disassociated environmental questions from those of social justice, but in this period he shows an increasing attention to environmental and ecological issues. He militated for academic and political action to understand the growing ecological crisis of globalizing modernity as produced by the same forces as Third World underdevelopment. This was a crucial part of his pedagogy and research at Vincennes,[37] and then his involvement in the events in Stockholm in 1972.

The geography department at Vincennes was directed in its early years by two leftist geographers, Robert Foeut, a human geographer, and Jean Cabot, a tropical geographer. Fouet had been nominated by Jean Dresch,[38] and it was he who accepted Castro's candidatute to work at Vincennes.[39] Others who worked in the department and who collaborated with Castro included younger geographers such as René Braque, who went on to work in the Geography department at Orléans, and Claude Collin Delavaud, who had already done fieldwork in Peru and went on to hold posts at the Sorbonne, the CNRS [The French National Centre for Scientific Research] and the *Institut des Haute Études de l'Amérique Latine* [The Institute of Latin American Studies] at the Sorbonne Nouvelle–Paris 3.[40]

Castro taught on many courses at Vincennes between 1968 and 1973. Colleagues who recall his work in Paris – specifically Magda Zanoni and Alain Bué – emphasize his support for younger scholars in experimenting with new, political approaches to human ecology.[41] He 'appreciated [his younger colleagues'] modest attempt to link theory and practice', and used his

35 Castro, 'Développement et Environnement'.

36 Castro, *Adónde va?* 22–24; Castro, 'Desarrollo, Ecologia, Desarme y Descolonización'; see also Josué de Castro, 'Conférence du CERN: Discours de Josué de Castro', May 1964, 224, CEHIBRA.JdC.

37 Magda Zanoni and Renato Carvalheira do Nascimento, 'Entrevista com Magda Zanoni', in *Josué de Castro: memória de um saber*, ed. Tânia Elias Magno da Silva, 1st ed. (Rio de Janeiro: Fundação Miguel de Cervantes, 2012), 425–26.

38 Alain Bué and Françoise Plet, 'Décès d'un Fondateur Du Département de Géographie de Vincennes-Paris 8: Robert Fouet (1926–2016)', geographie.univ-paris8.fr, 2016, geographie.univ-paris8.fr/?deces-de-robert-fouet.

39 Alain Bué and Françoise Plet, *Podcast département Géographie – Temps Communs (2014)*, podcast (Université Paris 8, 2014), accessed 18 June 2022, vimeo.com/260910658.

40 On the role of departments in the historiography of geography see Neil Smith, '"Academic War over the Field of Geography": The Elimination of Geography at Harvard, 1947–1951', *Annals of the Association of American Geographers* 77, no. 2 (1987): 155–72.

41 Alain Bué, 'Josué de Castro: Géographie de La Faim', archive.li, August 2010, accessed 18 June 2022, http://archive.li/Y4nrH.

reputation to enable radical approaches to teaching.[42] Documentation of the courses he taught or designed – in some cases their rewriting can be observed across multiple drafts – gives access to Castro's pedagogical practice and late thought. Some surviving course outlines are gnomic one-page documents, while others are fully developed prose descriptions making the case for a particular approach to a sub-discipline or area. One 'Introduction to Human Ecology' argues that 'the new geographical science cannot do without analyses of the environment and the application of ecological methods in the study of geographical spaces'.[43] These pithy comments, not formulated for academic publication, nevertheless constitute some evidence of Castro's relationship with the revolution that took place in disciplinary geography in the 1970s. They show Castro reckoning with changes in geography, but insisting on the value of a 'human ecology' and a regional approach within geographical science. We can see more clearly what he means in the detail of the course that covers what would become environmental geography.[44] The course covers 'the impact of man on the biosphere', pollution, demography, environmental degradation, the impact of development and growth, and the politics of protecting and restoring the environment.[45]

Another course on the 'Human Ecology of the Third World' from the early 1970s is a good example of his still-developing approach to human–environment relations. It covers familiar themes: the 'Guano Complex', the 'mangrove ecosystem and community of Recife in the Northeast of Brazil', sugar plantations, food chains and trophic resources, and 'environment and development at the regional scale' in the River Plate area of Argentina.[46] The course notes that there is a lack of clear data about the Third World and its ecologies. They want to develop an approach, nevertheless, that enables the analysis of relations between people, the biotic environment, the habitat, nature, and culture. Culture, they insist, can't be ignored. Alain Bué, who was a research assistant on the course, described how Castro taught the geography of hunger in his classes: he would ask students to limit their diets to only 1600 calories per day and then attempt to write a dissertation for the seminar, or undertake physical work.[47] This rather visceral approach was used to instil in students the wide-ranging effects of hunger. It seems unlikely that it would be an endorsed pedagogical method in many universities today.

42 Bué, 'Josué de Castro'.
43 Josué de Castro, 'Initiation a L'Ecologie Humaine' (Université de Paris VIII, undated), 300, CEHIBRA.JdC.
44 Noel Castree, David Demeritt, and Diana Liverman, 'Introduction: Making Sense of Environmental Geography', in *A Companion to Environmental Geography* (Hoboken, NJ: John Wiley & Sons, 2009), 1–15, doi:10.1002/9781444305722.ch1.
45 Castro, 'Initiation'.
46 Josué de Castro, Alain Bué, and Magda Zanoni, 'Ecologie Humaine du Tiers Monde' (Université de Paris VIII, undated), 166, CEHIBRA.JdC.
47 Bué, 'Josué de Castro'.

Castro connected a proto-environmental geography with a Third Worldist approach to underdevelopment. While avoiding a tendentious reading that sees Castro's work summed up in the gnomic form of a course syllabus, there are intriguing references to topics of lifelong concern. For instance, following ecosystems and biomass in part two, part three covers 'Trophic links. Biogeochemical cycles. Flows of energy and food chains'.[48] This seems to offer a development of the alternative intellectual history of metabolism that I have argued Castro can offer historians of political ecology.[49] References to the foundation of life on earth, 'living systems', and 'living matter' have connections with later vitalist turns in geographical inquiry.[50] A fuller course outline also exists. A collaboration with two of his younger colleagues, Alain Bué and Magda Zanoni, it shows a greater interest in modern ecology than any other document of Castro's career. It outlines ecological niches, auto-ecology, adaptation, synecology, population ecology, ecosystems, decomposition, edaphotopes (soil environments), climates, and energy fluxes. It shows Castro working through understandings of energy flows within food chains. Castro connects his own geography of hunger both with a biological science concerned with the somatic and cellular scales of living beings and with ecological and environmental science.[51] In his course on 'Geography of Food and Hunger' (Geographie de l'Alimentation et de la Faim), also from the early 1970s, Castro connects the study of hunger with the most basic processes of all living beings. As chapter 1 argued, this was an important idea in his early work across nutrition and geography, but it is explicit in a different way here. Hunger itself has a biological quality whose 'origin is in the relative richness in basic nutritional essentials on the inside of [...] cells, where the biochemical mechanisms of life take place'. This makes the biophysically relational geography of hunger clearer: the inside of cells and the environment are materially continuous with one another. Castro extends some of the essential formulations of a geography of hunger. Food has an 'energetic function', a 'plastic function' (to structure living materiality), and a 'regulatory function [...] to furnish the regulator elements of the metabolic process, that is to say, the ensemble of biochemical exchanges and transformations'. The course outline notes, though, that there is an important distinction to be made between the individual biochemical dynamics of hunger and the social qualities of 'hunger in the world',[52] which needs a multidisciplinary approach. Hunger, he argues, is a point of contact between different disciplines, including 'biogeography, psychology [and]

---

48 Castro, 'Initiation'.
49 Davies, 'Unwrapping the Oxo Cube'.
50 Castro, 'Initiation'.
51 Josué de Castro, Alain Bué, and Magda Zanoni, 'U.V. Ecologie Humaine du Tiers Monde' (Université de Paris VIII, 1972), 92, CEHIBRA.JdC.
52 Josué de Castro, 'U.V. Geographie de l'Alimentation et de la Faim (i)' (Université de Paris VIII, undated), 183, CEHIBRA.JdC.

bio-cybernetics'. It was this multidisciplinary optic, he argues, that 'gave birth to a geography of hunger, to a geopolitics of hunger, to a sociology of hunger'. All of this must be seen, however, in a political context: 'the struggle against hunger is worth something only if it is formulated within the optic of a struggle against the phenomenon of under-development'.[53] If Castro had fully developed these explorations they would have amounted to a new geography of hunger. Certainly they consist of an innovative approach to geography, particularly in a French context that Denis Gautier and Baptiste Hautdidier characterize as remaining 'wedded to conventional dichotomies (in the Vidalian tradition), especially in its teaching – human/physical, urban/rural, regional/general'.[54] Vincennes, of course, was only one site in wider changes in French geography in the aftermath of May '68.[55]

The course entitled 'Agrarian Structures and the Problem of Shantyowns in Latin America' (*Les Structures Agraires et le Problème des Bidonvilles en Amerique Latine*), connected agrarian structures – *minifundia* and *latifundia* – with urban poverty and '*bidonvilles*', a French term that roughly translates as 'favelas' or 'shanty towns'. The course description lays out a multidisciplinary approach to this rural-to-urban geography and suggests that it will be of interest to historians, sociologists, urbanists, and anthropologists. Students will approach the problem of urban poverty through studying 'the origin, evolution and current status of agrarian structures'.[56] In the second term Castro offers two further courses, on the Human Ecology of the Third World and on Continental Central America. The courses offer a snapshot of Castro's position in geographical history: still orientated by regional geography (re-formed, re-placed, and critiqued), but on the cusp of the formulations of political ecology.[57]

The reading lists, course outlines, and materials studied here are an idiosyncratic source for geographical research. They are unfinished, partial, formulaic, and institutionalized. Yet they are also full of potential for considering the actual historical undertaking of geographical work and, above all, the teaching of geography. Castro was a teacher at many stages of his life and wrote an introductory textbook for human geography in Brazil, published in *Ensaios da Geografia Humana* (Essays in Human Geography). He also collaborated in 1937 with the well-known Brazilian author Cecília Meireles on a children's book called *A Festa das Letras* [The Party of Letters], an educational book partly aimed at encouraging children to eat fruit.[58] Elsewhere in his archive he kept essays written by students at the University

53 Castro, 'U.V. Geographie de l'Alimentation et de la Faim (i)', 7.
54 Gautier and Hautdidier, 'Connecting Political Ecology and French Geography', 59.
55 On which see Olivier Orain, 'Mai 68 et Ses Suites En Géographie Française', *Revue d'histoire des Sciences Humaines*, 26 (February 2015): 209–42, doi:10.4000/rhsh.2406.
56 Castro, 'Initiation'.
57 As found in, for example, Bryant and Bailey, *Third World Political Ecology*.
58 Josué de Castro and Cecília Meireles, *A Festa Das Letras* (Porto Alegre: Globo, 1937).

of Brazil, as well as his course syllabi from the 1940s and 1950s.[59] The notes and course outlines from Vincennes are fragments of dialogic communication and pedagogy. As this book, in particular chapter 2, has argued, all of Castro's texts were amended, re-prefaced, and re-edited by Castro following their publication (the word is significant: public-ation). He even annotated and corrected published newspaper versions of interviews he had given. Texts reveal themselves as unstable and changing. These teaching texts are particularly contingent: they are written to serve an ephemeral purpose for students, colleagues, and the institution. They have very precise and particular publics at a specific moment in time and space. They would have circulated in particular ways: pinned on noticeboards, slipped into course handouts, and passed between students' hands. The geography in which they circulated was important: the corridors and lecture halls of a university explicitly seeking to reconstruct the meaning of the term, establishing new relationships between professors and students and new criteria for pedagogy, political commitment, and standards of truth.[60] Having written about the social function of universities[61] and been involved in Brazilian debates over the formation and structure of the new University of Brasília in the 1950s, it was not the first time Castro had been part of the birth of a new university with big dreams. The experimental university was a hive of activity, though not all of it rigorously co-ordinated. Full staff meetings were rare, and multiple strands of work coincided but did not necessarily interact. Yves Lacoste, for instance, conducted an evening research seminar on the Third World with students – including those from beyond Vincennes – but this seems to have had little overlap with Josué de Castro's research and teaching at the university.[62] Castro worked alongside not only young French geographers such as Alain Bué but also other young scholars such as the Argentine Moïses Ikonicoff, who worked at Vincennes in 1972–73 and would become a well-known figure in Argentine and French debates on dependency over the next decades.[63]

In the first semester of the 1972–73 academic year Castro taught three courses: on the agrarian structure of Latin America, an 'Introduction to Human Ecology', and an 'Introduction to Urban Ecology'. This latter is of particular interest. Castro's declaration of hours taught survives, in handwriting whose shakiness portends the ill health that was soon to lead to his death. In the 1973–74 academic year he was still listed as *professeur associé*

59 Various, 'Student Essays University of Brazil', 1940s, 258, CEHIBRA.JdC.
60 Dijan, *Vincennes*.
61 Josué de Castro, 'A Função Social das Universidades', in *Ensaios de Biologia Social* (São Paulo: Editôra Brasiliense, 1957), 121–32.
62 Bué and Plet, Podcast département Géographie – Temps Communs (2014).
63 See, for instance, Moises Ikonicoff, 'Technologie et Modele de Consommation Dans Le Tiers-Monde', *Revue Économique* 24, no. 4 (July 1973): 619, doi:10.2307/3499993.

[Associated Professor].[64] It seems, however, that, though Castro designed the course on Urban Ecology, he probably never taught it.[65] Listed elsewhere as also taught by Alain Bué and Magda Zanoni, the course studied open spaces and green areas in the city, with a focus on sites in Paris. Students were encouraged to investigate the urban ecologies of the city and to accompany the struggles of inhabitants being expelled by urban transformations. Castro brought a concern about urban dispossession connected to an analytical attention to urban nature, developed in his hometown of Recife to Paris in the early 1970s.[66] This opening – a lost predecessor of urban political ecology – is another foreshortened by Castro's death.

By the time of the *rentrée* in 1975–76, however, not only had Castro passed away but Bué and Zanoni had moved on. Yves Lacoste was an increasingly prominent figure in the department, and the structure of courses changed year on year. The central historiography of the geography department is dominated by Lacoste, who leaves Castro out of his account of those years. He suggests, indeed, that the impulse to teach on underdevelopment came from the presence of students from the Third World, but does not mention the presence of one of the world's leading Third Worldist geographical scholars in the new department.[67] Similarly, Lacoste makes no reference to Castro in his discussions of the founding of *Hérodote*, and his and his colleagues' efforts to resignify the term 'geopolitics' and replace it at the centre of a new radical geography. That Castro had done this two decades before, as discussed earlier in this book, seems to be of no interest to the French geographer.[68] Interestingly, by the 1975 brochure, '*ecologie politique*' was officially a course taught to all first-year geography undergraduates at Vincennes.[69] This opens onto a history of French political ecology that I do not have space to explore here. However, if Denis Gautier and Baptiste Hautdidier argue that the 'rich', but 'fissiparous', French tradition of *ecologie politique* 'has often been held back because of an insufficient regard for the role of politics in understanding human–environmental relations',[70]

64 Université paris 8, 'Programme de l'université Paris 8' (Octaviana, 74 1973), FVNP0221, Paris 8 V 56, accessed 18 June 2022, https://octaviana.fr/document/FVNP0221#?c=0&m=0&s=0&cv=0.

65 Josué de Castro, 'U.V. Introduction aux Problèmes du Sous-Développement' (Université de Paris VIII, 1973), 183, CEHIBRA.JdC.

66 Bué, 'Josué de Castro'.

67 Lacoste, 'Vincennes et Le Département de Géographie', 162–63.

68 See also Stéphane Rosière, 'La Géopolitique Au Brésil', in *De Récife à Reims, Récits Géographiques. Mélanges Offerts à Pernette Grandjean*, ed. M. Bazin, C. Fournet-Guérin, and Stéphane Rosière (Reims: Épure, 2013), 155–85.

69 Université paris 8, 'Institut de géographie : brochure de rentrée, 1975–1976 · Bibliothèque numérique Paris 8' (Octaviana, 76 1975), FVNP0236, Paris 8 V 57, accessed 18 June 2022, https://octaviana.fr/document/FVNP0236#?c=0&m=0&s=0&cv=0.

70 Gautier and Hautdidier, 'Connecting Political Ecology and French Geography', 57.

then perhaps Castro's role in this tradition is a fruitful area for further exploration. In particular in connection with the role of René Dumont, with whom Castro worked,[71] he can perhaps be seen as a precusor to the '*tiers mondiste*' trajectory of work in French geography.[72] In any case, following Castro's death, the story of geography at Vincennes is overtaken by the journal *Hérodote* and the emergence of the strong geopolitical school of French geography.

It appears – from the later documents of the geography department – that Yves Lacoste picked up the teaching of the course on underdevelopment that Castro had designed in 1973. The courses changed their emphasis under Lacoste and turned to the Maghreb. To some extent we can see the framing of the latter's geography of underdevelopment as, at least initially, in dialogue with Castro's. However, their relationship was apparently conflictual,[73] though Lacoste had written about Castro as early as 1962[74] and Castro used Lacoste's work in his own teaching. After Castro's death, rather than celebrating his former colleague or explicitly engaging in academic dialogue, Lacoste was publicly sceptical of Castro on the grounds, apparently, that he pulled his analytical punches about capitalism and North American imperialism. At a colloquium in 2004, Lacoste went so far as to suggest that the *Geopolítica da Fome* was a project put into Castro's mind by the American ambassador to Brazil after the publication of *Geografia da Fome*. Lacoste says, largely in passing, that 'they' – the American government – 'had it translated into 40 languages'.[75] The suggestion was that Castro was too close to the Americans and that the worldwide dissemination of *The Geography of Hunger* was an American scheme. I have found no other evidence for this. Lacoste seems to be suggesting that the Americans' ploy was to use the book to defuse the critique of capitalism. It is perhaps the case that the Geopolitics (the English *Geography of Hunger*) muddies the waters of analysis and is less politically sharp-elbowed than its predecessor. However, it is faintly ludicrous to claim that Castro lands in the North American camp. He called Robert MacNamara's US-driven policy of birth control 'almost genocidal'.[76] He praised Soviet agriculture,

71 For example, for the edition Castro and Feio, *O drama do Terceiro Mundo*.

72 Gautier and Hautdidier, 'Connecting Political Ecology and French Geography', 61–65.

73 Rosière, 'La Géopolitique Au Brésil'.

74 Yves Lacoste, 'Le Sous-Développement: Quelques Ouvrages Significatifs Parus Depuis Dix Ans', *Annales de Géographie* 71, no. 385 (1962): 247–78; see also Ferretti, 'A Coffin for Malthusianism'.

75 Sylvie Brunel et al., 'Nourrir Les Hommes, Nourrir La Planète. Les Géographes Se Mettent à Table' (Saint-Dié: Festival international de Géographie de Saint-Dié, 2004), accessed 18 June 2022, https://pedagogie.ac-orleans-tours.fr/fileadmin/user_upload/lhg/Archive/geopolitique_de_l_alimentation_2004.pdf.

76 Rosembuj, 'Josué de Castro: las dudas de un pacifista'.

called for a revolution in Latin America against the dominance of North American economic imperialism, and assisted anti-imperialist struggles.[77] If he was a stooge he was not a very good one. That he received American (and British) support – from his publisher – for the English version of *The Geography of Hunger* is clear. Where precisely the funds for that support came from the archive does not reveal, but his books sold tens of thousands of copies and Castro spent long months in negotiations with his US publisher over fees. Along with Castro's longstanding praxis against American state interests – witness, for example, his role in driving disarmament conferences at the UN fervently against American wishes, his work at the FAO in the teeth of American opposition, and his support for the Peasant Leagues – all of this renders it extremely unlikely that Castro was a tool of the CIA. Indeed, brief research in some of their own digitized archives suggests that the CIA internally saw Castro as an enemy. They listed an organization of which he was President in 1956 – 'The World Congress of Doctors for the Study of Present Day Living Conditions' – as a 'Communist-Front Organization'.[78] The embassy in Brazil in 1962 and 1963 described Castro as 'pro-Communist' in their 'Secret' weekly Intelligence Summaries.[79] Lacoste's accusation should, I think, be treated with a profound dose of scepticism. One of Castro's colleagues at the time, Magda Zanoni, argued that Lacoste effectively stole from Castro's ideas without crediting him, and recounts that Lacoste sought to marginalize Castro at the department in a manner that Castro was unable to resist thanks to periods of severe depression and deteriorating physical health in the early 1970s.[80] The broader problem with Lacoste's critique is that it withdraws Castro's own intellectual agency in a way reminiscent of many a colonial European treatment of Third World intellectuals. For Castro, like many Third Worldist intellectuals, the cold war was not the primary concern.[81] More importantly – and Lacoste is right to the limited extent that at times it can at times constitute a weakness in his analysis – Castro's analytical framework was not capital and his framework was not materialist. In terms of the writing and reception of his work he proactively pursued

---

77 Clodomir, 'Josué de Castro: Brasileiro e Cidadão Do Mundo'.

78 CIA, 'Directories of the International Communist-Front Organizations and Communist Societies of Friendship and Cultural Relations', February 1957, CIA-RDP78-00915R000600140008-2, General CIA Records, accessed 18 June 2022, https://www.cia.gov/library/readingroom/document/cia-rdp78-00915r000600140008-2.

79 CIA, 'Weekly Summary: Office of Current Intelligence', May 1963, CIA-RDP79-00927A004000100001-8, CIA General Files, accessed 18 June 2022, https://www.cia.gov/readingroom/search/site/CIA-RDP79-00927A004000100001-8.

80 Zanoni and Nascimento, 'Entrevista com Magda Zanoni'.

81 See Mark Philip Bradley, 'Decolonization, the Global South, and the Cold War, 1919–1962', in *The Cambridge History of the Cold War*, ed. Melvyn P. Leffler and Odd Arne Westad, vol. 1 (Cambridge: Cambridge University Press, 2010), 465.

contacts in both the socialist and capitalist worlds while resisting the Manicheanism of great power politics. In the early 1970s, in the emergence of international environmentalism, Castro found another outlet for this geopolitical framework.

Vincennes 1968–1973: Research, the Amazon and the Philosophy of Action

At Vincennes Castro not only taught but also conducted new research. He headed a research group on Ecology, a role he assumed after Jean Cabot moved on in 1970. Prior to his arrival, the focus of research had been on French regions. Castro helped shifted attention towards the Global South, and in particular an extensive research project on the Amazon.[82] In Magda Zanoni's account this emerged from Castro's engaged pedagogic practice.[83] Zanoni notes that this research group went on later to work on the environmental impacts of war in Vietnam (one of the outcomes of which was Yves Lacoste's well-known single-authored work on the topic[84]). The Amazon project, proposed by Castro but written collaboratively by graduate students and staff, sought interdisciplinary contributions. It was a collaboration between the university research group and the International Association on Living Conditions and Health, yet another international intellectual civil society body of which Castro was President. The group broke the traditional confines of the university, with members based in the OECD, UNESCO and other institutions. The Amazon research was collaborative – reports were signed by the group, rather than individuals – and functioned in French. It is an interesting episode in a prehistory of political ecology.

Although not claiming a universal history of the discipline, Tom Perreault, James McCarthy, and Gavin Bridge formulate the anglophone history of political ecology as emerging from a critique of cultural ecology and human ecology in the 1980s.[85] Here in the early 1970s in the politicized milieu of Vincennes we can see precisely such an approach being not only taught but formulated in research, as this group sought explicitly to make a political critique of human ecology.[86] How this work on the Amazon related to the history of French political ecology remains largely beyond the reach of this book, but the group also serves as a good example of how rigid linguistic

82 Josué de Castro and Alain Bué, 'Rappel des Activités de l'Equipe en 1970–71' (Université de Paris VIII, 1972), 158, CEHIBRA.JdC.
83 Zanoni, 'Josué de Castro'.
84 For example, Yves Lacoste, 'Bombing the Dikes: A Geographer's On-the-Site Analysis', The Nation 9 (1972): 298–301; Bowd and Clayton, 'Geographical Warfare in the Tropics'; see also Yves Lacoste, La géographie, ça sert, d'abord, à faire la guerre, éd. augmentée, La Découverte-poche (Paris: la Découverte, 2013).
85 Bridge, McCarthy, and Perreault, 'Editors' Introduction'.
86 Zanoni and Nascimento, 'Entrevista com Magda Zanoni'.

boundaries in the history of geography need to be unsettled. It worked in French but with lusophone, Polish, and other practitioners, with an intended international audience, initially with the Stockholm 1972 conference in mind, but with an eye on Latin American governments as well. Sidaway notes that 'western geographical knowledge did not develop in a vacuum, away from prior non-western geographies. It *depended* upon them.'[87] Equally we should emphasize the foundationally multi-lingual qualities of critical geography. These dependencies did not end with the emergence of radical geography in the second half of the twentieth century; the traffic across languages and traditions continues.

In terms of Stockholm 1972, the points of connection become blurry – how exactly the debates on demography and underdevelopment at and around that conference influenced the academic formulation of political ecology is not immediately legible. However, as clearly as Castro is part of the lusophone history of political ecology, he is part of its francophone history and should be part of its anglophone history. Furthermore, his episode at Vincennes inverts the traditional account of the direction of political ecological research, which sees Northern scholars in Northern institutions studying the South. Here we have a scholar from the South taking a Northern institution's gaze and turning it on the tropics. North–South dividing lines are ultimately less than helpful: the historical geographies of knowledge are not reducible to such abstractions.

The Amazon report laid out the social and ecological threats to the region, sought to build a network of concerned institutions and agencies, and began to propose potential solutions for an international response to these threats. Castro publicized the group's work in the press[88] as well as presenting it in Stockholm, where he took part in the civil society and independent sessions, held under the auspices of the Environment Forum.[89] At Stockholm, the Brazilian government responded aggressively – as they have recently, under President Jair Bolsonaro – to suggestions that the Amazon might be of international significance, emphasizing Brazilian sovereignty.[90] This gives Castro's role in the report a particular personal significance. The report begins by arguing that current attitudes to the role of underdeveloped countries in environmental issues is based on false premises and 'imprecise foundational concepts' of what 'the environment' and 'development' are:

the environment is not only the ensemble of material elements that

87 James D. Sidaway, 'The (Re)Making of the Western "Geographical Tradition"': Some Missing Links', *Area* 29, no. 1 (March 1997): 75, doi:10.1111/j.1475-4762.1997. tb00008.x.

88 Josué de Castro, 'To André Fontaine', Letter, June 1972, 303, CEHIBRA.JdC.

89 Josué de Castro, 'To Elisabeth Wettergren, Environment Forum, Stockholm', May 1972, 274, CEHIBRA.JdC.

90 Lars Emmelin, 'The Stockholm Conferences', *Ambio* 1, no. 4 (September 1972): 135–37.

compose the mosaics of geographical landscapes, acting continually upon one another. The environment is much more than that. Equally part of the environment are the economic structures and the structures of thought of human groups who live in different geographic spaces.[91]

The attention to the intersection, in place, between environment, development, 'structures of thought', and 'economic structures' is a precursor to what Peet and Watts would later outline in *Liberation Ecologies* as 'regional discursive formations'.[92] 'Ecology', Castro wrote in 1972, 'is the science of the future [...] the science of the "eco," of place'.[93] This is a situated knowledge, as chapter 4 explored. Castro argued that 'each place will have its own science, because science is not universal, it is local, it is a science of the region'.[94] This geographical understanding emphasizes the situatedness of knowledge, placing the scale of the region at the epistemological heart of his political ecology: an ecology of nature emergent from the particularities of place. Where regional geography's methodology was universalist – a pure geographical rationality that could be applied anywhere – Castro is proposing a more dialectical understanding of the relationship between science and place, in which geographical investigation is contingent on the dynamics of place. Significantly, this insight emerges in association with a lament for the genocide of indigenous peoples across Latin America; a lament for their lost culture and their lost science of place.[95] Here we can see a kinship between the regional political ecologies Enrique Leff has recently outlined and the importance of addressing power–knowledge relations in political ecology.[96] Again Castro's work foreshadows important later debates in geographical knowledge.

The concept of 'environment', the Amazon report argued, must include 'the total impact of man and his culture on all other environmental elements, and the impact of mesological factors on the integral life of the human group [...] encompass[ing] biological, physiological, economic and cultural aspects, all connected in the same fabric of a dynamic ecology in permanent transformation'.[97] The use of the term 'mesology' here is interesting. Mesology functions as a mediating concept, one that focuses on the relationships between organism and environment, rather than one or the other. It has recently become important for Augustin Berque, the geographer and

91 Josué de Castro, 'Proposition concernant une action concertée multinationale pour la defense de l'ecoysteme Amazonien' (Université de Paris VIII, 1972), 131, CEHIBRA.JdC.
92 Richard Peet and Michael Watts, 'Liberation Ecology: Development, Sustainability, and Environment in an Age of Market Triumphalism', in *Liberation Ecologies: Environment, Development, Social Movements*, ed. Richard Peet and Michael Watts (London and New York: Routledge, 2002), 15–16.
93 Castro, 'Développement et Environnement', 58.
94 Castro, 'Développement et Environnement', 28.
95 Castro, 'Développement et Environnement', 27–29.
96 Leff, 'Power–Knowledge Relations in the Field of Political Ecology'.
97 Castro, 'Proposition', 4.

philosopher, who uses it to translate the Japanese philosoper Watsuji's term *fudo*, drawing on a history of French *mésologie* deriving from a 'science of human milieux by the physician, statistician and demographer Louis-Adolphe Bertillon (1821–1883)'.[98] Castro, however, is more likely to have drawn the concept from other sources: either Brazilian, through Gilberto Freyre, or French, through Élisée Reclus.

Mesologia underpins Gilberto Freyre's approach, in particular his later works. In Freyre's hands *mesologia* was allied to a quasi-determinist analysis of tropical modernity.[99] For Reclus, on the other hand, *mésologie* allowed him to think through the differential kinds of changes occurring in environments.[100] For Isabelle Lefort and Philippe Pelletier it is precisely in his mesological concerns that Reclus' geographical investigations come closest to contemporary geography's movement beyond nature/society dualisms.[101] According to Berque, somewhat similarly, *mésologie* is part of an attempt to overcome such dualisms through an expanded ontology of being.[102] Corinne Pelluchon has developed an approach to mesology in order to treat the problem of nourishment 'not as a simple ecological and health issue, but as one extending to the entire chain of relation, taking food, human physiology and pleasure, life, joy, living environment, politics, and the relationship with society into account'.[103] Some affinities with Castro's project are clear. Perhaps the most interesting development of mesology [*mesologia*] is in Amílcar Cabral's work – what Reiland Rabaka has called Cabral's 'Revolutionary anticolonial mesology'[104] and Filipa César his 'agronomy of liberation'.[105] For Rabaka, mesology is a

98 Augustin Berque, 'Offspring of Watsuji's Theory of Milieu (F^udo)', *GeoJournal* 60, no. 4 (2004): 391, doi:10.1023/B:GEJO.0000042975.55513.f1.

99 Sergio B.F. Tavolaro, 'Gilberto Freyre and the Brazilian "Tropical Modernity": Between Originality and Deviation', *Sociologias* 15, no. 33 (August 2013): 282–317, doi:10.1590/S1517-45222013000200010.

100 Isabelle Lefort and Philippe Pelletier, 'Élisée Reclus ou la condition géographique: habiter la terre', *Annales de geographie* 704, no. 4 (2015): 338–50.

101 Lefort and Pelletier; though this is subject to some debate. See Bertrand Guest, 'Environmental Awareness and Geography: Reading Reclus Ecocritically?' in *Environmental Awareness and the Design of Literature*, ed. François Specq, 1st ed. (Leiden: Brill, 2016), 69–89.

102 Augustin Berque, 'The Perceptive Relation in Mesology: From the Functional Circle of Uexküll to Trajection', *Revue du MAUSS* 47, no. 1 (June 2016): 87–104; Berque, 'Offspring'.

103 Aoki Saburo, 'About Fragmentation and Divergence', *Inter Faculty* 7 (September 2016): ix; see also Corine Pelluchon, 'What Does It Mean to Replace Ecology with Mesology and Resources with Nourishment?' *Inter Faculty* 7, Fragmentation and Divergence (2016): 143–54.

104 Amílcar Cabral, *Resistance and Decolonization*, ed. Reiland Rabaka, trans. Dan Wood (Lanham, MD: Rowman & Littlefield International, 2016).

105 Filipa César, 'Meteorisations: Reading Amílcar Cabral's Agronomy of Liberation', *Third Text* 32, nos 2–3 (2018): 254–72.

'synonym' of ecology, but he notes that it 'also at one time meant the study of ways of attaining happiness. Etymologically, mesology refers to a discourse concerning mediality and the betweenness of things, and its historical double significance in regard to ecological and eudemonic matters helps to best characterize Cabral's political thought.' Cabral's praxis, he argues, 'involves the decolonization of adverse environmental conditions imposed on various forms of human and non-human life',[106] as well as being deeply embedded in the geographical and environmental realities of the spaces of decolonization. Following César and further exploration of mesology – Berque's, Pelluchon's, and, in particular, Cabral's – could be fruitful ground for anglophone political ecology, if the term's differentiation from existing understanding of ecology can be firmly established.

Returning to the Amazon report of 1972, however, mesology is used within a conception of the environment inseparable from the context of underdevelopment and colonialist economic formations. 'Underdeveloped countries who struggle to survive are forced to interest themselves in the problems of development and environment at the global scale, in order to defend themselves against the aggressions that their environment has been subjected to for centuries by colonialist metropoles, destroyers of their human condition.'[107] Here Castro has added a crucial component to his longstanding geography of hunger: colonialist development models are an attack on the human condition not only through hunger but through pollution and environmental degradation: 'the economic degradation of underdeveloped countries must be considered as a pollution of their human environment, provoked by the economic abuses of the dominant zones of the world economy'.[108]

The Amazon research project emerged as Castro and others were denouncing the Club of Rome's *Limits to Growth* report. Indeed, according to Alain Bué, Castro was asked by UNESCO to co-ordinate a response to the Club of Rome.[109] The Vincennes report contains a sophisticated conception of the plasticity of natural systems and their ability to respond to pollution and human activity, while noting that going 'beyond certain limits [... risks] provoking great, sometimes fatal, ruptures in the ecosystem'.[110] The report describes the environmental and developmental risks facing the Amazon, with particular reference to the importance of mangrove ecosystems as well as to the erosion of soils under plantation agriculture.[111] It outlines the considerations necessary for a 'balanced development' of the Amazon to be achieved, including warnings of pollution, deforestation, exploitation, and

106 Reiland Rabaka, 'Amílcar Cabral and Critical Theory', in *Resistance and Decolonization*, by Amilcar Cabral (Lanham, MD: Rowman & Littlefield International, 2016).
107 Castro, 'Proposition', 4.
108 Castro, 'Proposition', 5.
109 Personal communication, 26 January 2019.
110 Castro, 'Proposition', 5.
111 Castro, 'Proposition', 6–7.

avoiding at all costs the 'sub-proletarianization' of indigenous peoples, amid the risk of a long-term 'ethnocide'.[112] Even in the absence of a knowledge of climate change (although it does cite the forest's role in replenishing atmospheric oxygen), the report reads as an eerie foretaste of the devastation of the Amazon that was to pick up pace over ensuing decades. Castro and his colleagues were mounting 'a radical critique of the pressure-of-population-on-resources view of environment and point[ed] to the need for a rethinking of both conservation and development' that Peet and Watts credit Blaikie and Brookfield's work with achieving some fifteen years later, in the late 1980s.[113] Proving precedence is not particularly interesting, and others give various timelines of both political ecology[114] and critical development studies,[115] but it is significant that all of these concerns are at work in the geography department at Vincennes in the late 1960s. This is not to forge a *new* origin myth of political ecology or critical development studies; other alternative histories could be written. The point, rather, is to multiply intellectual histories in order to expand concepts and disciplinary categories. It is also to deepen an alternative story in which a constellation of influences forged a critical perspective on environment and development across languages and continents and out of anti-imperialist geographical practice.

In the Amazon report, addressing the UN Stockholm Conference's focus on 'action', Castro and his collaborators discuss practical steps to halt the destructive development of the Amazon and address the pollution and degradation of ecosystems. They insist that 'action, even in this extreme case, must be based on a set of knowledges adequately developed in a manner that can constitute the basis for a philosophy of action'. It is precisely *geography* that can provide this. Through its sophisticated, holistic interpretation of the dialectical interactions between the complex plasticities of ecosystems and the economic, political, and cultural dynamics of social and environmental transformation, geographical research is represented as the necessary prerequisite for political and economic action. This is a distinctive development from a persistent interest in hunger to a recognizably environmentalist – and political ecological – position. This is the late fruit of Castro's militant geography.

We can, in the Amazon report, see at least part of what Castro thought the role of the public geographer was, in terms of international environmental

112 Castro, 'Proposition', 18.
113 Peet and Watts, 'Liberation Ecology'.
114 Watts, 'Now and Then', 30–34.
115 On the history of critical development studies see David Simon, 'Postdevelopment', in *The International Encyclopedia of Geography: People, the Earth, Environment, and Technology*, ed. Noel Castree et al. (Chichester and Hoboken, NJ: John Wiley & Sons, 2017), 1–6, doi:10.1002/9781118786352.wbieg0263; and Robert Potter and Dennis Conway, 'Development', in *The SAGE Handbook of Geographical Knowledge*, ed. David Livingstone and John A. Agnew (Los Angeles: SAGE, 2011).

policy: to critique and challenge the terms by which 'environmental' and 'developmental' interventions proceeded. Castro, by 1972, had come to conceive of geography as a 'philosophy of action'. This can be placed alongside other understandings of the political role of geography, not least in the direction that Milton Santos later developed the concept of the 'active role of geography'.[116] If political ecology 'can be fruitfully understood as a terrain of debate over which the role of theory and practice come to be considered and contested', this version of geography as a philosophy of action is an important contribution.[117] Action was not only that of the UN or environmental agencies, but a broader political idea: 'struggles against underdevelopment cannot succeed if they do not take into consideration the environment within whose context one desires to change the mechanism and the speed of the process of development'.[118] In other words, environmental damage is a consequence of underdevelopment, and struggles for liberation must take into account the ecological complex within which they unfold. Geography as a 'philosophy of action' also constitutes an ecological contribution to strategic questions of anticolonial struggle. Much more work on the ecological thinking of anticolonial struggles would be productive for political ecology. Amílcar Cabral's work – his 'Revolutionary Anticolonial Mesology',[119] but more broadly his profound geographical instincts and deep empirical agronomic research – would be a good place to start.

These were all immediate concerns, but Castro's intellectual practice was always multi-faceted and anti-dogmatic. While pursuing this philosophy of action Castro did not limit himself to timely and 'policy-relevant' modes of intervention. On the contrary, he retained a belief in the value of humanist writing and research. Ever a maker of plans,[120] he had, at the same time as the report was being developed, sketched out a more ambitious writing project on the Amazon that would begin from 'the immoderation of nature' and 'the solitude of man' to analyse dreams of colonizing the 'green paradise' of the Amazon, its 'second discovery', and the threats of development. This fuller project, like many of his later ideas sketched out in notebooks and typescripts, was never undertaken.

116 Pedrosa, 'O Périplo Do Exílio de Milton Santos e a Formação de Sua Rede de Cooperação'; Adriana Bernardes et al., 'The Active Role of Geography: A Manifesto', *Antipode* 49, no. 4 (September 2017): 952–58, doi:10.1111/anti.12318.
117 Loftus, 'Political Ecology as Praxis', 180; Since the 1960s there have been many related calls. See, for instance, Bernardes et al., 'The Active Role of Geography'.
118 Castro, Bué, and Zanoni, 'Ecologie Humaine du Tiers Monde'.
119 Rabaka, 'Amílcar Cabral and Critical Theory'.
120 Josué de Castro, 'Sketch of Amazon Book Project' (handwritten notes, undated), 211, CEHIBRA.JdC.

Stockholm 1972: Underdevelopment and International Environmentalism

As well as constituting valuable reflections on the concept of the environment, the Amazon report was a political – and policy-orientated – intervention targeted at the UN Conference on the Human Environment in Stockholm in June 1972, the first major international conference on global environmental problem. The conference led to the founding of the UN Environment Programme[121] and was an undoubtedly important moment in the history of international environmentalism, often characterized as the beginning of the path towards sustainable development and the hegemony of liberal environmentalism.[122] However, a closer attention to the genesis, geographies, and politics of the conference shows that Stockholm was at the headwaters of a much more broadly contested political argument about the environment, development, and the politics of nature. The Stockholm process was always cleaved by politics: whether of the cold war and the status of East Germany in the negotiations, or in fundamental arguments over questions of environment and development. In Stockholm in that summer two kinds of event took place with different genealogies and spatialities: on the one hand a formal, interior world of official delegates – what Carl Death calls 'summit theatre'[123] – and on the other a mildly chaotic, sprawling world of unofficial events including hippies, deep ecologists, indigenous groups, and activist scholars.[124] These have different and competing histories. Their concerns and worldviews clashed. There were attempts to bridge the gap – as, for example, when the Secretary General of the Conference, Maurice Strong, sought to take part in civil society actions[125] – but the tensions between them provides a historical snapshot of the contested formal and subaltern geopolitics of environmental thinking that emerged before 1972 and has continued ever since. Video footage that remains of Stockholm, and reports about it,[126] demonstrate the cleavages between the inside and the outside of the conference hall and the importance of what Craggs and

121 John McCormick, *Reclaiming Paradise: The Global Environmental Movement* (Bloomington: Indiana University Press, 1991), 97–106.

122 Steven Bernstein, 'Liberal Environmentalism and Global Environmental Governance', *Global Environmental Politics* 2, no. 3 (2002): 1–16; Steven Bernstein, 'Ideas, Social Structure and the Compromise of Liberal Environmentalism', *European Journal of International Relations* 6, no. 4 (2000): 464–512.

123 Carl Death, 'Summit Theatre: Exemplary Governmentality and Environmental Diplomacy in Johannesburg and Copenhagen', *Environmental Politics* 20, no. 1 (2011): 1–19.

124 See the film Dean Evenson and Dudley Evenson, *Long Live Life Part 12 – United Nations Conference on the Human Environment Stockholm, Sweden 1972* (Bellingham, WA: Soundings of the Planet, 1972), accessed 18 June 2022, https://www.youtube.com/watch?v=jYC38S769VM.

125 Emmelin, 'The Stockholm Conferences'.

126 Evenson and Evenson, *Long Live Life*.

Mahoney call knowledge, performance, and protest in this moment of emergent environmental geopolitics.[127] In these dynamics we find Castro on the outside, taking his part in the heterogenous mix of voices of international environmental civil society.

Alain Bué, who travelled from Vincennes to Stockholm with Castro to take part in the conference and present the Amazon report, suggests that Castro was one of the authors of a response to the intergovernmental conference's announcement (which was later unpicked) of a moratorium on the killing of whales.[128] The response proposed a moratorium on the killing of humans. This became an important part of the declaration made outside the conference hall by activists.[129] The Environment Forum held the myriad organizations and individuals who flocked to Stockholm to try to influence proceedings, constituting one of the key founding moments of the international environmental movement not as a coherent or linear phenomenon but as a contested history of protest and struggle. On panels there Castro spoke virulently against the Club of Rome and its *Limits to Growth* report.[130] Perhaps more interestingly, Castro also gave an interview to French television in which he endorsed a somewhat dramatic – but now increasingly familiar[131]– element of ecological political discourse: fear, he said, was necessary, in the face of ecological disaster. All of this places Castro within the growing ecology movement, whose radical element got significant impetus from the gatherings around Stockholm.[132]

The Brussels newspaper *Le Soir* recounted the unsettling and clamorous meetings that echoed around the city outside the central conference. Its article – with the headline 'Josué de Castro: first, struggle against colonialism' – places Castro, and his anticolonial message, at the centre of this conflict.[133] Castro was also cited by UNESCO as one of the Environment Forum's spokespeople.[134] This is a misleading term, as the names reveal the internal contradictions in this emerging international environmental civil society: alongside Castro, UNESCO lists the incommensurate figures of

127 Craggs and Mahony, 'The Geographies of the Conference'.
128 Bué, 'Josué de Castro'.
129 Unknown, 'L'événement Stockholm', *Le Grand Virage*, April 1973.
130 Unknown, 'L'événement Stockholm'.
131 Erik Swyngedouw, 'Apocalypse Now! Fear and Doomsday Pleasures', *Capitalism Nature Socialism* 24, no. 1 (March 2013): 9–18, doi:10.1080/10455752.2012.759252.
132 Carl Death, 'Disrupting Global Governance: Protest at Environmental Conferences from 1972 to 2012', *Global Governance: A Review of Multilateralism and International Organizations* 21, no. 4 (2015): 579–98.
133 Anonymous, 'Josué de Castro: d'abord lutter contre le colonialisme', *Le Soir*, June 1972, 25, CEHIBRA.JdC.
134 UNESCO, 'Conferences Parallel to the United Nations Conference on the Human Environment' (United Nations Educational, Scientific and Cultural Organization, June 1973), 1, accessed 18 June 2022, http://unesdoc.unesco.org/images/0000/000044/004437EB.pdf.

Margaret Mead, Barry Commoner, and Paul Ehrlich. Ehrlich and Castro were on diametrically opposed ends of one of the key questions of the moment, population, about which Ehrlich and Commoner were also in the midst of a heated public dispute.[135] The *Time* magazine reporter recounted vigorous disputes:

> at the scientist's Environment Forum, Stanford Biologist Paul Ehrlich blamed half the world's environmental problems on increases in population. A woman biologist from Nigeria, aided by four burly colleagues, startled the audience by seizing Ehrlich's microphone and declaring that birth control was merely a way for the industrial powers to remain rich by preserving the status quo. Peace was restored only after Ehrlich conceded that the US should curb its own consumption of natural resources before urging population controls on developing countries. Brazilian Economist Josué de Castro fumes at the very mention of birth control. "Genocide of the unborn!" he charges.[136]

According to other reports Castro was even clearer, and framed population control in racial terms: it was a 'genocide against the coloured peoples of the world'.[137] The 'woman biologist from Nigeria' is almost certainly Dora Obi Chizea,[138] a member of the *Oi* group, who objected to the make-up of the forum. The split between a rightist, Malthusian ecologism and a leftist, Third Worldist environmentalism cut through the proceedings. The *Oi* group insisted on altering who spoke, when, and from what positions of power.[139] Further research on the other Third Worldist activists and thinkers involved in Stockholm in 1972 would be worthwhile to explore these trends, of which Castro's biography reveals only one. Paul Ehrlich reflected on these bothering scenes, arguing that there was 'a crying need for quiet conferences',[140] where politics would be kept on the sidelines. He does not refer to Castro by name, but attacks what he refers to as 'pseudo-leftists' and apparently ignorant 'third world' voices. He recalls, bitterly, the 'familiar accusations of genocide'.[141]

135 Michael Egan, *Barry Commoner and the Science of Survival: The Remaking of American Environmentalism* (Boston, MA: MIT Press, 2009), 133–34.

136 Friedel Ungeheuer, 'A Stockholm Notebook', *Time*, June 1972, sec. Environment, 25, CEHIBRA.JdC.

137 Anonymous, 'Man vs Man Not Man vs Nature, Commoner Tells Overflow Crowd' (unknown, 1972), 414, CEHIBRA.JdC; see also Rosembuj, 'Josué de Castro: las dudas de un pacifista'.

138 See Dora Obi Chizea, *Population and Africa: A Positive Programme* (Kenya: The African Environmental Association, 1974).

139 Tord Björk, 'The Emergence of Popular Participation in World Politics-United Nations Conference on Human Environment 1972', *Stockholm: University of Stockholm* 42, no. 2 (1996): 310–33.

140 Paul R. Ehrlich, 'A Crying Need for Quiet Conferences: Personal Notes from Stockholm', *Bulletin of the Atomic Scientists* 28, no. 7 (1972): 30–32.

141 Ehrlich, 'A Crying Need for Quiet Conferences', 31.

Ehrlich doesn't suggest that the repeated charges of genocide encouraged him to rethink any of his positions. International environmental civil society emerged already riven by conflict, with critical voices from the South demanding to be heard and emphatically changing the tenor and practice of debate. International environmentalism was neither a Northern invention nor a harmonious unity.[142]

In the aftermath of the conference, Castro published an important piece in the UNESCO magazine, *The Courier*.[143] Enrique Leff and Carlos Walter Porto-Gonçalves have recently traced from this piece a genealogy of Latin American political ecology through the 1970s and beyond.[144] The article was, in fact, very largely based on the unpublished Amazon report. As this chapter shows, it is therefore only one spring of a deeper source of geographical theory and geopolitical practice. Engaging in an international epistemological dispute over the environment and development, the article reworks and reiterates the arguments made in the Amazon report, emphasizing Castro's nuanced and multi-faceted understanding of the relationship between development and environment to argue that the most important cause of environmental degradation is underdevelopment. Here Castro makes a spatial and epistemic argument key to an anticolonial history of political ecology:

> if it is only recently that people have come to talk insistently about the pollution and degradation caused by economic growth, this is because Western civilization, with its scientific and ethnocentric approach, has always refused to see what is obvious: that the hunger and poverty of certain far-off regions form part of the social price mankind pays so that economic development may advance in a few economically and politically dominant regions.[145]

The history and theory of underdevelopment, in Castro's hands, becomes an environmental history too.

Conclusion

The strands of Latin American political ecology that Leff and Porto-Gonçalves identify have largely proceeded without anglophone political ecology paying great attention. At Stockholm in 1972 Castro was engaging in a resolutely international field, but his relations with anglophone critical scholarship and the various strands of New Left thinking remained surprisingly limited.

---

142 See, for example, McCormick, *Reclaiming Paradise*, 103–05.
143 Josué de Castro, 'Pollution Problem No. 1: Under-Development', *UNESCO Courier* 20 (January 1973): 22.
144 Carlos Walter Porto-Gonçalves and Enrique Leff, 'A Ecologia Política Na América Latina: A Reapropriação Da Natureza, a Reinvenção Dos Territórios e a Construção Da Racionalidade Ambiental', *Desenvolvimento e Meio Ambiente* 35 (2015): 70–71.
145 Castro, 'Pollution Problem No. 1', 20.

Though he gave many visiting lectures, and had a deep relationship with some British intellectuals and politicians, Castro did not work at any institutions based in the UK or the United States. Though I know of no equally traumatic exchange as that of Milton Santos' at UCL – his leaving a year-long appointment after eight days because of racism while trying to find housing in London – academic exchange and recognition in either Britain or the United States is a noteworthy missing feature of Castro's life, particularly after exile. Castro presented his work at anglophone international geographical conferences, as, for instance, in New York in 1970 at a conference of the American Geographical Society,[146] and he took part in seminars and conferences, but it seems that he somewhat lost interest in chasing a North American or British audience. There is a contrast between such later absences and the energy he applied to establishing nutritional and geographical networks in the United States in the 1940s and 1950s. Absences are difficult to interpret, but this is put into relief by his involvement in French circles, not only academically but as a writer and expert on Latin America in publications such as *Le Monde*[147] and *Le Monde Diplomatique*.[148]

There are some exceptions, and the archive reveals opaque but intriguing linkages. For example, the files in Recife contain a typescript of a televised lecture given by Peter Worsley – a sociologist and influential figure in the British New Left, particularly in relation to the idea of the third world,[149] at Manchester University in January 1969 on 'The Revolutionary Theories of Frantz Fanon'. It is addressed, by hand, from Worsley to Castro, and in it Worsley makes use of Castro's work on the Northeast while examining the significance of Fanon's conception of revolutionary action.[150] How and where Worsley and Castro met remains unclear.

It was only after his death that Castro attained a concrete place in the emergence of anglophone radical geography as such. A few important figures accompany this role, including Yves Lacoste, Milton Santos, Ben Wisner, and Keith Buchanan. Yves Lacoste had positioned himself as the *enfant*

146 Josué de Castro, 'La Production Mondiale et Sa Repartition', 1970, 92, CEHIBRA. JdC.

147 See, for example, Marcel Niedergang, 'L'Alliance Contre Le Progrès', *Le Monde*, September 1969; Niedergang, 'Josué de Castro avait longtemps crié dans le désert ...'.

148 See, for example, Josué de Castro, 'La formation humaine clé du développement', *Le Monde diplomatique*, 1968; Josué de Castro, 'Un danger pour la paix', *Le Monde diplomatique*, 1963; Josué de Castro, 'Révolution ou stagnation', *Le Monde diplomatique*, 1964; René Dumont, 'Tout pays déjà peuplé qui laisse accroître sa population de plus de 3 % par an prend une lourde responsabilité', *Le Monde diplomatique*, 1964.

149 Peter Worsley, 'The Revolutionary Theories of Frantz Fanon', January 1969, 317, CEHIBRA.JdC.

150 See, for example, Peter Worsley, 'Revolution of the Third World', *New Left Review* 12 (1961): 18; Peter Worsley, 'How Many Worlds?', *Third World Quarterly* 1, no. 2 (1979): 100–08.

terrible of French geography since the 1960s,[151] but it was not until 1976 that he published, through the radical publisher Maspero, his polemical *La Géographie, ça sert d'abord à faire la guerre* [Geography serves first of all to make war]. In that same year he also founded *Hérodote*, also published by Maspero. The influence of *Hérodote* in France was widespread, but in anglophone (and Italian and other) geography and geopolitics it was significant in one very particular sense: its interview with Michel Foucault in 1976 has been a key text for some branches of critical geography.[152] This interview also attests to the journal's roots in Vincennes.[153] Yet *Hérodote* largely remained a French-orientated project, with strictly limited engagement with anglophone debates.[154] The same is true reciprocally. Most anglophone geographers, with the exception of a few scholars of geopolitics such as Gearóid Ó Tuathail, overlooked the French geopolitical school, in what has been called 'a history of missed connections, occasional influence and mutual incomprehension if not outright indifference'.[155] Furthermore, Lacoste as a channel for Castro's influence is compromised by the antipathetic tenor of their relationship, outlined above.

Milton Santos, on the other hand, is a much more fruitful conduit. Santos linked perhaps the two most important early journals of radical geography, being involved in the early days of both *Hérodote* and *Antipode*.[156] In the second edition of *Hérodote* Santos engaged in a slightly frosty exchange with Lacoste, disputing Lacoste's characterization of Marx's silence on the question of space.[157] (The piece strongly bears out Ferretti's point that the relationship between French and Brazilian geography should not be considered a one-way traffic of influence North to South.[158]) But in spite of philosophical

---

151 Béatrice Giblin, 'Herodote et L'ecole Française de Geopolitique', *ACTA Geográfica, Boa Vista* Edición Espacial: Geografia Política e Geopolítica (2014): 51–61.

152 Calbérac, 'Close Reading Michel Foucault's and Yves Lacoste's Concepts of Space Through Spatial Metaphors'; see also Neil Smith and Cindi Katz, 'Grounding Metaphor: Towards a Spatialized Politics', in *Place and the Politics of Identity*, ed. Michael Keith and Steve Pile (London and New York: Routledge, 1993), 66–81.

153 Leslie W. Hepple, 'Yves Lacoste, Hérodote and French Radical Geopolitics', in *Geopolitical Traditions: Critical Histories of a Century of Geopolitical Thought*, ed. Klaus Dodds and David Atkinson (New York: Routledge, 2000), 268–301.

154 James D. Sidaway, 'The Geography of Political Geography', in *The SAGE Handbook of Political Geography*, ed. Kevin Cox, Murray Low, and Jenny Robinson (London: SAGE, 2008), 41–56.

155 Gautier and Hautdidier, 'Connecting Political Ecology and French Geography', 60.

156 Marina Amaral et al., 'Entrevista com o professor Milton Santos', *PADÊ: estudos em filosofia, raça, gênero e direitos humanos: UniCEUB, FACJS* 2, no. 1 (1980): 21.

157 Milton Santos, 'Silence de Marx? Silence Des Philosophes? Non, Silence Des Géographes!', *Hérodote* 2 (1976): 136–39.

158 Federico Ferretti, 'French–Brazilian Geography: The Influence of French Geography in Brazil by José Borzacchiello Da Silva', *Journal of Latin American Geography* 17, no. 2 (2018): 258–60, doi:10.1353/lag.2018.0035.

differences with Lacoste, Santos continued to publish in *Hérodote* in the late 1970s.[159] Santos also played an important role in bringing a Third Worldist Brazilian consciousness to *Antipode*'s work, editing issues of the journal while based at the University of Dar-Es-Salaam in 1973. Santos edited an early edition of *Antipode* on 'Geography, Marxism and Underdevelopment'. The edition responds to Harvey's *Social Justice and the City*, while also critiquing radical geography for its anglophone bias. Santos' piece in the edition was translated by Anne Buttimer from French, while Santos was working at an anglophone university in Dar Es Salaam. The negotiations of translation can't be overlooked here. Power and Sidaway argue that Santos was 'an agent through whom dependency ideas and geography were articulated, but the points of contact and circulation were complex'.[160] *Antipode* provided one of the vectors for this contact and circulation.[161] *Hérodote* in Paris provided another. Santos did not, however, cite Castro's work in these interventions. In this period Santos was developing a Marxist approach to social and spatial formations, in which Castro's less Marxist-orientated scholarship fits awkwardly. Nevertheless, as mentioned above, and in Ferretti and Pedrosa's work, we know that Castro and Santos were in contact, and at a foundational level the Pernambucan had been a key formative influence in the Bahian's geographical thought.

In *Antipode* there was an intermittent tradition of attempts to explore and analyse traditions of critical geography in other languages.[162] *Antipode*'s own roots were to some extent spatially diverse and multi-lingual. The first issues of the journal were edited by Ben Wisner, a political ecologist working on underdevelopment, risk, and disasters. Wisner was perhaps the anglophone geographer with the widest critical awareness of, and enthusiasm for, Josué de Castro's work,[163] and he worked with Milton Santos at the University of Dar Es Salaam between 1972 and 1974.[164] Castro is also referenced by David

159 For example, Milton Santos, 'De La Société Au Paysage. La Signification de l'espace Humain', *Hérodote: Revue de Géopolitique de l'agriculture*, 9 (1978): 66–73.

160 Power and Sidaway, 'The Degeneration of Tropical Geography', 598.

161 For assessment of Santos' role in this period of critical geography see Pedrosa, 'O Périplo Do Exílio de Milton Santos e a Formação de Sua Rede de Cooperação'; Davies, 'Milton Santos'; Melgaço, 'Thinking Outside the Bubble of the Global North'; Melgaço and Prouse, 'Milton Santos and the Centrality of the Periphery'.

162 Jacques Lévy, 'French Geographies of Today', *Antipode* 17, nos 2–3 (1985): 9–12; Steen Folke, 'The Development of Radical Geography in Scandinavia', *Antipode* 17, nos 2–3 (1985): 13–18.

163 See, for instance, Ben Wisner, 'Book Review: The Geography of Famine', *Progress in Geography* 6, no. 2 (June 1982): 271–77, doi:10.1177/030913258200600210; Wisner, Weiner, and O'Keefe, 'Hunger'; Ben Wisner, 'Does Radical Geography Lack an Approach to Environmental Relations?' *Antipode* 10, no. 1 (March 1978): 84–95, doi:10.1111/j.1467-8330.1978.tb00298.x; See also Carter, 'Population Control'.

164 Kirsten Johnson, Ben Wisner, and Phil O'Keefe, '"Theses on Peasantry" Revisited', *Antipode* 37, no. 5 (November 2005): 952, doi:10.1111/j.0066-4812.2005.00543.x; see

Slater in his articles on geography and underdevelopment.[165] Perhaps one of the reasons his influence never became fully fledged, however, was precisely the turn towards a Marxist theoretical basis for radical geography, closely associated with David Harvey's work, which took place in the first years of the 1970s. As Enrique Leff puts it in his account of the power–knowledge relations of political ecology, 'at play here is the recognition or not of academic peers, the attractiveness of some theories and disciplinary engagements that lead researchers to explore and accept some sources of inspiration and reject and disregard others when establishing their academic identity'.[166] However, as Sharad Chari has noted, it is worth picking apart the differences between North American schools: the Berkeley group were more orientated towards Third Worldist and agrarian studies approaches.[167] It is, therefore, perhaps not surprising that it is one of the key proponents of the Berkeley tendency, Michael Watts, who later credited Castro with being an important early thinker in this regard.[168] Watts' brilliant epic on famine references Castro a few times and, as mentioned above, gives him great rhetorical credit without deploying his work in theoretical or political exigesis.

Keith Buchanan, meanwhile, had been drawing on Castro's work from the early 1960s, discussing Castro's interventions not only with regard to population but on colonialism and underdevelopment.[169] In *Antipode* in 1973 he drew quite extensively on Castro in his piece on 'The White North and the Population Explosion', deploying Castro's anti-Malthusianism as well as his concern for environmental questions.[170] Perhaps the most important shared impulse, however, was the insistence on dealing with political and ideological questions within geographical inquiry, and on a radical humanist starting point for geography.[171] This was a position Buchanan became well

also Richard Peet, 'Radical Geography in the United States: A Personal History', *Antipode* 17, nos 2–3 (September 1985): 1–7, doi:10.1111/j.1467-8330.1985.tb00323.x; Joanne Sharp, 'Practising Subalternity: Postcolonial Tanzania, the Dar School and Pan-African Geopolitical Imaginations', in *Subaltern Geographies*, ed. Tariq Jazeel and Stephen Legg (Athens: University of Georgia Press, 2019).

165 Slater, 'Geography and Underdevelopment'; Slater, 'Geography and Underdevelopment – Part II*'.

166 Leff, 'Power–Knowledge Relations in the Field of Political Ecology', 229.

167 Sharad Chari, 'Trans-Area Studies and the Perils of Geographical "World-Writing"', *Environment and Planning D: Society and Space* 34, no. 5 (2016): 792–93.

168 Watts, *Silent Violence*, xix–xx.

169 Keith Buchanan, 'The Third World', *New Left Review* 18 (1963): 5; Keith Buchanan, *The Southeast Asian World: An Introductory Essay* (New York: Anchor Books, 1967); see also Noam Chomsky, *At War with Asia* (Oakland: AK Press, 2005), 11.

170 Keith Buchanan, 'The White North and the Population Explosion', *Antipode* 5, no. 3 (1973): 7–15.

171 Ray Watters, 'The Geographer as Radical Humanist: An Appreciation of Keith Buchanan', *Asia Pacific Viewpoint* 39, no. 1 (April 1998): 8, doi:10.1111/1467-8373.00051.

known for,[172] and it is one he shared deeply with Castro. These ebbs and flows of references, influence, and friendship put Castro alongside mainstream accounts of the emergence of anglophone critical geography. I have not had the space to explore the breadth and complex flows of these histories – particularly the francophone ones – or the multiple accounts of them.[173] Rather, I use Castro's biography as an opening, and as a synecdoche for a much more complex picture.

Castro was an anticolonial intellectual and the bearer of a militant geography. In anglophone geography there is a longstanding school of postcolonial geography,[174] increasing interest in subaltern studies,[175] and deepening deployment and investigation of decolonial approaches.[176] While drawing on all of these in different ways, it is worth emphasizing their distinction from anticolonial thought. This particular framework has a less rich contemporary

172 Tony Binns, 'Marginal Lands, Marginal Geographies', *Progress in Human Geography* 31, no. 5 (2007): 588.

173 For which see, for example, David Harvey, 'On the History and Present Condition of Geography: An Historical Materialist Manifesto', *The Professional Geographer* 36, no. 1 (1984): 1–11; Harvey, *Spaces of Capital*; Trevor J. Barnes, 'Retheorizing Economic Geography: From the Quantitative Revolution to the "Cultural Turn"', in *Theory and Methods: Critical Essays in Human Geography*, ed. Chris Philo (Routledge, 2017), 53–72; Trevor J. Barnes, 'Lives Lived and Lives Told: Biographies of Geography's Quantitative Revolution', *Environment and Planning D: Society and Space* 19, no. 4 (2001): 409–29; Trevor J. Barnes and Eric Sheppard, '"Nothing Includes Everything": Towards Engaged Pluralism in Anglophone Economic Geography', *Progress in Human Geography* 34, no. 2 (2010): 193–214; Trevor J. Barnes and Eric Sheppard, eds, *Spatial Histories of Radical Geography: North America and Beyond* (Hoboken, NJ: Wiley-Blackwell, 2019).

174 James D. Sidaway, 'Postcolonial Geographies: An Exploratory Essay', *Progress in Human Geography* 24, no. 4 (December 2000): 591–612, doi:10.1191/030913200100189120; Catherine Nash, 'Cultural Geography: Postcolonial Cultural Geographies', *Progress in Human Geography* 26, no. 2 (2002): 219–30; Andrew Sluyter, *Colonialism and Landscape: Postcolonial Theory and Applications* (Washington: Rowman & Littlefield, 2002); Sarah A. Radcliffe, 'Development and Geography: Towards a Postcolonial Development Geography?' *Progress in Human Geography* 29, no. 3 (2005): 291–98; Craggs, 'Postcolonial Geographies'.

175 Ananya Roy, 'Slumdog Cities: Rethinking Subaltern Urbanism', *International Journal of Urban and Regional Research* 35, no. 2 (March 2011): 223–38, doi:10.1111/j.1468-2427.2011.01051.x; Tariq Jazeel, 'Subaltern Geographies: Geographical Knowledge and Postcolonial Strategy', *Singapore Journal of Tropical Geography* 35, no. 1 (2014): 88–103; Dave Featherstone, 'Space, Subalternity, and Critique, or Which Subaltern Studies for Which Geography?' *Cultural Geographies* 24, no. 2 (2017): 341–46.

176 Sarah A. Radcliffe, 'Decolonising Geographical Knowledges', *Transactions of the Institute of British Geographers* 42, no. 3 (July 2017): 329–33, doi:10.1111/tran.12195; Esson et al., 'The 2017 RGS-IBG Chair's Theme'; Sam Halvorsen, 'Decolonising Territory: Dialogues with Latin American Knowledges and Grassroots Strategies', *Progress in Human Geography*, X (2018): 1–25.

geographical sub-field. We can point to anarchist geographers as a distinctive element of this history. Castro drew on both Élisée Reclus and Peter Kropotkin,[177] who, as Simon Springer put it, 'demonstrated long ago that geography lends itself well to emancipatory ideas',[178] and who both wrote about hunger in different ways. Throughout this book I have emphasized the political projects these intellectual developments were imbricated with. While the anticolonial is elided by some theorists with the decolonial,[179] I hold on to anticolonialism as a distinct mode of thinking and practice with a particular history and geography separate from, alongside, prior to, and distinct from not only decolonial thought but postcolonial theory and the Black radical tradition.[180] I prefer to retain a distinction in order, for instance, to discriminate between the tri-continental geographies of African anticolonial thought of scholars such as Aimé Césaire and Frantz Fanon (both born in Martinique), and the particular Latin American genealogies of decolonial thought, specifically those emerging from various Amerindian worldviews. There are many extremely important overlaps – the Atlantic trajectories of Paulo Freire and W.E.B. Du Bois being two examples, and the history of dependency theory being another – but holding these traditions apart, for analytical purposes, can give a clearer sense of their different scales and modes of theory and praxis.

The anticolonial project's focus on the nation state and pan-Africanist modes of internationalism and its particular historical geographies of solidarity and praxis[181] can be more productively put into dialogue with the pedagogical and communal inheritances of decolonial thought[182] or the anarchist roots of some anticolonial thought[183] if we do not entirely blur them. Certainly, it is important to distinguish these approaches from postcolonial (or postcolonial) thought, with its own (often Indian sub-continental) histories and its particular contributions to questions of representation, discourse, and histories of cultural practice.[184] There are hugely important intersections – Edward Said was both the rootstock of postcolonial criticism and an important anticolonial intellectual in the Palestinian cause – but nevertheless there are distinct traditions of thought at stake. Importantly, there are also cleavages within

---

177 Castro, *Geografia da Fome: O Dilema Brasileiro: Pão Ou Aço* (1946), 31–32.
178 Simon Springer, 'Anarchism! What Geography Still Ought To Be', *Antipode* 44, no. 5 (2012): 1613, doi:10.1111/j.1467-8330.2012.01034.x.
179 See, for instance, Nelson Maldonado-Torres, 'On the Coloniality of Being', *Cultural Studies* 21, nos 2–3 (2007): 261–62.
180 Reza, 'African Anti-colonialism'.
181 Featherstone, *Solidarity*.
182 Chela Sandoval, *Methodology of the Oppressed* (Minneapolis: University of Minnesota Press, 2000).
183 Springer, 'Anarchism!'; Federico Ferretti, 'L'egemonia Dell'Europa Nella Nouvelle Géographie Universelle (1876–1894) Di Elisée Reclus: Una Geografia Anticoloniale?', *Rivista Geografica Italiana*, Pacini Editore S.p.A, 117, no. 1 (2010): 65–92.
184 Mbembe et al., 'What Is Postcolonial Thinking?'

all these approaches. As Brent Hayes Edwards notes of 'cultures of black internationalism', they are '"adversarial" to themselves'.[185] It is productive to hold traditions apart to identify – perhaps counter-intuitively – what they have in common and their shared intellectual influences. This relates in particular to the distinctive ways in which anti, post, decolonial, and subaltern thought have related to the equally internally differentiated histories of Marxist thought. This is also to suggest that antitheses between 'Marxist' and 'postcolonial' approaches in geography might seem less irreconcilable if we explore new and shared histories of these traditions.[186] We might find other ways of working with what Gillian Hart calls 'an alternative spatio-historical Marxist postco-lonial approach'[187] through exploring such histories. Drawing the distinctions between traditions is to immediately break them down again: I have deliberately positioned Castro as an anticolonial thinker, but also as an important precursor of Latin American dependency theory, with its strong links with contemporary decolonial approaches. Traditions, after all, are made to be broken.

An influential branch of political ecology, inspired by decolonial and Black feminist thought, has opened up a path to making the anticolonial central to the discipline's analytical procedures and intellectual frameworks.[188] In this mould, Castro is a productive intellectual forebear: putting the anticolonial into political ecology is also a task for intellectual and disciplinary history. Guthman,[189] like Watts and many others, has described political ecology as emerging from the work of Blaikie and Brookfield on soil science in the 1980s. As this book has attempted to show, this genealogy for political ecology is foreshortened. A broader, more open intellectual history can be rerouted through Latin America, and the mobile worlds of an individual life, to unravel different sequences of explanation. Castro's work is one strand of a distinctive history of environmental thinking in Latin America whose relationship with European thought is one of interrelation, co-optation, and transformation. This book, therefore, insists on the relational history of counter-hegemonic thinking in the twentieth century. Indeed, Latin America has a claim to be the most significant site of all for the development of political ecology.[190] Attention to alternative, Latin American intellectual histories is part of a passage towards producing an anticolonial geography, and analysing Castro's life and work is one step along this path.

185 Edwards, *The Practice of Diaspora*, 7.
186 For example, Kate D. Derickson, 'Urban Geography I: Locating Urban Theory in the "Urban Age"', *Progress in Human Geography* 39, no. 5 (October 2015): 647–57, doi:10.1177/0309132514560961.
187 Gillian Hart, 'Relational Comparison Revisited: Marxist Postcolonial Geographies in Practice', *Progress in Human Geography* 42, no. 3 (2016): 373.
188 Heynen, 'Urban Political Ecology II'.
189 Julie Guthman, *Weighing in: Obesity, Food Justice, and the Limits of Capitalism* (Berkeley: University of California Press, 2011).
190 Porto-Gonçalves and Leff, 'Political Ecology in Latin America'.

Conclusion
Militant Geography

Tem que se entrenar, tem que se informar, tem que saber para onde corre o rio, não é? Tem que seguir o leito assim, tem que estar informado. Tem que saber quem é Josué de Castro, rapaz

[*You've got to train yourself up, you've got to inform yourself, you've got to know where the river runs, right? You've got to follow the river bed, you've got to be informed. You've got to know who Josué de Castro is, man*]

Chico Science, 1995[1]

Acho que pó Josué foi um gênio

[*I think old Josué was a genius*]

Milton Santos, 1998[2]

Eu sei o que é passar fome. Quando eu falo da fome não é porque eu li '*Geografia da Fome*' do Josué de Castro. Eu cito a fome, porque passei fome. – Lula, sobre a guerra contra a fome e a miséria que foram alicerces durante seu governo. #LulaPresidente

[*I know what it is to be hungry. I talk about hunger, because I've experienced hunger – Lula, on the war against hunger and poverty that were the foundation stones of his governments. #LulaPresidente*]

@Lulaoficial, 6.01 am, 21 August 2018[3]

1 Anonymous, 'Chico Science Fala Sobre Josué de Castro', Youtube, 1995, accessed 18 June 2022, https://www.youtube.com/watch?v=oT6-qCqZVec.
2 Santos, 'Entrevista explosiva'.
3 @lulaoficial, 'Eu Sei o Que é Passar Fome', social media, Lula official twitter account (blog), August 2018, accessed 18 June 2022, https://twitter.com/lulaoficial/status/103 1889130526003200?lang=en-gb.

Introduction

Photographs of Josué de Castro from the early 1970s show him looking old and drawn, beyond his sixty-five years. Death came to Castro in his office in Paris, in the form of a heart attack. His troubled relationship with the Brazilian state continued after he died. He had been trying to return to Brazil, and his family continued to fight bureaucratic barriers as they sought to move his body back to Brazil for burial. Eventually, posthumously, he was granted a passport. He was buried in the cemetery of São João Batista in Rio de Janeiro. But Castro's death is not really the end of this story. After he died his work took on new meanings and forms as it passed through the hands of military censorship, rural social movements, academic geographers, and urban musicians. I begin this conclusion with three quotations, from Chico Science, Milton Santos, and former President Lula. They show not only that Castro remains a presence in Brazilian political and cultural discourse today but how malleable his legacy can be. This book has bent Castro's work to speak to the concerns of anglophone critical geography as it is in the twenty-first century. The academic and institutional framework in which I write shapes my interpretation of his work, just as much as the lyrical mode of Chico Science's practice shapes his use of Castro and the respectively academic and political motivations of Santos and Lula structure theirs.

Josué de Castro was a global thinker, with global trajectories and intentions. Yet he has a particular significance in the intellectual history of Brazil and of the Northeast more specifically. As the epigraphs of this conclusion show, since his death in 1973 his legacy has been put to work by different sectors of Brazilian political, cultural, and intellectual life. In 1995 Chico Science was in his late twenties and one of Brazil's most famous musicians, the face and brain of the musical movement *mangue beat*, an afrociberdelic crush of hip-hop, funk, and Northeastern maracatu. *Mangue beat* insisted on the cultural dynamism of the urban Northeast, symbolized by the scuttling, scrabbling, ironic survivalism of the crab and the biological and cultural diversity of its urban mangrove forests. With his feet in the mud of the river Capibaribe, Chico Science called Josué de Castro the intellectual figurehead of this youthful, politically confrontational counterculture. Milton Santos was speaking in 1998, aged 72, as a professor in São Paulo, the most prominent geographer in Brazil, and a significant public intellectual. In a sweeping, synoptic interview with a group of younger geographers, during which he reflected on his work and the state of Brazilian disciplinary, political, and intellectual life, he called Josué de Castro a lost genius at the base of critical geography. Lula, another Northeasterner, positions the geography of hunger as the *alicerces*, the foundations, of his narrative of the Workers' Party's thirteen years of government. Lula continued to deploy Josué de Castro. Releasing a video about hunger, he said 'when I talk about hunger, I don't do it because I've read *A Geografia da Fome* by Josué de Castro. I talk about hunger, because I've experienced hunger.'[4] In simultaneously affirming and denying his reading of Castro, Lula deploys a Castroian idea, that knowledge of hunger is visceral and immanent. It recalls Castro's own insistence that 'it was not at the Sorbonne, or at any other seat of learning, that I came to know the anatomy of hunger, but rather in the marshy land of the poor parts of Recife'.[5]

Chico Science died in a car crash in 1997 at the height of his fame. Milton Santos passed away in 2001 as the *éminence grise* of Brazilian geography. Lula has become the charismatic roadblock, and only hope, of a Brazilian left in permanent crisis. Yet the ongoing relevance of the cultural politics of diversity, independent critical thought, and political resistance to imperialism and inequality could hardly be greater. Santos', Science's, and Lula's proclamations of Josué de Castro's legacy were assertions of the existence and power of an autocthonous, counter-hegemonic history of discourse emerging from the Northeast of Brazil. This is a geographical discourse embedded in the material social reality of the Northeast, and irreducibly central to global histories of knowledge.

One of this book's claims to value is straightforward: the history of geography has too often been told with white, European, or North American men at its centre.[6] It is high time to expand the discipline's transnational and polylingual sense of itself. Quite evidently – as the literature and resources cited in this book have hopefully made very clear – my work is not unique in this regard, but part of a much wider collective endeavour. However, the angle at which I come to this project helps offer something new: a biographical approach that broadens the history of geography to include anticolonial thought, praxis, and lives from the south. Analysing and writing about lives can function as a set of tools to enable geographers to tell a broader story about the discipline, its inheritances, and its lines of inquiry. This approach has involved following sets of connections between places and histories of knowledge. Whether in terms of the associations between Castro's urban geography and Recife, between the broader Northeast and the idea of the region, or between Vincennes and histories of political ecology, a biographical approach means following the mobile and undetermined relationships between space, social relations, and knowledge production embodied in the unpredictable routes of a person's life.

I have consistently positioned this book within the broad field of political ecology, in spite of its clear debt to a number of other fields of geographical thinking, from the postcolonial to the history of geography and historical geography. I retain the tenets of political ecology because I understand

---

4 @lulaoficial.

5 Castro, *Of Men and Crabs*, ix.

6 See, for instance, Charles Mayhew's first chapter in John Agnew and David N. Livingstone, eds, *The SAGE Handbook of Geographical Knowledge* (London: SAGE, 2011), or, indeed, the front cover of Geoffrey J. Martin, *All Possible Worlds: A History of Geographical Ideas* (Oxford: Oxford University Press, 2005).

Castro's work to be profoundly committed to a political understanding of socio-ecological relations in the context of global political economy. The implications for future work in political ecology are two-fold. First, I hope the book serves as an example for building more bridges between Latin American intellectual history and anglophone political ecology. Secondly, it offers a number of contributions to the methodology (historical, biographical) and theory (the corporeal, the regional) of political ecology. It suggests that work to expand, consolidate, and complicate political ecology can, as this book has, draw on a wide set of intellectual resources.

There are many other possible research trajectories that could emerge from Castro's biography. My contribution has focused on the history, theory, and praxis of geography and political ecology, working through the one part of geographical enquiry to contribute to another, with the purpose of expanding the discipline's conceptual frameworks. This has enabled a number of fresh insights and new directions for research in political ecology, the history of geography, and critical geography more broadly.

From a Geography of Hunger to a Geography of Survival

I want to return here to one of my most pressing concerns in the book: to rearticulate and reinterpret Castro's negative geography,[7] its starting point in the necessarily hungry human subject, and its meaning for geographical approaches to survival, metabolism, hunger, and the philosophy of liberation today. I undertake this further theoretical reflection here because it draws on the various different textures of the chapters that have preceded this. The question of the study of hunger in geography is intrinsic to, but not identical to, this book's exploration of Castro's idea of the geography of hunger and its ripples outward. Within anglophone geography itself we can, though, see some of Castro's influence in the early framing of *Antipode* as a journal of 'Studies in Survival and Radical Geography', as it announced itself in 1970.[8] In 1973 William Bunge published his 'geography of human survival',[9] and the recent interest in the geography of survival is a fresh return to an early interest of critical geography. As Nik Heynen puts it, 'radical geography should first and foremost be about recognizing that life depends on meeting material basic needs like food, water, shelter, etc. I think we must make meeting these fundamentals of life the core of our project, rather than taking them as somehow implied.'[10] Castro is an ally, a resource,

---

7 Castro, *Geography of Hunger*, 13.
8 Ben Wisner, 'Introduction: On Radical Methodology', *Antipode* 2, no. 1 (August 1970): 1–3, doi:10.1111/j.1467-8330.1970.tb00468.x; See also Noel Castree et al., *The Point is to Change It: Geographies of Hope and Survival in an Age of Crisis* (Malden, MA: John Wiley & Sons, 2010), p.3.
9 Bunge, 'The Geography of Human Survival'.
10 Heynen, '"But It's Alright, Ma, It's Life, and Life Only"', 920.

and a forebear for what Heynen calls this 'really radical geography'. This is not a reductionist politics but a scalar one: the demand for a world without hunger remains revolutionary and utopian. Through the blood and sugar of metabolism, the urban scuttle of the cycle of the crab, the ruptures of translation, the distension of regional geography, the chronic commitment of the intellectual, and the growing pains of political ecology, this brings us back with fresh eyes to the idea with which this book, and Josué de Castro, started: *a alma da fome é política*: the soul of hunger is politics.

Castro understands hunger as a negative drive that must be fulfilled for the human subject to be able to realize itself. It is the fundamental characteristic of life, both biologically and sociologically. As a drive, it is produced and satiated socially. With hunger as a core determinant, the figure of the human is not a liberal, possessive individual, but a socially and ecologically determined subject. The German Marxist philosopher Ernst Bloch wrote, in the first volume of *The Principle of Hope*, that 'very little, all too little has been said so far about hunger'.[11] Kathi Weeks notes that, for Bloch, hunger figures 'as a kind of minimal ontological force'[12] in his analysis. As I have tried to show throughout this book, for Castro this 'minimal ontological force' underpinned a philosophy of praxis in which the struggle against hunger was the first principle of politics and the right to eat was fundamental.[13] The primary object of politics should be 'before anything an economy of subsistence: give to each person the indispensable minimum'.[14] What kind of praxis this necessitated was an insistent question, at many scales. The myriad ways to tackle the geography of hunger – global social transformation, agrarian reform, school meals, synthetic vitamins, urban labour organization, international institutions, global campaigns – were the complex problems that drove his political praxis, just as hunger was the subject that drove his theoretical analysis. In practical, political terms we should draw a genealogy between Castro's humanism – grounded as it was in fierce local, national, and international debates over food and land – and the peasant movement *Via Campesina*'s 'sophisticated attempt at developing a grounded, localized and yet international humanism around the food system'.[15]

Nik Heynen has outlined what he sees as a '*really* radical geography' orientated towards survival:

> every child's life and death should be used to remind us all of what radical geography should first and foremost care about. The nameless and faceless

---

11 Ernst Bloch, *The Principle of Hope*, trans. N. Plaice, S. Plaice, and P. Knight, vol. 1 (Oxford: Blackwell, 1986), 65.
12 Weeks, *The Problem with Work*, 249.
13 Castro, *Ensaios de biologia social*, 188.
14 Castro, *Ensaios de biologia social*, 187.
15 Patel, 'Global Fascism Revolutionary Humanism', 81.

people represented as 'percent increase' in the demand for emergency food [...] can help us refocus our intellectual and political efforts, to reconfigure our radical compasses. All of these cases, profound and banal, should make us angry and tearful, outraged and determined.[16]

Heynen's 'Really Radical Geography' is explicitly Blochian, but his repetition of the staggering statistics of hunger also has a distinctively Castroian tenor to it: 'it is [not] doctrinaire to suggest that without food, human bodies cannot exist. This totalizing meta-reality cannot be disguised by difference, processes of othering or intellectual disagreement.'[17] Castro, Bloch, and Heynen share the idea that the beginning of utopia is a world without hunger, and persistently demanding that world is radicalism's opening gambit.

Insistence itself is central to how hunger as drive becomes a geography orientated towards survival. Bloch argues that 'sympathy with the starving is the only widespread sympathy there is [...] the cry of hunger is probably the strongest single cry that can be directly presented [...] the stomach is the first lamp into which oil must be poured'.[18] This recalls the concerns of chapter 3, and the aesthetics of moral and political revelation. The sympathy Bloch writes of derives from the fact that hunger is in part what is common – all of us have been hungry and all have demanded food urgently, not least as infants – and what is alien: the hunger of the starving is beyond the imagination of those who live satiated. Enrique Dussel's work suggests a way of translating hunger into a philosophical discourse through an interpellative figure[19] of the other expressing their hunger.[20] As I argued in chapter 3, this problematic of representing the hungry other was at the centre of some of the most dynamic Brazilian artistic and cinematic work of the twentieth century, and it crystallizes in the cry: a demand for recognition. For Enrique Dussel, the real is to be found in exteriority, that which is other to Being.

> Among the real things that retain exteriority to Being, one is found that has a history, a biography, freedom: another person [...] All of this acquires practical reality when someone says, 'I'm hungry!' The hunger of the oppressed, of the poor, is an effect of an unjust system. As such, it has no place in the system. [...] because it is negativity, 'lack of' [,] [...] non-being in the world. Hunger as such is the practical exteriority of, or

16 Heynen, '"But It's Alright, Ma, It's Life, and Life Only"', 919.
17 Heynen, '"But It's Alright, Ma, It's Life, and Life Only"', 921.
18 Bloch, *The Principle of Hope*, 1:65.
19 Enrique Dussel, 'Reason of the Other: "Interpellation" as Speech-Act', in Enrique Dussel, *The Underside of Modernity: Apel, Ricoeur, Rorty, Taylor, and the Philosophy of Liberation* (Atlantic Highlands, NJ: Humanities Press, 1996), 19–48.
20 See also Corine Pelluchon and Justin E.H. Smith, *Nourishment: A Philosophy of the Political Body* (London: Bloomsbury, 2019), 155–57.

the most subversive internal transcendentality against, the system: the total and insurmountable 'beyond'.[21]

As Nelson Maldonado-Torres puts it, 'it is the cry that animates the birth of theory and critical thought'.[22] In defending a humanist geography, Anne Buttimer defines humanism as 'the liberation cry of humanity'.[23] Buttimer does not address a specifically anticolonial humanism, or hunger as such, but her work remains a touchpoint for a radical humanist geography. The primal cry is that of hunger. From his earliest work Castro sought to attest to, and analyse, the cry of hunger. Attesting to hunger was itself a radical position.[24] Furthermore, his political and theoretical praxis was radical precisely because 'to satiate structurally the hunger of the oppressed is to change radically the system'.[25] As Castro understood social reality by 'develop[ing] a science from the manifestation of the lowest standard of living in its severest expression: hunger',[26] the geography of hunger as a negative geography is in syncopation with Enrique Dussel's philosophy of liberation, which begins from 'the negativity of starvation as a starting point'.[27] He 'begin[s] a philosophical discourse from the periphery, from the oppressed', taking 'geopolitical space seriously'. 'To be born', he wrote, 'at the North Pole or in Chiapas is not the same thing as to be born in New York City'.[28] In these formulations we can also see Castro's influence. In Paris in 1964 Dussel organized a series of seminars as a 'Latin American Week'. The central theme was Latin American Catholic Humanism. Castro took part, and it culminated in an edition of the magazine *Esprit* edited by Dussel.[29] In his piece, Castro wrote that 'total reality cannot be grasped from the outset, independent from the perspective of the viewer; reality seen from Moscow has nothing to do with reality seen from Washington.'[30] I dwell on Dussel here because through him we can see the broader significance of Castro's avowedly negative starting point. Dussel

21 Enrique Dussel, *Philosophy of Liberation*, trans. Aquilina Martinez and Christine Morkovsky (New York: Orbis Books, 1985), 41–42.
22 Maldonado-Torres, 'On the Coloniality of Being', 256.
23 Buttimer, 'Geography, Humanism, and Global Concern', 1.
24 Castree et al., *The Point is to Change It*, 12:2–3.
25 Dussel, *Philosophy of Liberation*, 41–42.
26 Anna Maria de Castro quoted in Paulo Gonçalves, '"Josué, nunca vi tamanho desgraça"', *A Nova Democracia* (blog), March 2004, accessed 18 June 2022, https://anovademocracia.com.br/no-17/870-josue-nunca-vi-tamanha-desgraca.
27 Enrique Dussel, 'From Critical Theory to the Philosophy of Liberation: Some Themes for Dialogue', *TRANSMODERNITY: Journal of Peripheral Cultural Production of the Luso-Hispanic World* (Fall 2011): 22; see also Maldonado-Torres, 'On the Coloniality of Being', 254–56.
28 Dussel, *Philosophy of Liberation*, 2.
29 See Enrique Dussel, 'Vers Une Histoire de l'Église d'Amérique Latine', *Esprit (1940–)*, 340, nos 7/8 (1965): 53–65; Castro, 'A La Recherche de l'Amérique Latine'.
30 Castro, 'A La Recherche de l'Amérique Latine', 66.

recalls his encounter with the Frankfurt School, whose 'anthropological materiality [...] was perceptibly close to our situation in an impoverished, starving, and suffering Latin America. In the Southern Cone, the multitude of demonstrations shouted: "bread, peace, and work!" three necessities that refer strictly to life, to the reproduction of its corporeal content.'[31] Castro's work on hunger was important in representing and framing this Latin American context. For instance, he is quoted at the opening of the deeply influential revolutionary film *Hora de los Hornos* [Hour of the Furnaces], by the Argentine filmmakers Fernando Solanas and Octavio Getino. For Dussel, the materiality of philosophy is 'corporeal vulnerability', established in dialogue with the Frankfurt School's 'negative' materiality.

To some extent this is well-trodden ground, but it is worth reiterating as the basis for a different kind of humanist geography. Alexander Weheliye has argued that 'once suffering that results from political violence severs its ties with liberal individualism, which would position this anguish in the realm of a dehumanizing exception, we can commence to think of suffering and enfleshment as integral to humanity'.[32] For Marx, being human is prefaced by suffering: 'to be sensuous is to *suffer*. Man as an objective, sensuous being is therefore a *suffering* being.'[33] Weheliye specifically understands hunger (for instance, drawing on C.L.R. James' hunger strike) as political violence, closely recalling one of Castro's key interventions, as well as Elaine Scarry's conception of pain. Hunger, as Marx had it, is the need of the body for something outside of itself: '*Hunger* is a natural *need*; it therefore needs a *nature* outside itself, an *object* outside itself, in order to satisfy itself, to be stilled. Hunger is an acknowledged need of my body for an *object* existing outside it, indispensable to its integration and to the expression of its essential being.'[34] The binary of self/world is overcome at the biophysical and ontological level. Castro's own humanism was built on the struggle of the hungry inhabitants of the marshy outskirts of Recife. In Alexander Weheliye's terms, 'the particular assemblage of humanity' that needs to ground an anticolonial humanism is '*habeas viscus*, which [...] insists on the importance of miniscule movements, glimmers of hope, scraps of food'.[35]

We can see Castro's humanism of the hungry through this lens of vulnerability and negativity. His humanism also echoes more recent formulations that base humanism on suffering and precarity. Hunger sets the terms of Castro's humanism and his geography. This is its negative orientation:

---

31 Dussel, 'From Critical Theory to the Philosophy of Liberation', 17.

32 Alexander G. Weheliye, *Habeas Viscus: Racializing Assemblages, Biopolitics, and Black Feminist Theories of the Human* (Durham, NC: Duke University Press, 2014), 14.

33 Karl Marx, *Economic and Philosophic Manuscripts of 1844* (Massachusetts: Courier Corporation, 2012), 157.

34 Marx, *Economic and Philosophic Manuscripts*, 157; see also Heynen, 'Bending the Bars of Empire', 409–10.

35 Weheliye, *Habeas Viscus*, 12.

The 'Geography of Hunger' may well strike the reader as a strange expression. For geography, in the usual sense of the word, has always dealt more with the positive and favourable aspects of the world than with its negative and unfavourable side. Geographers have studied the wealth of the earth and the victories of man rather than his deprivations and failures. In our own time, the science of 'human geography' has set out to write the epic of human toil [...] and to record everything that man, as a geographic factor, has done to alter his natural environment. The 'Geography of Hunger' takes up a different aspect of the relations between man and nature. It deals with precisely those things that man has not done, with the tasks for which he lacked the knowledge or the will. It explores the geographical possibilities of which he has not taken advantage, and the opportunities he has wasted. This, then, is a geography, not of human accomplishment, but of human poverty and distress.[36]

We do not need to accept Castro's characterization of the rest of human geography as an essentially celebratory science in order to see the significance of a geography that starts from waste, failure, 'poverty and distress'. Castro overturns the starting point of regional geography to turn geography into a negative science, attempting to understand the spatial, social, and natural production of lack, injustice, and bodily suffering. Elaine Scarry wrote:

> When one hears about another person's physical pain, the events happening within the interior of that person's body may seem to have the remote character of some deep subterranean fact, belonging to an invisible geography that, however portentous, has no reality because it has not yet manifested itself on the visible surface of the earth.[37]

Hunger and pain have much in common: but for Castro hunger is not an invisible geography, not an unreal fact, but a substantially real and mappable one, that can be seen and called to account in landscape, infrastructure, art, and politics. Doing so was a project that was laced with Castro's quasi-utopian hope that articulating the cry and demand of hunger – and its geography – could change the world. This hope was a necessary function of his radical humanism.

This radicalism was intimately tied to a conception of the human as metabolically connected to nature. This is the kind of radical humanism that Alexander Weheliye finds in Black feminist thought, a new humanism against 'the genocidal shackles of [liberal humanist subject] Man'. Here, humanity is 'hungered into being',[38] and begins from 'imagining the relational ontological totality of the human'.[39] (This 'relational ontological totality' of being has

36 Castro, *Geography of Hunger*, 13.
37 Scarry, *The Body in Pain*, 3.
38 Weheliye, *Habeas Viscus*, 136.
39 Weheliye, *Habeas Viscus*, 4.

kinship with the concerns of mesology and the question of space and nature as functions of being emergent from recent geographical work in France drawing on twentieth-century Japanese philosophy.[40]) A metabolic humanism is not a reduction to the body but an elevation of its constant reproduction through socio-natural processes in geographical space and inside scalar, social, political, and economic processes. This kind of humanism is not a shrinking but an expansive conception. It is a geographical humanism, based on a nutritional understanding of the body's relationship to its environment.

How does this relate to critiques of humanism in contemporary geography? Kristen Simonson has argued that 'the advance of anti-humanism and posthumanism within academic geography has primarily taken the form of (1) a travel from the self-containing subject towards subjectivities as relational effects of arrangements or assemblages, and (2) an emphasis on materiality or more broadly the "non-human" or "more-than-human"'.[41] I cannot excavate all these debates here, whether over Foucault and Hardt and Negri,[42] new or vital materialisms,[43] or over trans- and post-humanism.[44] I do, however, want to emphasize the importance of specificity in either attacks on humanism or attempts to move beyond it. Noel Castree and Catherine Nash rightly observe that 'the anti-humanistic embracing of posthumanism as an emergent or imminent historical condition also depends on the notion of the human as a once stable and coherent category'.[45] It depends, too, on humanism as a stable political philosophy or worldview, while it is in fact quite the contrary. Not all humanisms are equal, either politically, philosophically, or geographically; not all humanisms necessarily come with the same European Enlightenment, anthropocentric, and rationalist baggage.[46] Neil Badmington's critique of humanism's 'absolutist assumptions' posits an 'anthropocentric discourse' that 'relies upon a set of binary oppositions, such as human/inhuman, self/other, natural/cultural, inside/outside, subject/object, us/them, here/there, active/passive, and wild/tame'.[47] If humanism really were all this it certainly would be worth ditching. But it is not; it is a much more

40   Berque, 'Offspring'; Berque, 'The Perceptive Relation in Mesology'; Pelluchon, 'What Does It Mean to Replace Ecology with Mesology and Resources with Nourishment?'; R.S. Alexandre, 'Is Space a Part of Being? Reassessing Space through Japanese Thought', *Philosophy@lisbon: International EJournal, Centro de Filosofia Da Universidade de Lisboa*, 5 (2016): 145–59.

41   Kirsten Simonsen, 'In Quest of a New Humanism: Embodiment, Experience and Phenomenology as Critical Geography*', *Progress in Human Geography* 37, no. 1 (February 2013): 20, doi:10.1177/0309132512467573.

42   Pithouse, '"That the Tool"', 112–14.

43   Pithouse, '"That the Tool"', 114–16.

44   See Rosi Braidotti, *The Posthuman* (Oxford: Polity Press, 2012).

45   Nash, 'Cultural Geography', 501–02.

46   Buttimer, 'Geography, Humanism, and Global Concern', 7.

47   Neil Badmington, 'Mapping Posthumanism', *Environment and Planning A* 36 (2004): 1345.

complex set of historical narratives, philosophical positions, and political theories. For an anticolonial geography, it is productive to explore this legacy through the radical anticolonial movements that have made claims upon humanism,[48] and through Castro's own geographical humanism, which shared a moment, and a political project, with them.

A geographical humanism requires attention to the question of space and to the 'geography' in Castro's 'geography of hunger'. As I explored in the first chapter, across his career Castro moves between analyses of the body and analyses of space, maintaining the profound connection between the internal workings of the body and the expansive historical geographies of colonialism. This figures a scalar geometry of the human geographical subject.[49] The human metabolism is produced through its embeddedness in ecologies that materialize in it and pass through it,[50] and metabolism articulates the spatial, temporal, and ecological dynamics of survival in the body.[51] As Corinne Peluchon puts it, 'not only is the subject embodied and dependent on natural and cultural things that nourish his or her life [...] the subject is also always relational'.[52] The body is not a fixed space but a result of multiple processes and scales that take on meaning in relation to one another. This is not to say that everything is scale,[53] but to emphasize that the body is key to conceptualizing scale. It is key not as a fixed, ontological baseline for scalar thinking but precisely as relational and metabolic.

Just as Castro turned the nutritional science and politics of his day into the geography of hunger, contemporary scholars have undertaken to establish the spatial, social, and ecological politics immanent to new scientific understandings of hunger, public health, nutritional epigenetics, and contemporary metabolic diseases.[54] Thinking of these as 'metabolic geographies' is

---

48 Pithouse, '"That the Tool"', 107–08.

49 Erik Swyngedouw and Nikolas C. Heynen, 'Urban Political Ecology, Justice and the Politics of Scale', *Antipode* 35, no. 5 (2003): 898–918.

50 Erik Swyngedouw, 'Circulations and Metabolisms: (Hybrid) Natures and (Cyborg) Cities', *Science as Culture* 15, no. 2 (2006): 105–21; Matthew Gandy, 'Cyborg Urbanization: Complexity and Monstrosity in the Contemporary City', *International Journal of Urban and Regional Research* 29, no. 1 (2005): 26–49.

51 Heynen, '"But It's Alright, Ma, It's Life, and Life Only"'.

52 Pelluchon, 'What Does It Mean to Replace Ecology with Mesology and Resources with Nourishment?', 150.

53 See Neil Brenner, 'A Thousand Leaves: Notes on the Geographies of Uneven Spatial Development', in *Leviathan Undone? Towards a political economy of scale*, ed. Roger Keil and Rianne Mahon (Vancouver: UBC Press, 2009), 27–49.

54 See, for example, Becky Mansfield, 'Health as a Nature—Society Question', *Environment and Planning A* 40, no. 5 (2008): 1015–19; Julie Guthman, 'Doing Justice to Bodies? Reflections on Food Justice, Race, and Biology', *Antipode* 46, no. 5 (2014): 1153–71; Anthony Ryan Hatch, *Blood Sugar: Racial Pharmacology and Food Justice in Black America* (Minneapolis: University of Minnesota Press, 2016).

to connect the oscillating, dialectical force of metabolism with the spatial politics of food, nutrition, and hunger.[55] This reopens the question of how the open and relational body is implicated in the production of scale. Nikolas Rose argued that biopolitics has shifted to the molecular life of genetics from the eugenic and systemic scale of nineteenth-century science and early twentieth-century medicine.[56] The molecular, somatic, and eugenic scales are fixed, but the metabolic is interactive. Hannah Landecker describes nutritional epigenetics as instigating a new 'molecular understanding of the *environment* [which] answers a previous intense era of molecularization of the *body*, but is distinct from it because of the foregrounding of molecular inter-relation and critical timing rather than the search for answers in the structural enumeration of the molecules themselves'.[57] The metabolic scale of the body, in this conception of 'new metabolism', is both temporally sensitive and relational. Deploying a concept of metabolism emerging from critical nutritional thought is akin to approaches that embed the relational production of the body in the production of uneven environments and can, in Heynen's terms, 'bring the body back to life'[58] in radical geography.

The sensory relationship with the environment can be at the root of a different ecological politics of scale to the extent that bodies are materially relational, open, and unfinished.[59] Landecker reminds us not to demote the metabolic, ontologically relational body to a silent assumption.

> Thinking with nutritional metabolism troubles the boundary between body and environment. The *human* metabolism demarcates the impossible boundary between nature and culture not at the surface of bodies, but deep inside them [...] in the space and time that is not quite the organism nor quite the environment, but the moving zone in which the two become one.[60]

In terms of human*ism*, building from the discussion above, this is an expansive, ecological foundation. Susan Buck-Morss argues that the senses are the foundations of politics and aesthetics, but 'the nervous system is

---

55 Davies, 'Unwrapping the Oxo Cube'.

56 Nikolas Rose, 'The Politics of Life Itself', *Theory, Culture & Society* 18, no. 6 (December 2001): 1–30, doi:10.1177/02632760122052020.

57 Hannah Landecker, 'Food as Exposure: Nutritional Epigenetics and the New Metabolism', *BioSocieties* 6, no. 2 (2011): 170.

58 Nik Heynen, 'Bringing the Body Back to Life through Radical Geography of Hunger: The Haymarket Affair and Its Aftermath', *ACME: An International E-Journal for Critical Geographies* 7, no. 1 (2008): 32–44.

59 See Reecia Orzeck, 'What Does Not Kill You: Historical Materialism and the Body', *Environment and Planning D: Society and Space* 25, no. 3 (2007): 496–514.

60 Hannah Landecker, 'The Metabolism of Philosophy, In Three Parts', in *Dialectic and Paradox: Configurations of the Third in Modernity*, ed. Berhard Malmus and Ian Cooper (Bern: Peter Lang, 2013), 224, http://www.academia.edu/25940804/The_Metabolism_of_Philosophy_In_Three_Parts.

not contained within the body's limits. The circuit from sense-perception to motor response begins and ends in the world.'[61] So too the human metabolism; through it the body and the environment are materially connected. Elaborating the relational way in which bodies and environments are metabolically produced is therefore a key concern for political ecology.

Nik Heynen argues that 'in order to keep the notion of politics of scale sharp, we must take several steps back and ground these politics, and all other politics, in the processes of social reproduction, material inequality, corporal survival, and naked life'.[62] Castro's geography of hunger embeds the politics of scale in the body itself, and in particular in hunger as the base of a relational ontology of the body. This recalls the question of the sensory, as the mobile interface between body and world. But if hunger, as a metabolic relation, is a relation with the external, it is not as such a sensory relation. It is entirely experienced in bodies, apparently from the inside out, not the outside in. Unlike sensory experience, hunger is interoceptive.[63] It derives from stimuli channelled between the gastrointestinal and genitourinary systems and the brain and organized through the release of hormones. Hunger is felt, but not with senses. We might argue that interoception should also be considered, as Dawkins and Loftus put it for the senses, to be 'theoreticians of praxis'. They argue that 'against the anthropological humanism of Feuerbach, Marx argues for a relational understanding of the senses that is rooted in historically and geographically situated practices. Just as these practices (and the relationships that define and are defined by such practices) change, so do the senses.'[64] So does interoception. Bodies are historically and geographically situated, metabolism is mutable, and so is interoception. Indeed, Marx could be read as distinguishing between sensation and interoception in a passage quoted by Dawkins and Loftus: 'sense perception (see Feuerbach) must be the basis of all science. Only when science starts out from sense perception in the dual form of *sensuous consciousness* and *sensuous need* – i.e. only when science starts out from nature – is it real science.'[65] This distinction of sense perception's 'dual form' underpins the material relationality of the body. That is, the world is part of human being not only through the senses but through

61 Susan Buck-Morss, 'Aesthetics and Anaesthetics: Walter Benjamin's Artwork Essay Reconsidered', *October* 62 (1992): 12, doi:10.2307/778700.

62 Nik Heynen, 'Revolutionary Cooks in the Hungry Ghetto: The Black Panther Party's Biopolitics of Scale from Below', in *Leviathan Undone? Towards a Political Economy of Scale*, ed. Rianne Mahon and Roger Keil (Vancouver: UBC Press, 2009), 267.

63 Arthur D. Craig, 'How Do You Feel? Interoception: The Sense of the Physiological Condition of the Body', *Nature Reviews Neuroscience* 3, no. 8 (2002): 655.

64 Ashley Dawkins and Alex Loftus, 'The Senses as Direct Theoreticians in Practice', *Transactions of the Institute of British Geographers* 38, no. 4 (October 2013): 666, doi:10.1111/j.1475-5661.2012.00551.x.

65 Karl Marx, *Early Writings*, ed. Rodney Livingstone and Gregor Benton, trans. Lucio Colletti (Harmondsworth: Penguin, 1975), 355.

interoception and need. This allows us to think of bodily need not as part of a reductive idea of human sociality but as intimately connected to broader dynamics of human being, of aesthetics, of sensuousness, consciousness, and desire, all of which incorporate the world – the other, nature, society – into the self. We can return again to Enrique Dussel's philosophy of liberation:

> it is the materiality of the labourer's 'corporeality' (his body, his basic needs, his sensibility – [...] a sensibility of need, *of hunger*) from which all that is economic emerges, from which all economic science must be thought. From such a real and sensible corporeality of living labour everything must be ethically judged.[66]

It is along these lines that I understand a 'really radical geography' premised on survival.

In terms of political ecology, we might think of hunger as equivalent to environmental disease or toxicity: an internal production elicited by the body's absolute material entanglement with the world. It has, however, different spatialities and temporalities – immediate, diurnal – to the slow violence of toxicity. It also has more unqualified resolution: while the cancers caused by toxins may or may not be treatable, individual hunger – except in the most extreme of circumstances – can be effectively resolved immediately with the most basic of social and somatic interventions. Death from hunger opens a glaring schism between bodily survival and social processes. As a nutritionist, Castro was finely tuned to the biological specificities of social reproduction. By following not only food or calories but vitamins, minerals, and proteins, Castro allows us to tie a politics of social reproduction more intimately to the politics of agriculture, land, environmental justice, and global trade. These ties are complex and, when Castro constructed the cartography of hunger in the Northeast of Brazil, there was a different, perhaps more immediate, set of relations between landscape, ecology, and diet in culturally distinct regions. But that these ties are complex does not mean they are not there, and nor does it mean that the intellectual task has unrecognizably changed.

The scalar geometry of the geography of hunger takes us inside the body because the politics of social reproduction do not stop at the skin.[67] Turning to a geography of survival[68] has affinities to the idea of *rexistance*[69] as a way

---

66 Dussel, *Towards an Unknown Marx*, 203.

67 Archie Davies et al., 'The Body as Infrastructure', *Environment and Planning E: Nature and Space* 4.3 (2020): 799–817.

68 Bunge, 'The Geography of Human Survival'; Nik Heynen and Jason Rhodes, 'Organizing for Survival: From the Civil Rights Movement to Black Anarchism through the Life of Lorenzo Kom'boa Ervin', *ACME: An International E-Journal for Critical Geographies* 11, no. 3 (2012): 393–412; Don Mitchell and Nik Heynen, 'The Geography of Survival and the Right to the City: Speculations on Surveillance, Legal Innovation, and the Criminalization of Intervention', *Urban Geography* 30, no. 6 (2009): 611–32.

69 Carlos Walter Porto-Gonçalves and Milson Betancourt Santiago, 'Encrucijada

of capturing the movements in defence of life (resistance and existence) that characterize Latin American political ecology.[70] This is not to promote biologism, but to insist on the socialist feminist principle that the body relies, necessarily, on practices of care and social reproduction.[71] The body's relational ontology is metabolic: a socio-natural process that extends from the cell to the global food supply chain. The body is produced in relation to uneven socio-ecologies, and to other bodies. Understanding the subject of humanism in these terms chimes with Gramscian approaches to political ecology and the 'person' that 'cannot be divorced from the natural world and [...] cannot be understood outside of specific socio-natural relations in particular places and particular times'.[72] For political ecology this proposes that 'the subjects of politicized environments are actively produced through their interactions with those environments'.[73] For Josué de Castro, these interactions with environments were, crucially, fed by the biological forcing ground of hunger. Through the geography – and later the geopolitics – of hunger, he insisted on the historical and geographical specificities of this central relationship between nature and society.

The *homem-caranguejo* is a key exemplar of his mode of thinking. The historically and geographically specific figure is an episode in Castro's analysis of 'certain elements of the biological mechanism of adjustment of the Brazilian man to the natural and cultural settings of the country'.[74] By thinking about the *homem-caranguejo* in metabolic terms we can see how it is consistent with Castro's broader geographical humanism of hunger. The hunger that crabbing both holds at bay and maintains – the broth is never a satisfactory meal – is directly connected to the loss of land that Castro theorized and agitated against. The *homem-caranguejo* exists in the urban periphery as the product of a much more extensive geography of hunger. For Castro this hunger is intimately bodily, but inseparably spatial, political, and ecological: it is the defining relationship between man and nature. Through ingestion, nature becomes body, and this relationship is also a key constituent of identity. In this relation food is more than a metaphor: the 'miry milk' of crab broth that people live on in the mangroves is constituted by and constitutive of people's bodies, but also their social lives and cultural identities. There is something *unheimlich* about this anthropophagic crab broth: in Castro's formulation the

latinoamericana en Bolivia: el conflicto del TIPNIS y sus implicaciones civilizatorias' (La Paz: Editorial Autodeterminación, 2013), 64.

70 Leff, 'Power–Knowledge Relations in the Field of Political Ecology', 234–35.

71 See, for example, the essays in Meehan and Stauss, *Precarious Worlds*.

72 Alex Loftus, 'Gramsci, Nature, and the Philosophy of Praxis', in *Gramsci: Space, Nature, Politics*, ed. Alex Loftus et al. (Chichester: Wiley-Blackwell, 2012), 184, doi:10.1002/9781118295588.ch9.

73 Alex Loftus, 'A Time for Gramsci', in *International Handbook of Political Ecology*, ed. Raymond Bryant (Cheltenham: Edward Elgar Publishing, 2015), 95.

74 Castro, *Geografia da Fome: O Dilema Brasileiro: Pão Ou Aço* (1946), 31.

crabs are both foster brothers and dinner. But the entanglement of bodies and environments is always uncanny and uncomfortable.

Castro was a rich thinker of the body, what Adrienne Rich called, in 1984, the 'geography closest in'.[75] Rich developed this formulation, she says, 'not to transcend this body, but to reclaim it'.[76] Rich's phrase encapsulates the function of the body in Castro's humanism. Using Rich's radical feminist formulation, we must recognize Castro's failure to articulate any kind of feminist politics at all. The *homem-caranguejo* is an *homem*. Haraway argues that 'humanity is a modernist figure; and this humanity has a generic face, a universal shape. Humanity's face has been the face of man.'[77] This remains true of Castro's version *homem-caranguejo*. However, many crab-pickers were, and are, women.[78] As a hungry subject the *homem-caranguejo* is, like Haraway's, 'the figure of a broken and suffering humanity, signifying [...] a possible hope'.[79] 'From the start [...] in the midst of multiple translations and stagings',[80] the *homem-caranguejo*, like Haraway's figure of suffering humanity, is 'a trickster figure [...] who might trouble our notions [...] of "the human," while making us remember why we cannot not want this problematic universal'.[81] We should pull Castro's gendered subject from his grasp – translate, update, sublate it – if we are to put it to use in a new space and time. It can be one of many 'eccentric subjects [who] can call us to account for our imagined humanity, whose parts are always articulated through translation'.[82]

The *Geografia da Fome* develops an analytical framework in which food is an extraordinarily powerful signifier. Nature–society relations themselves are understood through an extensive analysis of the dietary practices of geographically and historically specific groups. The geography of hunger, and the *homem-caranguejo*, are both analytical tools and conditions to be resisted. The political, social, and ecological forces of hunger press towards *de*humanization[83]; the struggle *against* hunger, on the other hand, is humanizing.

The humanizing force of hunger returns us to the primacy of the practised response to hunger: producing and providing food. What we might call

75 Rich, 'Notes towards a Politics of Location', 212.
76 Rich, 'Notes towards a Politics of Location', 212–13.
77 Donna Haraway, 'Ecce Homo, Ain't (Ar'n't) I a Woman, and Inappropriate/d Others: The Human in a Post-Humanist Landscape', in *Feminists Theorize the Political*, ed. Judith Butler and Joan Wallach Scott (London and New York: Routledge, 1992), 86.
78 Elizabeth Farfán-Santos, *Black Bodies, Black Rights: The Politics of Quilombolismo in Contemporary Brazil* (Austin: University of Texas Press, 2016).
79 Haraway, 'Ecce Homo', 87.
80 Haraway, 'Ecce Homo', 89.
81 Haraway, 'Ecce Homo', 98.
82 Haraway, 'Ecce Homo', 98.
83 Preface by Josué de Castro in Robert de Montvalon, *Un milliard d'analphabètes le savoir et la culture* (Paris: Éditions du Centurion, 1965), 11.

metabolic politics – a politics of social reproduction – is premised on such practice. Alex Loftus proposes an environmentalism built on bodily praxis and everyday life, in which 'the environment is something *lived* as a simultaneously bodily and global process. The environment is as much the toxins circulating through the bodies of people of colour as it is a better, more just world to be struggled for.'[84] Castro's way of thinking about nutrition helps clarify the stakes and histories of how bodies are connected, and the multiple scales through which socio-natures are crystallized in the human metabolism. It opens out onto new historical paradigms, too, for anglophone scholars interested in histories of radical ecological thinking and praxis.

The spatial and bodily interpretation of hunger at the centre of Castro's thought is, like Rich's politics of locating the body, contoured by a struggle between the possessive 'I' and the communal 'we'.[85] Hunger is both 'mine' and 'ours'. Hunger – like pain – is felt deep in the body, but it is socially produced: it is in this sense both personal and communal. As Enrique Dussel put it, 'injustice is lived as pain'.[86] An anticolonial, humanist, metabolic politics seeks to act upon the relations between the hungry and the socio-spatial production of hunger. Such metabolic politics are less about food than about feeding. Heynen's analysis of the Black Panthers' breakfast club shows radical hunger politics at work, nourishing bodies in communities and households.[87] The legacy of Castro in the work of Betinho and *Ação Cidadania* similarly mobilized the radical potential of hunger.[88] Eating 'is never done alone',[89] and nourishment is a process that is never at rest.

Conclusion

Castro's anticolonial bent emphasizes the particular colonial – as well as capitalist – spatiality of hunger, which persists today. Dussel's philosophy of liberation emphasizes the originary power of the call of the hungry,[90] a call that Castro's political practice sought to articulate throughout his life. He did so in a way that brought to light the expanded geographies through which hunger came into being. Seeing the continuities between calls for

84 Loftus, *Everyday Environmentalism*, x.
85 Mary Eagleton, 'Adrienne Rich, Location and the Body', *Journal of Gender Studies* 9, no. 3 (2000): 299–312.
86 Dussel, 'From Critical Theory to the Philosophy of Liberation', 29.
87 Heynen, 'Bending the Bars of Empire', 410.
88 Francisco de Assis Guedes de Vasconcelos, 'Fome, Solidariedade e Ética: Uma Análise Do Discurso Da Ação Da Cidadania Contra a Fome, a Miséria e Pela Vida', *Hist Cienc Saude Manguinhos* 11, no. 2 (2004): 259–77.
89 Myra J. Hird, 'Digesting Difference: Metabolism and the Question of Sexual Difference', *Configurations* 20, no. 3 (2012): 233; see also Pelluchon, 'What Does It Mean to Replace Ecology with Mesology and Resources with Nourishment?' 151.
90 Dussel, 'From Critical Theory to the Philosophy of Liberation', 22.

land reform, struggles for the minimum wage, and free school meals brings to light the spatial politics Josué de Castro delineated. Castro's work has long been superseded at the level of scientific knowledge of nutrition, the natural science of the body, and geographical conceptions of space. Yet the fundamental insights of the geography of hunger remain profoundly enlightening and profoundly animating. Enlightening because if we start from a critical geographical approach to the metabolism of the human body we can see that it is socially, ecologically, and relationally produced. If we follow the sticky paths of blood and sugar, we can ask necessary questions about the ongoing functioning of capitalism and colonialism. We can still demand what Castro called 'nutritional emancipation'.[91] The geography of hunger and Castro's radical humanism are animating for a simpler reason, though no less bloody: if hunger – *all* hunger – is socially and politically produced, it must be subject to social and political refusal. This remains a radical starting point for a truly embodied political ecology: a metabolic humanism.

As a whole this book has brought forward an alternative intellectual history of critical geography. In a fashion, this is to offer a retrospective codification of geography as a political subject 'before' geography's political turn. Castro figures, then, as a kind of pioneer 'out of place' in relation both to the places in which geography's politicization is located and to the hegemonic dimensions of his own Brazilian intellectual context. The re-placing of Castro therefore reintroduces him to a differentially awakened geography and political ecology.[92] Aligned with movements and scholarship aiming to decolonize the history of geography,[93] and with accounts of the history of geography that emphasize the contributions and significance of many different actors in the development of geographical knowledge – from indigenous guides to female explorers[94] – this book has demonstrated that the history of twentieth-century geographical thought is transnational, polylingual, and mobile. I hope to offer, therefore, a historical dose of hope and optimism to scholars seeking an anticolonial geography to pit against the history and present of colonial and imperialist geographical practices. Josué de Castro's theory and praxis were varied, fluctuating, and at times internally incoherent. Yet they were held together by a profound counter-hegemonic commitment to make the world differently in the pursuit of equality and universal freedom from suffering. This commitment was organized around a lifelong struggle against hunger

91 Castro, *The Geopolitics of Hunger*, 195.
92 I am grateful to one of the book's anonymous reviewers for their characterisation of the book in these terms, which I have repurposed here.
93 Craggs in Craggs et al., 'Intervention: Reappraising David Livingstone's The Geographical Tradition'.
94 Maddrell, 'Scientific Discourse and the Geographical Work of Marion Newbigin'; Avril Maddrell, 'The "Map Girls". British Women Geographers' War Work, Shifting Gender Boundaries and Reflections on the History of Geography', *Transactions of the Institute of British Geographers* 33, no. 1 (2008): 127–48.

at all its scales. It proceeded through a geographical interpretation of the world and an equally lifelong engagement with the disciplinary practices of geographical work. This geographical work manifested inside institutions of higher education, through research and through teaching, but it was also felt through the countless forms of political activism and representational practice by which Castro turned his geographical worldview into agency for social and environmental transformation. Geography and political ecology need an anticolonial impetus, and they need to be constantly reinvented as emancipatory practices. Many resources for this reinvention can be found in their own history. If we have had enough of the legacies of 'geography militant'[95] – and we have – we can always reach, instead, for Castro's militant geography.

95 Driver, *Geography Militant.*

Index

Locators in *italics* refer to figures.

Printed and bound by CPI Group (UK) Ltd, Croydon, CR0 4YY

30/03/2023

03206961-0001